LIST OR MANIFEST OF ALIEN PASSENGERS FOR THE UNITED

ALL ALIENS, in whatsoever class they travel, MUST be fully listed and the master or commanding officer of each vessel carrying such passengers

"Celtic"   sailing from Liverpool   , 7th August, 1913

DEFINING DOCUMENTS
IN AMERICAN HISTORY

Immigration &
Immigrant Communities
(1650-2016)

NAME IN FULL		Age										
	Sophia	23										
	Jane	29						Sheffield				
	Hannah	29		Wife			Welsh Wales				
	Isidore	50					English England London				
	Mary	20										
	Bessie	37					English					
	Maud Louisa	35					England London				
	Mary Jane	35		Wife			Belfast				
	Mary	25					English U.S.A New Jersey				
	Mary Valenta	11										
	Ethel Kate	21					England Birmingham				
	Kathleen	26					Irish Ireland Londonderry				
	Arthur Ernest	27	m	Clerk	Yes Yes	English	U.S.A Toledo			NON IM
	Alice Ann	43	f	H'wife	do	do	England Southport			
	Arnold	17	m s	Turner	do	do	do do			
	Robert Cyril	15	m s	Scholar	do	do	do do			
	Norman	11	m s	do	do	do	do do			
	Reginald	9	m	do	do	do	do do			
	Edward	26	m	Salesman	do	do	U.S.A Brooklyn			NON IM
	Martha	39	f	H'wife	do	do	England London			
	Sophia	62	f		do	do	do Sheffield			
	Annie	69	f	H'keeper	do	do	do Bradford			
	Edie	19	f	Secretary	do	do	do do			
	Thomas John	29	m	Miner	do	Welsh Wales Llanberis			
	Wilfred Ewart	28	m		do	English England Sutton			
	John Moyle	30	m	Farmer	do	do	do Helston			
	Fred	37	m	Joiner	do	do	do Manchester			
	Tom	22	m s	Weaver	do	do	do Preston			
	Harry	16	m s	do	do	do	do			

75

* Last permanent residence is the country in which the alien has last resided for one year or more.
† List of races will be found on the back of this sheet.

s to whom
d to collect head tax

DEFINING DOCUMENTS
IN AMERICAN HISTORY

Immigration & Immigrant Communities (1650-2016)

Editor

James S. Pula, PhD

SALEM PRESS
A Division of EBSCO Information Services, Inc.
Ipswich, Massachusetts

GREY HOUSE PUBLISHING

Publisher's Cataloging-In-Publication Data
(Prepared by The Donohue Group, Inc.)

Names: Pula, James S., 1946- editor.
Title: Immigration & immigrant communities (1650-2016) / editor, James S. Pula, PhD.
Other Titles: Immigration and immigrant communities (1650-2016) | Defining documents in American history (Salem Press)
Description: [First edition]. | Ipswich, Massachusetts : Salem Press, a division of EBSCO Information Services ; [Amenia, New York] : Grey House Publishing, [2017] | Series: Defining documents in American history | Includes bibliographical references and index.
Identifiers: ISBN 978-1-68217-285-8 (hardcover)
Subjects: LCSH: Immigrants--United States--History--Sources. | United States--Emigration and immigration--Government policy--Sources. | United States--Ethnic relations--History--Sources.
Classification: LCC JV6450 .I46 2017 | DDC 304.873--dc23

FIRST PRINTING
PRINTED IN THE UNITED STATES OF AMERICA

Contents

IN THEIR OWN WORDS: IMMIGRANT DESCRIPTIONS

ANTI-IMMIGRANT RHETORIC

FEDERAL LEGISLATION

EXECUTIVE AND JUDICIAL ACTIONS

APPENDIXES

Publisher's Note

Defining Documents in American History series, produced by Salem Press, consists of a collection of important historical primary source documents by a diverse range of important figures from history, dealing with a broad range of subjects in American history, along with thoughtful commentary and analysis by contemporary scholars and writers. This established series offers twenty-two titles including *Exploration & Colonial America* (1492-1755), *The American West* (1836-1900), *The Civil War* (1860-1865), *The Cold War* (1945-1991), and *The Vietnam War* (1956-1975).

This current volume, *Defining Documents in American History: Immigration & Immigrant Communities (1650-2016)*, offers in-depth analysis of a broad range of historical documents and historic events that shaped the lives of immigrants and immigrant communities throughout American history, from Adriaen van der Donck's description of the New Netherlands in 1650 to President Franklin D. Roosevelt's Executive Order 9066 in 1942 that led to the incarceration of people of Japanese ancestry during World War II to the opinions of Supreme Court Justices Anthony Kennedy and Antonin Scalia in 2012 regarding the case of *Arizona v. United States* concerning states' rights related to the enforcement of federal immigration laws to the 2016 Supreme Court decision in *United States v. Texas*. The material is organized under four broad categories:

- **In Their Own Words: Immigrant Descriptions**
- **Anti-Immigrant Rhetoric**
- **Federal Legislation**
- **Executive and Judicial Actions**

Historical documents provide a compelling view of this and other important aspects of American history. Designed for high school and college students, the aim of the series is to advance historical document studies as an important activity in learning about history.

Essay Format

Immigration & Immigrant Communities contains thirty-one primary source documents—some in their entirety. Documents are supported by a critical essay, written by historians and teachers, that includes a Summary Overview, Defining Moment, Author Biography, Document Analysis, and Essential Themes. Readers will appreciate the diversity of the collected texts, including congressional acts, letters, presidential vetos, political and religious sermons, laws and executive orders, government acts, and Supreme Court decisions, among other genres. An important feature is the close reading of the primary source that develops evidence of broader themes, such as the author's rhetorical purpose, social or class position, point of view, and other relevant issues. In addition, essays are organized by section themes, listed above, highlighting major issues of the period, many of which extend across eras and continue to shape life as we know it around the world. Each section begins with a brief introduction that defines questions and problems underlying the subjects in the historical documents. A brief glossary included at the end of each document highlights keywords important in the study of the primary source. Each essay also includes a Bibliography and Additional Reading section for further research.

Appendixes

- **Chronological List** arranges all documents by year.
- **Web Resources** is an annotated list of websites that offer valuable supplemental resources.
- **Bibliography** lists helpful articles and books for further study.

Contributors

Salem Press would like to extend its appreciation to all involved in the development and production of this work. The essays have been written and signed by scholars of history, humanities, and other disciplines related to the essays' topics. Without these expert contributions, a project of this nature would not be possible. A full list of contributor's names and affiliations appears in the front matter of this volume.

Editor's Introduction

"Once I thought to write a history of the immigrants in America," recalled historian Oscar Handlin. "Then I discovered that the immigrants *were* American history." Indeed, the history of the United States is the history of the peoples who moved there to create a society, a nation, bringing with them their own familiar cultures and traditions that they reshaped for use in their new environment and which, in turn remodeled that society itself. The most accepted theory of the population of North America is that the very first inhabitants were themselves immigrants, crossing the Bering Sea on a land bridge millennia ago from northeastern Asia to be joined thousands of years later by new arrivals from Europe, Africa, and other lands, making North America a multicultural region long before the establishment of the United States as an independent nation. It is this pattern that continues to repeat itself from the establishment of American independence until today.

By the time of the first United States census in 1790, the more than 3,929,000 recorded inhabitants included 2,100,000 of English descent, 300,000 Irish and Scots-Irish, 270,000 Germans, 150,000 Scots, 100,000 Dutch, 15,000 French, 10,000 Welsh, 2,000 Swedes, 2,000 Jews, with smaller representations from many other nationality and ethnic groups. At the same time, the census recorded 757,208 people of African ancestry, some 19.3 percent of the total population. Of course, most of these were not immigrants of their own free will.

Between 1790 and the eve of the Civil War in 1860, immigration to America grew from a small stream to a massive wave. In the first decade after ratification of the Constitution, 1790-1800, approximately 50,000 immigrants arrived in America. From that time until 1830, the number coming per decade tripled: 70,000 in 1801-10; 114,000 in 1811-20; and 151,000 in 1821-30. Beginning in 1816, about seventy percent of all European travelers entered the United States through the port of New York City. Most arrived in "steerage," the cheapest class of travel. Until the advent of the large passenger liners toward the end of the nineteenth century, most came in ships built to carry cargo rather than people. The average passage before the Civil War was about 44 days at sea, with some lasting as long as four months due to inclement weather. Overcrowding was standard, with poor ventilation and poor food. Upon arrival in America there were no public facilities or officials to assist the newcomers. If no one met them, they were let loose in the city with nowhere to turn for assistance. This led to the formation of the Irish Emigrant Aid Society in New York City in 1817 as the first ethnic attempt to assist fellow countrymen. In an era before government support facilities, individual groups increasingly developed societies to assist their own in the transition to American life.

In an early effort to regulate immigration, New York passed a law in 1824 requiring ships' captains to post a bond to guarantee that arriving immigrants would not become paupers or public charges. Later, a head tax of $1 per immigrant was levied, on steerage passengers only, to support an immigrant hospital. In 1849, however, in the "Passenger Cases" brought against New York and Massachusetts, the U.S. Supreme Court, by a vote of 5-4, declared the "head tax" on aliens to be unconstitutional. Its reasoning was that the power to regulate commerce rested exclusively with the Federal government. In 1847 New York established the "State Board of Commissioners of Immigration" to address immigration issues, and in 1855 "Castle Garden" was established on the southern tip of Manhattan Island as a reception center for new arrivals. There, newcomers could exchange money at fair rates, obtain food, review lists of approved boarding houses, and obtain other information. Later, Castle Garden would be replaced by Ellis Island in New York Harbor as the primary immigration center in the United States. In the two decades between 1820 and 1840, the largest single group of immigrants was from Ireland (43 percent), followed closely by those from the various German states (27 percent), England (18 percent), and the nations of northern Europe (11 percent).

Beginning in the 1830s, massive immigration from Ireland, followed in the late 1840s by huge migrations from Germany, saw arrivals reach never before imagined numbers: 599,000 in 1831-40; 1,713,000 in 1841-50; and 2,314,000 in 1851-60. By the mid-1850s, with a total population that stood slightly less than thirty million, nearly ten percent of the population had arrived within the previous decade. The overwhelming majority of Irish were Catholic, while German immigration contained in addition to Catholics, large numbers of Lutherans and other Protestants, significant numbers of

Jews, and a sizeable minority of "freethinkers," groups that were either anti-clerical, anti-religious, or both. Germans arriving after 1848 included a large number of political radicals who wanted to remake society. Failing in Germany, they brought their penchant for reform to America where they supported the anti-slavery movement, women's rights, and other causes.

The dramatic rise in immigration led to a corresponding rise in "nativism," a growing concern that immigration should be regulated to preserve "the American way of life." The Irish were Catholic, while America was overwhelmingly Protestant. In 1776 there were little more than 25,000 Catholics in the rebellious colonies, but that number increased dramatically to 1,750,000 by 1850 and 3,103,000 in 1860, making Catholics the single largest religious group in the country. The Irish also tended to stay in the large cities where they landed, or close by, where they competed for jobs, housing and services. Because of this, they were blamed for the poverty and rising crime rates in the cities and an anti-Catholic bias grew rapidly, including violence and mob actions in some cities. German migration included new strains of Protestantism such as the Lutherans, but also large numbers of Catholics and Jews, both of which continued to be antithetical to mainstream Protestants. The Germans also spoke a different language that they proved reluctant to give up, and had cultural habits, like having picnics on Sunday, which seemed odd if not downright sacrilegious to more conservative English-American Protestants. All of this heightened fears that continued immigration would take away jobs from "real Americans" and submerge American culture in what one writer referred to as the "pollution and degradation of European hordes."

The first nativist political convention, convened in Philadelphia in 1845, resulted in the formation of the "American Party" with a platform arguing for opposition to Catholics and the foreign-born being able to vote or hold elective office, as well as stricter naturalization requirements. The American Party, also known as the "Know-Nothing Party," reached its zenith of influence in 1854-55 when it counted three million supporters out of a total population of over twenty million. Thus, as immigration increased, so did nativism, but so also did the diversity of the United States.

With the conclusion of the Mexican War, "ethnicity" became a major issue. Although the overriding issue of the day was whether the "Mexican Cession," the lands taken from Mexico as a result of the war, would en-

ter the nation as "free" or "slave" states, the Treaty of Guadalupe-Hidalgo that ended the war also had a profound effect on the American cultural makeup. Along with the new areas under American control, which would become the states of Texas, New Mexico, Arizona, Nevada, and California, came tens of thousands of Spanish-speaking peoples and indigenous people. All had considerably different cultures and historical traditions than the rest of the American population. Of course, these people could not strictly be considered "immigrants." After all, they had not moved, control of the land on which they lived had changed hands.

Following the Civil War Southern and Eastern Europeans flocked to the unskilled labor positions in the expanding textile, steel, mining and other industries. By 1910, 58 percent of unskilled industrial workers were foreign-born, two-thirds of those being from the "New Immigration," chiefly Italians, Poles, and others from those regions. Numbers increased to the peak year of 1907 when more than a million people entered the country. It has been estimated that some 10 million people entered the United Stated between 1860 and 1890, and another 18 million between 1890 and 1920, a total of over 28 million people. About 80 percent of these settled in the northeast. New York City's population grew from just over one million in 1860 to over three million by 1900, while the dramatic rise in Chicago's population reflects not only increased immigration but also the massive westward movement: 100,000 in 1860, 503,000 in 1880, and 1,700,000 in 1900. Between 1860 and 1910, the urban population rose from 6.2 million to 42 million, an astounding 677 percent of its 1860 size. By 1890, New York City had become the largest immigrant center in the world and in the 18 largest American cities fully 60 percent of all males were of foreign birth.

As in previous eras, this enormous influx of people, most of whom were somehow perceived as "different," led to a renewed upsurge in nativism stoked by the American Federation of Labor's fears of competition and lowering wage scales combined with the racism attending the growing popularity of eugenics and Social Darwinism. While the reaction in the eastern portion of the nation was against those from Southern and Eastern Europe, that on the west coast was aimed at the Chinese. The discovery of gold and work on the railroads brought 14,000 Chinese to California by 1852. This number increased to 37,000 in 1855 and 290,610 by 1880. Of the 10,000 workers employed constructing the Central Pacific Railroad, some 9,000 were Chinese. By the 1870s, most of the railroads had been completed, mining was gradually closed to many Asians, and the economic panic of 1873 brought increasing calls for the restriction of the Chinese. The result was the first exclusionary immigration law in American history bases on national origins, the "Chinese Exclusion Act" of 1882.

Similarly, political pressure led to restrictions on Southern and Eastern European immigration as well. In 1887 the anti-Catholic American Protective Association was formed in the Midwest. In 1894, Senator Henry Cabot Lodge and a number of other New Englanders formed the Immigration Restriction League in Boston to push for a literacy test as a requirement for admission to the U.S., and other immigration "reforms." Opponents of the 1906 literacy test bill hoped to postpone or prevent its passage by calling for the establishment of the United States Immigration Commission, also known as "Dillingham Commission" after its chair, Sen. William P. Dillingham of Vermont. The Commission's findings supported the proponents of restriction, officially declaring for the first time that there was a distinct difference between what it labeled the "new" immigration from Southern and Eastern Europe and the previous groups from Northwestern Europe that it termed the "old" immigration. Restriction of the former, it concluded, was "demanded by economic, moral, and social conditions." This led to passage of severe restrictions on the entry of people from countries of the "new" immigration through legislation adopted in 1921 and 1924, as well as a cap on total immigration from outside the Western Hemisphere. Whereas nearly 880,000 people a year arrived in the first decade of the twentieth century, the new law reduced the maximum annual number to only 164,667.

World War II brought some exceptions to the rigid quotas with the War Brides Act of 1945 and the Displaced Person Acts of 1948 and 1950, but even when the immigration laws were revised under the McCarran-Walter Act in 1952 the previous nationality quotas were kept. They would not be discarded until the Immigration Act of 1965. In the meantime, arrivals from the Western Hemisphere foreshadowed a new "mass migration" from Latin America akin to that of the "new" immigration during the period between 1870 and 1920. By 2010 the U.S. census recorded a total population of 311,591,919. Of these, 40,381,574 (or 13.0 percent) were of foreign birth including 18,788,300 Hispanics (6.0 percent) of whom 11,691,632 were born in Mexico (3.8 percent). Mirroring the same cycle that is typical of American history, these new arrivals were also met with growing nativism and calls for restriction, generally using iterations of the same recycled arguments.

In this volume we attempt to present a cross section of documents for the study of what Oscar Handlin aptly note was the heart of American history. We begin with the immigrants themselves, providing a collection of first-hand commentaries on the process of immigration, the construction of immigrant communities, and protests of unfair treatment. We follow this by selections taken from those who opposed unrestricted immigration because without understanding their motivations one cannot understand the issues and their consequences. Since American immigration policy is defined by law, the third section includes a collection of federal legislation either designed specifically to address immigration or effecting it whether intended or not. Finally, immigration policy can be influenced by both the executive and judicial branches of government so we have included texts from both that have played important roles in how the legislation adopted by Congress is interpreted or enforced.

We hope that these documents not only provide for a better understanding of immigration issues, but an incentive for further study of this continually evolving subject.

James S. Pula, PhD

Contributors

Jakub Basista, PhD
Jagiellonian University

Martin Bunton, DPhil
University of Victoria

K. P. Dawes, MA
Chicago, IL

Amber R. Dickinson, PhD
Oklahoma State University

Justus D. Doenecke, PhD
New College of Florida

Ashleigh Fata, MA
University of California, Los Angeles

Gerald F. Goodwin, PhD
Bloomington, IN

Aaron Gulyas, MA
Mott Community College

David Conrad Johnson, PhD
Elmhurst College

Mark Joy, PhD
University of Jamestown

Esther Katz, PhD, and Cathy Moran Hajo, PhD
Margaret Sanger Papers Project, New York University

Tom Lansford, PhD
University of Southern Mississippi

David W. Levy, PhD
University of Oklahoma

Scott A. Merriman, PhD
Troy University

Nicole Mitchell, PhD
University of Alabama, Birmingham

Scott C. Monje, PhD
Tarrytown, NY

Michael J. O'Neal, PhD
Moscow, ID

Lisa Paddock, PhD
Cape May, NJ

William S. Pettit, Phd
Stone Mountain, GA

Luca Prono, PhD
Bologna, Italy

Jonathan Reese, PhD
Colorado State University, Pueblo

Steven Schroeder, PhD
University of Chicago

David Simonelli, PhD
Youngstown State University

Robert N. Stacy, MA
Leominster, MA

Stephen K. Stein, PhD
University of Memphis

William N. Tilchin, PhD
Boston University

Kevern J. Verney, PhD
Edge Hill University

Donald A. Watt, PhD
Middleton, ID

Zachary Williams, PhD
University of Akron

DEFINING DOCUMENTS
IN AMERICAN HISTORY

Immigration &
Immigrant Communities
(1650-2016)

IN THEIR OWN WORDS: IMMIGRANT DESCRIPTIONS

Scholars have long sought to describe and explain the human experience of migration. Yet, we can do no better by way of understanding than to read the words that these intrepid people left behind. Fortunately, letters and other sources abound that describe nearly every phase of the migration process, both for individuals and discreet groups of people. The documents in Part I, arranged in chronological order, fall into four categories, descriptions of: the Atlantic crossing, the individual experience, the immigrant communities, and their protests of anti-immigrant thought and action.

A Voyage to America provides a description of some of the hazards of the Atlantic crossing during the early nineteenth century when sailing ships took weeks to make the perilous voyage and the lack of government regulation allowed unscrupulous ship captains and others to prey upon the unwary and helpless. Andreas Geyer, Jr., sent by the German Society of Philadelphia to investigate the conditions under which Germans made the crossing, details in his report some of the more flagrant abuses to which people might be subject by corrupt shipping agents and government officials.

Once in North America, immigrants had to adjust to their new surroundings to create for themselves the new life they sought when they decided to leave their native lands. *A Description of New-Netherland*, Kleindeutschland *in the 1850s*, and *How the Other Half Lives* detail different aspects of the integration of immigrants into their adopted society. In the first, Adriaen van der Donck, an agent for the Dutch West India Company, describes in a letter the nature of the new colony of New Netherland, its economy, and its potential. As a company employee, his letter represents not only a description of the early Dutch colony but an exceptionally

early example of public relations; that is, an effort to promote further emigration from the Dutch Republic to its North American colony through positive descriptions of the climate, resources, and abundant opportunities. Documents such as this could be found throughout American history, with more marketing expertise, and perhaps less honesty, as time passed.

Over time, as the population of North America increased and urban areas developed, immigrants began to settle in specific areas within the cities to create ethnic neighborhoods. In *Kleindeutschland*, Theodor Griesinger describes the German settlement in New York City in the 1860s. A neighborhood that could easily pass for a German city, what was often referred to as *"Kleindeutschland"* contained German restaurants, stores, churches, theaters, newspapers, and all of the other distinctive cultural elements one might find in Munich, Heidelberg, or Berlin. It was an area where one could live comfortably with little or no English, secure in the knowledge that your immediate needs could be taken care of in your native language. Although Griesinger's descriptions were of a German settlement, they could easily apply to any such ethnic enclave. Yet all was not necessarily positive in these miniature European villages within the American urban landscape. In *How the Other Half Lives*, Jacob Riis records the abject poverty and hopelessness often found in some of these same communities by the end of the nineteenth century when overcrowding and neglect from building owners and local governments combined to produce urban ghettos. Taken from his highly regarded work of pioneering photojournalism, this excerpt from *How the Other Half Lives* balances Griesinger's more positive account with what can happen to poor immigrants struggling to merely survive from day to day.

Individual experiences of course varied. In *Letter from an Irish Immigrant*, John F. Costello's letter home to his family in Ireland sets forth his homesickness, comparisons between his life in America with that in Ireland, suggestions that his family and friends inclined to migrate join him, and a plea for them to send him letters with news of the family. This is an excellent example of this typical form of immigrant letter. On the other hand, *How I Found America*, written by Anzia Yezierska, a Polish-Jewish émigré from the Russian Empire, provides vivid details on the reasons for her migration and what she encountered on entry into the United States. Her work also includes valuable descriptions of the family conflicts that could emerge with migration and the heartache of dreams unfulfilled.

The final segment of Part I provides examples of immigrant protests. In *A Chinese Letter to Governor John Bigler*, Chinese community leader Norman Asing responds to a defamatory letter about his group written by California Governor John Bigler. In the process he asserts Chinese loyalty to America and their contributions to the United States while at the same time appealing to the ideals of the Declaration of Independence and the Constitution as magnets appealing to the Chinese. As such, it is a classic example of immigrant response to prejudice and discrimination. A much more in depth protest appears in *A Polish American Protest of Immigration Restriction* where several Polish American organizations banded together to craft an appeal to Congress to vote against proposed legislation that would make it much harder for future immigrants to enter the country and become naturalized citizens. An excellently presented and argued case, it relies on providing evidence that Poland was a cultured and civilized nation with a constitution as liberal as the United States, that Polish immigrants had contributed substantially to the development of America, and that they only sought to enjoy the same freedoms that other citizens enjoyed and which brought them to American in the first place.

Bartolomeo Vanzetti's speech is a little different in that, having been convicted of armed robbery and murder, the Italian immigrant anarchist links his conviction with the wave of anti-foreign sentiment prevalent in the 1920s. A very famous case that is still argued today, Vanzetti's comments provide an interesting perspective on the era of the post-World War I "Red Scare" and the anti-immigrant public attitude shaped by the terror campaign waged by anarchist leader Luigi Galleani. The final selection, An Address by Cesar Chávez, also deals with public perceptions. In it, César Chávez addresses a meeting of the farmers union that he founded, detailing the reasons for the struggle, the successes of the largely Mexican workers' organization to date, and its goals. In this respect it is also an example of an organized immigrant attempt to influence public policy not unlike *A Polish American Protest of Immigration Restriction*.

■ A Description of New-Netherland

Date: 1650
Author: Adriaen van der Donck
Genre: Letter

Summary Overview

Early European exploration was largely motivated by the concept of "mercantilism," the idea that establishing profitable trade routes to Asia would yield wealth and political power. As a commercial nation, the Dutch formed the United East India Company, a joint stock enterprise, in 1602. It was this group that hired Henry Hudson to explore along the North American coast to find the elusive water route to the riches of Asia. When the sought-after route proved elusive, the Dutch recognized that trading with the indigenous people might provide commercial success, offering pots, pans, cloth, beads, and other finished goods for valuable furs.

In 1615 the Dutch established Fort Nassau as a trading post near modern Albany, New York. Six years later the Dutch government chartered the West India Company (WIC) with exclusive rights to manage New Netherland, the name they gave their new colony, including a monopoly on trade. Recognizing that the colony's fertile lands could result in agricultural profits, the WIC appointed Pieter Minuit as director with the mission of obtaining land from the indigenous people and inducing settlers to move to the New World. One of their strategies was to offer huge tracts of land to "patroons" on the condition that they obtain at least fifty families to settle on and make the land grant productive. The patroons enjoyed almost complete authority on their land to appoint local administrators, including court officials, and otherwise rule as they saw fit as long as they obeyed Dutch law. The settlers were effectively tenant farmers who worked the land of the patroon in exchange for either a fixed rent, a portion of the profit from the crop, or both.

Defining Moment

The rich farmlands proved quite productive, but the population of New Netherland remained small. In 1630 the entire New Netherland colony numbered only about 300, rising to 500 by 1640 and an estimat-ed 800 to 1,000 in 1650. While the fur trade proved quite lucrative, if the colony was to return the profits to investors as originally envisioned, clearly the number of settlers had to be increased dramatically. Part of the reason for the slow growth was the new director, Willem Kieft, who arrived in 1638. Charged with cutting costs and increasing profits, he first attempted to extract tribute from the nearby indigenous tribes then, on the pretext that a colonist had been murdered, he launched military strikes on nearby indigenous settlements, killing the inhabitants, carrying off anything of value, and burning the villages. Naturally, this sparked a very destructive war.

Opposition to Kieft's policies soon emerged, both because of his destructive policy toward the indigenous peoples and his authoritarian attitude toward the settlers themselves. When appeals to Kieft and to the WIC failed to bring any changes, representatives of the settlers submitted a protest directly to the Dutch government. Written by Adriaen van der Donck, the document demanded that a new director be appointed and the rights of the colonists as Dutch citizens be respected. The result of this unprecedented action was the appointment of a new director, Pieter Stuyvesant, in 1647. Charged with expanding the population and increasing profits, among his initiatives was the construction of a wall to protect New Amsterdam (on the line of modern Wall Street), a canal to promote irrigation and trade (along modern Broad Street and Broadway), and expansion of the colony into surrounding farmland. In these efforts he had a ready ally in van der Donck who took on the role of head cheerleader for the colony.

Author Biography

Adriaen van der Donck was born into a well-to-do family in the Netherlands, about 1618. After completing legal studies at the University of Leiden in 1641 he spurned the practice of his new profession in the

Dutch Republic in favor of accepting a position managing Rensselaerwijck, the patroonship of the wealthy Kiliaen van Rensselaer, one of the founders and directors of the West India Company. Once in New Netherland, van der Donck proved to be an able administrator but often took the side of the tenants in disagreements with the patroon. He also spent a considerable amount of time exploring nearby lands, learning the local indigenous languages, and neglecting the patroon's business. Not surprisingly he soon found himself without employment.

Moving to New Amsterdam, van der Donck arrived in the midst of the war provoked by Director Kieft. Perhaps because of his understanding of indigenous languages and customs, Kieft tapped van der Donck to assist in negotiating an end to the disruptive conflict. When the resulting discussions succeeded, Kieft rewarded van der Donck with 24,000 acres of land north of Manhattan Island in modern Yonkers. The legal expert immediately

repaid his benefactor by secretly leading a group of dissatisfied colonists who petitioned the WIC to remove Kieft. With the arrival of the director's replacement, Pieter Stuyvesant, van der Donck gained appointment as a member an advisory board created to represent the interests of the inhabitants to Stuyvesant. Seeking more freedom and a representative form of government as in the Dutch Republic, van der Donck soon left for Europe to plead the case of the colonists against Stuyvesant's dictatorial style. As part of his written presentation he included a glowing description of New Netherland designed to encourage numbers of prospective colonists to set sail for America.

Van der Donck returned to New Netherland, but died sometime between late 1655 and early 1656. The cause of death is unknown, but it may have occurred during an indigenous raid on his estate that occurred during this time.

HISTORICAL DOCUMENT

When, and by whom, New-Netherlands was first discovered

This country was first found and discovered in the year of our Lord 1609; when, at the cost of the incorporated East India Company, a ship named the Half-Moon was fitted out to discover a westerly passage to the kingdom of China. This ship was commanded by Hendrick Hudson, as captain and supercargo, who was an Englishman by birth, and had resided many years in Holland, during which he had been in the employment of the East India Company. This ship sailed from the Canary Islands, steering a course north by west; and after sailing twenty days with good speed, land was discovered, which, by their calculation, lay 320 degrees by west. On approaching the land, and observing the coast and shore convenient, they landed, and examined the country as well as they could at the time, and as opportunity offered; from which they were well satisfied that no Christian people had ever been there before, and that they were the first who by Providence had been guided to the discovery of the country.

Why this country is called New-Netherlands

We have before related, that the Netherlanders, in the year 1609, had first discovered this country, of which they took possession as their own in right of their discovery, and finding the country fruitful and advantageously situated, possessing good and safe havens, rivers, fisheries, and many other worthy appurtenances corresponding with the Netherlands, or in truth excelling the same; for this good reason it was named New-Netherlands, being as much as to say, another or a new-found Netherlands. Still the name depended most upon the first discovery, and upon the corresponding temperatures of the climates of the two countries, which to strangers is not so observable. We notice also that the French in the same quarter of the new world, have named their territory Canada or Nova Francia, only because they were the first Europeans who possessed the lands in those parts, for the temperature of the climate is so cold and wintry, that the snow commonly lies on the earth four or five months in succession and from four to five feet deep, which renders it costly to keep domestic animals there; and although this country lies no farther than fifty degrees north, still the air in winter is so fine, clear and sharp there, that when the snow once falls, which it commonly does about the first of December, it does not thaw away except by the power of the sun in April. If a shower of rain happens to fall in winter, (which is seldom,) then it forms a hard crust on the surface of the snow, that renders the travelling difficult for man and beast. The air there is clear and dry, and the snow seldom melts or thaws away suddenly.

The Swedes also have a possession on the south (Delaware) river, which they name New-Sweden. The climate of this place by no means corresponds with that of Sweden, as it lies in latitude 39 degrees north. But, although they have formed a settlement there, still their title is disputed, for they can show no legal right or claim to their possessions.

The country having been first found or discovered by the Netherlanders, and keeping in view the discovery of the same, it is named the New-Netherlands. That this country was first found or discovered by the Netherlanders, is evident and clear from the fact, that the Indians or natives of the land, many of whom are still living, and with whom I have conversed, declare freely, that before the arrival of the Lowland ship, the Half-Moon, in the year 1609, they (the natives) did not know that there were any other people in the world than those who were like themselves, much less any people who differed so much in appearance from them as we did. Their men on the breasts and about the mouth were bare, and their women like ours, hairy; going unclad and almost naked, particularly in summer, while we are always clothed and covered. When some of them first saw our ship approaching at a distance, they did not know what to think about her, but stood in deep and solemn amazement, wondering whether it were a ghost or apparition, coming down from heaven, or from hell. Others of them supposed her to be a strange fish or sea monster. When they discovered men on board, they supposed them to be more like devils than human beings. Thus they differed about the ship and men. A strange report was also spread about the country concerning our ship and visit, which created great astonishment and surprise amongst the Indians. These things we have

frequently heard them declare, which we hold as certain proof that the Netherlanders were the first finders or discoverers and possessors of the New-Netherlands. There are Indians in the country, who remember a hundred years, and if there had been any other people here before us, they would have known something of them, and if they had not seen them themselves, they would have heard an account of them from others. There are persons who believe that the Spaniards have been here many years ago, when they found the climate too cold to their liking, and again left the country; and that the maize or Turkish corn, and beans found among the Indians, were left with them by the Spaniards. This opinion or belief is improbable, as we can discover nothing of the kind from the Indians. They say that their corn and beans were received from the southern Indians, who received their seed from a people who resided still farther south, which may well be true, as the Castilians have long since resided in Florida. The maize may have been among the Indians in the warm climate long ago; however, our Indians say that they did eat roots and the bark of trees instead of bread, before the introduction of Indian corn or maize.

Of the limits of the New-Netherlands, and how far the same extend

New-Netherlands is bounded by the ocean or great sea, which separates Europe from America, by New-England and the Fresh (Connecticut) river, in part by the river of Canada, (the St. Lawrence,) and by Virginia. Some persons who are not well informed, name all North-America Virginia, because Virginia from her tobacco trade is well known. These circumstances, therefore, will be observed as we progress, as admonitions to the readers. The coast of New-Netherlands extends and stretches mostly north-east and south-west. The sea-shore is mostly formed of pure sand, having a dry beach. On the south side, the country is bounded by Virginia. Those boundaries are not yet well defined, but in the progress of the settlement of the country, the same will be determined without difficulty. On the north-east the New-Netherlands abut upon New-England, where there are differences on the subject of boundaries which we wish were well settled. On the north, the river of Canada stretches a considerable distance, but to the north-west it is still undefined and unknown. Many of our Netherlanders have been far into the country, more than seventy or eighty miles from the river and sea-shore. We also frequently trade with the Indians, who come more than ten and twenty days' journey from the interior, and who have been farther off to catch beavers, and they know of no limits to the country, and when spoken to on the subject, they deem such enquiries to be strange and singular. Therefore we may safely say, that we know not how deep, or how far we extend inland. There are however many signs, which indicate a great extent of country, such as the land winds, which domineer much, with severe cold, the multitudes of beavers, and land animals which are taken, and the great numbers of water-fowl, which fly to and fro, across the country in the spring and fall-seasons. From these circumstances we judge that the land extends several hundred miles into the interior; therefore the extent and greatness of this province are still unknown.

Of the forelands and sea-havens
The coast of New-Netherlands extends south-west and northeast, as before mentioned, and is mostly clean and sandy, drying naturally; and although the bare, bleak and open sea breaks on the beach, still there is good anchorage in almost every place, because of the clean, sandy bottom. There seldom are severe gales from the sea, except from the southeast, with the spring tides. When the winds blow from the north-west, which domineer the strongest, then there is an upper or windward shore, with smooth water and little danger. For those reasons, the coast is as convenient to approach at all seasons, as could be desired. The highlands, which are naturally dry, may be seen far at sea, and give timely warning.

The forelands are generally double, and in some places broken into islands, (affording convenient situations for the keeping of stock,) which would lead seamen to suppose, on approaching the shore, that the same were the main land, when the same are islands and forelands, within which lie large meadows, bays, and creeks, affording convenient navigable passages, and communications between places.

It has pleased God to protect against the raging sea those parts of the coast which have no double foreland, with natural barriers of firm, strong, and secure stone foundations, that preserve the coast from the inundations of the mighty ocean, (which are ever to be feared,) where the coast, if not thus protected, might be lessened and destroyed; particularly the nearest sea lands, against which the sea acts with most violence. Nature has secured those positions with firm, high, and accommodated rocky heads and cliffs, which are as perfect formations, as the arts and hands of man, with great expense, could make the same.

There are many and different sea havens in the New-Netherlands, a particular description of which would form a work larger than we design this to be; we will therefore briefly notice this subject, and leave the same for the consideration of mariners and seamen. Beginning at the south and terminating at Long Island, first comes Godyn's bay, or the South (Delaware) bay, which was the first discovered. This bay lies in 39 degrees north latitude, being six (Dutch) miles wide and nine miles long, and having several banks or shoals, but still possessing many advantages; convenient and safe anchorages for ships, with roomy and safe harbours. Here also is a good whale fishery. Whales are numerous in the winter on the coast, and in the bay, where they frequently ground on the shoals and bars; but they are not as fat as the Greenland whales. If, however, the fishery was well-managed, it would be profitable. After ascending the bay nine miles, it is terminated in a river, which we name the South river, to which we will again refer hereafter, and pass on to the bay, wherein the East and North rivers terminate, and wherein Staten Island lies; because the same is most frequented, and the country is most populous, and because the greatest negotiations in trade are carried on there; and also because it is situated in the centre of the New-Netherlands. Hence it is named *quasi per excellentiam*, "The Bay." But before we speak more at large of this place, we will attend to the places, and their advantages, which lie between this bay and the South bay.

Between those two bays, the coast, almost the whole distance, has double forelands, with many islands, which in some places lie two or three deep. Those forelands as well as the islands, are well situated for seaboard towns, and all kind of fisheries, and also for the cultivation of grain, vineyards, and gardening, and the keeping of stock, for which purposes the land is tolerably good. Those lands are now mostly overgrown with different kinds of trees and grape-vines; having many plums, hazel-nuts and strawberries, and much grass. The waters abound with oysters, having many convenient banks and beds where they may be taken.

Besides the many islands which lie between the aforesaid bays, many of which are highland, there are also several fine bays and inland waters, which form good sea harbours for those who are acquainted with the inlets and entrances to the same, which at present are not much used; particularly the Bear-gat, Great and Little Egg Harbours, Barnegat, &c., wherein the anchorages are safe and secure. But as New-Netherlands is not yet well peopled, and as there are but few Christians settled at those places, these harbours are seldom used, unless the winds and weather render it necessary for safety.

The before-mentioned bay, wherein Staten Island lies, is the most famous, because the East and North rivers empty therein, which are two fine rivers, and will be further noticed hereafter. Besides those, there are several kills, inlets, and creeks, some of which resemble small rivers, such as the Raritan, Kill van Col, Neuversinck, &c. Moreover, the said bay affords a safe and convenient haven from all winds, wherein a thousand ships may ride in safety inland. The entrance into the bay is reasonably wide or roomy, without much danger, and easily found by those who have entered the same, or are well instructed. We can also easily, if the wind and tide suit, in one tide sail and proceed from the sea to New-Amsterdam, (which lies five miles from the open sea,) with the largest ships fully laden; and in like manner proceed from New-Amsterdam to

sea. But the outward bound vessels usually stop at the wateringplace under Staten Island, to lay in a sufficient supply of wood and water, which are easily obtained at that place. We also frequently stop far in the bay behind Sand Point (Sandy Hook) in waiting for the last passengers and letters, and to avail ourselves of the wind and tide.

Along the seacoast of Long Island, there are also several safe, commodious inlets for small vessels, which are not much frequented by us. There also are many spacious inland bays, from which, by the inlets, (at full tide,) the sea is easy of access; otherwise those are too shallow. The same also are not much frequented by us. With population several of the places would become important, which now, for brevity's sake, we pass over.

Between Long Island and the main land, there are throughout many safe and convenient places for large and small vessels; which may be occupied, if necessary. For in connection with the whole river which is held by many to be a bay, there are in the main land and in the island opposite to the same, many safe bays, harbours, and creeks, which are but little known to us, and which the English, by their devices have appropriated. Although this subject is spoken of in the remonstrances of the New-Netherlands, we will pass over it without waking the sleepers, and attend briefly to the most important rivers, waters, and creeks. ...

Of the East River

This river is thus named, because it extends eastward from the city of New-Amsterdam. By some this river is held to be an arm of the sea, or a bay, because it is very wide in some places, and because both ends of the same are connected with, and empty into the ocean. This subtility notwithstanding, we adopt the common opinion and hold it to be a river. Be it then a river or a bay, as men may please to name it, still it is one of the best, most fit and most convenient places and most advantageous accommodations, which a country can possess or desire, for the following reasons:—Long Island, which is about forty miles in length, makes this river. The river, and most of the creeks, bays and inlets joining the same, are navigable in winter and in summer without much danger. This river also affords a safe and convenient passage at all seasons to those who desire to sail east or west; and the same is most used, because the outside passage is more dangerous. Most of the English (of New-England) who wish to go south to Virginia, to South river, or to other southern places, pass through this river, which brings no small traffic and advantage to the city of New-Amsterdam. This also causes the English to frequent our harbours, to which they are invited for safety. Lastly, this river is famous on account of its convenient bays, inlets, havens, rivers, and creeks, on both sides, to wit, on the side of Long Island and on the side of the fast or main land. In the Netherlands, no such place is known. Of this and the other rivers of New-Netherlands, enough has been said, in our opinion, for this time and for our purpose.

Of the several Waters, and their Diversity

In this place we will briefly notice the waters, before we notice other matters. In general, we say, to describe per species would take too long, and draw us from our original plan. We find in New-Netherlands many fine waters, kills, brooks and streams which are navigable, large and roomy, as well on the sea-board as far inland: also many runs of water, sprouts, stream-kills and brooks having many fine falls, which are suitable for every kind of milling work. Inland, there are also several standing waters and lakes, as large as small seas, also large rivers abounding with fish. The rivers have their origin in sprouts which flow from valleys, and in springs, which connected form beautiful streams. But inasmuch as a report has already been published of a principal part of the waters, near the sea, and of the rivers before mentioned, there still remain several which deserve the names of rivers. There are also several inland waters; some are large, and others of less dimensions, which mostly lie near the sea-shores south of the North River; many of which are navigable and roomy kills and creeks suitable for inland navigation; and those by the industry of man are susceptible of great betterments and improvements, as may be seen by the chart of the New-Nether-

lands. There also are, as before remarked, several falls, streams and running brooks, suitable for every kind of water-work for the convenience and advantage of man, together with numerous small streams and sprouts throughout the country, serving as arteries or veins to the body, running in almost every direction, and affording an abundance of pure living water. Those are not numerous near the sea-shore, where the water in some places is brackish, but still the same is of service, and is drank by the wild and domestic animals. Many of the springs run into the rivers, and thence into the sea. In addition to those, there are also many fine springs and veins of pure water inland and in places where no other water can be obtained, as upon the mountains, high elevated rocks and cliffs, where like veins the water flows out of fissures and pours down the cliffs and precipices, some of which are so remarkable that they are esteemed as great curiosities. Other streams rise in bushy woods, through which the summer sun never shines, which are much trodden by the wild beasts, and wherein the decayed leaves and rotting vegetation falls, all which tend to render the water foul. Those however in their course again become clear and wonderfully pure. Some of them possess the extraordinary quality of never freezing in the bitterest cold weather, when they smoke from their natural warmth, and any frozen article immersed in those waters thaws immediately. If the unclouded sun shone on those springs for whole days with summer heat, the water would still remain so cold that no person would bear to hold his hand in it for any length of time in the hottest weather. This peculiarity makes these waters agreeable to men and animals, as the water may be drank without danger; for however fatigued or heated a person may be who drinks of these waters, they do no injury in the hottest weather. The Indians, gunners, and other persons use those waters freely at all seasons, and I have never heard that any pleurisy or other disease had been caused by their use.

The Indians inform us that there are other waters in the country differing in taste from the common water, which are good for many ailments and diseases. As this is intimated by the Indians, therefore we do not place full confidence in the information, not knowing the facts; yet we deem the reports probable, because the land abounds in metals and minerals, through which spring veins may filter and partake of the mineral qualities, and retain the same.

It is a great convenience and ease to the citizens of New-Netherlands, that the country is not subject to great floods and inundations, for near the sea, or where the water ebbs and rises, there are no extraordinary floods. The tide usually rises and falls from five to six feet perpendicular, in some places more, in others less, as by winds and storms affected. The flood and ebb tides are strong but not rapid. Sometimes where the wind blows strong from the sea, at spring tides the water rises a foot or two higher than usual; but this is not common, hence, of little inconvenience. But, at the colony of Rensselaerwyck, Esopus, Catskill, and other places, from which the principal upper waters flow, they are entirely fresh at those places. The lowlands are sometimes overflowed once or twice in a year when the wind and current are in opposition; but even then, they who guard against those occurrences in time suffer but little. Sometimes the water may wash out a little in places, but the land is manured by the sediment left by the water. Those floods do not stand long; as they rise quick, they also again fall off in two or three days. …

Of the wood, the natural productions and fruits of the land

The New-Netherlands, with other matters, is very fruitful, and fortunate in its fine woods; so much so, that the whole country is covered with wood, and in our manner of speaking, there is all too much of it, and in our way. Still it comes to hand to build vessels and houses, and to enclose the farms &c. The oak trees are very large; from sixty to seventy feet high without knots, and from two to three fathoms thick, being of various sizes. There are several kinds of oak, such as white, smooth bark, rough bark, grey bark and black bark. It is all durable wood, being as good as the oak of the Rhine or the Weser when properly worked, according to the opinion of our woodcutters, who are judges of timber and are saw-

yers. The nut-wood grows as tall as the oak, but not so heavy. It is probable that this kind of wood will be useful for many purposes, it grows straight and is tough and hard. We now use it for cogs and rounds in our mills and for threshing-flails, swivel-trees and other farming purposes. It also is excellent firewood, surpassing every other kind, and setting at naught our old adage, "The man is yet to come, who can find better wood to burn than oak." This wood is far better as well for heat as duration. It possesses a peculiar sap, which causes it to burn freely, whether green or dry. If we draw it up out of the fresh water where it has lain a long time, still, on account of its hardness, it is even then uncommonly durable on the fire. We all agree, that no turf, or other common fuel is equal to nut-wood. When it is dry, it keeps fire and sparkles like matches. Our women prefer nut-coals to turf for their stoves, because they last longer, and are not buried in ashes. This kind of wood is found all over the New-Netherlands in such abundance, that it cannot become scarce in the first hundred years with an increased population. There also is oak and ash enough to supply its place for many purposes. The land also is so natural to produce wood, that in a few years large trees will be grown, which I can say with certainty from my own observation; and that unless there be natural changes or great improvidence, there can be no scarcity of wood in this country.

It has happened when I have been out with the natives, (Wilden, for so we name those who are not born of Christian parents,) that we have come to a piece of young woodland. When I have told them, in conversation, that they would do well to clear off such land, because it would bear good corn, that they said, "it is but twenty years since we planted corn there, and now it is woods again." I asked them severally if it were true, when they all answered in the affirmative. This relation was also corroborated by others. To return to the subject: this woodland was composed of oak, nut and other kinds of wood, but principally of oak and nut; and there were several trees in the same which were a fathom in circumference. The wood was so closely grown that it was difficult to pass through it on horseback. As the wood appeared young and thrifty, I give credit to the relation of the natives. I have also observed that the youngest woodlands are always covered closest with wood, and where the growth is small, the woods are so thick as to render walking through the same difficult. But where the woods are old, the timber is large and heavy, whereby the underwood is shaded, which causes it to die and perish.

The Indians have a yearly custom (which some of our Christians have also adopted) of burning the woods, plains and meadows in the fall of the year, when the leaves have fallen, and when the grass and vegetable substances are dry. Those places which are then passed over are fired in the spring in April. This practice is named by us and the Indians, "bush burning," which is done for several reasons; first, to render hunting easier, as the bush and vegetable growth renders the walking difficult for the hunter, and the crackling of the dry substances betrays him and frightens away the game. Secondly, to thin out and clear the woods of all dead substances and grass, which grow better the ensuing spring. Thirdly, to circumscribe and enclose the game within the lines of the fire, when it is more easily taken, and also, because the game is more easily tracked over the burned parts of the woods.

The bush burning presents a grand and sublime appearance. On seeing it from without, we would imagine that not only the dry leaves, vegetables and limbs would be burnt, but that the whole woods would be consumed where the fire passes, for it frequently spreads and rages with such violence, that it is awful to behold; and when the fire approaches houses, gardens, and wooden enclosures, then great care and vigilance are necessary for their preservation, for I have seen several houses which have recently been destroyed, before the owners were apprized of their danger.

Notwithstanding the apparent danger of the entire destruction of the woodlands by the burning, still the green trees do not suffer. The outside bark is scorched three or four feet high, which does them no injury, for the trees are not killed. It however sometimes happens that in the thick pine woods, wherein the fallen trees lie across each other, and

have become dry, that the blaze ascends and strikes the tops of the trees, setting the same on fire, which is immediately increased by the resinous knots and leaves, which promote the blaze, and is passed by the wind from tree to tree, by which the entire tops of the trees are sometimes burnt off, while the bodies remain standing. Frequently great injuries are done by such fires, but the burning down of entire woods never happens. I have seen many instances of wood-burning in the colony of Rensselaerwyck, where there is much pine wood. Those fires appear grand at night from the passing vessels in the river, when the woods are burning on both sides of the same. Then we can see a great distance by the light of the blazing trees, the flames being driven by the wind, and fed by the tops of the trees. But the dead and dying trees remain burning in their standing positions, which appear sublime and beautiful when seen at a distance.

Hence it will appear that there actually is such an abundance of wood in the New-Netherlands, that, with ordinary care, it will never be scarce there. There always are, however, in every country, some people so improvident, that even they may come short here, and for this reason we judge that it should not be destroyed needlessly. There, however, is such an abundance of wood, that they who cultivate the land for planting and sowing can do nothing better than destroy it, and thus clear off the land for tillage, which is done by cutting down the trees and collecting the wood into great heaps and burning the same, to get it out of their way. Yellow and white pine timber, in all their varieties, is abundant here, and we have heard the Northerners say (who reside here) that the pine is as good here as the pine of Norway. But the pine does not grow as well near the salt water, except in some places. Inland, however, and high up the rivers, it grows in large forests, and it is abundant, and heavy enough for masts and spars for ships. There also are chestnuts here, like those of the Netherlands, which are spread over the woods. Chestnuts would be plentier if it were not for the Indians, who destroy the trees by stripping off the bark for covering for their houses. They, and the Netherlanders also, cut down the trees in the chestnut sea-son, and cut off the limbs to gather the nuts, which also lessens the trees. We also find several kinds of beech trees, but those bear very little. Amongst the other trees, the water-beeches grow very large along the brooks, heavier and larger than most of the trees of the country. When those trees begin to bud, then the bark becomes a beautiful white, resembling the handsomest satin. This tree retains the leaves later than any other tree of the woods. Trees of this kind are considered more ornamental and handsomer than the linden trees for the purpose of planting near dwelling-houses. We can give no comparison with this species of trees, and can give the same no better name to make the wood known. There also is wild ash, some trees large; and maple trees, the wood resembling cedar; white-wood trees, which grow very large,—the Indians frequently make their canoes of this wood, hence we name it Canoe-wood; we use it for flooring, because it is bright and free of knots. There are also two kinds of ash, with linden, birch, yew, poplar, sapine, alder, willow, thorn trees, sassafras, persimmon, mulberry, wild cherry, crab, and several other kinds of wood, the names of which are unknown to us, but the wood is suitable for a variety of purposes. Some of the trees bear fruit. The oak trees in alternate years bear many acorns of the chestnut species. The nuts grow about as large as our persimmons, but they are not as good as ours. The mulberries are better and sweeter than ours, and ripen earlier. Several kinds of plums, wild or small cherries, juniper, small kinds of apples, many hazelnuts, black currants, gooseberries, blue India figs, and strawberries in abundance all over the country, some of which ripen at half May, and we have them until July; blueberries, raspberries, black-caps, &c., with artichokes, ground-acorns, ground beans, wild onions, and leeks like ours, with several other kinds of roots and fruits, known to the Indians, who use the same which are disregarded by the Netherlanders, because they have introduced every kind of garden vegetables, which thrive and yield well. The country also produces an abundance of fruits like the Spanish capers, which could be preserved in like manner.

GLOSSARY

Brackish: Water is said to be brackish if it has a noticeably higher salt content than fresh water, but less than sea water. This typically occurs with the mixture of fresh and sea water in coastal estuaries or in inland water that originates in salty soil or mineral deposits. The word's origin is the Dutch word "brak."

Forelands: A piece of land such as a cape, a headland, an island, or an earthen promontory that separates the mainland from an ocean or sea. From the old English word "forlonde," this would typically be a landform that provides some protection from the sea for an anchorage.

Kill: At the time New Netherland was established, the Dutch word "kill" meant a creek or stream. It survives today in American place names such as Catskill, Fishkill, and Schuylkill.

Patroon: The holder of a significant land grant in New Netherland who also enjoyed "manorial" rights akin to those of feudal princes. Known as patroonships, these tracts of land were usually worked by tenant farmers who paid for the right to farm the patroon's land.

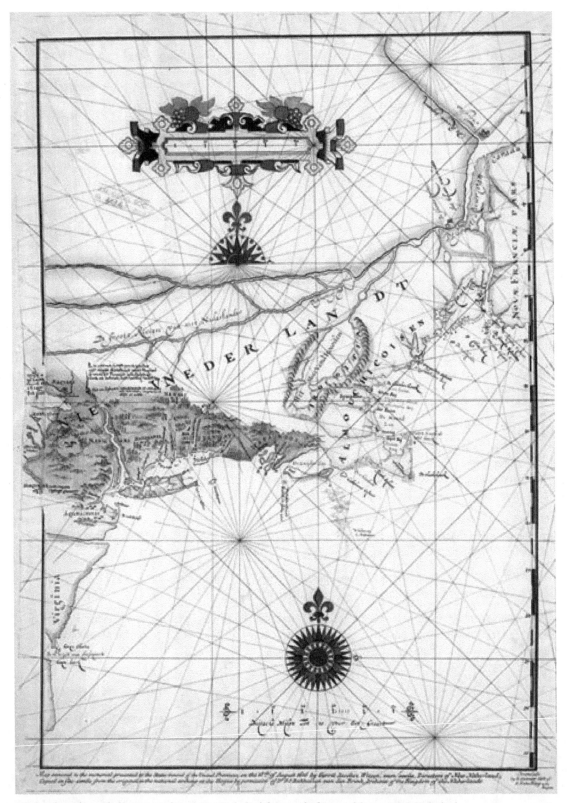

Map based on Adriaen Block's 1614 expedition to New Netherland, featuring the first use of the name New Netherland

Explanation and Analysis of the Document

Van der Donck opens his description with an explanation of the colony's founding, beginning with the voyage of Henry Hudson to find a new trade route to China. Given the international situation of the day, it was important for the Dutch to show that their claims to the land included in New Netherland were original and not simply an attempt to assert entitlement to land already explored by another European power. For this reason he is careful to state that upon first reaching land the explorers "examined the country" and concluded that "no Christian people had ever been there before, and that they were the first who by Providence had been guided to the discovery of the country." Based on this, van der Donck claimed possession of the land for "the Netherlanders" dating to 1609 under the "right of discovery."

After establishing ownership, van der Donck briefly describes the indigenous people, their dress, and their reactions to the arrival of Europeans. In this he is careful to point out that the oldest of them could not remember ever before seeing anyone resembling the Dutch in appearance, which he uses as further proof of the Dutch claim to the land. This leads logically to the next portion of the report which defines the extent of the Dutch claim. In this he is not shy to define an exceptionally vast area from the St. Lawrence River to Virginia and east to the Fresh River (today the Connecticut River). Van der Donck next turns to a description of the coastal areas or "forelands" which was important for reassuring ship captains that there were ample anchorages safe from any inclement ocean weather. Among the potential economic benefits of the ocean in this area were fisheries, oyster beds and abundant whales during the winter months. The nearby lands are portrayed as covered with vines bearing grapes, plums, hazelnuts, and strawberries, but the description also includes grass and emphasizes that the land is "tolerably good" for "cultivation of grain, vineyards, and gardening, and the keeping of stock."

With the major trading post, New Amsterdam, located on Manhattan Island, van der Donck takes great care to describe in detail the large harbor, the rivers, and the other natural features around what today is New York Harbor that might make it attractive to both settlers and commercial traffic. He notes specific places that would be good for establishing settlements and also comments on the many waterways that would provide sufficient flow for establishing milling operations.

To support a future population he carefully describes the many sources of fresh water, while observing that the indigenous people speak of the existence of mineral waters and even the brackish waters nearer the coastline can be used for watering livestock.

With wood in short supply in the Dutch Republic, van der Donck describes in some detail the abundance of woods in New Netherland, comparing the oak favorably with that found along the Rhine and Weser Rivers in the German states. The hardness of some of the woods made them excellent for a variety of purposes, while the "nut-wood" produced "excellent firewood" superior in both "heat" and "duration." The report stresses the abundance of the various woods, speculating that even with an enlarged population "it cannot become scarce in the first hundred years." Adding to this were van der Donck's conversations with the natives which indicated that land once cleared quickly began to grow new trees so as to replenish the supply.

Van der Donck's description of "bush burning" presents a valuable first-hand account of the indigenous practice designed to make hunting game easier while at the same time clearing away dead underbrush so that trees may grow better in the ensuing spring. But he also notes that care must be taken that the fires did not reach cabins. Among the other advantages of the forest areas were the abundance of various nuts and fruits including acorns, chestnuts, mulberries, plums, cherries, apples, currants, blueberries, raspberries, hazelnuts, gooseberries, figs and strawberries. Other wild foods included onions, leeks, beans, and edible wild roots.

Clearly, van der Donck's descriptions provide a very positive portrait of New Netherland designed to attract both settlers and investors in the Dutch colony.

Essential Themes

Adriaen van der Donck's description of the New Netherland colony is the earliest detailed account that we have of the Dutch settlement. Since it was used to attract colonists to the New World it focuses on the positive aspects of the colony, what it had to offer to potential settlers and investors, rather than any of the problems or dangers they might encounter. Nevertheless, with this caveat, the information it contains remains important not only as a description but for what it reveals about what the promoters of the colony believed were its most attractive features. According to

Charles Gehring, director of the New Netherland Institute and the foremost authority on early documents relating to the colony, the van der Donck document is "the fullest account of the province, its geography, the Indians who inhabited it, and its prospects.... It has been said that had it not been written in Dutch, it would have gone down as one of the great works of American colonial literature."

Large portions of van der Donck's report were used as the basis for some of Russell Shorto's acclaimed *The Island at the Center of the World: The Epic Story of Dutch Manhattan and the Forgotten Colony That Shaped America*. Shorto portrays him as a very important colonial figure largely forgotten today because his work was in Dutch and so it went unnoticed by the English once they took possession of the colony. For historians, it remains an important source not only for life in the early colony but, along with van der Donck's other works, for descriptions of indigenous peoples, the interaction of Dutch colonists and traders with these peoples, and other aspects of colonial Dutch life.

Bibliography and Further Reading

Van Cleaf Bachman, *Peltries or Plantations: The Economic Policies of the Dutch West India Company in New Netherland, 1623-1639* (Baltimore: Johns Hopkins Press, 1969).

Jaap Jacobs, *New Netherland: A Dutch Colony in Seventeenth-Century America* (Ithaca, NY: Cornell University Press, 2009).

Oliver A. Rink, *Holland on the Hudson. An Economic and Social History of Dutch New York* (Ithaca, NY: Cornell University Press, 1986).

Russell Shorto, *The Island at the Center of the World: The Epic Story of Dutch Manhattan and the Forgotten Colony That Shaped America* (New York: Doubleday, 2004).

■ A Voyage to America

Date: April 27, 1805
Author: Andreas Geyer, Jr.
Genre: Letter

Summary Overview

Before the age of steam, immigrants wishing to cross the Atlantic to the "New World" had to endure a lengthy and dangerous voyage across the ocean in small wooden ships that were at the mercy of the winds to fill their sails enough to push them through the water. Too little wind and the ship was becalmed making the voyage longer and possibly even threatening to outlast the supply of food and drink. Too much wind, such as a major storm, and the vulnerable ship might be sunk with everyone aboard.

The ships themselves were built for carrying cargo so passenger space was limited. Fortunate indeed was a well-to-do passenger who could find a ship with a cabin and afford the cost of securing the accommodation. The typical immigrant was housed in a cargo hold on the ship which was either a large open area or, on the better ships, temporary partitions that divided the space into smaller compartments. Since this was located on the same level as the steering mechanisms it came to be referred to as "steerage." Often travelers had only a bench to sit on and these, or bunks made of wood, on which to sleep. Some had straw-filled mattresses, but passengers were expected to bring their own pillows, blankets, or whatever else they needed.

Conditions aboard ship varied, but generally they were crowded, lacked proper ventilation and sanitation, and took on the odors of the people and cargo being carried. More often than not the passenger spaces were infested with rats, fleas, lice, and other vermin making for a decidedly unhealthy atmosphere in which diseases spread quickly. In 1800 the average Atlantic crossing took six weeks, but depending on the weather could stretch to as much as fourteen weeks, in which case provisions might run out before reaching land. In the end, much depended on the ship's captain.

Defining Moment

Prior to the 1820s when the British government began to actively regulate ships carrying passengers, travel was done mostly at the mercy of the ship owner and the captain of the vessel. Conditions varied greatly and there were many opportunities for the unwary to be abused or exploited. For example, if a voyage took longer than travelers expected they might run out of provisions and the captain could then increase profits from the voyage by selling food and drink at greatly inflated prices. Or if it were cold on the ocean and the traveler did not bring a blanket these could also be sold at exorbitant prices. Female passengers were particularly vulnerable, especially if traveling alone.

Particularly at risk were people referred to as "redemptioners." In colonial times when a person signed on as an apprentice to learn a trade they incurred an obligation to the master craftsman doing the training that had to be satisfied. Once this was done, the apprentice was said to be "redeemed" and had then settled the obligation. The same concept was used for indentured servants who obligated themselves to provide their labor for a certain number of years in return for passage to America and often some other considerations such as a piece of land of their own when the obligation was completed.

In Germany this practice usually took one of two forms. There was the traditional indentured servant who negotiated the terms of the indenture prior to leaving Europe, but there was also another type of traveler sometimes referred to as a "free-willer" who, in return for passage, gave the ship's captain permission to arrange an indenture for the traveler once the ship arrived in America. The latter left the immigrant particularly vulnerable to unscrupulous exploitation. One study found that German redemptioners paid almost twice as much for passage as did English equivalents and that while the average debt amounted to about a half-year's salary for the typical Philadelphia laborer the redemptioner was usually required to work three to four years to satisfy the debt. Once in America they had no way to return to Europe and could not leave the ship, or the place where they were held, until they agreed to the conditions under which the captain had sold them.

Author Biography

Andreas Geyer, Jr., was sent by the German Society of Philadelphia to Perth Amboy, New Jersey, to look into rumors of abusive treatment of German immigrants during their voyage from Europe. Located in Philadelphia, the Society was founded in 1764 to assist German immigrants and today claims to be the oldest German cultural organization in the United States. Geyer was born in Philadelphia in 1772. His father served as an officer in the American Revolution including the Battles of Trenton, Princeton, Germantown, and Monmouth. He became a bookseller and an officer in the German Society of Philadelphia where he was a member of the St. Michael's-Zion German Lutheran Congregation. The younger Geyer was no doubt detailed to this mission because of his father's prominence in the German Society.

HISTORICAL DOCUMENT

SIR: Having just returned from the errand sent upon by you and the other officers of the German Society, relative to the German Redemptioners lately arrived at Perth Amboy, I have thought proper without loss of time to communicate to you in writing, for your and their information, how far I proceeded with the business entrusted me, respecting the said German redemptioners.

I left the city on Friday last, and in the evening arrived at New Brunswick, when I waited on Mr. Robert Eastburn[1], and presented him the letter you addressed him. Mr. Eastburn appears to be a gentleman of humanity and of feeling. After he read the letter, he observed a willingness to accompany me to Amboy; he did so the next morning, as also did Mr. Kladey. Both of them behaved with the greatest politeness towards me, and with great liberality towards the German Redemptioners at Amboy. Immediately on our arrival at Amboy we went to the river with an intention of going on board the ship General Wayne, or with an expectation of seeing some of the redemptioners on shore. However, we saw none of them at the time, and the ship was weighing anchor, and soon after set sail for New York. By enquiry we found the passengers were deposited in the Jail of Amboy, however not closely confined, having permission granted them by the agent to walk about the place or town. From what I could learn, the captain began to be uneasy, as some of the inhabitants had spoken to him with respect to the malconduct exercised by him towards those unhappy beings, and resolved to leave Amboy and go to New York.

I went to visit those unfortunate people, and in truth they may be called unfortunate. And I must confess I have seen a number of vessels at Philadelphia with redemptioners, but never did I see such a set of miserable beings in my life. Death, to make use of the expression, appeared to be staring them in the face. The complaints were numerous which they made against the captain respecting the bad treatment they received from him on and during the passage. The complaints which I conceive are of the greatest importance I shall briefly state. My intention was to have had them confirmed with their oaths, but as they are made by every one of the passengers I thought it unnecessary. They are that they left Hamburg some time in November last, and arrived at Tonningen, where lay the ship General Wayne, John Conklin, Master, bound for New York, with whom they entered into a certain agreement, on condition that he, the said Conklin, would take them to New York, that during the passage they should be allowed a certain quantity of bread, meat, peas, fish, vinegar, butter, potatoes, tobacco, etc., as also a dram in the morning, as will appear by a reference to the agreement itself, each passenger having one. About fourteen days after they left Tonningen they put into an English port near Portsmouth, where they remained about four weeks ; that during that time a British recruiting officer came on board the ship, when the captain informed them that they now had an opportunity of enlisting, that those who so chose to do might, as the recruiting officer was on board the ship. Ten men consented, and entered their names, giving to the other passengers their reasons for so doing, namely, that, having been already put on allowance by the captain, they were apprehensive that, should they stay on board the ship, they should be starved before they arrived in America. Amongst those that enlisted was a man who had a wife and child on board the ship; that eight days after they had thus entered their names they were taken from the ship by the recruiting officer, although some of them wished to withdraw their names, but to no effect; go they must. The woman and her child are now at Amboy, lamenting the loss of the husband and father.

On the last day of their remaining in this British port, the same recruiting officer came the third time on board the ship, when the mate called four or five of the passengers by name, and told them, in the presence of the captain, they must be soldiers and go with the officer. They replied they had no intention of being soldiers, they wished to go to America; whereupon the captain and mate seized one of them by name Samuel Vogel, and threw him into the boat belonging to the recruiting officer, which was alongside of the ship. However, Vogel got back again into the ship, went below, and hid himself, but was again compelled to come forward with his clothes, when the recruiting officer, observing him weep, declared he would not have him, and left the ship, mentioning that he should not have again come on board had not the captain, the day before, pressed him so to do. The captain was highly dissatisfied with these men for refusing to go, and declared that they should not have anything to eat on board the ship, that they might starve, and ordered one of them to be flogged for refusing, which was performed, too, in a cruel manner. That the whole of the passengers, when at this British port, complained to the captain that the treatment they received was not such as was agreed to between them at Tonningen. He replied they were not then in Tonningen, neither were they in America, but in England. They then set sail, and after fourteen days had elapsed the captain informed them that they would get nothing to eat except bread and meat. After this each person received two biscuits, one pint of water, and the eighth part of a pound of meat per day. This regulation continued for two or three weeks, when they one and all declared they could not any longer exist on the small allowance they received; that they must, without doubt,

perish. The hunger and thirst being at this time so great, and the children continually crying out for bread and drink, some of the men, resolved, at all events, to procure bread, broke open the apartment wherein it was kept, and took some. This was discovered by the captain, as were also those who did the same, when each of them was ordered to, and actually did, receive, after being first tied, a number of lashes on their bare backs well laid on. The whole of the passengers were also punished for this offence. The men received no bread, the women but one biscuit. This continued for nine days, when the men were again allowed one biscuit per day; however, the captain would at least make or proclaim a fast day. In this situation their condition became dreadful, so much so that five and twenty men, women, and children actually perished for the want of the common necessaries of life, in short, for the want of bread. The latter were ten in number, all at the time at the breasts of their mothers. The hunger was so great on board that all the bones about the ship were hunted up by them, pounded with a hammer and eaten; and what is more lamentable, some of the deceased persons, not many hours before their death, crawled on their hands and feet to the captain, and begged him, for God's sake, to give them a mouthful of bread or a drop of water to keep them from perishing, but their supplications were in vain; he most obstinately refused, and thus did they perish. The cry of the children for bread was, as I am informed, so great that it would be impossible for man to describe it, nor can the passengers believe that any other person excepting Captain Conklin would be found whose heart would not have melted with compassion to hear those little inoffensive ones cry for bread. The number of passengers, when the ship arrived at Amboy, amounted to one hundred and thirty-two. Fifty-one remain there still; the others have been disposed of.

The passengers further state that they did not receive the tobacco, the fish, nor the potatoes, as they ought to have received, and which they were entitled to as by their contract with the captain, neither did they receive their dram but four or five times during their passage, and no butter after they left the British port until within three or four days ago.

The foregoing are the principal causes of complaint, and indeed they appear very serious ones too to me. However, I having heard those complaints, and understanding from a number of citizens of Amboy that the captain's intention was to take the ship to New York, leave her, as also the State of New York, and go to his native State, Rhode Island, I was at a loss to know how to act or what to do, as my instructions were not for New York. However, after reflection I determined to push on for New York, and there inform the German Society of his conduct. I did so, and on Sunday arrived there, when, after some little enquiry, I found the President of the society, Mr. Philip I. Arcularius.[2] To him I communicated the whole of this disagreeable affair. His feelings can be more easily conceived than described. He, however, gave directions to have the officers of the society summoned to meet the next day, which was done, and they all attended, excepting one of the assistants, and, after hearing the circumstances relative to those unfortunate people, they appointed three of their members, officers, to act in such way as they should, after taking legal advice, think best to bring the captain to that punishment which his conduct should merit.

[1] Robert Eastburn (1742–1815) was a merchant and realtor who lived in New Brunswick, New Jersey. He was also a member of the Society of Friends (Quakers).

[2] Philip I. Arcularius was a tanner and currier who was also the first president of the German Society of the City of New York when it was founded in 1804.

GLOSSARY

Dram: A drink of whiskey or some other liquor equivalent to one-eighth of a liquid ounce. In popular use it can simply mean a small drink.

Flogged: To be beaten, usually on the back with a whip or stick. Aboard ship at that time it would often be done with a "cat-o'-nine-tails" which was a whip made from nine ropes fastened to a single grip.

Redemptioner: An immigrant who paid for passage to America by selling labor such as an indentured servant.

Explanation and Analysis of the Document

Upon Geyer's arrival in Perth Amboy he found some of the recently-arrived German redemptioners in jail or under order not to leave the city. This was not unusual and implied no wrong-doing on their part. It only meant that these were "free-willers" who had not yet settled their obligation and were most likely awaiting the time when their labor would be sold to find out where they would be going and for whom they would be working. In Geyer's retelling the captain left the port quickly to avoid criticism, but this might also have been a routine departure to load a new cargo. If captains could not quickly arrange for the placement of "free-willers" they often engaged an agent to handle the process for them so that they could continue on their voyage.

Geyer reported finding a very "miserable" group of people who had apparently suffered greatly during the ocean voyage through no small fault of the ship's captain. Chief among the immigrants' complaints was that Captain Conklin had breached the contract they had signed with him by not providing the amount or type of food promised, instead providing them with a greatly reduced ration of biscuit, a small amount of meat, and water. The survivors of the ordeal claimed that twenty-five of their number perished from hunger on the voyage, but one wonders if this might have been an exaggeration or if the deaths might rather have come from disease because the ship's captain would be losing money on every passenger whose labor he could not sell when the vessel reached port.

Another passenger complaint was that when the vessel stopped in England the captain allowed British recruiting officers to come aboard to enlist men from among the group into the British army. Some who refused were punished by being deprived of their food allowance. British "impressment gangs" were a very real threat at that time, especially in seaports. These groups of roving recruiters attempted to sign men up for the British armed forces through whatever means they could, and in some cases outright kidnapping was reported. A favorite tactic of these "press gangs" for the British army was to frequent taverns where they would ply a likely candidate with drink until he did not realize what he was signing. Then, once his name or mark was on the paper there was no way the victim could rescind the enlistment. Since Great Britain depended so much on the Royal Navy to protect its essential overseas trade, recruitment for the navy could be even more extreme, especially in the seaports where men with sailing experience might be found. In fact, impressment of Americans by British authorities was one of the causes that led to the War of 1812. It is unlikely that Captain Conklin would have allowed the recruiters onboard unless he had some arrangement with them, perhaps a "finder's fee" of sorts for anyone who agreed to enlist. Support for this conclusion may be seen in the attempt by both the captain and the recruiting party to force some men into military service.

A search of available records indicates that Captain Conklin went to New York from Perth Amboy, then home to New England. No further information has surfaced on whether Captain Conklin was ever prosecuted.

Essential Themes

Crossings of the Atlantic Ocean in the age of sailing ships were filled with danger from the forces of nature, but these were often supplemented with man-made endangerments. Although the experience described in this document may be an extreme case of cruelty inflicted on vulnerable passengers, it was not uncommon during this era for ship owners or captains to take advantage of travelers in as many ways as they could devise. Often this came in the form of inflated prices for provisions or other necessities once onboard. The "free-will" redemp-

tioners were particularly vulnerable since they often had no specific contractual agreement for their labor prior to sailing and were thus at the mercy of the captain once they arrived in America. With little choice at that point their labor could be sold for whatever the captain could get, requiring them to work for as long as the purchase agreement stated.

In the Royal Navy flogging was then a standard punishment for some shipboard offenses. It was unusual, however, for this to be used against passengers even in the case of theft as described in Geyer's report. The Royal Navy began to limit the practice in the 1860s and eventually eliminated it in 1881. Flogging was also used in the United States Navy. Senator John P. Hale of New Hampshire pushed a bill through Congress to abolish it in September 1850.

Bibliography and Further Reading

Frank Ried Diffenderffer, *The German Immigration into Pennsylvania Through the Port of Philadelphia from 1700 to 1775 and the Redemptioners* (Baltimore: Genealogical Publishing Co., 1977).

Farley Grubb, "The Auction of Redemptioner Servants, Philadelphia, 1771-1804: An Economic Analysis," *The Journal of Economic History*, Vol. 48, no. 3 (September 1988), 583-603.

Cheesman A. Herrick, *White Servitude in Pennsylvania: Indentured and Redemption Labor in Colony and Commonwealth* (New York: Negro University Press, 1969).

John Frederick Whitehead, Johann Carl Büttner, Susan E Klepp, Farley Ward Grubb, and Anne Pfaelzer De Ortiz, *Souls for Sale: Two German Redemptioners Come to Revolutionary America: the Life Stories of John Frederick Whitehead and Johann Carl Büttner* (University Park, PA: Pennsylvania State University Press, 2006).

A Chinese Letter to Governor John Bigler

Date: 1852
Author: Norman Asing
Genre: Letter

Summary Overview

To the Chinese, California was Gam Saan, "Gold Mountain." Following the discovery of that precious metal they flocked to America's Pacific coast to seek their fortune just as others did from Mexico, the eastern United States, and Europe. By 1852 Chinese miners could be found throughout California and had penetrated into the Rouge River Basin in Oregon, while small communities began to form in places like San Francisco, although they were heavily male-oriented with very few females arriving during this time. Although these communities numbered much less than ten percent of the Chinese population, they did attract the attention of an English visitor to the city, J. D. Borthwick, who left this description: "There were Chinamen in all the splendor of sky-blue or purple figured silk jackets, and tight yellow continuations, black satin shoes with thick white soles, and white gaiters; a fan in the hand, and a beautifully plaited glossy skullcap, with a gold knob on the top of it. [These] were the swell Chinamen; the lower orders of the Celestials were generally dressed in the immensely wide blue calico jackets and bags, for they really could not be called trousers, and on their heads they wore enormous wickerworks ... which would have made very fine clothes-baskets."

Early interactions between Chinese, who many referred to as "Celestials" because of their religious references to the "Celestial Kingdom," and other groups tended mostly toward the positive despite the occasional difficulties as might be expected when dissimilar cultures meet for the first time. Chinese businesses naturally catered to their countrymen, but appear to have been frequented by members of other groups as well and the Chinese community was invited to participate in the public ceremonies attending the admission of California into the Union in 1850. In the same year a Caucasian asserted that in his remote mining camp "Were it not for the Chinese we might have starved the first year," while the San Francisco newspaper *Daily Alta California* wrote that "These celestials make excellent citizens and we are pleased to notice their daily arrival in large numbers."

Defining Moment

With the dramatic increase in Chinese immigration in the early 1850s the initial positive or ambivalent feelings of Californians toward this new group began to change. Soon the same *Daily Alta California* that had welcomed the Chinese began, under a new editor, describing them as "morally a far worse class to have among us than the negro. They are idolatrous in their religion—in their disposition cunning and deceited [sic], and in their habits libidinous and offensive." Chinese miners became increasingly unwelcome, with some communities banning them altogether. The state enacted a Foreign Miners' License Tax of $20 per month in response to demands for "protection" by Caucasian miners. The tax applied to those from Mexico, Central and South America as well.

Anti-Chinese sentiment intensified dramatically in April 1852 when Governor John Bigler publicly expressed his concern about "the present wholesale importation to this country, of immigrants from the Asiatic quarter of the globe. ... I allude particularly, to a class of Asiatics known as 'Coolies,' who are sent here, as I am assured, and as is generally believed, under contract to work in our mines for a term; and who, at the expiration of the term, return to their native country." The governor particularly objected to "the exportation by them of the precious metals which they dig up from our soil without charge and without assuming any of the obligations imposed on citizens." The Chinese, he argued, could not assimilate and were incapable of becoming Americans so action ought to be taken to "check this tide of Asiatic immigration." This official sanction of a negative view of the Chinese as "coolies" fed into the rising calls for Chinese restriction or outright expulsion.

Norman Asing, a Chinese leader in San Francisco, responded to the governor's attack in a letter "To His Excellency Gov. Bigler" published in the *Daily Alta California* on May 5, 1852.

Author Biography

Norman Asing is one of those shadowy figures that appear out of the obscure mists of history, play their part, then disappear as mysteriously as they appear. Very little is certain about his youth. At some unknown time, in some unknown place in the Huangliang Du region along the Pearl River delta in southeastern China a boy name Sang Yuen (or was it Yuan Sheng, or Chen Yannquig?) came into the world. Somehow, around 1820 he left the port of Macao, perhaps as a seaman. Landing in New York, he moved to South Carolina where he became a merchant, somewhere along the way acquiring the name Norman Asing.

By 1849 Asing was in San Francisco where he opened the Macao and Woosung Restaurant, believed by some to be the first Chinese restaurant in the city. Elected chair of the first Chinese mutual aid society in America in the same year, when the "first reported Chinese New Year celebration in the United States" was held on February 1, 1851, he hosted "a grand feast" at his home. On George Washington's birthday in 1852 he led a Chinese group in a parade behind a red banner with the words "China Boys." He is known to have led local Chinese delegations that took part in the funeral procession for President Zachary Taylor and the celebration of California's admittance to the American Union, and to have served as an interpreter for his fellow Chinese.

By 1854 Asing was listed in the city directory as a "foreign consul" which would seem to indicate that he served as a go-between linking the local Chinese community with its homeland. It appears that his political control over the Chinese residents, which at least one scholar likened to that of a big city "boss," eventually led him to extorting money from its businessmen, and perhaps attempts to extend this to the greater business population. Historian Gunther Barth describes him as a very strict boss, whose community leadership was marked by "shrewdness, belligerency, and ruthlessness." Whatever the truth, he eventually fades from the picture, his date and place of death as yet unknown.

HISTORICAL DOCUMENT

Sir:

I am a Chinaman, a republican, and a lover of free institutions; am much attached to the principles of the government of the United States, and therefore take the liberty of addressing you as the chief of the government of this State. Your official position gives you a great opportunity of good and evil. Your opinions through a message to a legislative body have weight, and perhaps none more so with the people, for the effect of your late message has been thus far to prejudice the public mind against my people, to enable those who wait the opportunity to hunt them down, and rob them of the rewards of their toil. You may not have meant that this should be the case, but you can see what will be the result of your propositions.

I am not much acquainted with your logic, that by excluding population from this State you enhance its wealth. I have always considered that population was wealth; particularly a population of producers, of men who by the labor of their hands or intellect, enrich the warehouses or the granaries of the country with the products of nature and art. You are deeply convinced you say "that to enhance the prosperity and preserve the tranquility of this State, Asiatic immigration must be checked." This, your Excellency, is but one step towards a retrograde movement of the government, which, on reflection, you will discover; and which the citizens of this country ought never to tolerate. It was one of the principal causes of quarrel between you (when colonies) and England; when the latter pressed laws against emigration, you looked for immigration; it came, and immigration made you what you are—your nation what it is. It transferred you at once from childhood to manhood and made you great and respectable throughout the nations of the earth. I am sure your Excellency cannot, if you would, prevent your being called the descendant of an immigrant, for I am sure you do not boast of being a descendant of the red man. But your further logic is more reprehensible. You argue that this is a republic of a particular race—that the Constitution of the United States admits of no asylum to any other than the pale face. This proposition is false in the extreme, and you know it. The declaration of your independence, and all the acts of your government, your people, and your history are all against you.

It is true, you have degraded the Negro because of your holding him in involuntary servitude, and because for the sake of union in some of your states such was tolerated, and amongst this class you would endeavor to place us; and no doubt it would be pleasing to some would-be freemen to mark the brand of servitude upon us. But we would beg to remind you that when your nation was a wilderness, and the nation from which you sprung barbarous, we exercised most of the arts and virtues of civilized life; that we are possessed of a language and a literature, and that men skilled in science and the arts are numerous among us; that the productions of our manufactories, our sail, and workshops, form no small share of the commerce of the world; and that for centuries, colleges, schools, charitable institutions, asylums, and hospitals, have been as common as in your own land. That our people cannot be reproved for their idleness, and that your historians have given them due credit for the variety and richness of their works of art, and for their simplicity of manners, and particularly their industry. And we beg to remark, that so far as the history of our race in California goes, it stamps with the test of truth the fact that we are not the degraded race you would make us. We came amongst you as mechanics or traders, and following every honorable business of life. You do not find us pursuing occupations of degrading character, except you consider labor degrading, which I am sure you do not; and if our countrymen save the proceeds of their industry from the tavern and the gambling house to spend it on farms or town lots or on their families, surely you will admit that even these are virtues. You say "you desire to see no change in the generous policy of this government as far as regards Europeans." It is out of your power to say, however, in what way or to whom the doctrines of the Constitution shall apply. You have no more right to propose a measure for checking immigration, than you have the right of sending a message to the Legislature on the subject. As far as regards the color and complexion of our race, we are perfectly aware that our population have been a little more tan than yours.

Your Excellency will discover, however, that we are as much allied to the African race and the red man as you are yourself, and that as far as the aristocracy of skin is concerned, ours might compare with many of the European races; nor do we consider that your Excellency, as a Democrat, will make us believe that the framers of your declaration of rights ever suggested the propriety of establishing an aristocracy of skin. I am a naturalized citizen, your Excellency, of Charleston, South Carolina, and a Christian, too; and so hope you will stand corrected in your assertion "that none of the Asiatic class" as you are pleased to term them, have applied for benefits under our naturalization act. I could point out to you numbers of citizens, all over the whole continent, who have taken advantage of your hospitality and citizenship, and I defy you to say that our race have ever abused that hospitality or forfeited their claim on this or any of the governments of South America, by an infringement on the laws of the countries into which they pass. You find us peculiarly peaceable and orderly. It does not cost your state much for our criminal prosecution. We apply less to your courts for redress, and so far as I know, there are none who are a charge upon the state, as paupers.

You say that "gold, with its talismanic power, has overcome those natural habits of non-intercourse we have exhibited." I ask you, has not gold had the same effect upon your people, and the people of other countries, who have migrated hither? Why, it was gold that filled your country (formerly a desert) with people, filled your harbours with ships and opened our much-coveted trade to the enterprise of your merchants.

You cannot, in the face of facts that stare you in the face, assert that the cupidity of which you speak is ours alone; so that your Excellency will perceive that in this age a change of cupidity would not tell. Thousands of your own citizens come here to dig gold, with the idea of returning as speedily as they can.

We think you are in error, however, in this respect, as many of us, and many more, will acquire a domicile amongst you.

But, for the present, I shall take leave of your Excellency, and shall resume this question upon another occasion which I hope you will take into consideration in a spirit of candor. Your predecessor pursued a different line of conduct towards us, as will appear by reference to his message.

I have the honor to be your Excellency's very obedient servant, Norman Asing

GLOSSARY

Asylum: Protection granted by a government to someone who has left their native country to escape harm or political persecution.

Cupidity: A strong desire for wealth or possessions; greed.

Emigration: The act of moving out of a country or region, as opposed to immigration which is the act of moving into an area.

Granaries: Buildings in which threshed grain is stored.

Explanation and Analysis of the Document

Asing begins his letter by identifying himself as a "China-man," but immediately asserting his love for "free institutions" and his loyalty to the principles of the United States. He observes that as governor, Bigler's words have great impact with the general populace and in this instance acted to "prejudice the public mind against my people." He then proceeds to demolish the governor's arguments.

While Bigler asserted that excluding the Chinese would increase the state's wealth, Asing argues that population *is* wealth. He correctly notes that British changes in the open immigration law was one of the issues enumerated as a complaint in the Declaration of Independence and that the nation developed as immigration increased. After cleverly pointing out that the governor himself was the descendent of immigrants, he argues that in "all the acts of your government" there is no support for the idea that the country is "a republic of a particular race." This is not entirely correct since the Immigration Act of 1790 limited citizenship to "white persons."

Next, Asing argues that Bigler is attempting to include the Chinese in the same category as the "Negro" which, he correctly observes, has been "degraded" by being held in "involuntary servitude" for the sake of maintaining the union of the states. He then refers to the myriad of Chinese achievements in art, literature, science, industry, and other fields of endeavor, all achieved when North America "was a wilderness, and the nation from which you sprung barbarous." As far as the Chinese who came to California, they included "mechanics or traders, and

[those] following every honorable business life. You do not find us pursuing occupations of degrading character, except you consider labor degrading, which I am sure you do not."

Asing reminds Bigler that as governor of a state he has no authority over immigration law, which is a federal responsibility under the Constitution. He contradicts Bigler's claim that "none of the Asiatic class" have applied for the benefits of citizenship by noting that he himself is Chinese, a Christian, and a naturalized citizen. "I could point out to you numbers of citizens, all over the whole continent, who have taken advantage of your hospitality and citizenship, and I defy you to say that our race have ever abused that hospitality or forfeited their claim.... You find us peculiarly peaceable and orderly." Asing's claim of citizenship is interesting since under federal law naturalization was limited to "white people," yet it is possible that he could have been a citizen since some of the courts in the east, where he spent his first years in the U.S., were known to occasionally grant naturalization to Asians.

To Bigler's charge that gold has "overcome those natural habits of non-intercourse," Asing asks "has not gold had the same effect upon your people, and the people of other countries, who have migrated hither?" In this and other aspects of life, "white" people are no different than others. With this well-reasoned and lucid letter, Asing not only established himself as a leader of the Chinese community, but displayed an intimate knowledge of the cultural values of his adopted nation which he adroitly uses to frame his arguments.

Essential Themes

The exchange between Governor Bigler and Norman Asing is an excellent example of two essential themes that recur throughout the history of immigration in the United States. The first is "nativism" which from time to time surfaces to demand restriction or exclusion of various peoples. The governor's arguments, together with the pronouncements of the *Daily Alta California*'s editor, touch on nearly all of the traditional anti-immigrant arguments. The Chinese (or in other generations the Irish, Germans, Italians, Poles, Mexicans, etc.) were morally beneath "Americans," their religious beliefs were strange and "idolatrous," and their inclinations dishonest. Bigler's argument that Chinese immigrants lowered the economic prosperity can be found in many iterations throughout American history, as can the belief that they drain valuable resources from the country—in this case by exporting gold, in others through remissions to their native country.

Asing's response also reflects classic immigrant responses to nativist criticisms. He stresses his loyalty to the United States and the principles of freedom, while mentioning that he is a citizen. He points with pride to the accomplishments of his group in their homeland, then refers to their good citizenship and contributions to their adopted country. And he couches all of this in the symbolism of the Declaration of Independence, the Constitution, and the notion of liberty. Look at any group seeking acceptance in America and you will find the same general responses.

Bibliography and Further Reading

Gunther Barth, *Bitter Strength: A History of the Chinese in the United States, 1850-1870* (Cambridge, MA: Harvard University Press, 1964).

Yong Chen, *Chinese San Francisco, 1850-1943: A Trans-Pacific Community* (Stanford: Stanford University Press, 2000).

Ping Chiu, *Chinese Labor in California, 1850-1880* (Madison: State Historical Society of Wisconsin, 1963).

Ronald Takaki, *Strangers From a Different Shore* (Boston: Little, Brown and Company, 1989).

Judy Yung, Gordon H. Chang, and Him Mark Lai, eds., *Chinese American Voices: From the Gold Rush to the Present* (Berkeley: University of California Press, 2006).

Liping Zhu, *A Chinaman's Chance: The Chinese on the Rocky Mountain Mining Frontier* (Boulder, CO: University Press of Colorado, 1997).

■ *Kleindeutschland* in the 1850s

Date: 1863
Author: Theodor Griesinger
Genre: Book Excerpt

Summary Overview

Colonial North America was largely a rural, agricultural nation. By the beginning of the American Revolution in 1775 there were only five cities with a population of more than 10,000—Philadelphia (40,000), New York (25,000), Boston (16,000), Charleston (12,000), and Newport (11,000). All of them were seaports with their economies largely dependent on commerce. Almost 96 percent of the total population resided in small towns or farming areas with most making a living as subsistence farmers.

Although these were English colonies, there was considerable diversity within them. New England included Scots-Irish, especially along the early frontier areas, and Dutch settlers in western Connecticut. New York had large Dutch and German populations, as well as a myriad of people in New York City. New Jersey contained an influential Scots-Irish population, along with both Catholic and Presbyterian Irish. Pennsylvania included a French community in Philadelphia and heavily German districts outside the city. Scots-Irish farmers predominated in many of the backcountry areas of the South. In Virginia, until they were supplanted by slaves, Irish and English indentured servants provided the primary labor force on the colony's plantations. In the Carolinas, many of the English settlers arrived from the Barbados, bringing African slaves with them, while Charleston contained a large French community. By the time of the first United States census in 1790, the approximately 2,800,000 people included 1,300,000 of English descent, 180,000 Scots and Scots-Irish, 156,000 Germans, 54,000 Dutch, 44,000 Irish, and 13,000 French, with a scattering of other groups.

Defining Moment

Following American independence, the largest immigrant group was the Irish. Between 1820 and 1840, 43 percent of those arriving were Irish with Germans next at 27 percent. Severe agricultural failures in 1829-30 prompted German emigration which was further stimulated by high rents and taxes in the 1840s, as well as democratic and nationalistic revolts in 1830, 1846 and 1848. Many of these settled in New York, Philadelphia, and the emerging western cities like Cincinnati, Milwaukee, Chicago, and St. Louis, but large numbers purchased farm lands in the Midwest. They were the largest single immigrant group every year but three between 1854 and 1894, and are estimated to have been the largest group to migrate during the 19th century with over five million people. In 1851, 221,253 Germans arrived, with the 1910 census revealing 8,282,618 people listing "Germany" as their "country of origin." By 1900, Germans constituted the largest single ethnic group in 27 different states.

Germans arriving in the 1830s contained a large number of farmers and so-called "Latin Farmers," educated people who sought an idyllic bucolic life in the open farmlands of the American west (today's Midwest). Germans arriving after 1848 were generally referred to as the "Forty-Eighters" because they included a large number of political revolutionaries and reformers who participated in the 1848 uprisings. Because of their numbers, their relative economic position, and the fact that they were spread over such a wide area of the United States, the Germans became a significant political force in mid-nineteenth century America. They were also large enough to create recognizable German communities, both rural and urban, where one could find a full array of businesses and services that did not require speaking English. In New York, some 200,000 Germans constituted almost one-fourth of the city's population by 1860 including 120,000 in the German *"Kleindeutschland"* section from the Bowery to the East River and as far north as Houston and Fourteenth Streets. Only Berlin and Vienna had larger German-speaking populations than New York. In 1863 Theodor Griesinger published *Land und*

Leute in Amerika: Skizzen aus dem amerikanischen Leben (Stuttgart: A. Kröner) in which he described what it was like to live in this island of Germany in America.

Author Biography

Karl Theodor Griesinger was a "Forty-Eighter." Born in Kirnbach in the Black Forest region in 1809, he studied theology in Tübingen but soon embarked on a career as a novelist, humorist, and editor of *Der schwäbische Humorist* (The Swabian Humorist). During the 1848 revolutions he founded and edited *Die Volkswehr* (The People's Army), a liberal democratic publication in Baden that led to his arrest and trial on charges of treason. After serving a term in prison he emigrated to North America in 1852, staying for five years during which he made observations of the local New York German community, as well as other places in America.

Griesinger eventually returned to Stuttgart in 1857 where he continued his literary and journalistic career, much of which involved work based on his observations in America—*Lebende Bilder aus Amerika* (Living Images from America), *Emigrantengeschichten* (Emigrant Stories), *Die alte Brauerei, oder Kriminalmysterien aus New York* (The Old Brewery, or Crime Mystery from New York). He also wrote about the Vatican, the Jesuits, and several other books, but brought criticism upon himself for some later anti-Semitic writings. He passed away in Stuttgart in 1884 after publishing numerous books including commentaries on North America including the extract below.

HISTORICAL DOCUMENT

The traveler who passes up Broadway, through Chatham Street, into the Bowery, up Houston Street, and thence right to First Avenue will find himself in a section which has very little in common with the other parts of New York. The arrangement of the streets and the monotony of the brownstone dwellings are similar, but the height and detail of the houses, the inhabitants, and their language and customs differ greatly from those of the rest of New York. This is *"Kleindeutschland,"* or *"Deutschländle,"* as the Germans call this part of the city....

The first floor of the houses along these avenues serves as a grocery or shoemaker's shop, or even an inn; but the upper floors still house from five to 24 families, in some buildings as many as 48.... On each floor of such buildings there are eight apartments, four on the street side and four on the back. Naturally the apartments are very small: a living room with two windows and a bedroom with no windows—that is all. The room with the two windows is 10 feet by 10 feet, and such apartments rent for five to six dollars a month. Apartments in buildings where only ten or twelve families reside rent for eight to nine dollars. These apartments contain a comfortable living room, with three windows, and two bedrooms. According to the standards of the German workingman, one can live like a prince for ten to fourteen dollars a month. Apartments at this price contain two bedrooms, two living rooms, one of which is used for a kitchen, and sufficient room for storing coal and wood.

That is how the Germans live in *Kleindeutschland.* But they are satisfied-happy, contented, and, most significantly, among their own people.... *Deutschländle* certainly deserves its name, because 15,000 German families, comprising 70,000 to 75,000 people, live here. New York has about 120,000 German-born inhabitants. Two-thirds of these live in *Kleindeutschland.* They come from every part of Germany, although those from Northern Germany are rarer than those from the southern part, and Hessians, people from Baden, Württemburgers, and Rhenish Bavarians are most numerous.

Naturally the Germans were not forced by the authorities, or by law, to settle in this specific area. It just happened. But the location was favorable because of its proximity to the downtown business district where the Germans are employed. Moreover, the Germans like to live together; this permits them to speak their own language and live according to their own customs. The cheapness of the apartments also prompted their concentration. As the first Germans came into *Kleindeutschland*, the Irish began to move and the Americans followed because they were ashamed to live among immigrants.

Life in *Kleindeutschland* is almost the same as in the Old Country. Bakers, butchers, druggists—all are Germans. There is not a single business which is not run by Germans. Not only the shoemakers, tailors, barbers, physicians, grocers, and innkeepers are German, but the pastors and priests as well. There is even a German lending library where one can get all kinds of German books. The resident of *Kleindeutschland* need not even know English in order to make a living, which is a considerable attraction to the immigrant.

The shabby apartments are the only reminder that one is in America. Tailors or shoemakers use their living rooms as workshops, and there is scarcely space to move about. The smell in the house is not too pleasant, either, because the bedrooms have no windows, and there is a penetrating odor of sauerkraut. But the Germans do not care. They look forward to the time when they can afford a three-room apartment; and they would never willingly leave their beloved *Kleindeutschland*. The Americans who own all these buildings know this. That is why they do not consider improving the housing conditions. They like the Germans as tenants because they pay their rent punctually, in advance, and keep the buildings neat and clean. The landlords are interested in keeping the German tenants crowded together because such buildings bring more profit than one-story houses....

There are more inns in *Kleindeutschland* than in Germany. Every fourth house is an inn, and there is one for every 200 people. To the stranger, coming for the first time into the section, it would appear that there was nothing but beer saloons. Actually, an immense quantity of beer is consumed. Since the German does not care for brandy there is not a single hard liquor saloon in *Kleindeutschland*. Wine is too expensive, so the resident has to be content with beer.

One who has not seen the *Deutschländle* on a Sunday, does not know it at all. What a contrast it presents to the American sections, where the shutters are closed,

and the quiet of a cemetery prevails! On Sundays the ... churches are full, but there is nevertheless general happiness and good cheer. The Protestant Germans do not indulge in much religious observance. They profess to be freethinkers, and do not go to church very often. On the other hand, the Catholic church on Third Street is always overcrowded. It was built from the voluntary contributions of the German workingmen. Saving the money out of their weekly pay, they have built the second largest, and the most beautiful, church in New York City. It has a big tower and three bells, and nearby is a school which the German children attend and where classes are conducted in German. All this has been accomplished through the monthly contributions of the German workingmen, who take great pride in their school and their church.

On Sunday the movement in the streets is like that in a dovecote. People go from the inn to the church and back to the inn again. Everyone wears his Sunday clothes and is in high spirits. In the afternoon, on days when the weather is good, almost everybody leaves town and goes on a picnic. On Sunday night there is still more merriment in *Kleindeutschland*. The inns are crowded, even with women. There is music, in spite of the laws against making noise on Sunday.

The Germans have a *Volkstheater*, although the name theatre can hardly be applied to this long hall where the consumption of beer and cheese is a major activity. At the end of the hall is a small stage; and the performances are not real plays as much as entertainment by comedians whom the proprietor hires to amuse his customers. Their ribald songs receive the enthusiastic applause of the audience. The people enjoy themselves immensely; the entertainment costs only ten cents, and one gets a free beer now and then. Such is the way Sunday is celebrated in *Kleindeutschland*.

GLOSSARY

Brownstones: The term refers to a reddish-brown form of sandstone often used for construction, especially in 19th century American cities. Because of the prevalence of the material for housing in New York City, the label became synonymous with the structures themselves.

Deutschländle: Little Germany, the ethnic German area of New York City, began taking shape around 1840. It reached its peak between about 1870 and 1880 after which second generation Germans began slowly moving away as new economic opportunities became available.

Freethinkers: A person who rejected religious doctrine. This was especially prevalent in Germany during the 19th century when the ideals of tolerance and humanism caused many to reject organized religion.

Kleindeutschland: This was a more frequently used term for *Deutschländle* (see above).

Volkstheater: A German term meaning "People's Theater," in the context of the letter it referred to the ethnic theaters offering public performances.

Document Analysis

The excerpt describes the distinctive 19th century immigrant community in which most people lived wither in tenements or in brownstones, both of which typically became overcrowded as the influx of immigrants outpaced the available living space. Apartments of course came in different sizes and configurations with differing rents to match. In Griesinger's descriptions, a rent of $6 for a 100 square foot apartment (10 feet by 10 feet) in 1863 would be the equivalent of about $117 in 2015 dollars. Some had windows and some did not, some had kitchens and some did not. Regardless of the size, the number of families and people crowded into the limited space led to serious problems with sanitation and the spread of contagious diseases, a situation that became much worse by the end of the century.

Griesinger explains that the housing often had bakeries, butchers, and other businesses located on the ground floor, with residential space in the floors above. Most of the commercial establishments specialized in ethnic favorites that would appeal to their customers, recreating as near as possible the traditional ambiance of Old World villages. Within the larger of these ethnic communities people from different areas of Germany settled near others from the same region so that some city blocks contained mostly Bavarians or Rhinelanders or any other region, creating smaller, more individualized ethnic enclaves within what appeared to outsiders to be a homogenous German community.

As the reading suggests, this ethnic segregation was largely voluntary. Economics played a role with new arrivals seeking affordable—that is, cheap—housing, but immigrants who had only limited English skills generally preferred to settle among those who shared their language and traditions, thus easing to some extent the

transition to an alien society and culture. In the natural evolution of these urban sub-communities, over time one group would become upwardly mobile while other new arrivals would take their place. In this way early German communities might evolve into Italian settlements, and these in turn later into Mexican districts.

Griesinger also observes the differences in Sunday customs between the Germans and the surrounding community. Whereas the "American sections" are characterized by church services but otherwise being as quiet as a cemetery, the Germans are divided between those who attend church and those who do not. Regardless of whether the Germans are religious or not, the atmosphere is one of "general happiness and good cheer." Residents "go from the inn to the church and back to the inn again." The taverns are "crowded" with both men and women with music contributing to the gaiety. In good weather Sunday afternoon picnics are the norm. Whether the activities are indoor or outdoor, they are quite different than the non-Germans who most often considered Sunday activities other than church to be inappropriate. Perhaps most improper of all, at least in the eyes of those outside the community, were the Sunday theater performances which often included comedians, loud applause, and even "ribald" songs. All of this further set *Kleindeutschland* apart from the general community in which it existed while fueling interethnic tensions and nativist reactions. This portrait of New York's German community could easily be substituted for almost any urban ethnic enclave in the 19th or 20th centuries with only the substitution of specific ethnic-related terms and traditions.

Essential Themes

Griesinger's descriptions of Kleindeutschland are typical of the varied ethnic communities that began forming in 19th century America. German and Irish areas of cities emerged in the antebellum era, while distinctively Italian, Polish, Jewish, and other ethnic neighborhoods developed during the period of the great migration, 1870-1920. On the Pacific coast, Chinese communities developed in San Francisco and elsewhere, while the latter 20th century saw the rise of Mexican and other Hispanic districts.

To a greater or lesser extent, depending on the size of the ethnic population, these were all relatively self-sustaining communities where a person could live, work, and conduct the normal activities of daily life in the person's native language without having to learn English except, perhaps, for a few workplace phrases depending on the nature of the employment. Ethnic areas formed small, more intimate communities within the more anonymous sprawl of the cities. Ethnic theaters, newspapers, businesses, churches, and social clubs made the new immigrants feel at home, while politicians often courted ethnic leaders for the votes they could deliver. The latter sometimes brought recognition and status to the community, but perhaps the most important aspect was that the otherwise powerless individual immigrant could count on the community and its political and religious leaders for support in times of need. These were, in many respects, recreations of the small rural villages of the Old World and excellent examples of how they adapted their cultural traditions to support themselves in America.

Bibliography and Additional Reading

Tyler Anbinder, *City of Dreams: The 400-year Epic History of Immigrant New York* (Boston: Houghton Mifflin Harcourt, 2016).

Robert Ernst, *Immigrant Life in New York City, 1825-1863* (New York: King's Crown Press, 1949).

Stanley Nadel, *Little Germany: Ethnicity, Religion, and Class in New York City, 1845-80* (Urbana: University of Illinois Press, 1990).

Richard O'Connor, *German-Americans: An Informal History* (Boston: Little, Brown, 1968).

Carl Frederick Wittke, *Refugees of Revolution: The German Forty-Eighters in America* (Philadelphia: University of Pennsylvania Press, 1952).

■ Letter from an Irish Immigrant

Date: January 11, 1883
Author: John F. Costello
Genre: Letter

Summary Overview

The population density of Ireland was one of the largest in Europe during the 1830s. Absentee landlords controlled the vast majority of Irish land, making it virtually impossible for the Irish to purchase farms, while at the same time increasing rents and taxes made small farmers unable to compete with large estates and often forced those who did own land to sell it and become landless tenant farmers. These economic factors, coupled with a lack of any real political opportunities and the religious annoyance of Catholics having to pay taxes to support the Anglican Church, led many to think of migration elsewhere. The great "Potato Famine" of 1845-49 only spurred on a movement that had already begun. Between 1845 and 1855, an estimated 750,000 Irish died of famine and disease, while another two million left their homeland. Historians have estimated that nearly half of the entire population of Ireland migrated elsewhere during the nineteenth century, almost four million to the United States forming the largest single group migration prior to 1850.

Most of the Irish settled in the large northeastern port cities, especially New York and Boston, because they were too poor to travel elsewhere. They took unskilled positions in factories or work as common laborers, settling into the cheapest tenements they could find. Tenements grew to be grossly overcrowded, often with entire extended families living in one room or a basement, causing diseases to spread rapidly. Sanitation and fire protection were rudimentary at best. Life for most of these early Irish immigrants was at or below subsistence level, making each day a dreary life-and-death existence.

Defining Moment

Though generally poor and ill-educated, the early Irish immigrants prior to the Civil War had two advantages that helped them accommodate to their new surroundings. First, they were used to dealing with British control in Ireland so in this strange new world they fell back on some of the same survival tactics they had used in the "Old Country" to assist them in their adjustment to life in urban America. The other advantage the Irish had was that they spoke English. Very soon American politicians began appealing for the votes of Irish immigrants, and a close relationship developed between the Irish and American urban politics. While political reformers and Nativists bemoaned the "selling of Irish votes" that kept political machines in power, the relationship was not one-dimensional. The Irish received significant benefit for their political support. In return, political bosses helped them to obtain what they needed most—jobs. Politicians obtained city employment for constituents, push-cart licenses for their supporters, fixed minor problems with the police, sent Christmas turkeys, provided coal in the winter, paid rents and provided food in emergencies, appeared at their constituents' funerals, saw to it that presents arrived when babies were born, arranged for housing, and in dozens of other ways courted the Irish vote with services and support the immigrants could obtain nowhere else. By 1855, fully 34 percent of the registered voters in New York City were Irish. In time, the Irish themselves grew in political power to control most of the big-city political machines throughout the northeast from Boston through Chicago.

Over time, too, the Irish began to move up the socioeconomic ladder in American, while later arrivals coming from a more prosperous Ireland often came with sufficient funds to make them more mobile. Both of these circumstances led to more mobility, with some Irish of the immigrant or second generation moving as far west as the Pacific coast.

Author Biography

John Francis Costello was a native of Croagh, Limerick County, Ireland, where he was born on November 27, 1860. He arrived in the United States as a steerage passenger aboard the 4,588 ton single-screw ship *Helvetia* listed as a laborer. His letter was dated from Seattle on January 11, 1883. Exactly how or why he journeyed to the northwest is unknown, but he settled in Seattle, Washington. The return address on a letter he sent home was that of a Mr. P. Hayes who was the author's uncle. He owned a farm where Costello was living at the time the letter was written.

Costello was a very literate man who became a naturalized citizen on August 29, 1888, married Mary Bridget Costello, and acquired enough money to purchase a farm in White River, King County. He died on November 24, 1930, in Seattle. He was the grandfather of John and Leo Costello who were active members of the Irish Heritage Club of Seattle.

HISTORICAL DOCUMENT

Dear Father Mother Sister and Brothers,

I once more take the opportunity of addressing ye a few lines from the far and distant shores of Puget Sound hoping they will find ye and uncle & family in as good health as I am at present. I expect ye are of the opinion by this time that I never did intend to write again to ye but I hope ye will excuse my laziness and I promise to be a better boy for the future even if I don't write very often. It's often I think of ye & Cousins & Uncle and all my old Companions. To speak in truth, my last thought going to bed at night and first arising in the morning are of home. The thoughts of it everlastingly haunts my mind.

I often think if I were back in the Atlantic States I would be home to ye every Christmas, but we are so far West here that if we attempted to go any further we would walk into the Pacific Ocean. Its often I laugh when I think about school at home when James McDonnell used to ask me point out Vancouver Island for him, I told Mike the day I landed here. If he were out here now I could lay his hand on it. But at one time it was my last thought I would ever see such places as I have seen.

But then I still think I am in as good a country as there is in the world today for a poor man. The majority of what men is in the country have risen from their own industry. Any man here that will work and save his earnings, and make use of his brains can grow rich. This was one extraordinary good year that's past, on all kinds of work in general but especially hop raisers & loggers. Hops were ($1) one dollar per pound my Uncle has 17 tons. He sold some for 60 cents, and holds 8 tons unsold. Yet his brother in law John Burns; sold 12 tons at $1 per pound in San Francisco.

Burns is a man that worked many a day for 8 and 10d in Ireland and he is worth more than William Power today. He has 9 men working for him; and paying them upwards of 30 dollars a month per man: and they are not starved with the hunger like half the Gentlemen to home. There are no Gentlemen here. If a farmer in Ireland made 3 or 4 thousand dollars in a year you couldn't walk the road with them. You would have to go inside the fence or they would ride over you.

I would like to know what the boys about to be wasting their time around Croagh. They have nothing to do there but to go to work for somebody; and sooner then I would work for a farmer in Ireland, I would cut off my good right hand. I don't think little of Ireland by talking so, for it's the dearest spot upon the earth to me,

For as true as the needle by magnet love lead
My sad heart points faithfully back to Ireland
In vain all the charms of creation may woo
While away from thy shores,
Oh my sweet sainted sireland

There is one thing certain if they ever do come out here. For many a long month they will wish they stopped at home. But home sickness is something that's natural. I often get a relapse of it but somehow there seems to be no cure only to stand it. I often thinks that I would give $200 for to be at home again for the short space of one day. But when you cannot have what you like, you must learn to like what you have. I have seen fellows here who have been back 4 times to Ireland and still intend to be buried there. I am sure I don't know where I will be buried though neither do it bother me any yet. I suppose the greater portion of the boys around Croagh are all leaving there.

I heard that John Hayes & J. Cahill went to Australia. I think this is a better Country than Australia. I wish ye would send me their addresses if possible. I also understand that Jas. Hogan with others intended to go to Australia. I don't see why they wouldnt come out here. Wages is good, work and Land plenty but a wild looking Country, all woods, trees: Some of them I have seen 14 and 15 feet in diameter. If that was in Croagh the people would class it one of the seven wonders of world.

I would leave but account of the wages. Then I am getting the highest wages paid on a ranch. The only dislike I have is the hours are so long. In the morning now I do be up and have 50 head of cattle, pair of horses fed 6 cows milked and breakfast and then it is not day. There are none but Mike and I working here now during the winter. He is in town for the last few days. I do be cutting cord wood all alone by myself in the woods during the day. Often I sits down and think of everybody I wished well to home. Indeed I do be thinking of ye when ye don't least expect it. I felt kind of forlorn all last summer. Not a letter did I get from anybody belong to me. But I have made up my mind that it won't be my fault or they will write next year.

When Sunday comes takes a rifle or shotgun, go out to hunting. Wild animals of all description abound here. And as for wild ducks they are as thick as the cows to home. Also pheasants grouse you can take your gun, or four if you want to, and nobody will ask where is your license. All you went is money enough to buy a gun. To sum all up this is a free Country. If they see such men as Meade Fitzgerald here they would tie them and drown them in the river.

I must conclude by wishing ye & Cousin & Uncle a fond adieu.

Respectfully yours
J F Costello

---

[1]This is probably a reference to William Powers who owned Powers Irish Whiskey.

[2] Joseph J. Cahill, a son of the Cahill mentioned in the letter as going to Australia, served as Premier of the Australian State of New South Wales from 1952 to 1959.

GLOSSARY

10d: A reference to English coinage in circulation in Ireland which would indicate a value of 10 pence.

Adieu: Derived from the Anglo-French expression "a dieu" (to God), in common usage it means farewell.

Ye: This is an archaic Old English form for "thou" or "you" when referring to a person, but in popular usage it was sometimes used in place of "the" such as in "ye old tavern."

Document Analysis

John Costello's letter to his immediate family in Ireland betrays, in its first paragraph, the typical immigrant's longing for the sight of family and friends left behind. In his case he appears to feel this all the more because of his location on the West coast which, because of the great distances, does not even permit an occasional visit to his native land. But unlike some who succumb to depression, Costello is able to follow with a pleasant memory from his school days at home showing that, while longing to see his family, he was not despondent about his circumstances.

The emigrant has remained positive, he explains, because of his view of America as a land where a person can succeed through individual effort and intelligence. As an example he cites his uncle and a brother-in-law, both of whom were very successful raising hops for sale and logging. He especially contrasts the experience of John Burns, the brother-in-law, in Ireland where he was a laborer as opposed to the United States where he is affluent and owns a business employing nine men. They are, he asserts, "not starved with the hunger like half the Gentlemen to home." In this respect he asks about "the boys about to be wasting their time" in his home village with no prospects "but to go to work for somebody; and sooner then I would work for a farmer in Ireland, I would cut off my good right hand." Yet, Costello is also quick to reassure his family that "I don't think little of Ireland by talking so, for it's the dearest spot upon the earth to me." He emphasizes this by inserting a poem which, though in this case wistfully longing for Ireland, could describe any immigrant's love for the native land. Costello provides an excellent description of how homesickness can afflict an immigrant in a new land, explaining that it can often recur without any apparent remedy other than "to stand it" because "when you cannot have what you like, you must learn to like what you have."

Costello also comments on friends who have gone to Australia, believing that the United States is better because wages are good, in fact, what keeps him from returning to Ireland despite the long work day is the high wages. He closes with another sentiment typical of this type of letter, reassuring his family that they are constantly in his thoughts and scolding them for not writing to him more often. The latter is of course yet another illustration of the immigrant's loneliness and longing for the only tangible thing that keeps him tied to his previous life, precious words from his family.

Essential Themes

Immigrant letters home served important purposes in the immigration process. Letters sent home by early immigrants are valuable sources for exploring the reasons why people left their original country, what they expected to find in their adopted land, and the reality of what they experienced once the journey was completed. Often they were a major contributing factor to chain migration from villages or regions to specific locations in America if an early arrival wrote positively about the new land and the opportunities available there. This would prompt family members, friends, or acquaintances to make the decision to follow, leading to the settling of small communities or city neighborhoods by people from the same country or region or village within a country.

Unwilling to admit failure, unsuccessful immigrants might embellish the extent of their success which could also cause people to migrate with unrealistic expectations. In John Costello's letter we see all of the homesickness that beset most immigrants, as well as the inevitable comparison between the native and adopted country, the suggestion that those inclined to search for a better life join him in America, and finally the plea for his family to write. In all of these factors, Costello's letter is typical of the genre regardless of the origin of the document's author.

Bibliography and Additional Reading

Michael Coffey and Terry Golway, *The Irish in America* (New York: Hyperion, 1997).

Michael Glazier, ed., *The Encyclopedia of the Irish in America* (Notre Dame, IN: University of Notre Dame Press, 1999).

John F Keane, *Irish Seattle* (Charleston, SC: Arcadia Publishers, 2007).

Timothy J. Meagher, *The Columbia Guide to Irish American History* (New York: Columbia University Press, 2005).

William V. Shannon, *The American Irish: A Political and Social Portrait* (Amherst: University of Massachusetts Press, 1989).

William E. Watson and Eugene J. Halus, Jr., *Irish Americans: The History and Culture of a People* (Santa Barbara, CA: ABC-CLIO, 2014).

How the Other Half Lives

By Jacob A. Riis

Original Cover of 1890 edition of *How the Other Half Lives*

How the Other Half Lives

Date: 1890
Author: Jacob Riis
Genre: Book Excerpt

Summary Overview

Following the Civil War, immigration began to increase slowly until the mid-1870s when a massive influx of people began that lasted until the beginning of World War I in 1914. Some 28 million people entered the United Stated between 1860 and 1920. About 80 percent of these settled in the northeast, the area from Boston to Washington (DC), then west to St. Louis and north to Chicago and Milwaukee. Between 1860 and 1910, the urban population rose from 6.2 million to 42 million, an astounding 677 percent of its 1860 size! Due in large part to this human influx, the 1920 census found, for the first time, more than half of America's population residing in cities—the United States had become an urban nation.

New York City's population more than tripled from about one million in 1860 to over three million by 1900. By 1890 it had become the largest immigrant center in the world. But with the rapid rise of the city came a plethora of unwanted problems that horrified many Americans—overcrowding, lack of proper sanitation and other urban facilities, and an increase in poverty, crime, and disease. One of the prominent complaints was the seeming alliance between immigrants and urban political machines. In an era when public social services were largely non-existent, immigrants arriving in the nation's seaports sought assistance wherever they could find it. Often this was from politicians eager to court the votes of the newcomers. In return, politicians could offer assistance in obtaining jobs, housing, naturalization, support in times of financial or emotional need such as the death of a family member, various social services, personal access to authority, and deference to ethnic pride. Many people believed this alliance led to the urban evils they decried causing them to condemn not only political bosses but also the immigrants.

single square mile sometimes ten to fifteen people into a tenement apartment originally meant to house two to four people. Chinese, Czechs, Hungarians, Irish, Italians, Jews, Lithuanians, Poles, Russians, Slovaks, and a myriad of other religious and ethnic peoples competed for jobs, housing, and services in these horribly congested streets, hoping to eke out a narrow subsistence living for themselves and their families.

The story of one immigrant who arrived in 1870 was the story of many, if not most. He arrived aboard a steamship with $40 in his pocket, but within five days both his pockets and his stomach were empty. Luckily, he found work as a carpenter for a few days, then moved from one job to another, eventually finding temporary work on a farm, but was soon unemployed again. Homeless, he slept on a tombstone one night, in a street the next, eating discarded food from Delmonico's Restaurant and whatever else he could scavenge. A brief stint selling flatirons took him to Chicago, but he lost everything to swindlers and found himself back in New York no better off than before.

Just when all seemed hopeless, he made the acquaintance of an editor from the *New York Tribune* who recommended him for a temporary position as a police reporter, perhaps because of his familiarity with the crime-ridden Lower East Side. Or perhaps it was because no one else wanted to venture into Mulberry Street, then known as "Death's Thoroughfare," the main avenue about which radiated the other streets forming the notorious Five Points neighborhood, the worst of the worst of New York slums. It was the break he finally needed. The impoverished young man had taken his first step along a roadway that would lead to fame based on his own experiences and those of his fellow immigrants. His name was Jacob Riis.

Defining Moment

By 1880 the Lower East Side of Manhattan Island was already home to some 334,000 people squeezed into a

Author Biography

Born in Ribe, Denmark, on May 3, 1849, Jacob Riis arrived in New York in 1870 where he worked at various jobs before being hired as a police reporter by the *South Brooklyn News* in 1873. Covering mostly the city's Lower East Side, a neighborhood of closely packed tenements serving the poor, most of whom were recent immigrants, Riis was greatly impressed by the extreme poverty and the deplorable living conditions he encountered. His realistic reporting led him to positions with the *New York Tribune* (1877-88) and the *New York Evening Sun* (1888-99) where he continued his efforts to bring the plight of tenement dwellers before the public.

A self-taught photographer, Riis became a pioneer photojournalist capturing the stark everyday reality of life in the overcrowded, disease-ridden tenement neighborhoods. In 1890 he published *How the Other Half Lives: Studies Among the Tenements of New York* in which he combined text, statistics, and drawings based on his photographs to depict the deplorable conditions and hopelessness of the city's slums. One of the people immediately impressed by the volume was the New York City police commissioner, Theodore Roosevelt, who is said to have told Riis "I have read your book, and I have come to help." And he did. Accompanying Riis on walking tours of the tenement areas, Roosevelt was largely responsible for influencing city officials to begin passing legislation to address some of the worst conditions in the immigrant neighborhoods.

Although his most famous work was the groundbreaking *How the Other Half Lives*, he went on to author several more books of the same genre including *Children of the Poor* (1892), *The Battle With the Slum* (1902), *Children of the Tenements* (1903), and the autobiographical *The Making of an American* (1901). Before he passed away on May 26, 1914, in Barre, Massachusetts, Riis had inspired a generation of reform-minded journalists, often referred to derisively as "muckrakers," who used his style of realism to pen exposés on the Chicago meat packing industry, New York city political corruption, sweatshops, the unfair business practices of many corporate leaders, and a host of other issues of social reform.

HISTORICAL DOCUMENT

CHAPTER I

GENESIS OF THE TENEMENT

The first tenement New York knew bore the mark of Cain from its birth, though a generation passed before the waiting was deciphered. It was the "rear house," infamous ever after in our city's history. There had been tenant-houses before, but they were not built for the purpose. Nothing would probably have shocked their original owners more than the idea of their harboring a promiscuous crowd; for they were the decorous homes of the old Knickerbockers, the proud aristocracy of Manhattan in the early days. It was the stir and bustle of trade, together with the tremendous immigration that followed upon the war of 1812 that dislodged them. In thirty-five years the city of less than a hundred thousand came to harbor half a million souls, for whom homes had to be found.

It was thus the dark bedroom, prolific of untold depravities, came into the world. It was destined to survive the old houses. In their new role, says the old report, eloquent in its indignant denunciation of "evils more destructive than wars," "they were not intended to last. Rents were fixed high enough to cover damage and abuse from this class, from whom nothing was expected, and the most was made of them while they lasted. Neatness, order, cleanliness, were never dreamed of in connection with the tenant-house system, as it spread its localities from year to year; while redress slovenliness, discontent, privation, and ignorance were left to work out their invariable results, until the entire premises reached the level of tenant-house dilapidation, containing, but sheltering not, the miserable hordes that crowded beneath smouldering, water-rotted roofs or burrowed among the rats of clammy cellars." Yet so illogical is human greed that, at a later day, when called to account, "the proprietors frequently urged the filthy habits of the tenants as an excuse for the condition of their property, utterly losing sight of the fact that it was the tolerance of those habits which was the real evil, and that for this they themselves were alone responsible."

Within the memory of men not yet in their prime, Washington had moved from his house on Cherry Hill as too far out of town to be easily reached. Now the old residents followed his example; but they moved in a different direction and for a different reason. Their comfortable dwellings in the once fashionable streets along the East River front fell into the hands of real-estate agents and boarding-house keepers; and here, says the report to the Legislature of 1857, when the evils engendered had excited just alarm, "in its beginning, the tenant-house became a real blessing to that class of industrious poor whose small earnings limited their expenses, and whose employment in workshops, stores, or about the warehouses and thoroughfares, render a near residence of much importance." Not for long, however. As business increased, and the city grew with rapid strides, the necessities of the poor became the opportunity of their wealthier neighbors, and the stamp was set upon the old houses, suddenly become valuable, which the best thought and effort of a later age has vainly struggled to efface. Their "large rooms were partitioned into several smaller ones, without regard to light or ventilation, the rate of rent being lower in proportion to space or height from the street; and they soon became filled from cellar to garret with a class of tenantry living from hand to mouth, loose in morals, improvident in habits, degraded, and squalid as beggary itself."

Still the pressure of the crowds did not abate, and in the old garden where the stolid Dutch burgher grew his tulips or early cabbages a rear house was built, generally of wood, two stories high at first. Presently it was carried up another story, and another. Where two families had lived ten moved in. The front house followed suit, if the brick walls were strong enough. The question was not always asked, judging from complaints made by a contemporary witness, that the old buildings were "often carried up to a great height without regard to the strength of the foundation walls." It was rent the owner was after; nothing was said in the contract about either the safety or the comfort of the tenants. The garden gate no longer swung on its rusty hinges. The shell-paved walk had become an alley; what the rear house had left of the garden, a "court" Plenty such are yet to be found in the Fourth Ward, with here and there one of the original rear tenements.

Worse was to follow. It was "soon perceived by estate owners and agents of property that a greater percentage of profits could be realized by the conversion of houses and blocks into barracks, and dividing their space into smaller proportions capable of containing human life within four walls. . . . Blocks were rented of real estate owners, or 'purchased on time,' or taken in charge at a percentage, and held for under-letting." With the appearance of the middleman, wholly irresponsible, and utterly reckless and unrestrained, began the era of tenement building which turned out such blocks as Gotham Court, where, in one cholera epidemic that scarcely touched the clean wards, the tenants died at the rate of one hundred and ninety-five to the thousand of population; which forced the general mortality of the city up from 1 in 41.83 in 1815, to 1 in 27.33 in 1855, a year of unusual freedom from epidemic disease, and which wrung from the early organizers of the Health Department this wail: "There are numerous examples of tenement-houses in which are lodged several hundred people that have a pro rata allotment of ground area scarcely equal to two-square yards upon the city lot, court-yards and all included." The tenement-house population had swelled to half a million souls by that time, and on the East Side, in what is still the most densely populated district in all the world, China not excluded, it was packed at the rate of 290,000 to the square mile, a state of affairs wholly unexampled. The utmost cupidity of other lands and other days had never contrived to herd much more than half that number within the same space. The greatest crowding of Old London was at the rate of 175,816. Swine roamed the streets and gutters as their principal scavengers.

The death of a child in a tenement was registered at the Bureau of Vital Statistics as "plainly due to suffocation in the foul air of an unventilated apartment," and the Senators, who had come down from Albany to find out what was the matter with New York, reported that "there are annually cut off from the population by disease and death enough human beings to people a city, and enough human labor to sustain it." And yet experts had testified that, as compared with uptown, rents were from twenty-five to thirty per cent. higher in the worst slums of the lower wards, with such accommodations as were enjoyed, for instance, by a "family with boarders" in Cedar Street, who fed hogs in the Stellar that contained eight or ten loads of manure; or "one room 12 x 19 with five families living in it, comprising twenty persons of both sexes and all ages, with only two beds, without partition, screen, chair, or table." The rate of rent has been successfully maintained to the present day, though the hog at least has been eliminated.

Lest anybody flatter himself with the notion that these were evils of a day that is happily past and may safely be forgotten, let me mention here three very recent instances of tenement-house life that came under my notice. One was the burning of a rear house in Mott Street, from appearances one of the original tenant-houses that made their owners rich. The fire made homeless ten families, who had paid an average of $5 a month for their mean little cubby-holes. The owner himself told me that it was fully insured for $800, though it brought him in $600 a year rent. He evidently considered himself especially entitled to be pitied for losing such valuable property. Another was the case of a hard-working family of man and wife, young people from the old country, who took poison together in a Crosby Street tenement because they were "tired." There was no other explanation, and none was needed when I stood in the room in which they had lived. It was in the attic with sloping ceiling and a single window so far out on the roof that it seemed not to belong to the place at all. With scarcely room enough to turn around in they had been compelled to pay five dollars and a half a month in advance. There were four such rooms in that attic, and together they brought in as much as many a handsome little cottage in a pleasant part of Brooklyn. The third instance was that of a colored family of husband, wife, and baby in a wretched rear rookery in West Third Street. Their rent was eight dollars and a half for a single room on the top-story, so small that I was unable to get a photograph of it even by placing the camera outside the open door. Three short steps across either way would have measured its full extent.

There was just one excuse for the early tenement house builders, and their successors may plead it with nearly as good right for what it is worth. "Such," says an official report, "is the lack of houseroom in the city that any kind of tenement can be immediately crowded with lodgers, if there is space offered." Thousands were living in cellars. There were three hundred underground lodging-houses in the city when the Health Department was organized. Some fifteen years before that the old Baptist Church in Mulberry Street, just off Chatham Street, had

been sold, and the rear half of the frame structure had been converted into tenements that with their swarming population became the scandal even of that reckless age. The wretched pile harbored no less than forty families, and the annual rate of deaths to the population was officially stated to be 75 in 1,000. These tenements were an extreme type of very many, for the big barracks had by this time spread east and west and far up the island into the sparsely settled wards. Whether or not the title was clear to the land upon which they were built was of less account than that the rents were collected.

If there were damages to pay, the tenant had to foot them. Cases were "very frequent when property was in litigation, and two or three different parties were collecting rents." Of course under such circumstances "no repairs were ever made." The climax had been reached. The situation was summed up by the Society for the Improvement of the Condition of the Poor in these words: "Crazy old buildings, crowded rear tenements in filthy yards, dark, damp basements, leaking garrets, shops, outhouses, and stables converted into dwellings, though scarcely fit to shelter brutes, are habitations of thousands of our fellow-beings in this wealthy, Christian city." "The city," says its historian, Mrs. Martha Lamb, commenting on the era of aqueduct building between 1835 and 1845, "was a general asylum for vagrants." Young vagabonds, the natural offspring of such "home" conditions, overran the streets. Juvenile crime increased fearfully year by year. The Children's Aid Society and kindred philanthropic organizations were yet unborn, but in the city directory was to be found the address of the "American Society for the Promotion of Education in Africa." . . .

CHAPTER XXV

HOW THE CASE STANDS

WHAT, then, are the bald facts with which we have to deal in New York?

I. That we have a tremendous, ever swelling crowd of wage-earners which it is our business to house decently.

II. That it is not housed decently.

III. That it must be so housed here for the present, and

for a long time to come, all schemes of suburban relief being as yet utopian, impracticable.

IV. That it pays high enough rents to entitle it to be so housed, as a right.

V. That nothing but our own slothfulness is in the way of so housing it, since "the condition of the tenants is in advance of the condition of the houses which they occupy" (Report of Tenement-house Commission).

VI. That the security of the one no less than of the other half demands, on sanitary, moral, and economic grounds, that it be decently housed.

VII. That it will pay to do it. As an investment, I mean, and in hard cash. This I shall immediately proceed to prove.

VIII. That the tenement has come to stay, and must itself be the solution of the problem with which it confronts us.

This is the fact from which we cannot get away, however we may deplore it. Doubtless the best would be to get rid of it altogether; but as we cannot, all argument on that score may at this time be dismissed as idle. The practical question is what to do with the tenement. I watched a Mott Street landlord, the owner of a row of barracks that have made no end of trouble for the health authorities for twenty years, solve that question for himself the other day. His way was to give the wretched pile a coat of paint, and put a gorgeous tin cornice on with the year 1890 in letters a yard long. From where I stood watching the operation, I looked down upon the same dirty crowds camping on the roof, foremost among them an Italian mother with two stark-naked children who had apparently never made the acquaintance of a wash-tub. That was a landlord's way, and will not get us out of the mire.

The "flat" is another way that does not solve the problem. Rather, it extends it. The flat is not a model, though it is a modern, tenement. It gets rid of some of the nuisances of the low tenement, and of the worst of them, the overcrowding—if it gets rid of them at all—at a cost that takes it at once out of the catalogue of "homes for the poor," while imposing some of the evils from which they suffer upon those who ought to escape from them.

There are three effective ways of dealing with the tenements in New York:

I. By law.

II. By remodelling and making the most out of the old houses.

III. By building new, model tenements.

Private enterprise—conscience, to put it in the category of duties, where it belongs—must do the lion's share under these last two heads. Of what the law has effected I have spoken already. The drastic measures adopted in Paris, in Glasgow, and in London are not practicable here on anything like as large a scale. Still it can, under strong pressure of public opinion, rid us of tile worst plague-spots. The Mulberry Street Bend will go the way of the Five Points when all the red tape that binds the hands of municipal effort has been unwound. Prizes were offered in public competition, some years ago, for the best plans of modern tenement-houses. It may be that we shall see the day when the building of model tenements will be encouraged by subsidies in the way of a rebate of taxes. Meanwhile the arrest and summary punishment of landlords, or their agents, who persistently violate law and decency, will have a salutary effect. If a few of the wealthy absentee landlords, who are the worst offenders, could be got within the jurisdiction of the city, and by arrest be compelled to employ proper overseers, it would be a proud day for New York. To remedy the overcrowding, with which the night inspections of the sanitary police cannot keep step, tenements may eventually have to he licensed, as now the lodging-houses, to hold so many tenants, and no more; or the State may have to bring down the rents that cause the crowding, by assuming the right to regulate them as it regulates the fares on the elevated roads. I throw out the suggestion, knowing quite well that it is open to attack. It emanated originally from one of the brightest minds that have had to struggle officially with this tenement-house question in the last ten years. In any event, to succeed, reform by law must aim at making it unprofitable to own a bad tenement. At best, it is apt to travel at a snail's pace, while the enemy it pursues is putting the best foot foremost.

In this matter of profit the law ought to have its strongest ally in the landlord himself, though the reverse is the case. This condition of things I believe to rest on a monstrous error. It cannot be that tenement property that is worth preserving at all can continue to yield larger returns, if allowed to run down, than if properly cared for and kept in good repair. The point must be reached, and soon, where the cost of repairs, necessary with a house full of the lowest, most ignorant tenants, must overbalance the saving of the first few years of neglect; for this class is everywhere the most destructive, as well as the poorest paying. I have the experience of owners, who have found this out to their cost, to back me up in the assertion, even if it were not the statement of a plain business fact that proves itself. I do not include tenement property that is deliberately allowed to fall into decay because at some future time the ground will be valuable for business or other purposes. There is unfortunately enough of that kind in New York, often leasehold property owned by wealthy estates or soulless corporations that oppose all their great influence to the efforts of the law in behalf of their tenants.

There is abundant evidence, on the other hand, that it can be made to pay to improve and make the most of the worst tenement property, even in the most wretched locality. The example set by Miss Ellen Collins in her Water Street houses will always stand as a decisive answer to all doubts on this point. It is quite ten years since she bought three old tenements at the corner of Water and Roosevelt Streets, then as now one of the lowest localities in the city. Since then she has leased three more adjoining her purchase, and so much of Water Street has at all events been purified. Her first effort was to let in the light in the hallways, and with the darkness disappeared, as if by magic, the heaps of refuse that used to be piled up beside the sinks. A few of the most refractory tenants disappeared with them, but a very considerable proportion stayed, conforming readily to the new rules, and are there yet. It should here be stated that Miss Collins's tenants are distinctly of the poorest. Her purpose was to experiment with this class, and her experiment has been more than satisfactory. Her plan was, as she puts it herself, fair play between tenant

and landlord. To this end the rents were put as low as consistent with the idea of a business investment that must return a reasonable interest to be successful. The houses were thoroughly refitted with proper plumbing. A competent janitor was put in charge to see that the rules were observed by the tenants, when Miss Collins herself was not there. Of late years she has had to give very little time to personal superintendence, and the care-taker told me only the other day that very little was needed. The houses seemed to run themselves in the groove once laid down. Once the reputed haunt of thieves, they have become the most orderly in the neighborhood. Clothes are left hanging on the lines all night with impunity, and the pretty flower-beds in the yard where the children not only from the six houses, but of the whole block, play, skip, and swing, are undisturbed. The tenants, by the way, provide the flowers themselves in the spring, and take all the more pride in them because they are their own. The six houses contain forty-five families, and there "has never been any need of putting up a bill." As to the income from the property, Miss Collins said to me last August: "I have had six and even six and three-quarters per cent. on the capital invested; on the whole, you may safely say five and a half per cent. This I regard as entirely satisfactory." It should be added that she has persistently refused to let the corner-store, now occupied by a butcher, as a saloon; or her income from it might have been considerably increased.

Miss Collins's experience is of value chiefly as showing what can be accomplished with the worst possible material, by the sort of personal interest in the poor that alone will meet their real needs. All the charity in the world, scattered with the most lavish hand, will not take its place. "Fair play" between landlord and tenant is the key, too long mislaid, that unlocks the door to success everywhere as it did for Miss Collins. She has not lacked imitators whose experience has been akin to her own. The case of Gotham Court has been already cited. On the other hand, instances are not wanting of landlords who have undertaken the task, but have tired of it or sold their property before it had been fully redeemed, with the result that it relapsed into its former bad condition faster than it had improved, and the tenants with it. I am inclined to think that such houses are liable to fall even below the average level. Backsliding in brick and mortar does not greatly differ from similar performances in flesh and blood.

Backed by a strong and steady sentiment, such as these pioneers have evinced, that would make it the personal business of wealthy owners with time to spare to look after their tenants, the law would be able in a very short time to work a salutary transformation in the worst quarters, to the lasting advantage, I am well persuaded, of the landlord no less than the tenant. Unfortunately, it is in this quality of personal effort that the sentiment of interest in the poor, upon which we have to thus given is too apt to be wasted along with the sentiment that prompted the gift.

Even when it comes to the third of the ways I spoke of as effective in dealing with the tenement-house problem, the building of model structures, the personal interest in the matter must form a large share of the capital invested, if it is to yield full returns. Where that is the case, there is even less doubt about its paying, with ordinary business management, than in the case of reclaiming an old building, which is, like putting life into a defunct newspaper, pretty apt to be up-hill work. Model tenement building has not been attempted in New York on anything like as large a scale as in many other great cities, and it is perhaps owing to this, in a measure, that a belief prevails that it cannot succeed here. This is a wrong notion entirely. The various undertakings of that sort that have been made here under intelligent management have, as far as I know, all been successful.

From the managers of the two best-known experiments in model tenement building in the city, the Improved Dwellings Association and the Tenement-house Building Company, I have letters dated last August, declaring their enterprises eminently successful. There is no reason why their experience should not be conclusive. That the Philadelphia plan is not practicable in New York is not a good reason why our own plan, which is precisely the reverse of our neighbor's should not be. In fact it is an argument for its success. The very reason why we cannot house our working masses in cottages, as has been done in Philadelphia—viz., that they must live on Manhattan Island, where the land is too costly for small houses—is the best guarantee of the success of the model tenement house, properly located and managed. The drift in tenement building, as in everything else, is toward concentration, and helps smooth the way. Four families on the floor, twenty in the house, is the rule of to-day. As the crowds increase, the need of guiding this drift into safe channels becomes more urgent. The larger the scale upon which the model tenement is planned, the more certain the promise of success. The utmost ingenuity cannot build a house for sixteen or twenty families on a lot 25 × 100 feet in the middle of a block like it, that shall give them the amount of air and sunlight to be had by the erection of a dozen or twenty houses on a common plan around a central yard. This was the view of the committee that awarded the prizes for the best plan for the conventional tenement, ten years ago. It coupled its verdict with the emphatic declaration that, in its view, it was "impossible to secure the requirements of physical and moral health within these narrow and arbitrary limits." Houses have been built since on better plans than any the committee saw, but its judgment stands unimpaired. A point, too, that is not to be overlooked, is the reduced cost of expert superintendence—the first condition of successful management—in the larger buildings.

The Improved Dwellings Association put up its block of thirteen houses in East Seventy-second Street nine years ago. Their cost, estimated at about $240,000 with the land, was increased to $285,000 by troubles with the contractor engaged to build them. Thus the Association's task did not begin under the happiest auspices. Unexpected expenses came to deplete its treasury. The neighborhood was new and not crowded at the start. No expense was spared, and the benefit of all the best and most recent experience in tenement building was given to the tenants. The families were provided with from two to four rooms, all "outer" rooms, of course, at rents ranging from $14 per month for the four on the ground floor, to $6.25 for two rooms on the top floor. Coal lifts, ash-chutes, common laundries in the basement, and free baths, are features of these buildings that were then new enough to be looked upon with suspicion by the doubting Thomases who predicted disaster. There are rooms in the block for 218 families, and when I looked in recently all but nine of the apartments were let. One of the nine was rented while I was in the building. The superintendent told me that he had little trouble with disorderly tenants, though the buildings shelter all sorts of people. Mr. W. Bayard Cutting, the President of the Association, writes to me:

"By the terms of subscription to the stock before incorporation, dividends were limited to five per cent. on the stock of the Improved Dwellings Association. These dividends have been paid (two per cent. each six months) ever since the expiration of the first six months of the buildings operation. All surplus has been expended upon the buildings. New and expensive roofs have been put on for the comfort of such tenants as might choose to use them. The buildings have been completely painted inside and out in a manner not contemplated at the outset. An expensive set of fire-escapes has been put on at the command of the Fire Department, and a considerable number of other improvements made. I regard: the experiment as eminently successful and satisfactory, particularly when it is considered that the buildings were the first erected in this city upon anything like a large scale, where it was proposed to meet the architectural difficulties that present themselves in the tenement-house problem. I have no doubt that the experiment could be tried to-day with the improved knowledge which has come with time, and a much larger return be shown upon the investment. The results referred to have been attained in spite of the provision which prevents the selling of liquor upon the Association's premises. You are aware, of course, how much larger rent can be obtained for a liquor saloon than for an ordinary store. An investment at five per cent. net upon real estate security worth more than the principal sum, ought to be considered desirable."

The Tenement House Building Company made its "experiment" in a much more difficult neighborhood, Cherry Street, some six years later. Its houses shelter many Russian Jews, and the difficulty of keeping them in order is correspondingly increased, particularly as there are no ash-chutes in the houses. It has been necessary even to shut the children out of the yards upon which the kitchen windows give, lest they be struck by something thrown out by the tenants, and killed. It is the Cherry Street style, not easily got rid of. Nevertheless, the houses are well kept. Of the one hundred and six "apartments," only four were vacant in August. Professor Edwin R. A. Seligman, the secretary of the company, writes to me: "The tenements are now a decided success." In the three years since they were built, they have returned an interest of from five to five and a half per cent. on the capital invested. The original intention of making the tenants profit-sharers on a plan of rent insurance, under which all earnings above four per cent. would be put to the credit of the tenants, has not yet been carried out.

A scheme of dividends to tenants on a somewhat similar plan has been carried out by a Brooklyn builder, Mr. A. T. White, who has devoted a life of beneficent activity to tenement building, and whose experience, though it has been altogether across the East River, I regard as justly applying to New York as well. He so regards it himself. Discussing the cost of building, he says: "There is not the slightest reason to doubt that the financial result of a similar undertaking in any tenement-house district of New York City would be equally good. . . . . High cost of land is no detriment, provided the value is made by the pressure of people seeking residence there. Rents in New York City bear a higher ratio to Brooklyn rents than would the cost of land and building in the one city to that in the other." The assertion that Brooklyn furnishes a better class of tenants than the tenement districts in New York would not be worth discussing seriously, even if Mr. White did not meet it himself with the statement that the proportion of day-laborers and sewing-women in his houses is greater than in any of the London model tenements, showing that they reach the humblest classes.

Mr. White has built homes for five hundred poor families since he began his work, and has made it pay well enough to allow good tenants a share in the profits, averaging nearly one month's rent out of the twelve, as a premium upon promptness and order. The plan of his last tenements . . . may be justly regarded as the beau ideal of the model tenement for a great city like New York. It embodies all the good features of Sir Sydney Waterlow's London plan, with improvements suggested by the builder's own experience. Its chief merit is that it gathers three hundred real homes, not simply three hundred families, under one roof. Three tenants, it will be seen, everywhere live together. Of the rest of the three hundred they may never know, rarely see, one. Each has his private front door. The common hall, with all that it stands for, has disappeared. The fire-proof stairs are outside the house, a perfect fire-escape. Each tenant has his own scullery and ash-flue. There are no air-shafts, for they are not needed. Every room, under the admirable arrangement of the plan, looks out either upon the street or the yard, that is nothing less than a great park with a play-ground set apart for the children, where they may dig in the sand to their heart's content. Weekly concerts are given in the park by a brass band. The drying of clothes is done on the roof, where racks are fitted up for the purpose. The outside stairways end in turrets that give the buildings a very smart appearance. Mr. White never has any trouble with his tenants, though he gathers in the poorest; nor do his tenements have anything of the "institution character" that occasionally attaches to ventures of this sort, to their damage. They are like a big village of contented people, who live in peace with one another because they have elbowroom even under one big roof.

Enough has been said to show that model tenements can be built successfully and made to pay in New York, if the owner will be content with the five or six per cent. He does not even dream of when investing his funds in "governments" at three or four. It is true that in the latter case he has only to cut off his coupons and cash them. But the extra trouble of looking after his tenement property, that is the condition of his highest and lasting success, is the penalty exacted for the sins of our fathers that "shall be visited upon the children, unto the third and fourth generation." We shall indeed be well off, if it stop there. I fear there is too much reason to believe that our own iniquities must be added to transmit the curse still further. And yet, such is the leavening influence of a good deed in that dreary desert of sin and suffering, that the erection of a single good tenement has the power to change, gradually but surely, the character of a whole bad block. It sets up a standard to which the neighborhood must rise, if it cannot succeed in dragging it down to its own low level.

And so this task, too, has come to an end. Whatsoever a man soweth, that shall he also reap. I have aimed to tell the truth as I saw it. If this book shall have borne ever so feeble a hand in garnering a harvest of justice, it has served its purpose. While I was writing these lines I went down to the sea, where thousands from the city were enjoying their summer rest. The ocean slumbered under a cloudless sky. Gentle waves washed lazily over the white sand, where children fled before them with screams of laughter. Standing there and watching their play, I was told that during the fierce storms of winter it happened that this sea, now so calm, rose in rage and beat down, broke over the bluff, sweeping all before it. No barrier built by human hands had power to stay it then. The sea of a mighty population, held in galling fetters, heaves uneasily in the tenements. Once already our city, to which have come the duties and responsibilities of metropolitan greatness before it was able to fairly measure its task, has felt the swell of its resistless flood. If it rise once more, no human power may avail to check it. The gap between the classes in which it surges, unseen, unsuspected by the thoughtless, is widening day by day. No tardy enactment of law, no political expedient, can close it. Against all other dangers our system of government may offer defence and shelter; against this not. I know of but one bridge that will carry us over safe, a bridge founded upon justice and built of human hearts.

I believe that the danger of such conditions as are fast growing up around us is greater for the very freedom which they mock. The words of the poet, with whose lines I prefaced this book, are truer to-day, have far deeper meaning to us, than when they were penned forty years ago:

"—Think ye that building shall endure
Which shelters the noble and crushes the poor?"

GLOSSARY

Burgher: In general, a citizen of a borough or town, especially someone of the merchant class. In The Netherlands and Dutch New Amsterdam (now New York) a person who had the "burgher right" was considered to be a citizen and was therefore able to engage in trade and commerce and participate in the political system.

Garret: A small, cramped, but habitable attic at the top of a home or other building such as a tenement.

Knickerbocker: A Dutch term referring to the style of trousers worn in the 1600s where the men's pants were rolled up to a position just below the knee. This was in use among the Dutch settlers in what later became New York, so the term in colloquial use refers to a person from New York City.

Mark of Cain: This term derives from Genesis 4 in the Bible where God states that Cain, the first-born son of Adam and Eve, will be cursed because he killed his brother Abel. In modern use it refers to someone who is cursed or otherwise destined for misfortune.

Tenement: A multiple-family lodging that is usually substandard and located in an older area occupied by the poor. In New York they were sometimes referred to as "walk-ups" because they lacked an elevator. In 1869, New York State defined the tenement as "any house or building, or portion thereof, which is rented, leased let or hired out, to be occupied, or is occupied as the home or residence of three families or more living independently of each other, and doing their cooking upon the premises, or by more than two families upon any floor, so living and cooking, but having a right in the halls, stairways, yards, water-closets or privies, or some of them."

Explanation and Analysis of the Document

Riis begins the first chapter by tracing the origin of the New York City tenements, linking them with the antebellum influx of immigrants who were crowded into some of the older mansions abandoned by their original owners who moved to more affluent areas. In his analysis, the owners of these properties took no care to make sure they were well kept up, instead they invested as little as possible while charging whatever rents the traffic would bear in an effort to maximize profit. The lack of maintenance led to deterioration of the structure, the surroundings, and the living conditions which led to inflated death rates. Although the deplorable conditions were largely due to the practices of real estate agents and tenement owners, both of these groups and the general public tended to blame them on the poor who lived there.

The author provides a detailed, realistic account of how older homes were subdivided, or additional floors were added from above, to accommodate more and more people as the demand for housing increased. This led to the erection of new structures, of cheap construction, to house an even larger number of people. The result was the most densely packed area on earth with 290,000 people per square mile compared with the most overcrowded areas of London which were at 175,816 per square mile. Despite the deplorable conditions, rents averaged 25 to 30 percent higher than in the more affluent areas of the city and in addition residents were liable to pay for any damages despite the overcrowded conditions. He supports his assertions with examples taken from his own observations and reports of organizations such as the Society for the Improvement of the Condition of the Poor.

The second portion of the reading, taken from Chapter XXV, described conditions at the time that Riis wrote.

He argues that "the security of the one no less than of the other half [of society] demands, on sanitary, moral, and economic grounds, that it be decently housed." While he would prefer to dispense with the tenements altogether, he recognizes that this would not be feasible because of the demand for housing. With this in mind, he proposes that the "practical" solution is to find a way to ameliorate the conditions. After rejecting some half-measures that would not solve the problem, he proposes three interrelated approaches. First, by using the law to impose requirements for habitable housing because "the arrest and summary punishment of landlords, or their agents, who persistently violate law and decency, will have a salutary effect." This would also take the form of increased government regulation of the tenements coupled with vigorous inspection and prosecution for violations. Second, by remodeling the older houses to make "the most out of the houses" which, he argues, would also be profitable to the property owner in the long run. Third, he proposes holding a contest to design the best modern hosing unit, and to provide tax incentives for "building new, model tenements." Whether renovating an existing older building or constructing a new facility, Riis argues that the landlord will benefit financially by making the living conditions as habitable as possible, although he acknowledges this may take more investment for existing structures than for wholly new construction.

The author concludes with a discussion of some of the features that ought to be included in tenement buildings, both for health and safety. "Whatsoever a man soweth," Riis concludes, "that shall he also reap. I have aimed to tell the truth as I saw it. If this book shall have borne ever so feeble a hand in garnering a harvest of justice, it has served its purpose."

Essential Themes

How the Other Half Lives is a pioneering effort in the new field of photojournalism as well as an early example of the investigative reporting that underlay many of the reform movements between 1880 and 1920. Beyond this, Riis brought attention to the deplorable urban slums that concerned the growing Progressive movement, while at the same time diverging from most of those in that movement by blaming real estate agents and tenement owners for the conditions rather than placing the blame at the feet of the poor residents.

The book also includes commentary on the moral issues relating to poverty, appealing to the same religious beliefs in social activism that motivated the antebellum reform movements after the Second Great Awakening. In this sense it may also be relevant to note the resurgence of church attendance during this era and the popularity of missionary work among many of the Christian denominations between 1880 and World War I. Riis's appeal fit squarely into this context.

Finally, by influencing persuasive people such as Theodore Roosevelt and other emerging Progressives, Riis was able effect real social change through both individuals and government organizations.

Bibliography and Further Reading

Alexander Alland, Sr., *Jacob A. Riis: Photographer and Citizen* (Millerton, NY: Aperture Book, 1993).

Tom Buk-Swienty, *The Other Half: The Life of Jacob Riis and the World of Immigrant America* (New York: W. W. Norton & Company 2008).

Keith Gandal, *The Virtues of the Vicious: Jacob Riis, Stephen Crane, and the Spectacle of the Slum* (New York: Oxford University Press, 1997).

Janet B. Pascal, *Jacob Riis: Reporter and Reformer* (New York: Oxford University Press, 2005).

Richard Plunz, *A History of Housing in New York City* (New York: Columbia University Press, 1990).

Bonnie Yochelson and Daniel Czitrom, *Rediscovering Jacob Riis: Exposure Journalism and Photography in Turn-of-the-Century New York* (New York: New Press, 2007).

■ A Polish American Protest of Immigration Restriction

Date: 1898
Author: Franciszek Jablonski
Genre: Petition

Summary Overview

By 1890 the percentage of immigrants in the American population reached 14.7, up from 9.7 in 1850. Most of the increase was due to the mass migration of peoples from Eastern and Southern Europe, a significantly different origin than the previous majority from Northern and Western Europe. With not only the increase in number but the diversity in cultural origin as well, anti-immigrant feelings rose dramatically. Although there continued to be economic arguments in favor of restricting immigration, these were now joined with racial animus. Writing in the liberal journal *Chautauquan* in 1888, E. A. Hempstead bemoaned the influx of "ignorant laborers" noting that the recently excluded Chinese possessed "no more terrors than Hungarian, or Polish, or Italian cheap labor." In the same year the U.S. House of Representatives organized a Select Committee to investigate the effects of immigration. Its final report likewise concluded that the time had come "to select the good from the bad, and to sift the wheat from the chaff." That was exactly what members of Congress proposed to do.

In 1895, Massachusetts Senator Henry Cabot Lodge, a founding member of the Immigration Restriction League, proposed a bill that would require potential immigrants to pass a literacy test for entrance into the United States. The bill passed the House by the overwhelming vote of 205 to 35 and the Senate 34 to 31. However, the success was short-lived. President Grover Cleveland quickly vetoed the proposed law as "a radical departure" from traditional policy, noting that "the time is quite within recent memory when … immigrants who, with their descendants, are now numbered among our best citizens." The bill was, he said, "illiberal, narrow, and un-American." But the veto did not cool the ardor of its proponents.

Defining Moment

Henry Cabot Lodge was not a man to give up easily. In the wake of the veto he continued to pursue adoption of the measure, explaining that "It is found, in the first place, that the illiteracy test will bear most heavily upon the Italians, Russians, Poles, Hungarians, Greeks, and Asiatics, and very lightly, or not at all, upon English-speaking emigrants or Germans, Scandinavians, and French. In other words, the races most affected by the illiteracy test are those whose emigration to this country has begun within the last twenty years and swelled rapidly to enormous proportions, races with which the English-speaking people have never hitherto assimilated, and who are most alien to the great body of the people of the United States."

Lodge's continuing efforts, and his direct assault on specific groups, led to an influx of petitions being mailed to Congress opposing the measure. Nor did they only originate with the nationalities he named. Germans, Catholics, Jews, and a host of others presented their arguments why the literacy test ought to be defeated. Among those strenuously opposing the bill was the Polish American community. By the 1890s some 100,000 Poles were arriving in the United States every year, settling mostly in the large industrial cities of the northeast and the mining communities of Pennsylvania and West Virginia. The Polish language press was full of editorials against the pending bill and the major ethnic organizations came together to send to Congress "A Memorial of the Polish-American Organizations of the United States in reference to the proposed Lodge Immigration Bill, now pending in the American House of Representatives."

Author Biography

The memorial was approved by several Polish American organizations acting through a joint executive committee. The organizations included the Polish National Alliance of the United States of North America, the Polish Roman Catholic Union of America, the Polish Association of America, the Polish Turners Alliance of America, the Polish Alliance of the State of Ohio, the United Polish

Singers of America, the Polish Young Men's Alliance of America, the Second Polish Military Corps of America, and the Civic Board. These reflect a wide variety of fraternal associations including both the nationalist-oriented Polish National Alliance and the religious-focused Polish Roman Catholic Union which were then in a struggle for hegemony over the Polish immigrant communities and seldom cooperated in anything. This is an indication of how important the issue was to them.

The executive committee that drew up the memorial was headed by Franciszek H. Jablonski who was also the president of the Polish National Alliance and the guiding hand behind the effort. Arriving in Chicago around 1885 from his native Poland, Jablonski had been educated in theology in Poznań and the University of Louvain in Belgium. Becoming a teacher and Polonia activist, he was elected editor of *Zgoda* (Harmony), a periodical published by the Polish National Alliance. In 1897 he gained election as president of the fraternal organization where his close connections to Polish organizations in Europe proved very valuable. He later edited *Dziennik Związkowy* (Alliance Daily), the PNA's organizational newspaper founded in 1908, but he passed away in Chicago only one month into this position.

HISTORICAL DOCUMENT

The persistent and studied efforts of reckless and sensational writers and agitators to belittle and traduce the character of American citizens, of Polish descent and nativity, has led to the formation of a committee, consisting of representatives of all the large Polish-American organizations throughout the United States, for the purpose of removing in a measure the erroneous impression, which prevails in certain quarters, in regard to the Polish people. While this agitation was confined to articles of sensational writers and wild rantings of irresponsible demagogues, it was deemed the part of wisdom to treat the movement with dignified silence. The statements of certain individuals, who view the subject with eyes which are jaundiced with prejudice, that the Slavonic race is totally depraved and is without a single redeeming feature, are too absurd to merit a reply.

It remained however for the honorable senator from Massachusetts to dignify these gross misrepresentations with his scholarly and well-known literary attainments by including them in his report to the Senate recommending the passage of Senate Bill No. 112, commonly known as the Lodge Immigration Bill. The damage done to the reputation of Polish-American citizens by this report is incalculable. Were the statements therein contained allowed to pass unchallenged, some future historian in his researches might discover this remarkable document, and accepting the figures and pretended facts therein cited as true, use it as a basis of his views on the effects of immigration in the United States.

We exceedingly regret that the time at the disposal of this committee was too limited to collate all the necessary data to refute the allegations of the report so far as they relate to the Polish people. We however respectfully invite the attention of the American public to a few facts hurriedly sketched in this memorial.

To fairly adjudge the character of a race it is imperatively necessary to know their past history, their present condition at home, and their conduct in their adopted country. For this reason we have subdivided this memorial into three chapters, in which we briefly treat of "Poland during the days of Independence"; "Poland under the reign of her despoilers," and "The Poles in America."

I. Poland During the Days of Her Independence.

For many centuries Poland was the predominant power of Eastern Europe. Situated on the border of European civilization, her peculiar mission among the family of nations was to repel the repeated invasions and depredations of hordes of savage Mongols, Tartars, Muscovites and Turks who frequently threatened to overrun Europe and destroy her institutions. She was justly called the cavalier nation of Europe, the bulwark of Christianity and modern civilization. From the reign of Boleslas the Great (992-1025) to the date of the first partition of Poland (1772) her arms alone repelled ninety-one Tartar invasions, any one of which, if successful, would have disastrously affected, if not jeopardized, the civilization of Europe. For the cause of Christianity, the brave chivalrous king Wladislas Warnenczyk at Warna in 1444 sacrificed his life, and the great warrior king Stefan Batory repelled the savage armies of Ivan the Terrible, and drove them back to the wild steppes of Russia. To prevent the eventual subjugation of Europe to the fanatical rule of the Mussulman[,] John III Sobieski met the Turkish forces at Vienna and forever established the supremacy of the Cross over the Crescent. ...

Though martial in her character, Poland in no small degree cultivated the finer arts of peace. To the civilized world she gave the first example of religious toleration. "They had" said the great publicist, Sir James Mackintosh, in his "An account of the Partition of Poland," "another singularity of which they might justly have been proud. Soon after the Reformation, they had set the first example of that true religious liberty, which equally admits the members of all sects to the privileges, the offices and dignities of the commonwealth. For nearly a century they have afforded a secure asylum to those obnoxious sects of Anabaptists and Unitarians, whom all other states excluded from toleration; and the Hebrew nation, proscribed everywhere else, found a second country, with protection for their learned and religious establishments in this hospitable and tolerant land."

At an early age she took a prominent part in the advancement and dissemination of learning in Europe. To the astronomical world she gave Copernicus. The first two centers of learning in central Europe were the University of Prague, in Bohemia, and the University of Cracow in Poland. As early as the fifteenth century we find in the Polish literature such names as that of Jan Dlugosz (Longinus), the famous historian, and while, little later the names of Jan Kochanowski (1503-1584), the prince of Polish poets and Casimir Sarbiewski (Sarbievius) the Polish Petrarch, stand pre-eminent among their contemporaries. In the sister Slavonic nation, Bohemia, John Komensky (Comenius) won fame as one of the earliest reformers of educational methods.

The government of Poland was republican in form. Its fundamental idea and object was to secure to the Polish people the greatest possible individual liberty. Absolute slavery was never recognized. In 1347, in the historic statutes of Wislica, measures were adopted for the betterment of the condition of the peasantry. In 1413, by humane means alone, without the slightest bloodshed,

the Polish people Converted to Christianity the powerful pagan nation of Lithuania numbering over two millions inhabitants. A union was effected between these two great nations which subsequently in 1569 became indissoluble and was based upon the theory, to use the quaint language of the historic pact, of "free with free and equals with equals."

The Polish kings were elected by the representative deliberative assemblies of the nation, the diet and senate. Their powers were limited. The power of enacting laws, levying taxation and declaring war was vested solely in the diet. The main defect of the constitution was the provision which invited foreign intrigue, corruption and intervention into the land by permitting foreign princes to compete for the crown of Poland. ...

[In] 1772, when in pursuance of a pre-concerted arrangement, without the slightest pretext of right, without the formality of declaring war, in open violation of the laws of God and man, Russia, Prussia and Austria marched their troops into Poland, parceled off among themselves large portions of her dominions and then compelled the protesting diet to ratify their unparalleled robbery. This was the first partition of Poland. It was the most flagrant violation of the laws of nations recorded in the annals of man. To aggravate the enormity of their crime, to perpetuate the unfortunate existing state of affairs, these unscrupulous despoilers exacted from the unwilling diet a pledge that no attempt would be made to alter the old impotent constitution.

At the time of the first partition, the surface of Poland exceeded that of France and the number of her inhabitants was estimated at eighteen millions; a population probably exceeding that of the British Islands or of the Spanish Peninsula at that date. Of these about twelve millions were Roman Catholics, three millions were Orthodox Schismatics, one million Protestants and the remainder Jews or Mussulmen.

Realizing the great dangers which surrounded them and fearing further aggrandizement, by their treacherous neighbors upon their territories and liberties, the brave people aroused themselves from their lethargy buried all their feuds and dissensions and proceeded peacefully and harmoniously to strengthen their government. On May 3rd, 1791, after four years of careful deliberation the Polish diet promulgated a new constitution, which for the liberality and wisdom of its provisions compares favorably with the Magna Charta of England or our own Federal Constitution. In its main features it resembles the Constitution of the United States. It guaranteed civil and religious liberty to all alike. It declared everyone to be equal before the law. It greatly ameliorated the condition of the peasantry. The crown was made hereditary, while the pernicious liberum veto was abolished. The government was divided into three co-ordinate branches: the executive, legislative and judicial.

It was enthusiastically received by the nation and was adopted with singular unanimity. "The course of this glorious revolution" says Sir James Mackintosh, "was not dishonoured by popular tumult, by sanguinary excesses, or by political execution. History will one day do justice to that illustrious body and hold out to posterity their work as a perfect model of a most arduous reformation."

In England it was hailed with delight. Fox declared it to be one of the noblest boons conferred upon man, while Edmund Burke exclaimed: "Mankind must rejoice at the great change which has taken place in Poland. It has destroyed anarchy and slavery."

This enthusiasm, however, was not shared by the despotic ruler of Russia. She declared it to be the work of hot headed Jacobins who had no regard for the ancient order of things. Before the constitution could be fully put into operation she poured the vast armies into Poland. The perfidious king of Prussia, violating solemn treaties which he made previously with the diet to protect the constitution, followed her ignoble example. Together these despots proceeded to destroy this masterpiece of statesmanship.

At this critical stage there appeared upon the scene a hero, whose spotless character, sterling virtues, splendid statesmanship and great military genius, makes him a worthy pupil of George Washington. The heroic struggle of the Polish people under the leadership of Thaddeus Koscius[z]ko forms one of the most thrilling and sanguinary events in the history of the world. All that lofty patriotism, undaunted courage and superb generalship could accomplish was done. Not until they were overpowered by overwhelmingly greater numbers and their intrepid leader fell, covered with wounds, did the proud Polish spirit yield and was the name of Poland erased from the maps of Europe.

"Thus" says Sir James Mackintosh, "fell the Polish people, after a wise and virtuous attempt to establish liberty and a heroic struggle to defend it, by the flagitious wickedness of Russia, by the foul treachery of Prussia, by the unprincipled accession of Austria, and by the short-sighted as well as mean-spirited acquiescence of all the other nations of Europe." …

II. Poland Under the Rule of her Despoilers

Immediately after the dismemberment of Poland, the three partitioning powers adopted towards their unfortunate subjects, a policy of relentless persecution and oppression. Every method, which heartless tyranny and blind fanaticism could devise, was resorted to in order to crush the national spirit, eradicate the native customs and extirpate the Polish language. Numerous libraries, art galleries, schools and seats of learning, rich with the accumulation of centuries, were despoiled of their treasures and closed for the purpose of keeping the Polish people in the lowest state of ignorance and preventing them from participating in the progress and advancement of the world. Strenuous efforts were made, and are still being made, to Russianize and Germanize the unhappy compatriots of Sobieski, Koscius[z]ko, Pulaski and Chopin. Yet notwithstanding all the harsh and inhuman means which have been employed by these oppressors of Poland, the national spirit of her people seems invincible. Although hundreds of thousands of noble minded and public spirited men and women have been confined in subterranean prisons, transported to Siberia and doomed to pass their remaining days in banishment, amid hardship and poverty, for no other crime than that of loving the faith and land of their fathers, and although the wearing of the native picturesque costumes has been interdicted and the speaking of the Polish language has been prohibited and in many instances has been made a penal offense, the love of the Polish people for their Country, its traditions, literature and faith increases as time advances. The literature of Poland reached its zenith in the present century. …

The intolerant policy of religions and political persecution was also evidenced immediately after the first partition when, of the 1900 Churches of the Uni[a]tes, 1200 were given to Russians and converted into Schismatic Churches. The protesting communicants of these houses of worship were arrested, persecuted and exiled to Siberia because they refused to accept the Empress Catherine as the head of their Church. The same policy has been pursued without cessation throughout the present century. It formed the subject of extensive debates in the English parliament of 1830, 32, 34 & 36. It was also discussed in the French parliament. But no definite action was taken.

In 1863 when the Polish insurrection broke out in Russia, Muraview, styled by his own countrymen the "Hangman" was appointed Governor of Lithuania. Between June 8-th and December 28-th, 1803, this executioner ordered eleven priests to be hung or shot, and thousands were deported to Siberia. In 1864 he confiscated 24 churches, in 1865, 26 and in 1867—140 churches. …

In all civilized communities patriotism is understood as love of one's native land and zeal for her general welfare and safety. In Russia it has a different meaning. There, it means devotion to the "sacred" person of the Czar,—the absolute autocrat in all secular and religious matters, and who claims the exclusive power to dispose, according to his whim, not only of the life, liberty and property of his subjects, but also of their souls. Enlightenment and absolutism can never thrive together. Despotism can only be maintained and preserved by keeping the great masses of people in the most abject state of intellectual, political and physical bondage. The knout and sword, not reason, humanity or justice, are the weapons by which the monstrous sway of Czarism can be sustained. The sentiments, aspirations and hopes of the Polish people are so antagonistic to the tendencies and spirit of Russian institutions as to be irreconcilable. To the narrow and intolerant mind of the average Russian it is inconceivable that the Polish people do not readily become reconciled to their lot and renounce the faith, language and traditions of their fathers and blindly accept, as benefactors, the tyrants who have persecuted, butchered and robbed their fathers and brethren. No means have been left untried to bring about this result. Estates have been confiscated and given to Russian favorites in order to impoverish the people and make them dependent upon the liberality and generosity of their persecutors. The purchase of

reality by Polish speaking subjects, for the same reason, was interdicted. To retard the growth of Polish literature and to suppress the national sentiment, most rigid decrees were promulgated. Thousands of ardent sons and daughters of Poland were fined, imprisoned and transported sometimes even without the formality of a trial—for singing patriotic songs, or expressing the natural yearnings of their heart.

In Wilno in 1803 the following decree was issued: "Whoever in whatsoever kind of public place (street, alley, park, restaurant, store etc.) shall in any conversation use the Polish language, he or she shall for the first offense pay 25 rubles, the second 50 rubles, the third 150 rubles. Further contumacy shall be punished by administrative process and eventual transportation. Non-acquaintance with any language other than the Polish will not be accepted as an excuse." This decree is in effect until the present date. It was posted in all public highways and shops.

To fully realize the monstrous nature of this decree, we must bear in mind that a husband, wife, brother, sister, father or mother on meeting each other in a public place could not even inadvertently express the natural emotions of their heart in the language taught them from the cradle without running imminent risk of being overheard by someone of the numerous spies, Cossacks and Police officials, who swarm the country, and be dragged before some servile tool of the government. ...

In the limited number of schools which the government established, only the Russian language is taught. All books are coloured so as to imbue the children with hatred for the creed, language and traditions of their forefathers and instill into their minds a love for the Czar. They are taught that the Czar is the Kind Father of all; that he is the only lawful law-giver, the fountain head of the real faith and the only true and absolute ruler of all the lands from the Baltic to the Pacific Ocean. Oppression begets resistance. Is it to be wondered, that the true Polish parent in his anxiety to prevent the mind of his child from being poisoned by such un-European Asiatic, ancient and false doctrines, should prefer to keep his child at home and let him be content with such meager knowledge as he may obtain in the home circle or at schools which are clandestinely conducted by patriotic clergymen and brave men and women? To the tyranny and attempts of the Russian government to Russianize Poland is due the large number illiterates in that unhappy land. …

In Prussian Poland the condition of the Polish subjects cannot be regarded as having been greatly improved. Although compulsory education laws were enacted, the Polish language was and still is excluded from the schools. The rising generation is deprived of the opportunity of becoming acquainted with the literature which is of paramount interest to them and which reveals such untold treasures as that of their native land. The harsh measures for Germanization of the Polish provinces adopted by the early Prussian statesmen having proven futile, a little over a decade ago Prince Bismarck resorted to a heroic remedy, by striking a powerful blow at their economic condition. Over thirty-five thousand Poles were suddenly expelled from their native land. Laws were enacted for the purchase of large estates, which were to be transferred exclusively in parcels to German colonists. As late as 1886, 100,000,000 marks was appropriated by the German Reichstag for this purpose. During the month of February, 1898, the German government asked for an additional appropriation of 100,000,000 marks for the same purpose.

Under the patronage of the government, societies were formed for the purpose of boycotting Polish merchants, traders and manufacturers. In the present year (1898) a powerful movement has been inaugurated to compel all Polish papers to be printed both in the Polish and German languages. Thus by forcing them to unnecessarily increase their expenses for printing and paper, it is expected to place the Polish press at a great disadvantage in competing with the German papers and so in a measure destroy their utility. …

The attitude of the Austrian government towards its Slavonic subjects is not much better. The same policy of repression is continually pursued. The recent riotous demonstrations in the Austrian parliament against the cabinet of the late prime minister Badeni for making the Slavonic language in certain Slavonic dis- tricts co-ordinate with the German, amply proves with what intolerance the German people regards the Slavonic race and to what shameful tactics they will resort to keep them in subjugation.

III.   Poles in America

In view of the merciless persecution of the Polish people under the rule of their despoilers, it is not strange that they should emigrate in such large numbers to the land of freedom, for which their compatriots, Koscius[z]ko and Pulaski, fought and bled during the American revolution, in order that they might enjoy those advantages, economical and political, which are unjustly denied to them at home. It is true that among them a certain percentage of illiterates may be found, though the number is by no means as great as claimed by the Honorable Senator from Massachusetts in his report to the Senate. Illiteracy, though greatly to be deplored, is not per se a crime. We must further respectfully insist that the figures cited by the Hon. [Henry Cabot] Lodge in his report on the Immigration question are not, so far as they relate, to the Polish people, reliable. The sources from which they have been obtained are not the most trustworthy. Under the heading of Poles, are included other elements with which the Polish people have nothing in common.

Experience in this country soon teaches the illiterate the advantages of education, and self-interest will dictate to him the necessity of learning to read and write. A visit to the homes of the Polish people in this country will convince the impartial observer that they are cleanly, orderly and law-abiding people. They have established at great expense numerous schools in which the English language is taught. They have founded libraries and heartily support their own press as well as papers published in the English language.

Owing to their thrifty and industrious habits they soon become property owners and cheerfully contribute their share of taxes for the support of the government. Socialistic and anarchistic doctrines never receive any encouragement from them. For this country and its institution they entertain the profoundest respect.

The limited time at our disposal did not enable us to gather complete statistics in order to refute the figures quoted by the Honorable Senator from Massachusetts. We have, however, been able to secure a large number of commendatory testimonials from officials who by reason of their position come most closely in contact with the people and are best qualified to judge their character. The officials we refer to are the mayors and police officials of large cities. Of the large number received, we will subjoin only the following extracts from letters sent to Mr. F. H. Jablonski, President of the Polish National Alliance of the United States of North America and chairman of the Joint Committee for drafting this memorial:

Detroit. Jan. 24, 1898.—The Polish citizens of Detroit are probably more numerous to the population of the city than in any other city in the United States. One section in our city is inhabited exclusively by Polish families. it must he conceded that taking into consideration their condition as very recent immigrants to this country, poor, unskilled and ignorant of the ways of our people they are advancing very rapidly. We have already in our community Poles whose native ability brought them to a high plane in business lines and it must he said that their record for peacefulness and good citizenship is above reproach. It is gratifying for me to say that there is no Pole in this city, however old, sickly or dependent, who does not prefer to earn his bread by honest labor. Conditions of the times in Detroit, as I suppose elsewhere, have brought thousands of families to a state of privation.

—William C. Maybury, Mayor.

Manistee, Mich., Jan. 24, 1898.—We have a Polish population in this county of over 5000 souls. There are within the city limits over (500 Polish school children between the ages of 5 to 16 years. The total number of arrests in this (Manistee) county was 288 for 1897. The total population of the county is about 30,000. We think that there are but few counties of like population that can show such record for peace and good order. I do not think that the number of Polish people arrested is equal to their proportion, and as a rule those of that nationality arrested are charged with misdemeanors and minor offenses. It has been stated by some who are prejudiced, politically or otherwise, that Polish people furnish more than their quota of arrests, but records do not show this, but prove the contrary.

Personally I have found our Polish citizens to be peaceable and law-abiding people, frugal and industrious and progressive. A great many of them own their homes and some have acquired considerable other property. Quite a number have purchased farm lands in this vicinity and are developing the country and prospering personally. There are of course some exceptions to the general rule, but the exceptions are no more numerous comparatively with them than with Americans or any other nationality.

I have always maintained that Polish people by reason of their past history and their being at present practically without a nation are especially and peculiarly adapted to our institutions and so to become loyal, patriotic and intelligent American citizens without any other national attachments to divide their patriotic zeal.

—Thos. Smuarthwaite, Mayor.

Milwaukee, Jan. 25, 1898.—The Polish-Americans in this city are very industrious and have a fair reputation.

—F. Baringer. Secretary

Toledo. Ohio. Jan. 25, 1898.—We have very little bother with Polish-American residents of this city, they quarrel among themselves, mostly church troubles but are very peaceful with other citizens. Total number of arrests for 1897 are 4673, out of which 100 to 150 would be fair average for the Polish people.

—C. H. Durian, Sec'y of Police.

New York. Jan. 29,. 1898.—In reply to your request to be informed as to the reputation of the Polish people of this city for peacefulness, industry and integrity, it is my personal opinion that they possess all these traits and are a very desirable class of immigrants.

—John J. Nagle, M. D. Chief of the Bureau of Municipal Statistics

From the metropolis of the State in which the Honorable Senator from Massachusetts discovered, according to his Senate report, such a astonishingly-large and alarming proportion of criminals among the Polish people we received the following letters:

Boston, Jan. 25, 1898.—I am directed by His Honor, Mayor Quincy, to acknowledge the receipt of yours of the 25th with reference to the character of the Polish-American residents in our community. I am pleased to say that though we have a fairly large number of Poles in our community their demeanor is so exemplary that it rarely happens that any one is before our police court even on a trivial charge. We have a Polish Roman Catholic church in the district of our city called South Boston, and we find the communicants exemplary in every way. I think I may say that it is the opinion of the citizens of Boston that the Poles, far from being a detriment, are a positive addition to our community in the direction of morality and good citizenship.

—Thos. A. Mullen, Secretary

Boston, Jan. 28, 1898.—We have mailed you a copy of the annual report of the Board of Police for the city of Boston for the year of 1897. On page 30, you will find from the statistics that the number of arrests of Polish-American residents is small as compared with the other.

The captain of one of our police districts in which the largest number of arrests is made each year states that the number of arrests of the Polish-Americans is smaller in proportion to the number of residents than that of some of the other nationalities. He also states that their reputation for peacefulness and industry is very fair, and that many of them are very good farm lands.

—A. P. Martin, Chairman of Board of Police

Omaha. Feb. 4, 1898.—Replying to your communication of recent date asking for a statement of the reputation for peacefulness, industry and integrity which the Polish American residents bear in our community, I would say that we regard our Polish-American population very highly for the various qualities you have mentioned. They are peaceful, law-abiding citizens and there is no class of workmen in this city who bear a better reputation for industry than do they. They are honest and trustworthy and have the confidence of the community.

—Frank E. Moores, Mayor.

LANSING, Feb. 8. 1898.—The Polish people of Detroit have always been very peaceable citizens and are one of the most industrious classes of foreigners that come to our cities. They are always glad to work and are not usually particular as to the kind of work, as long as they can earn an honest dollar. When one takes into consideration the training which they have had in their own country I think they are a very good people and entitled to a great deal of credit. I might say also that I have a great expectations from the Poles, that is from the next generation, as almost any other class of people we have here. They have a very strong physique fitting them for all kinds of labor and they are very quick and willing to learn.

—H. S. Pingree, Governor [of Michigan]

Buffalo, Jan. 24, 1898.—In reply to your communication of January 21, in which you request a brief statement as to the reputation for peacefulness, industry and integrity that the Polish-American residence bears in this community. I take pleasure in saying that the general reputation of the class of citizens referred to and in the respect indicated in your note, is subject of constant and favorable comment. The Polish-American population of Buffalo is very large and has for years been notable for industry, thrift and good citizenship.

—Conrad Diehl, Mayor.

Chicago. Feb. 3rd. 1898. – In response to your request for an expression of opinion from me as to the character and standing of the Polish population of Chicago, it gives me great pleasure to bear testimony to the fact, that the Polish residents of this city are on the whole, among the most industrious and reputable of our citizens. They are law-abiding and industrious, and deserve great credit for the manly manner in which on their arrival in this country, they struggle against and overcome, the difficulties that confront them.

—Carter H. Harrison, Mayor.

P. S. I am informed that the Polish population of Cook County is over 175,000.

At some future day this committee expects to furnish to the Congress and the American Public reliable statistics of the real status of the Polish people in America. Suffice it for the present to say that viewing the subject from either a moral, economical or political standpoint, we fail to perceive the necessity for the enactment of the proposed immigration bill. The wonderful resources of this country have not been fully developed, and it certainly cannot be contended that the late industrial stagnation and financial depression was due to an overcrowded labor market.

Finally we respectfully submit that while the Polish people are oppressed in their native land and are denied the privilege of learning to read and write in their native tongue the same consideration should be shown to them as is shown by this bill to the unfortunate Cubans struggling for liberty and the semi-civilized Hawaiians.

Appealing to the exalted sense of justice and humanity of the members of Congress and the American Public in general, we, representatives of all the large Polish-American organizations of the United States respectfully ask that the Lodge Immigration bill be not adopted.

GLOSSARY

Bulwark: A defensive wall, barricade, embankment, or other such fortification.

Jacobin: Derived from the radical Jacobin faction during the French Revolution, the term is often applied to any radical or extremist group.

Knout: A whip used for flogging or, as a verb, to flog.

Mussulman: From the Persian word *musulmān,* this is an archaic term for Muslim.

Schismatic: Usually used in reference to religious groups, the term refers to a person who promoted division, discord, or separation.

Document Analysis

The Polish protest begins by providing some context for the issue while at the same time castigating those "irresponsible demagogues" who disparage Poland and the Poles. It then focuses specifically on the catalyst that prompted the joint action of the various Polish organizations, the immigration bill that Senator Henry Cabot Lodge had introduced into the U.S. Senate surrounded by demeaning comments about the Southern and Eastern Europeans he assured listeners would be largely eliminated by the proposed literacy test.

To oppose the Lodge bill the Polish organizations used a three-fold approach: praising the contributions of a free Poland to European civilization, informing readers of the suffering of Poles under the foreign occupiers during the partitions, and then providing evidence and endorsements designed to depict Poles as decent, law-abiding citizens. In the first instance the authors of the protest promoted the idea of Poland as the safeguard of Christian Europe against the "savage Mongols, Tartars, Muscovites and Turks," buttressing the claim with historical incidents designed to substantiate Polish contributions to Europe's security over several centuries. Next, they moved on to show that Poles had always welcomed others to their lands, especially the Jewish people who, though "proscribed everywhere else, found a second country, with protection for their learned and religious establishments in this hospitable and tolerant land."

To address the primary question of "literacy," the Poles took pains to mention the preeminent contributions of Copernicus [Mikołaj Kopernik] to world science, as well as other important scholars and the fact that the Jagiellonian University in Kraków was the second oldest university in Eastern Europe. Then too, since Lodge asserted that Poles knew nothing of democracy and a republican form of government, the authors emphasized that the Polish crown had been elective for centuries, the legislature was republican in form with a "deliberative" assembly, and the powers of the monarch were greatly circumscribed by the legislature. Slavery never existed in free Poland, religious and ethnic toleration were codified into law, and its written constitution was compared favorably by scholars with the famous English Magna Carta.

Despite this sterling record, Poland succumbed to partition by its stronger neighbors—Austria, Prussia, and Russia—in the last decades of the 18th century. Enlightenment was replaced with "relentless persecution and oppression" the authors explained. "Every method, which heartless tyranny and blind fanaticism could devise, was resorted to in order to crush the national spirit, eradicate the native customs and extirpate the Polish language." Those who resisted were imprisoned or, if in the Russian-occupied area, condemned to Siberia. Against these outrages the Poles rose in 1794, 1830-31, 1846, and 1863, only to have their aspirations for freedom dashed each time. It was through these experiences, the authors asserted, that Poles certainly knew the value of freedom, it was because of the lack of freedom and a representative republic under the partitioning powers that Poles came to America seeking the very things that Lodge claimed they neither understood nor valued.

Turning to the Polish experience in America, the protest pointed to the assistance given to the American colonists in their own fight for freedom by the Poles Kazimierz Pułaski and Tadeusz Kościuszko, the latter of whom designed the fortress at West Point where the United States Military Academy is today. The new immigrants are "orderly and law-abiding people" and value education as proved by the fact that they "have established at great expense numerous schools in which the English language is taught. They have founded libraries and heartily support their own press as well as papers published in the English language."

Finally, as proof of the good character of Polish immigrants, the authors of the protest gathered a number of endorsements from political leaders around the country attesting to their good behavior and positive contributions to their communities. These came from leaders such as the mayors of Buffalo, Chicago, Detroit, Milwaukee, and other cities, along with a selection of governors and of police and other city officials. All of these were selected to bolster the Polish argument that the Lodge bill rested on ill-informed and false information.

Essential Themes

All too often immigrant groups in America are pictured as helpless pawns caught up in a strange new culture with which they cannot relate. This view was reinforced by historian Oscar Handlin's popular history of immigration, *The Uprooted*, where, as the title suggests, he views newcomers largely as people "uprooted" from their pasts, rootless in a new society. This interpretation was challenged by John Bodnar who argued, in *The Transplanted*, that European immigrants did not lose their cultural traditions when the migrated, they merely "transplanted" and adapted them to their new environment. The Polish American protest of the literacy bill presented here stands as an excellent example of coordinated joint action, erudite argumentation, and ethnic pride. As an act of collection action it can also be traced back to a similar nineteenth-century Polish custom usually labeled "organic work"; that is, a self-help ethic brought from the Old Country and applied to the problems the immigrants found in their newly adopted land.

In another sense this also fits well into a long pattern of immigrant protest and other actions taken in response to conditions they found in America. Irish immigrant leaders held dinners and rallies and published newspapers to support the unsuccessful Young Ireland Rebellion of 1848 and established local chapters of the Ancient Order of Hibernians to protect Irish interests. German "Forty-Eighters" formed political and social groups, distributed newspapers, and actively promoted the interests of their group, especially easy immigration laws and cheap western lands for homesteaders. There were, in fact, numerous and recurring mutual expressions of cooperation with Irish, Germans, Poles, and other groups attending and otherwise supporting each other's causes.

Bibliography and Additional Reading

Victor Greene, *For God and Country: The Rise of Polish and Lithuanian Ethnic Consciousness in America, 1860-1919* (Madison: State Historical Society of Wisconsin, 1975).

Edward R. Kantowicz, *Polish American Politics in Chicago: 1888-1940* (Chicago: University of Chicago Press, 1975).

Donald E. Pienkos, *PNA: A Centennial History of the Polish National Alliance of the United States of North America* (Boulder: East European Monographs, distributed by Columbia University Press, 1984)

James S. Pula, *Polish Americans: An Ethnic Community* (New York: Twayne Publishers, 1995).

How I Found America

Date: 1920
Author: Anzia Yezierska
Genre: Book Extracts

Summary Overview

Sometimes known as the Great Migration, the period between 1870 and the outbreak of World War I in 1914 witnessed an enormous surge in immigration peaking in 1907 when more than a million people entered the United States in that single year. About eighty percent of the new arrivals settled in the region east of the Mississippi Rover and north of the Ohio River and Mason-Dixon Line. New York City's population alone grew from about one million in 1860 to over three million by 1900 taxing the ability of the city to provide adequate housing and services for the exploding population. The result of the overcrowding was a rapid deterioration in sanitation, the spread of virulent epidemics, and the every-present danger of fires in the poorer tenement sections of the city.

Largely dominated by peoples from Southern and Eastern Europe, these new groups brought with them unfamiliar languages and traditions and practitioners of non-Protestant religions such as Catholicism, Judaism, and various forms of the Orthodox faith. Ethnic communities grew within the cities, featuring theater productions, musical organizations, newspapers, holidays, foods, and eventually even athletic teams and schools. These distinctive neighborhoods provided their members with familiarity, cultural cohesiveness, and group support in their transition to a new nation, a new workplace environment, and a new cultural landscape. They also provided authors with new material for works of fiction and non-fiction, as well as supplying detractors with ammunition to fuel negative nativism.

Defining Moment

As early as 1890 New York became the largest immigrant center in the world. Most prominent among the newcomers were Italians and Poles, although if one counted those of the Jewish religion regardless of the country of origin then they would rank second between the two nationality groups. Competition for jobs, housing, influence, and other factors of urban life often added to the tensions of cultural transition for these and other groups sharing the same experience. This simmering mixture of ethnic and cultural traditions struggling to find a place in its new environment produced its own unique, dynamic urban culture.

It should not be surprising that this cauldron of cultural transformation produced a number of writers and other observers who attempted to chronicle and explain this vibrant interaction. Perhaps the best known of these was Jacob Riis, an immigrant from Denmark who gained prominence through his documentary photography of the impoverished living conditions in New York's congested tenement neighborhoods that was published in 1890 as *How the Other Half Lives: Studies Among the Tenements of New York*. Among other noteworthy works from this era are Abraham Cahan's *The Rise of David Lavinsky* and Henry Roth's *Call It Sleep*. Born in modern Belarus, Cahan describes the immigrant experience, the process of Americanization, and Jewish culture in New York in a work based on his own experiences, while Roth, a native of the Ukraine, also uses the Lower East Side as a backdrop for exploring his experiences growing up in the tenements. Another immigrant who left a largely autobiographical account of immigrant life was Anzia Yezierska.

Author Biography

Born into a Jewish family in Mały Płock, a small village in northeastern Poland that was then within the Russian Empire, Anzia Yezierska was the daughter of a Talmudic scholar who, in the tradition of the Orthodox religious community, devoted his time to study rather than economic endeavor. Responsibility for providing for the family fell on her mother. Her date of birth is unknown but believed to be in the early 1880s. Around 1890 her family moved to the United States, following in the footsteps of her elder brother who migrated several years previously. Settling into a crowded tenement in the immigrant section on the Lower East Side of New York City, Yezierska found that her burning desire for an education appeared no easier to satisfy in her new surroundings than it was in Eastern Europe.

Forced to leave elementary school for employment, she grew increasingly unhappy with her family's poverty which interfered with her obtaining the education she craved. Frequent arguments with her father, who failed to support her ambitions, caused her to move to the Clara de Hirsch Home for Working Girls where she was able further her education. Although she apparently never completed a high school course of study, she managed to not only gain entrance to the Teacher's College at Co-

lumbia University but to obtain a scholarship as well. After completing her studies she taught elementary school from 1908 to 1913 and began to write fiction. Although she married, in 1916 she left her husband to move to San Francisco where she became a social worker.

Following a divorce she returned to New York where she resumed writing, relying heavily on her own experiences to examine issues of acculturation against the backdrop of the Jewish immigrant community. Focusing especially on the struggles of Jewish women, informed by her own experiences, her works are rich in detailed realism, often appearing as thinly veiled autobiographical reflections. After a long literary career, she passed away after suffering a stroke in Ontario, California, on November 21, 1970.

HISTORICAL DOCUMENT

Part I

Every breath I drew was a breath of fear, every shadow a stifling shock, every footfall struck on my heart like the heavy boot of the Cossack.

On a low stool in the middle of the only room in our mud hut sat my father—his red beard falling over the Book of Isaiah open before him. On the tile stove, on the benches that were our beds, even on the earthen floor, sat the neighbors' children, learning from him the ancient poetry of the Hebrew race.

As he chanted, the children repeated:

"The voice of him that crieth in the wilderness,
Prepare ye the way of the Lord.
Make straight in the desert a highway for our God

"Every valley shall be exalted,
And every mountain and hill shall be made low,
And the crooked shall be made straight,
And the rough places plain.

"And the glory of the Lord shall be revealed,
And all flesh shall see it together."

Undisturbed by the swaying and chanting of teacher and pupils, old Kakah, our speckled hen, with her brood of chicks, strutted and pecked at the potato-peelings which fell from my mother's lap, as she prepared our noon meal.

I stood at the window watching the road, lest the Cossack come upon us unawares to enforce the ukaz of the Czar, which would tear the bread from our mouths: "No Chadir [Hebrew school] shall be held in a room used for cooking and sleeping."

With one eye I watched ravenously my mother cutting chunks of black bread. At last the potatoes were ready. She poured them out of the iron pot into a wooden bowl and placed them in the center of the table.

Instantly the swaying and chanting ceased, the children rushed forward. The fear of the Cossacks was swept away from my heart by the fear that the children would get my potato.

The sentry deserted his post. With a shout of joy I seized my portion and bit a huge mouthful of mealy delight.

At that moment the door was driven open by the blow of an iron heel. The Cossack's whip swished through the air. Screaming, we scattered.

The children ran out—our livelihood gone with them.

"Oi weh," wailed my mother, clutching her breast, "is there a God over us—and sees all this?"

With grief-glazed eyes my father muttered a broken prayer as the Cossack thundered the ukaz: "A thousand rubles fine or a year in prison if you are ever found again teaching children where you're eating and sleeping."

"Gottuniu!" pleaded my mother, "would you tear the last skin from our bones? Where else can we be eating and sleeping? Or should we keep chadir in the middle of the road? Have we houses with separate rooms like the Czar?"

Ignoring my mother's entreaties the Cossack strode out of the hut. My father sank into a chair, his head bowed in the silent grief of the helpless.

"God from the world"—my mother wrung her hands—"is there no end to our troubles? When will the earth cover me and my woes?"

I watched the Cossack disappear down the road. All at once I saw the whole village running toward us. I dragged my mother to the window to see the approaching crowd.

"Gewalt! What more is falling over our heads?" she cried in alarm.

Masheh Mindel, the water-carrier's wife, headed a wild procession. The baker, the butcher, the shoemaker, the tailor, the goat-herd, the workers of the fields, with their wives and children, pressed toward us through a cloud of dust.

Masheh Mindel, almost fainting, fell in front of the doorway." A letter from America!" she gasped.

"A letter from America!" echoed the crowd, as they snatched the letter from her and thrust it into my father's hands.

"Read! Read!" they shouted tumultuously.

My father looked through the letter, his lips uttering no sound. In breathless suspense the crowd gazed at him. Their eyes shone with wonder and reverence for the only man in the village who could read.

Masheh Mindel crouched at his feet, her neck stretched toward him to catch each precious word of the letter.

"To my worthy wife, Masheh Mindel, and to my loving son, Susha Feifel, and to my precious darling daughter, the apple of my eye, the pride of my life, Tzipkeleh!

"Long years and good luck on you! May the blessings from heaven fall over your beloved heads and save you from all harm!

"First I come to tell you that I am well and in good health. May I hear the same from you.

"Secondly, I am telling you that my sun is beginning to shine in America. I am becoming a person—a business man.

"I have for myself a stand in the most crowded part of America, where people are as thick as flies and every day is like market-day by a fair. My business is from bananas and apples. The day begins with my pushcart full of fruit, and the day never ends before I count up at least $2. 00 profit – that means four rubles. Stand before your eyes… I…Gedalyeh Mindel, four rubles a day, twenty-four rubles a week!"

"Gedalyeh Mindel, the water-carrier, twenty-four rubles a week.…" The words leaped like fire in the air.

We gazed at his wife, Masheh Mindel—a dried-out bone of a woman.

"Masheh Mindel, with a husband in America—Masheh Mindel, the wife of a man earning twenty-four rubles a week!"

We looked at her with new reverence. Already she was a being from another world. The dead, sunken eyes became alive with light. The worry for bread that had tightened the skin of her cheek-bones was gone. The sudden surge of happiness filled out her features, flushing her face as with wine.

The two starved children clinging to her skirts, dazed with excitement, only dimly realized their good fortune by the envious glances of the others.

"Thirdly, I come to tell you," the letter went on, "white bread and meat I eat every day just like the millionaires.

"Fourthly, I have to tell you that I am no more Gedalyeh Mindel—*Mister* Mindel they call me in America.

"Fifthly, Masheh Mindel and my dear children, in America there are no mud huts where cows and chickens and people live all together. I have for myself a separate room with a closed door, and before any one can come to me, I can give a say, 'Come in,' or 'Stay out,' like a king in a palace.

"Lastly, my darling family and people of the Village of Sukovoly, there is no Czar in America."

My father paused; the hush was stifling. No Czar—no Czar in America! Even the little babies repeated the chant: "No Czar in America!"

"In America they ask everybody who should be the President, and I, Gedalyeh Mindel, when I take out my Citizens papers, will have as much to say who shall be the next President in America, as Mr. Rockefeller the greatest millionaire."

"Fifty rubles I am sending you for your ship-ticket to America. And may all Jews who suffer in Goluth from ukazes and pogroms live yet to lift up their heads like me, Gedalyeh Mindel, in America."

Fifty rubles! A ship-ticket to America! That so much good luck should fall on one head! A savage envy bit me. Gloomy darts from narrowed eyes stabbed Masheh Mindel.

Why should not we too have a chance to get away from this dark land? Has not every heart the same hunger for America? The same longing to live and laugh and breathe like a free human being? America is for all. Why should only Masheh Mindel and her children have a chance to the new world?

Murmuring and gesticulating the crowd dispersed.

Each one knew every one else's thought: How to get to America. What could they pawn? From where could they borrow for a ship-ticket?

Silently we followed my father back into the hut from which the Cossack had driven us a while before.

We children looked from mother to father and from father to mother.

"Gottuniu! The Czar himself is pushing us to America by this last ukaz." My mother's face lighted up the hut like a lamp.

"Meshugeneh Yidini!" admonished my father, "Always your head in the air. What—where—America? With what money? Can dead people lift themselves up to dance?"

"Dance?" The samovar and the brass pots rang and reëchoed with my mother's laughter." I could dance myself over the waves of the ocean to America."

In amazed delight at my mother's joy we children rippled and chuckled with her.

My father paced the room—his face dark with dread for the morrow.

"Empty hands—empty pockets—yet it dreams itself in you America."

"Who is poor who has hopes on America?" flaunted my mother.

"Sell my red quilted petticoat that grandmother left for my dowry," I urged in excitement.

"Sell the feather beds, sell the samovar," chorused the children.

"Sure we can sell everything—the goat and all the winter things," added my mother; "it must be always summer in America."

I flung my arms around my brother and he seized Bessie by the curls, and we danced about the room crazy with joy.

"Beggars!" laughed my mother, "why are you so happy with yourselves? How will you go to America without a shirt on your back—without shoes on your feet?"

But we ran out into the road, shouting and singing: "We'll sell everything we got—we'll go to America."

"White bread and meat we'll eat every day—in America! In America!"

That very evening we fetched Berel Zalman, the usurer, and showed him all our treasures, piled up in the middle of the hut.

"Look, all these fine feather beds, Berel Zalman," urged my mother; "this grand fur coat came from Nijny itself. My grandfather bought it at the fair."

I held up my red quilted petticoat, the supreme sacrifice of my ten-year-old life.

Even my father shyly pushed forward the samovar. "It can hold enough tea for the whole village."

"Only a hundred rubles for them all," pleaded my mother; "only enough to lift us to America. Only one hundred little rubles."

"A hundred rubles? Pfui!" sniffed the pawnbroker." Forty is overpaid. Not even thirty is it worth."

But coaxing and cajoling my mother got a hundred rubles out of him.

Steerage—dirty bundles—foul odors—seasick humanity—but I saw and heard nothing of the foulness and ugliness around me. I floated in showers of sunshine; visions upon visions of the new world opened before me.

From lips to lips flowed the golden legend of the golden country:

"In America you can say what you feel—you can voice your thoughts in the open streets without fear of a Cossack."

"In America is a home for everybody. The land is your land. Not like in Russia where you feel yourself a stranger in the village where you were born and raised—the village in which your father and grandfather lie buried."

"Everybody is with everybody alike, in America. Christians and Jews are brothers together."

"An end to the worry for bread. An end to the fear of the bosses over you. Everybody can do what he wants with his life in America."

"There are no high or low in America. Even the President holds hands with Gedalyeh Mindel."

"Plenty for all. Learning flows free like milk and honey."

"Learning flows free."

The words painted pictures in my mind. I saw before me free schools, free colleges, free libraries, where I could learn and learn and keep on learning.

In our village was a school, but only for Christian children. In the schools of America I'd lift up my head and laugh and dance—a child with other children. Like a bird in the air, from sky to sky, from star to star, I'd soar and soar.

"Land! Land!" came the joyous shout.

"America! We're in America!" cried my mother, almost smothering us in her rapture.

All crowded and pushed on deck. They strained and stretched to get the first glimpse of the "golden country," lifting their children on their shoulders that they might see beyond them.

Men fell on their knees to pray. Women hugged their babies and wept. Children danced. Strangers embraced and kissed like old friends. Old men and women had in their eyes a look of young people in love.

Age-old visions sang themselves in me—songs of freedom of an oppressed people.

America!—America!

Part II

Between buildings that loomed like mountains, we struggled with our bundles, spreading around us the smell of the steerage. Up Broadway, under the bridge, and through the swarming streets of the ghetto, we followed Gedalyeh Mindel.

I looked about the narrow streets of squeezed-in stores and houses, ragged clothes, dirty bedding oozing out of the windows, ash-cans and garbage-cans cluttering the sidewalks. A vague sadness pressed down my heart— the first doubt of America.

"Where are the green fields and open spaces in America?" cried my heart." Where is the golden country of my dreams?"

A loneliness for the fragrant silence of the woods that lay beyond our mud hut welled up in my heart, a longing for the soft, responsive earth of our village streets. All about me was the hardness of brick and stone, the stinking smells of crowded poverty.

"Here's your house with separate rooms like in a palace." Gedalyeh Mindel flung open the door of a dingy, airless flat.

"Oi weh!" my mother cried in dismay. "Where's the sunshine in America?"

She went to the window and looked out at the blank wall of the next house. "Gottuniu! Like in a grave so dark...."

"It ain't so dark, it's only a little shady." Gedalyeh Mindel lighted the gas. "Look only"—he pointed with pride to the dim gaslight. "No candles, no kerosene lamps in America, you turn on a screw and put to it a match and you got it light like with sunshine."

Again the shadow fell over me, again the doubt of America!

In America were rooms without sunlight, rooms to sleep in, to eat in, to cook in, but without sunshine. And Gedalyeh Mindel was happy. Could I be satisfied with just a place to sleep and eat in, and a door to shut people out—to take the place of sunlight? Or would I always need the sunlight to be happy?

And where was there a place in America for me to play? I looked out into the alley below and saw pale-faced children scrambling in the gutter. "Where is America?" cried my heart.

My eyes were shutting themselves with sleep. Blindly, I felt for the buttons on my dress, and buttoning I sank back in sleep again—the deadweight sleep of utter exhaustion.

"Heart of mine!" my mother's voice moaned above me. "Father is already gone an hour. You know how they'll squeeze from you a nickel for every minute you're late. Quick only!"

I seized my bread and herring and tumbled down the stairs and out into the street. I ate running, blindly pressing through the hurrying throngs of workers—my haste and fear choking each mouthful.

I felt a strangling in my throat as I neared the sweatshop prison; all my nerves screwed together into iron hardness to endure the day's torture.

For an instant I hesitated as I faced the grated window of the old dilapidated building—dirt and decay cried out from every crumbling brick.

In the maw of the shop, raging around me the roar and the clatter, the clatter and the roar, the merciless grind of the pounding machines. Half maddened, half deadened, I struggled to think, to feel, to remember—what am I—who am I—why was I here?

I struggled in vain—bewildered and lost in a whirlpool of noise.

"America—America—where was America?" it cried in my heart.

The factory whistle—the slowing-down of the machines—the shout of release hailing the noon hours.

I woke as from a tense nightmare—a weary waking to pain.

In the dark chaos of my brain reason began to dawn. In my stifled heart feelings began to pulse. The wound of my wasted life began to throb and ache. My childhood choked with drudgery—must my youth too die—unlived?

The odor of herring and garlic—the ravenous munching of food—laughter and loud, vulgar jokes. Was it only I who was so wretched? I looked at those around me. Were they happy or only insensible to their slavery? How could they laugh and joke? Why were they not torn with rebellion against this galling grind—the crushing, deadening movements of the body, where only hands live and hearts and brains must die?

A touch on my shoulder. I looked up. It was Yetta Solomon from the machine next to mine.

"Here's your tea."

I stared at her, half hearing.

"Ain't you going to eat nothing?"

"Oi weh! Yetta! I can't stand it!" The cry broke from me. "I didn't come to America to turn into a machine. I came to America to make from myself a person. Does America want only my hands – only the strength of my body – not my heart – not my feelings – my thoughts?"

"Our heads ain't smart enough," said Yetta, practically. "We ain't been to school like the American-born."

"What for did I come to America but to go to school—to learn—to think—to make something beautiful from my life...."

"Sh-sh! Sh-sh! The boss—the boss!" came the warning whisper.

A sudden hush fell over the shop as the boss entered. He raised his hand.

Breathless silence.

The hard, red face with pig's eyes held us under its sickening spell. Again I saw the Cossack and heard him thunder the ukaz.

Prepared for disaster, the girls paled as they cast at each other sidelong, frightened glances.

"Hands," he address us, fingering the gold watch-chain that spread across his fat belly, "it's slack in the other trades and I can get plenty girls begging themselves to work for half what you're getting—only I ain't a skinner. I always give my hands a show to earn their bread. From now on, I'll give you fifty cents a dozen shirts instead of seventy-five, but I'll give you night-work, so you needn't lose nothing." And he was gone.

The stillness of death filled the shop. Each one felt the heart of the other bleed with her own helplessness.

A sudden sound broke the silence. A woman sobbed chokingly. It was Balah Rifkin, a widow with three children.

"Oi weh!" She tore at her scrawny neck. "The bloodsucker—the thief! How will I give them to eat—my babies—my babies—my hungry little lambs!"

"Why do let him choke us?"

"Twenty-five cents less on a dozen—how will we be able to live?"

"He tears the last skin from our bones!"

"Why didn't nobody speak up to him?"

"Tell him he couldn't crush us down to worse than we had in Russia?"

"Can we help ourselves? Our life lies in his hands."

Something in me forced me forward. Rage at the bitter greed tore me. Our desperate helplessness drove me to strength.

"I'll go to the boss!" I cried, my nerves quivering with fierce excitement. "I'll tell him Balah Rifkin has three hungry mouths to feed."

Pale, hungry faces thrust themselves toward me, thin, knotted hands reached out, starved bodies pressed close about me.

"Long year on you!" cried Balah Rifkin, drying her

eyes with a corner of her shawl.

"Tell him about my old father and me, his only bread-giver," came from Bessie Sopolsky, a gaunt-faced girl with a hacking cough.

"And I got no father or mother and four of them younger than me hanging on my neck." Jennie Feist's beautiful young face was already scarred with the gray worries of age.

America, as the oppressed of all lands have dreamed America to be, and America *as it is,* flashed before me—a banner of fire! Behind me I felt masses pressing—thousands of immigrants—thousands upon thousands crushed by injustice, lifted me as on wings.

I entered the boss's office without a shadow of fear. I was not I—the wrongs of my people burned through me till I felt the very flesh of my body a living flame of rebellion.

I faced the boss.

"We can't stand it!" I cried. "Even as it is we're hungry, Fifty cents a dozen would starve us. Can you, a Jew, tear the bread from another Jew's mouth?"

"You, fresh mouth, you! Who are you to learn me my business?"

"Weren't you yourself once a machine slave—your life in the hands of your boss?"

"You—loaferin—money for nothing you want! The minute they begin to talk English they get flies in their nose....A black year on you—trouble-maker! I'll have no smart heads in my shop! Such freshness! Out you get... out from my shop!"

Stunned and hopeless, the wings of my courage broken, I groped my way back to them—back to the eager, waiting faces—back to the crushed hearts aching with mine.

As I opened the door they read our defeat in my face.

"Girls!" I held out my hands. "He's fired me."

My voice died in the silence. Not a girl stirred. Their heads only bent closer over their machines.

"Here, you! Get yourself out of here!" The boss thundered at me. "Bessie Sopolsky and you, Balah Rifkin, take out her machine into the hall....I want no big-mouthed Americanerins in my shop."

Bessie Sopolsky and Balah Rifkin, their eyes black with tragedy, carried out my machine.

Not a hand was held out to me, not a face met mine. I

felt them shrink from me as I passed them on my way out.

In the street I found I was crying. The new hope that had flowed in me so strong bled out of my veins. A moment before, our togetherness had made me believe us so strong—and now I saw each alone—crushed—broken. What were they all but crawling worms, servile grubbers for bread?

I wept not so much because the girls had deserted me, but because I saw for the first time how mean, how vile, were the creatures with whom I had to work. How the fear for bread had dehumanized their last shred of humanity! I felt I had not been working among human beings, but in a jungle of savages who had to eat one another alive in order to survive.

And then, in the very bitterness of my resentment, the hardness broke in me. I saw the girls through their own eyes as if I were inside of them. What else could they have done? Was not an immediate crust of bread for Balah Rifkin's children more urgent than truth—more vital than honor?

Could it be that they ever had dreamed of America as I had dreamed? Had their faith in America wholly died in them? Could my faith be killed as theirs had been?

Gasping from running, Yetta Solomon flung her arms around me.

"You golden heart! I sneaked myself out from the shop—only to tell you I'll come to see you to-night. I'd give the blood from under my nails for you—only I got to run back—I got to hold my job—my mother—"

I hardly saw or heard her—my senses stunned with my defeat. I walked on in a blind daze—feeling that any moment I would drop in the middle of the street from sheer exhaustion.

Every hope I had clung to—every human stay—every reality was torn from under me. I sank in bottomless blackness. I had only one wish left—to die.

Was it then only a dream—a mirage of the hungry-hearted people in the desert lands of oppression—this age-old faith in America—the beloved, the prayed-for "golden country?"

Had the starved villagers of Sukovoly lifted above their sorrows a mere rainbow vision that led them—where—where? To the stifling submission of the sweatshop or the desperation of the streets!

"O God! What is there beyond this hell?" my soul

cried in me. "Why can't I make a quick end to myself?"

A thousand voices within me and about me answered:

"My faith is dead, but in my blood their faith still clamors and aches for fulfillment—*dead generations whose faith though beaten back still presses on—a resistless, deathless force!*

"In this America that crushes and kills me, their spirit drives me on—to struggle—to suffer—but never to submit."

In my desperate darkness their lost lives loomed—a living flame of light. Again I saw the mob of dusty villagers crowding around my father as he read the letter from America—their eager faces thrust out—their eyes blazing with the same hope, the same age-old faith that drove me on—A sudden crash against my back. Dizzy with pain I fell—then all was darkness and quiet.

I opened my eyes. A white-clad figure bent over me. Had I died? Was I in the heaven of the new world—in America?

My eyes closed again. A misty happiness filled my being.

"Learning flows free like milk and honey," it dreamed itself in me.

I was in my heaven—in the schools of America—in open, sunny fields—a child with other children. Our lesson-books were singing birds and whispering trees—chanting brooks and beckoning skies. We breathed in learning and wisdom as naturally as flowers breathe in sunlight.

After our lessons were over, we all joined hands skipping about like a picture of dancing fairies I had once seen in a shop-window.

I was so full of the joy of togetherness—the great wonder of the new world; it pressed on my heart like sorrow. Slowly, I stole away from the other children into silent solitude, wrestling and praying to give out what surged in me into some form of beauty. And out of my struggle to shape my thoughts beautifully, a great song filled the world.

"Soon she's all right to come back to the shop—yes, nurse?" The voice of Yetta Solomon broke into my dreaming.

Wearily I opened my eyes. I saw I was still on earth.

Yetta's broad, generous face smiled anxiously at me. "Lucky yet the car that run you over didn't break your hands or your feet. So long you got yet good hands you'll soon be back by the machine."

"Machine?" I shuddered. "I can't go back to the shop again. I got so used to sunlight and quiet in the hospital I'll not be able to stand the hell again."

"Shah!—Shah!" soothed Yetta. "Why don't you learn yourself to take life like it is? What's got to be, got to be. In Russia, you could hope to run away from your troubles to America. But from America where can you go?"

"Yes," I sighed. "In the blackest days of Russia, there was always the hope from America. In Russia we had only a mud hut; not enough to eat and always the fear from the Cossack, but still we managed to look up to the sky, to dream, to think of the new world where we'll have a chance to be people, not slaves."

"What's the use to think so much? It only eats up the flesh from your bones. Better rest...."

"How can I rest when my choked-in thoughts tear me to pieces? I need school more than a starving man needs bread."

Yetta's eyes brooded over me. Suddenly a light broke. "I got an idea. There's a new school for greenhorns where they learn them anything they want...."

"What—where?" I raised myself quickly, hot with eagerness. "How do you know from it—tell me only—quick—since when—"

"The girl next door by my house—she used to work by cigars—and now she learns there."

"What does she learn?"

"Don't get yourself so excited. Your eyes are jumping out from your head."

I fell back weakly: "Oi weh! Tell me!" I begged.

"All I know is that she likes what she learns better than rolling cigars. And it's called 'School for Immigrant Girls.'"

"Your time is up. Another visitor is waiting to come in," said the nurse.

As Yetta walked out, my mother, with the shawl over her head, rushed in and fell on my bed kissing me.

"Oi weh! Oi weh! Half my life is out from me from fright. How did all happen?"

"Don't worry yourself so. I'm nearly well already and will go back to work soon."

"Talk not work. Get only a little flesh on your bones. They say they send from the hospital people to the country. Maybe they'll send you."

"But how will you live without my wages?"

"Davy is already peddling with papers and Bessie is selling lolly-pops after school in the park. Yesterday she brought home already twenty-eight cents."

For all her efforts to be cheerful, I looked at her pinched face and wondered if she had eaten that day.

Released from the hospital. I started home. As I neared Allen Street, the terror of the dark rooms swept over me. "No—no—I can't yet go back to the darkness and the stinking smells," I said to myself. "So long they're getting along without my wages, let them think I went to the country and let me try out that school for immigrants that Yetta told me about."

So I went to the Immigrant School.

A tall, gracious woman received me, not an employee, but a benefactress.

The love that had rushed from my heart toward the Statue in the Bay, rushed out to Mrs. Olney. She seemed to me the living spirit of America. All that I had ever dreamed America to be shone to me out of the kindness of her brown eyes. She would save me from the sordidness that was crushing me I felt the moment I looked at her. Sympathy and understanding seemed to breathe from her serene presence.

I longed to open my heart to her, but I was so excited I didn't know where to begin.

"I'm crazy to learn!" I gasped breathlessly, and then the very pressure of the things I had to say choked me.

An encouraging smile warmed the fine features.

"What trade would you like to learn—sewing machine operating?"

"Sewing-machine operating?" I cried. "Oi weh!" I shuddered. "Only the thought 'machine' kills me. Even when I only look on clothes, it weeps in me when I think how the seams from everything people wear is sweated in the shop."

"Well, then"—putting a kind hand on my shoulder—"how would you like to learn to cook? There's a great need for trained servants and you'd get good wages and a pleasant home."

"Me—a servant?" I flung back her hand. "Did I come to America to make from myself a cook?"

Mrs. Olney stood abashed a moment. "Well, my dear," she said deliberately, "what would you like to take up?"

"I got ideas how to make America better, only I don't know how to say it out. Ain't there a place I can learn?"

A startled woman stared at me. For a moment not a word came. Then she proceeded with the same kind smile. "It's nice of you to want to help America, but I think the best way would be for you to learn a trade. That's what this school is for, to help girls find themselves, and the best way to do is to learn something useful."

"Ain't thoughts useful? Does America want only the work from my body, my hands? Ain't it thoughts that turn over the world?"

"Ah! But we don't want to turn over the world," Her voice cooled.

"But there's got to be a change in America!" I cried. "Us immigrants want to be people—not 'hands'—not slaves of the belly! And it's the chance to think out thoughts that makes people."

"My child, thought requires leisure. The time will come for that. First you must learn to earn a good living."

"Did I come to America for a living?"

"What did you come for?"

"I came to give out all the fine things that was choked in me in Russia. I came to help America make the new world....They said, in America I could open up my heart and fly free in the air—to sing—to dance—to live—to love....Here I got all those grand things in me, and America won't let me give nothing."

"Perhaps you made a mistake in coming to this country. Your own land might appreciate you more." A quick glance took me in from head to foot. "I'm afraid that you have come to the wrong place. We only teach trades here."

She turned to her papers and spoke over her shoulder. "I think you will have to go elsewhere if you want to set the world on fire."

GLOSSARY

Greenhorn: In the urban communities a newly arrived immigrant unfamiliar with local customs was referred to as a "greenhorn."

Pogrom: In Russia, or areas under the control of the Russian Empire, an officially sanctioned or tolerated attack on

Jews or other ethnic groups was called a "pogrom." These were often begun to take pressure off the government by directing blame for complains to the minority group.

Samovar: A metal container used for the heating of water, usually in the preparation of tea or other beverages.

Steerage: Steerage was the name applied to the lowest deck of a ship where the cargo was carried. Because this is where passengers with the cheapest tickets were also accommodated, the term came to mean someone of the lowest class.

Sweatshop: Factories that paid low wages, demanded long hours of work, and provided dangerous, unhealthy working conditions were referred to as "sweatshops."

Ukaz: Often written as "ukase" in English, this Russian word was the equivalent of an edict. When issued by the government or a religious leader it had the force of law.

Usurer: A term referring to a person who lends money at exceptionally high interest rates.

Document Analysis

The selections appearing here are taken from Anzia Yezierska's *Hungry Hearts* (Boston: Houghton Mifflin, 1920), a collection of short stories largely based on her own experiences or those of her relatives. The story begins with the protagonist and her family gathered about listening to readings from the Book of Isaiah while the narrator sits by the window charged with alerting the gathering should Cossacks, the czar's enforcers, appear. It was against the law to study the Hebrew religion in any room used for cooking or sleeping. This established very clearly the kind of restrictions placed on Jews in the Russian Empire, a fact of life brought home more intensely when the appearance of black bread and potatoes distract the lookout from her duty. Reality returned quickly as a Cossack's "iron heel" smashed in the door to announce a fine and imprisonment should the infraction ever be repeated. This single opening scene serves to establish the fear in which the family lives their daily lives. It also established what historians of immigration would call "the push," the reasons why a person might choose to leave their native land to migrate to another country.

The turning point in the first portion of the excerpt comes in the form of a letter from America. Taken to the only person in the village who can read, its contents prove explosive, changing the family's life forever. Read aloud, it is from a neighbor who moved to America several years earlier. It speaks of good health, being a successful businessman making the unheard of sum of twenty-four rubles a week—it seemed like a dream. But there was more: he enjoyed white bread and meat "every day just like the mil-lionaires," he has a private room with a door, people call him "mister," and best of all "there is no Czar in America." Compared to the local village, America seemed like heaven. This form of enthusiastic letter was commonplace during this time when emigrants were often prone to exaggerated embellishments to demonstrate to friends and relatives how well they were doing. Historians recognize them as a major factor in encouraging the chain migration of families and friends from rural villages to urban America. The glowing reports also provided the "pull" factor. Having determined the negative factors that convinced people to leave their native lands, there remained to be established the "pull" factors that drew them to decide on *where* they wished to move. Letters such as this often provided the last missing piece of the migration equation.

With the decision made, the family scrapes together the minimum requirement for steamship tickets by selling off its possessions. The narrator hastily skims over the steerage passage with its "foul odors," its "seasick humanity," its "foulness and ugliness," choosing to concentrate instead on the promise of America. In America "you can say what you feel," there "Christians and Jews are brothers together," there is no "worry" in America, no "fear," and "learning flows free like milk and honey." Learning — how she yearned for it!

And finally the cry "Land!" They had made it. But then came the shock, the first realization that perhaps her fondest hopes had been in vain. Her first impression of "narrow streets of squeezed-in stores and houses, ragged clothes, dirty bedding oozing out of windows, ash-cans and garbage-cans cluttering the sidewalks" brought a

THE CEDAR RAPIDS EVENING GAZET

Cinderella Story of A Servant Girl

ANZIA YEZIERSKA LEAVES POTS AND PANS FOR FAME AND RICHES.

HUNGRY heart. Anzia Yezierska.

Join them and you have the Cinderella-like story of filmdom's newest author.

She was an immigrant girl from Poland. Poor. Unlettered. But ambitious.

Worked in a garment factory. Was a cook. A domestic Stranger in a strange land, she was hungry-hearted.

Life to her was as seamy as the inner side of the garments on which she labored, as dark as the skillets she scrubbed.

She set about to feed the craving of her soul. She would write! She would make others happy!

She was more proficient as cook than writer. She earned a scholarship in a domestic science school.

Now her story in her own words:

"Before the term was half over I went to the instructor and said, 'I had enough of cooking—I want better to write.'

"'Write? Bah! You'll starve to death.'

"'If I can't write in American English, I'll write in immigrant English, but write I must,' I answered."

She went to school at night after long days of toil. Then "Hungry Hearts" was accepted. Fame and success bounded to her.

A dinner was given in her honor recently at the Waldorf-Astoria. Less than two years ago, Anzia Yezierska visited that hotel. She entered then through the dark, underground servants' tunnel.

"I was so down and out I did not have the spunk to ask for work as a waitress," she says. "I knew I didn't look good enough for that.

"All I asked was for a job as scullery maid, dishwasher or scrub-woman. And even this was refused me."

Now—she is under contract to Goldwyn. She's out at Culver City assisting in the filming of "Hungry Hearts."

And what is takes to make those pictures realistic, Anzia Yezierska can tell—for they are pictures of Anzia Yezierska's heart.

ANZIA YEZIERSKA, FILMDOM'S NEWEST AUTHOR.

STAR DUST

Marguerite Maxwell, Ziegfeld Follies beauty, makes her film debut in Mildred Harris' "Playthings of Desire."

Betty Ross Clarke, who appears in Arbuckle comedies, lived on an Indian reservation in North Dakota when a little girl. She later was a "Russian" dancer in vaudeville.

Bessie Love is to have an important role in Dickens' "Old Curiosity Shop," which is to be filmed in London this spring.

Elliott Dexter has the lead in "The Witching Hour."

Buster Keaton got his front name from Houdini, the handcuff king, when Houdini saw him fall down a flight of stairs.

Gladys Leslie is to return to the silver sheet, playing opposite Lionel Barrymore in a forthcoming production.

For the sake of art Bull Montana is to be called Jack Montana after this. He was "Ferre, the Ape Man" in "Go and Get It" and his right name is Luigi Montagni.

"Forfaiture," the first grand opera adapted from a movie, has been given its premiere in Paris. It was adapted from "The Cheat," directed by Cecil DeMille with Fanny Ward as the star in 1915.

Anzia Yezierska featured in an article in the *Cedar Rapids Evening Gazette*, March 5th, 1921.

sense of "doubt." Was coming to America the right decision after all? The crowded apartments, the lack of sunlight inside, the brick and stone outside and the omnipresent "smells of crowded poverty" were completely alien to her hopes, her expectations. What a striking description of the cultural shock experienced by so many immigrants from rural Europe arriving for the first time in a large urban metropolis.

Instead of education she had to find employment to survive. But to rebel against the low wages and arbitrary treatment proved impossible. When she voiced even mild protest she was summarily fired. Finally she tried to pursue her dream of an education at an "Immigrant School," only to find that assistance was readily available but *only* to those content with learning to sew or cook or some other domestic skill. When the frustrated immigrant confided that she wanted to deal in ideas, to think, she was told that they only taught "trades."

Yezierska's powerful representation of the conflict between the emigrant's hopes and the immigrant's reality, picturesquely portrayed in the idioms and cultural replications of Lower East Side Jewish culture, form an excellent description of the stages through which a person went in the long journey from the hopes of the homeland to the reality of the adoptive land.

Essential Themes

Yezierska's work is characterized by the intertwining of explorations of immigrant, Jewish, and female life in New York's Lower East Side tenement district. Her use of dialect in depicting Jewish life, her selection of descriptive terminology, and the reflections of the narrator of her stories combine to produce a vivid ethnic experience that at once enriches readers from a different cultural heritage and vividly describes life in the turbulent early twentieth-century immigrant communities. The selections from *Hungry Hearts* presented here clearly illustrate the conflicts that can emerge within the family from the traditional patriarchal structure of East European Jewish society, the anguish of dreams unfulfilled, and the constant struggle of a family living on a day-to-day basis.

Yezierska's use of a female protagonist highlights the distinct gender experience as she negotiates the uncertain waters from immigrant greenhorn to acceptance in the new environment. In doing so, she especially illuminates the one-sided view of many immigrant aid organizations interested in providing assistance only if the immigrant is willing to accept preparation for low-paying, low-status occupations that the aid providers believe suitable for what modern scholars would label "the other." In this, they are a reflection of the particular broader genre of ethnic immigrant writers who attempted to portray their own experiences both to other members of their communities and to the general public.

Bibliography and Additional Reading

Sally Ann Drucker, "Yiddish, Yidgin & Yezierska," *Modern Jewish Studies Annual*, Vol. VI (1987), 99-113.

Louise Henriksen, *Anzia Yezierska: A Writer's Life* (New Brunswick: Rutgers University Press, 1988).

Carol B. Schoen, *Anzia Yezierska* (Boston: Twayne, 1982).

Anzia Yezierska, *How I found America: Collected Stories of Anzia Yezierska* (New York: Persea Books, 1991).

Anzia Yezierska, *Hungry Hearts and Other Stories* (New York: Persea Books, 1985).

Anzia Yezierska, *The Open Cage: An Anzia Yezierska Collection* (New York: Persea Books, 1979), Alice Kessler-Harris, ed.

◼ Bartolomeo Vanzetti's Final Courtroom Statement

Date: April 9, 1927
Author: Bartolomeo Vanzetti
Genre: Speech

Summary Overview

The Bolshevik Revolution in November 1917 replaced the tsar with a socialist government. A year later the end of World War I was accompanied by an attempted socialist uprising in Germany, unrest in England and France, and other revolutionary movements. Even before the war Americans were suspicious and fearful of European anarchists, socialists, and other radicals that many believed were behind the violence that broke out during American labor strikes. After the Bolshevik takeover in Russia, the Communist Third International formed in March 1919 to promote the spread of revolution to other nations. With this, Americans came to fear all the more that anarchists and socialists coming from Europe would spread violent revolution to the U.S.

In April 1919 at least 36 bombs were sent through the U.S. mail. Two months later, followers of the Italian anarchist Luigi Galleani launched a series of bombings across the U.S. aimed at politicians, judges and business leaders. Some 30 bombs exploded in eight cities. A surge of popular opinion directed against radicals and foreigners in general was fanned by officials like Senator Kenneth D. McKellar who proposed sending radicals to a penal colony in Guam and the religious revivalist Billy Sunday, the most successful evangelist of the day, who wanted to "stand [radicals] up before a firing squad."

In August 1919, under increasing pressure because of the series of bombings, Attorney General Alexander M. Palmer received $500,000 to establish an anti-radical division within the Department of Justice. Palmer appointed J. Edgar Hoover head of the new agency. Under his leadership, the so-called "Palmer Raids" were launched on suspected anarchists, socialists, and communists, the first taking place on November 7 against the Union of Russian Workers where some 250 people were arrested. Hoover's men searched the U.S. mail, organizational offices and the homes of officials, jailing the latter under the Sedition Act. All socialist mail was ordered confiscated. In January 1920, over 4,000 communists were arrested in one night with all of the aliens being deported. Aliens everywhere, radical or not, lived under the specter of suspicion.

Defining Moment

In the midst of this postwar Red Scare paymaster Frederick "Frank" Parmenter of the Slater and Morrill Shoe Company, accompanied by guard Alessandro "Alex" Berdardelli, carried the business's payroll down Pearl Street in South Braintree, Massachusetts. It was a routine they performed on a regular basis in those days when wages were paid in cash at the end of each week. There was nothing different about April 15, 1920, to distinguish it from any other day except that the two would not live to complete their brief walk. Along the way two men approached, one of whom extracted a gun from under his coat and fired several shots into the guard. Parmenter tried to run but fell to more shots only yards away. The two assailants jumped into a dark colored Buick touring car that stopped for them, then sped off with their loot.

A similar robbery attempt the previous December in a nearby city was believed by police to be the work of Italian anarchists Ferruccio Coacci and Mario "Mike" Buda. Coacci was under deportation order and soon left, but authorities found that Buda owned an automobile that was then being repaired. When Buda arrived to pick up his car he was accompanied by three other Italians—Riccardo Orciani, Nicola Sacco, and Bartolomeo Vanzetti. Buda soon left for Italy while Orciani had witnesses that said he was at work at the time of the robbery and murder. The other two were soon apprehended. Both denied owning any guns, but both were found to have loaded pistols. Sacco also possessed some obsolete cartridges of the same type left at the murder scene. Vanzetti had a nickel-plated .38-caliber Harrington & Richardson revolver identical to the one taken from the slain guard Berardelli. Both denied any connection to anarchism. On May 5 the two were charged with murder. They were

69

indicted on September 14, found guilty on July 14, 1921, and were electrocuted on August 23, 1927. Bartolomeo Vanzetti made his last statement in court on April 9, 1927.

Author Biography

Bartolomeo Vanzetti was born in 1888 in Villafalletto, Italy, in the Piedmont region about 37 miles south of Turin and 12 miles north of Cuneo. The son of a farmer, he left school to begin an apprenticeship but after his mother died in 1907 he emigrated to the United States the following year. Landing in New York City, he worked at various jobs over the next several years there and in Connecticut and Massachusetts. Eventually, in 1912, he found employment as a laborer in Springfield, Massachusetts, but by the next year had moved to Plymouth. Vanzetti was apparently quite disappointed with the United States, expecting to find a better life than he left behind in Italy. Instead he was discouraged by the poverty and appalled by working conditions and the ill-treatment of workers. Over the years he gravitated to anarchism, a philosophy no doubt reinforced by Vincenzo Brini in whose home he lived in Plymouth. He began subscribing to Luigi Galleani's periodical *Cronaca Sovversiva* (Subversive Chronicle), a periodical that Nicola Sacco not only read but for which he also wrote. Vanzetti met Sacco at an anarchist meeting and the two became friends.

When the United States entered World War I Vanzetti and Sacco left for Mexico to avoid possible conscription into the army, but before leaving Vanzetti filled out paperwork to apply for citizenship. The two returned once the war ended with Vanzetti once again taking up residence with the Brinis. He earned a living at that time as a fish peddler until he was arrested, along with Sacco, in 1920.

HISTORICAL DOCUMENT

What I say is that I am innocent, not only of the Braintree crime, but also of the Bridgewater crime. That I am not only innocent of these two crimes, but in all my life I have never stole and I have never killed and I have never spilled blood. That is what I want to say. And it is not all. Not only am I innocent of these two crimes, not only in all my life have I never stole, never killed, never spilled blood, but I have struggled all my life, since I began to reason to eliminate crime from the earth.

Everybody that knows these two arms knows very well that I did not need to go in between the street and kill a man to take the money. I can live with my two arms and live well. But besides that, I can live even without work with my arm for other people. I have had plenty of chance to live independently and to live what the world conceives to be a higher life than not to gain our bread with the sweat of our brow....

Well, I want to reach a little point farther, and it is this ... not only have I struggled hard against crimes, but I have refused myself the commodity or the glory of life, the pride of life of a good position, because in my consideration it is not right to exploit man. I have refused to go into business because I understand that business is a speculation on profit upon certain people that must depend upon the business man, and I do not consider that that is right and therefore I refuse to do that.

Now, I should say that I am not only innocent of all these things ... not only have I struggled all my life to eliminate crimes, the crimes that the official law and the official moral condemns, but also the crime that the official moral and the official law sanctions and sanctifies,—the exploitation and the oppression of the man by the man, and of there is reason why I am here as a guilty man, if there is a reason why you in a few minutes can doom me, it is this reason and none else.

I beg your pardon. There is more good man I ever cast my eyes upon since I lived, a man that will last and will grow always more near and more dear to the people, as far as into the heart of the people, so long as admiration for the goodness and for sacrifice will last. I mean Eugene Debs. I will say that even a dog that killed the chickens would not have found an American jury to convict it with the proof that the Commonwealth produced against us. That man was not with me in Plymouth or with Sacco where he was on the day of the crime. You can say that it is arbitrary, what we are saying, that he is good and he applied to the other his own goodness, that he is incapable of crime, and he believed that everybody is incapable of crime.

Well, it may be like that but it is not, it could be like that but it is not, and that man has a real experience of court, of prison and of jury. Just because he want the world a little better he was persecuted and slandered from his boyhood to his old age, and indeed he was murdered by the prison. He know, and not only he but every man of understanding in the world, not only in this country but also in other countries, men that we have provided a certain amount of a record of the times, they are all still slick with us, the flower of mankind of Europe, the better writers, the greatest thinkers of Europe, have pleaded in our favor. The scientists, the greatest scientists, the greatest statesmen of Europe, have pleaded in our favor. The people of foreign nations have pleaded in our favor.

It is possible that only a few on the jury, only two or three men, who would condemn their mother for worldly honor and for earthly fortune; is it possible that they are right against what the world, the whole world has to say it is wrong and that I know that it is wrong? If there is one that I should know it, if it is right or wrong, it is I and this man. You see it is seven years that we are in jail. What we have suffered during these seven years no human tongue can say, and yet you see me before you, not trembling, you see me looking you in your eyes straight, not blushing, not changing color, not ashamed or in fear.

Eugene Debs say that not even a dog—something like that—not even a dog that kill the chickens would have been found guilty by American jury with the evidence that the Commonwealth have produced against us. I say that not even a leprous dog would have his appeal refused two times by the Supreme Court of Massachusetts—not even a leprous dog.

They have given a new trial to Madeiros[1] for the reason that the Judge had either forgot or omitted to tell the jury that they should consider the man innocent until found guilty in the court, or something of that sort. That man has confessed. The man was tried and has confessed, and the court give him another trial. We have proved that there could not have been another Judge on the face of the earth more prejudiced and more cruel than you have been against us. We have proven that. Still they refuse the new trial. We know, and you know in your heart, that you have been against us from the very begin-

ning, before you see us. Before you see us you already know that we were radicals, that we were underdogs, that we were the enemy of the institution that you can believe in good faith in their goodness—I don't want to condemn that-and that it was easy on the time of the first trial to get a verdict of guiltiness.

We know that you have spoke yourself and have spoke your hostility against us, and your despisement against us with friends of yours on the train, at the University Club of Boston, on the Golf Club of Worcester, Massachusetts. I am sure that if the people who know all what you say against us would have the civil courage to take the stand, maybe your Honor—I am sorry to say this because you are an old man, and I have an old father-but maybe you would be beside is in good justice at this time.

When you sentenced me at the Plymouth trial you say, to the best of my memory, of my good faith, that crimes were in accordance with my principle,—something of that sort,—and you take off one charge, if I remember it exactly, from the jury. The jury was so violent against me that they found me guilty of both charges, because there were only two. But they would have found me guilty of a dozen charges against your Honor's instructions. Of course, I remember that you told them that there was no reason to believe that if I were the bandit I have intention to kill somebody, so that they will take off the indictment of attempt to murder. Well, they found me guilty of what? And if I am right, you take out that and sentence me only for attempt to rob with arms,—something like that. But, Judge Thayer, you give more to me for that attempt of robbery than all the 448 men that were in Charlestown, all of those that attempted to rob, all those that have robbed, they have not such a sentence as you gave me for an attempt at robbery....

We were tried during a time that has now passed into history. I mean by that, a time when there was a hysteria of resentment and hate against the people of our principles, against the foreigner, against slackers, and it seemed to me—rather, I am positive of it, that both you and Mr. Katzmann[2] has done all what it were in your power to order to work out, in order to agitate still more the passion of the juror, the prejudice of the juror, against us....

But the jury were hating us because we were against the war, and the jury don't know that it makes any difference between a man that is against the war because he believes that the war is unjust, because he hate no country, because he is a cosmopolitan, and a man that is against the country in which he is, and therefore a spy, and he commits any crime in the country in which he is in behalf of the other country in order to serve the other country. We are not men of that kind. Katzmann know very well that. Katzmann know that we were against the war because we did not believe it that the war is wrong, and we believe this more now after ten years that we understood it day by day,—the consequences and the result of the after war. We believe more now than ever that the war was wrong, and we are against war more now than ever, and I am glad to be on the doomed scaffold if I can say to mankind, "Look out; you are in a catacomb of the flower of mankind. For what? All that they say to you, all that they have promised to you—it was a lie, it was an illusion, it was a cheat, it was a fraud, it was a crime. They promised you liberty. Where is the liberty? They promised you prosperity. Where is the prosperity? They have promised you elevation. Where is the elevation?

From that day that I went in Charlestown, the misfortune, the population of Charlestown has doubled in number. Where is the moral good that the War has given to the world? Where is the spiritual progress that we have achieved from the War? Where are the security of life, the security of the things that we possess for our necessity? Where are the respect for human life? Where are the respect and admiration for the good characteristics and the good of human nature? Never as now before the war there have been so many crimes, so many corruptions, so many degeneration as there is now....

When two or three women from Plymouth come to take the stand, the woman reach that point where this gentleman sit down over there, the jury were sit down in their place, and Katzmann asked this woman if they have not testified before for Vanzetti, and they say, yes, and he tell them, "You cannot testify." They left the room. After that they testified just same. But in the meanwhile he tell to the jury that I have been tried before. That I think is not to make justice to the man who is looking after the true, and it is a frameup with which he has split my life and doomed me.

It was also said that the defense has put every obstacle to the handling of this case in order to delay the case. That sound weak for us, and I think it is injurious because it is not true. If we consider that the prosecution, the State, has employed one entire year to prosecute us, that is, one of the five years that the case has last was taken by the prosecution to begin our trial, our first trial. That the defense make an appeal to you and you waited, or I think that you were resolute, that you had the resolute in your heart when the trial finished that you will refuse every appeal that we will put up to you. You waited a month or a month and a half and just lay down your decision on the eve of Christmas—just on the evening of Christmas. We do not believe in the fable of the evening of Christmas, neither in the historical way nor in the church way. You know some of our folks still believe in that, and because we do not believe in that, it don't mean that we are not human. We are human, and Christmas is sweet to the heart of every man. I think that you have done that, to hand down your decision on the evening of Christmas, to poison the heart of our family and of our beloved. I am sorry to be compelled to say this, but everything that was said on your side has confirmed my suspicion until that suspicion has changed to certitude. So that you see that one year it has taken before trying us.

That the defense, in presenting the new appeal, has not taken more time that you have taken in answer to that. Then there came to the second appeal, and now I am not sure whether it is the second appeal or the third appeal where you wait eleven months or one year without an answer to us, and I am sure that you have decide to refuse u a new trial before the hearing for the new appeal began. You take one year to answer it or eleven months,—something like that. So that you see that out of the five years, two were taken by the State from the day of our arrest to the trial, and then one year to wait for your answer on the second or third appeal.

Then on another occasion that I don't remember exactly now, Mr. Williams was sick and the things were delayed not for fault of the defense but on account of the fault of the prosecution. So that I am positive that if a man take a pencil in his hand and compute the time taken by the prosecution in prosecuting the case, and the time that was taken by the defense to defend this case, the prosecution has taken more time than the defense, and there is a great consideration that must be taken in this point, and it is that my first lawyer betrayed us,—the whole American population were against us. We have the misfortune to take a man from California, and he came here, and he was ostracized by you and by every authority, even by the jury, and is so much so that no part of Massachusetts is immune from what I would call the prejudice,—that is, to believe that each people in each place of the world, they believe to be the better of the world, and they believe that all the other are not so good as they. So of course the man that came from California into Massachusetts to defend two of us, he must be licked if it is possible, and he was licked all right. And we have our part too.

What I want to say is this: Everybody ought to understand that the first of the defense has been terrible. My first lawyer did not stick to defend us. He has made no work to collect witnesses and evidence in our favor. The record in the Plymouth Court is a pity. I am told that they are almost one-half lost. So the defense had a tremendous work to do in order to collect some evidence, to collect some testimony to offset and to learn what the testimony of the State has done. And in this consideration it must be said that even if the defense take double time of

the State without delay, double time that they delay the case it would been reasonable, whereas it took less than the State

Well, I have already say that I not only am not guilty of these two crimes, but I never commit a crime in my life,—I have never steal and I have never kill and I have never spilt blood, and I have fought against the crime, and I have fought and I have sacrificed myself even to eliminate the crimes that the law and the church legitimate and sanctify.

This is what I say: I would not wish to a dog or to a snake, to the most low and misfortunate creature of the earth—I would not wish to any of them what I have had to suffer for things that I am not guilty of. But my conviction is that I have suffered for things that I am guilty of. I am suffering because I am a radical; I have suffered because I was an Italian, and indeed I am an Italian; I have suffered more for my family and for my beloved than for myself; but I am so convinced to be right that if you could execute me two times, and if I could be reborn two other times, I would live again to do what I have done already.

[1] Celestino Madeiros confessed to the crime for which Sacco and Vanzetti were found guilty, stating that they were not involved in it. At the time he was in jail charged with a different murder. From this, an alternative theory was developed by some researchers linking the Braintree crime with a Rhode Island-based gang headed by Joe Morelli whose appearance was similar to Sacco.

[2] Frederick Katzmann was the Norfolk and Plymouth County District Attorney who prosecuted the case.

GLOSSARY

Catacomb: An underground passageway normally full of turns, especially an underground cemetery along whose corridors are recessed tombs.

Cosmopolitan: A person whose world view goes beyond the local or provincial; a person familiar and comfortable with other cultures.

Eugene Debs: Debs was a socialist labor leader and a founding members of the Industrial Workers of the World. He ran for president of the United States five times on the Socialist Party of America ticket, including 1920 when he campaigned from his jail cell.

Leprous: Infected with leprosy, a disease that seriously damages nerves and the skin causing painful roughness and lesions in the flesh.

Slackers: This was a term used during World War I for people who did not enlist or evaded the draft.

Document Analysis

Vanzetti begins by immediately stating that he is innocent of any crime, not only the one for which he was convicted, but that in his entire life he has "never stole" and "never killed" and "never spilled blood." In fact, he asserts, ever since he reached the age of reason he has struggled to "eliminate crime from the earth." From here, his message becomes more of a political statement than an explanation of why the evidence proves him innocent. It is clear that the crime he claims to be struggling against is his perception of the exploitation of workers. He is a working man, he says, who does not need to steal to support himself; more importantly, he contends that he has shunned good positions and going into business because he did not want to profit from other people. This is an interesting statement. Aside from a reflection of his political beliefs, he seems to believe that it was his choice to live a difficult life of day-to-day living rather than blaming it on his lack of education, his immigrant status, or other factors.

After establishing his bona fides as a poor member of the working class, he continues with his political declaration. Not only has he fought crime, he has also fought against legally sanctioned "exploitation" and "the oppression of the man by the man." This, he maintains, is why he was found guilty, because of who he is as a member of what he sees as an exploited class. He likens himself to Eugene Debs, the socialist labor leader, who, "because he want the world a little better he was persecuted and slandered" and jailed.

Vanzetti shows his awareness of the outpouring of support for him from around the world. In fact, the lengthy trial and post-trial appeals became a world-wide *cause célèbre* among the left and other supporters. Vanzetti then goes back to commenting on his own suffering in prison, astutely trying to portray himself as the aggrieved party and reinforcing his basic argument that he was convicted for reasons other than the evidence which he claimed was lacking. From here he briefly states why he believes he was unjustly convicted. He blames the prejudice of the judge for his conviction, an issue that has actually gained much support over the years from people who have reviewed the court transcripts. He complains that his appeal for a new trial has been denied even though it is clear to him that the judge had been "against us from the very beginning…. Before you see us you already know that we were radicals, that we were underdogs, that we were the enemy of the institution" the judge believes in. In fact, Judge Thayer did deny a new trial, as did the

Massachusetts Supreme Court. He then refers to the Red Scare, complaining that he and Sacco "were tried during a time that has now passed into history. I mean by that, a time when there was a hysteria of resentment and hate against the people of our principles, against the foreigner, against slackers, and it seemed to me—rather, I am positive of it, that [you have] done all what it were in your power to order to work out, in order to agitate still more the passion of the juror, the prejudice of the juror, against us."

Vanzetti also mentions his stand against World War I, trying to explain that he was not spying or in any way disloyal to the United States, he only left the country because he did not support the war. And he reaffirmed his opposition which he claims is justified in view of the results of the conflict. From there he argues that his defense was "terrible" and his first attorney "made no work to collect witnesses and evidence in our favor." Finally, he concludes by reiterating his innocence, claiming that he "never commit[ed] a crime in my life. … But my conviction is that I have suffered for things that I am guilty of. I am suffering because I am a radical; I have suffered because I was an Italian, and indeed I am an Italian…."

Essential Themes

The Sacco and Vanzetti trial mirrored the major immigration issues of the early 1920s including the rise of nativism and the fear of radicalism. Probably the latter did play some part in the trial, especially since the defendants were firmly linked with not only radicalism but specifically with the Italian anarchist Luigi Galleani who was behind the series of bombings which were fresh in everyone's minds as the trial progressed. The fact that they both lied about not possessing guns when arrested and that those guns were at least circumstantially tied to the crime certainly did not help. And, despite his statements that he was not violent and believed in peace, from his jail cell Vanzetti wrote "I will try to see Thayer death before his pronunciation of our sentence" and called on his anarchist associates for "revenge, revenge in our names and the names of our living and dead." This was certainly different than the public posture he projected at the trial.

Conversely, Vanzetti's criticism of the judge as biased was well taken. In fact, a special commission appointed by the governor of Massachusetts did censure Judge Webster Thayer for his conduct of the trial. Prior to the trial he was on record as speaking against Bolshevism and anarchism which he called a threat to American institutions. He also supported repression of free speech for radicals and was quoted *after* the trial as commenting: "Did you see what I did with those anarchistic bastards the other day? I guess that will hold them for a while!" Despite the censorship, the commission still upheld the verdict.

Following the trial and the executions, Galleani's followers embarked on a lengthy series of bombings, many of them aimed at witnesses, jurors, and even Judge Thayer himself. In the latter case he escaped injury when a bomb destroyed his home injuring his wife and housekeeper. Of course, this only served to heighten anti-immigrant feelings during the remainder of the decade.

Bibliography and Additional Reading

Paul Avrich, *Sacco and Vanzetti: The Anarchist Background* (Princeton: Princeton University Press, 1991)

Francis Russell, *Sacco and Vanzetti: The Case Resolved* (New York: Harper & Row, 1986).

James E. Starrs, "Once More Unto the Breech: The Firearms Evidence in the Sacco and Vanzetti Case Revisited," *Journal of Forensic Sciences*, 1986, 630-54, 1050-78.

Susan Tejada, *In Search of Sacco & Vanzetti: Double Lives, Troubled Times, & the Massachusetts Murder Case that Shook the World* (Boston: Northeastern University Press, 2012).

Moshik Temkin, *The Sacco-Vanzetti Affair: America on Trial* (New Haven: Yale University Press, 2009)

William Young and David E. Kaiser, *Postmortem: New Evidence in the Case of Sacco and Vanzetti* (Amherst, MA: University of Massachusetts Press, 1985).

CONTACT: Tor Torland, Info Officer
630 Sansome Street, San Francisco
YUkon 6-3111, Ext. 647

Mr Robertson

FOR IMMEDIATE RELEASE

File
Mexican Program

RECEIVED
AUG 4 1959
REGIONAL ATTORNEY
SAN FRANCISCO

FEDERAL STOP-ORDER ON INDIO FARMER

    SAN FRANCISCO, August 3: Joseph Munoz, a member of the Coachella Valley
Farmers Association in Indio, has been refused further authorization to employ
Mexican farm workers in a decision made public today by the U.S. Department of
Labor.

    Under the terms of public law 78 and the international agreement between
the governments of the U.S. and Mexico, Mexican nationals may be imported to work
on our farms only if it has been determined by authorities that there are not
enough American workers in a specific area to fill farm-labor needs there.

    Munoz was found to be using Mexican nationals to sort tomatoes in his pack-
ing shed despite repeated warnings by the U. S. Labor Department and the California
Department of Employment that American workers were available for the jobs.

    Glenn E. Brockway, regional director of the Labor Department's employment
security bureau, issued his decision in a letter to the Coachella Valley Farmers
Association. Brockway said, in part:

    "All authorizations issued to the Coachella Valley Farmers Association to
contract Mexican national workers are hereby revoked with respect to the employment
of Mexican national workers by the said Joseph Munoz."

    The federal stop-order also specified that because of Munoz's "repeated
failure to give preference in employment to United States domestic workers", no
authorizations would be granted him in future to use Mexican nationals.

    The move came as part of the U.S. Labor Department's continuing policy of
strictly policing the foreign-labor importation program so as to ensure first
preference for farm jobs to American citizens.

#####

USDL-IX-59856

■ An Address by César Chávez

Author: César Chávez
Date: November 9, 1984
Genre: Speech

Summary Overview

Following the Civil War, commercial agriculture began to expand in the Midwest and on the Pacific coast. With the increased need for labor, owners began relying on Asian workers to the extent that by the mid-1880s about 87.5 percent were of Chinese ancestry. With the Chinese Exclusion Act in 1882 the lack of these people caused owners in the southwest and Pacific coast to rely more heavily on Mexicans. During World War I, producers pressured Congress to adopt a guest worker program which brought an estimated 70,000 Mexican migrant workers to the agricultural fields. However, with the Great Depression the large number of foreclosures forced displaced Caucasian farmers into competition for these jobs, reducing wages to the barest of subsistence levels. To relieve some of the pressure on wages and unemployment, the U.S. government actively pursued a policy of "Mexican Repatriation" especially directed at people in California, Colorado, and Texas. Estimates on the number of those returned to Mexico vary wildly from about 500,000 to two million.

The onset of World War II created a labor crisis resulting in the same federal government reversing policy to establish the "Bracero Program" to attract Mexican agricultural workers. This program, which lasted from 1942 until 1964, provided temporary guest worker visas. Despite the labor shortage, wages remained low and the treatment of workers was often abusive. Reacting to these conditions, in 1962 César Chávez and Dolores Huerta cooperated in organizing the National Farm Workers Association, which later became the United Farm Workers. The movement to organize farm workers had begun.

Defining Moment

During the 1970s, jurisdictional disputes between the United Farm Workers (UFW) and the Teamsters' Union consumed time and resources that could have been better used in assisting workers. While gaining some early success, Chávez's union lost ground to the Teamsters when the latter signed agreements with lettuce producers that effectively cut the UFW out of negotiations and resulted in some of its membership leaving to join the Teamsters.

When the long-standing dispute was finally resolved, Chávez organized a protest march from San Francisco to the Ernest and Julio Gallo Winery in Modesto, a distance of about 110 miles. Although it began slowly with a small core of people, by the time it concluded newspapers reported over 15,000 marchers. Despite this success, the influence and membership of the UFW began to decline as Chávez was increasingly at odds with his union leadership over issues such as moving the organization's headquarters away from the farms and his opposition to forming union locals, preferring instead to have a centralized headquarters.

When the California Labor Relations Board ran out of money and the state legislature refused to appropriate funds to keep it open, Chávez organized a movement to place on the state ballot Proposition 14, which would guarantee the right of the union to organize farm workers even if it had to send representatives onto private land. It was defeated by a 2 to 1 majority further damaging the UFW's status as a labor representative.

By the early 1980s membership in the UFW was shrinking. The union held its Seventh Constitutional Convention in September 1984. Chávez used the occasion to attempt to link his movement with the greater Civil Rights struggle.

Author Biography

Born in to a Mexican immigrant family in Yuma, Arizona, on March 31, 1927, César Chávez grew up feeling the sting of anti-Mexican prejudice. When only ten years old his family lost their home in the Great Depression and moved to California to work as laborers in the state's agricultural fields. To assist his family, Chávez dropped out of school in the seventh grade to go to work. Aside from two years in the navy, he toiled in the fields until 1952 when he took a position with the Community Service Organization where he acquired his initial experience with labor organization and voter registration. By 1958 he was the organization's national director.

In 1962 he urged that the Community Service Organization undertake a pilot program to organize farm workers, but the idea was rejected. Chávez resigned, joined forces with Dolores Huerta who had founded the Agricultural Workers Association in 1960, and the two of them established the National Farm Workers Association. Chávez contributed an energetic leadership style and vibrant speaking style while Huerta provided administrative ability and tenacious bargaining skills. Together they led the new organization into a series of strikes against grape producers in the 1960s and 1970s. The most successful effort was the five-year Delano strike which led to calls for a nationwide boycott on grapes.

Early successes led to the famous Salad Bowl Strike against lettuce and grape producers which became the largest agricultural labor strike in U.S. history. The work stoppage led to passage of the California Agricultural Labor Relations Act, which instituted collective bargaining for farmworkers. Later, Chávez played a leading role in the inclusion of amnesty provisions into the Immigration Reform and Control Act of 1986. However, in the 1980s membership in the United Farm Workers began to decline and it lost an attempted strike in 1988. Chávez died in San Luis, Arizona, on April 23, 1993. Following his death President Bill Clinton awarded him the Medal of Freedom.

HISTORICAL DOCUMENT

Twenty-one years ago last September, on a lonely stretch of railroad track paralleling U.S. Highway 101 near Salinas, 32 Bracero farm workers lost their lives in a tragic accident.

The Braceros had been imported from Mexico to work on California farms. They died when their bus, which was converted from a flatbed truck, drove in front of a freight train.

Conversion of the bus had not been approved by any government agency. The driver had "tunnel" vision.

Most of the bodies lay unidentified for days. No one, including the grower who employed the workers, even knew their names.

Today, thousands of farm workers live under savage conditions—beneath trees and amid garbage and human excrement—near tomatoe fields in San Diego County, tomatoe fields which use the most modern farm technology.

Vicious rats gnaw on them as they sleep. They walk miles to buy food at inflated prices. And they carry in water from irrigation pumps.

Child labor is still common in many farm areas.

As much as 30 percent of Northern California's garlic harvesters are under-aged children. Kids as young as six years old have voted in state-conducted union elections since they qualified as workers.

Some 800,000 under-aged children work with their families harvesting crops across America. Babies born to migrant workers suffer 25 percent higher infant mortality than the rest of the population.

Malnutrition among migrant worker children is 10 times higher than the national rate.

Farm workers' average life expectancy is still 49 years—compared to 73 years for the average American.

All my life, I have been driven by one dream, one goal, one vision: To overthrow a farm labor system in this nation which treats farm workers as if they were not important human beings.

Farm workers are not agricultural implements. They are not beasts of burden—to be used and discarded.

That dream was born in my youth. It was nurtured in my early days of organizing. It has flourished. It has been attacked.

I'm not very different from anyone else who has ever tried to accomplish something with his life. My motivation comes from my personal life—from watching what my mother and father went through when I was growing up; from what we experienced as migrant farm workers in California.

That dream, that vision, grew from my own experience with racism, with hope, with the desire to be treated fairly and to see my people treated as human beings and not as chattel.

It grew from anger and rage—emotions I felt 40 years ago when people of my color were denied the right to see a movie or eat at a restaurant in many parts of California.

It grew from the frustration and humiliation I felt as a boy who couldn't understand how the growers could abuse and exploit farm workers when there were so many of us and so few of them.

Later, in the '50s, I experienced a different kind of exploitation. In San Jose, in Los Angeles and in other urban communities, we—the Mexican American people—were dominated by a majority that was Anglo.

I began to realize what other minority people had discovered: That the only answer—the only hope—was in organizing. More of us had to become citizens. We had to register to vote. And people like me had to develop the skills it would take to organize, to educate, to help empower the Chicano people.

I spent many years—before we founded the union—learning how to work with people.

We experienced some successes in voter registration, in politics, in battling racial discrimination—successes in an era when Black Americans were just beginning to assert their civil rights and when political awareness among Hispanics was almost non-existent.

But deep in my heart, I knew I could never be happy unless I tried organizing the farm workers. I didn't know if I would succeed. But I had to try.

All Hispanics—urban and rural, young and old—are connected to the farm workers' experience. We had all lived through the fields—or our parents had. We shared that common humiliation.

How could we progress as a people, even if we lived in the cities, while the farm workers—men and women of our color—were condemned to a life without pride?

How could we progress as a people while the farm workers—who symbolized our history in this land—were denied self-respect?

How could our people believe that their children could become lawyers and doctors and judges and business people while this shame, this injustice was permitted to continue?

Those who attack our union often say, 'It's not really a union. It's something else: A social movement. A civil rights movement. It's something dangerous.'

They're half right. The United Farm Workers is first and foremost a union. A union like any other. A union that either produces for its members on the bread and butter issues or doesn't survive.

But the UFW has always been something more than a union—although it's never been dangerous if you believe in the Bill of Rights.

The UFW was the beginning! We attacked that historical source of shame and infamy that our people in this country lived with. We attacked that injustice, not by complaining; not by seeking hand-outs; not by becoming soldiers in the War on Poverty.

We organized!

Farm workers acknowledged we had allowed ourselves to become victims in a democratic society—a society where majority rule and collective bargaining are supposed to be more than academic theories or political rhetoric. And by addressing this historical problem, we created confidence and pride and hope in an entire people's ability to create the future.

The UFW's survival—its existence-was not in doubt in my mind when the time began to come—after the union became visible—when Chicanos started entering college in greater numbers, when Hispanics began running for public office in greater numbers—when our people started asserting their rights on a broad range of issues and in many communities across the country.

The union's survival—its very existence—sent out a signal to all Hispanics that we were fighting for our dignity, that we were challenging and overcoming injustice, that we were empowering the least educated among us—the poorest among us.

The message was clear: If it could happen in the fields, it could happen anywhere—in the cities, in the courts, in the city councils, in the state legislatures.

I didn't really appreciate it at the time, but the coming of our union signaled the start of great changes among Hispanics that are only now beginning to be seen.

I've travelled to every part of this nation. I have met and spoken with thousands of Hispanics from every walk of life—from every social and economic class.

One thing I hear most often from Hispanics, regardless of age or position—and from many non-Hispanics as well—is that the farm workers gave them hope that they could succeed and the inspiration to work for change.

From time to time you will hear our opponents declare that the union is weak, that the union has no support, that the union has not grown fast enough. Our obituary has been written many times.

How ironic it is that the same forces which argue so passionately that the union is not influential are the same forces that continue to fight us so hard.

The union's power in agriculture has nothing to do with the number of farm workers under union contract. It has nothing to do with the farm workers' ability to contribute to Democratic politicians. It doesn't even have much to do with our ability to conduct successful boycotts.

The very fact of our existence forces an entire industry—unionized and non-unionized—to spend millions of dollars year after year on improved wages, on improved working conditions, on benefits for workers.

If we're so weak and unsuccessful, why do the growers continue to fight us with such passion?

Because so long as we continue to exist, farm workers will benefit from our existence—even if they don't work under union contract.

It doesn't really matter whether we have 100,000 members or 500,000 members. In truth, hundreds of thousands of farm workers in California—and in other states—are better off today because of our work.

And Hispanics across California and the nation who don't work in agriculture are better off today because of what the farm workers taught people about organization, about pride and strength, about seizing control over their own lives.

Tens of thousands of the children and grandchildren of farm workers and the children and grandchildren of poor Hispanics are moving out of the fields and out of the barrios—and into the professions and into business and into politics. And that movement cannot be reversed!

Our union will forever exist as an empowering force among Chicanos in the Southwest. And that means our power and our influence will grow and not diminish.

Two major trends give us hope and encouragement.

First, our union has returned to a tried and tested weapon in the farm workers' non-violent arsenal—the boycott!

After the Agricultural Labor Relations Act became law in California in 1975, we dismantled our boycott to work with the law.

During the early- and mid-'70s, millions of Americans supported our boycotts. After 1975, we redirected our efforts from the boycott to organizing and winning elections under the law.

The law helped farm workers make progress in overcoming poverty and injustice. At companies where farm workers are protected by union contracts, we have made progress in overcoming child labor, in overcoming miserable wages and working conditions, in overcoming sexual harassment of women workers, in overcoming dangerous pesticides which poison our people and poison the food we all eat.

Where we have organized, these injustices soon pass into history.

But under Republican Governor George Deukmejian, the law that guarantees our right to organize no longer protects farm workers. It doesn't work anymore.

In 1982, corporate growers gave Deukmejian one million dollars to run for governor of California. Since he took office, Deukmejian has paid back his debt to the growers with the blood and sweat of California farm workers.

Instead of enforcing the law as it was written against those who break it, Deukmejian invites growers who break the law to seek relief from the governor's appointees.

What does all this mean for farm workers?

It means that the right to vote in free elections is a sham. It means that the right to talk freely about the union among your fellow workers on the job is a cruel hoax. It means the right to be free from threats and intimidation by growers is an empty promise.

It means the right to sit down and negotiate with your employer as equals across the bargaining table—and not as peons in the field—is a fraud. It means that thousands of farm workers—who are owed millions of dollars in back pay because their employers broke the law—are still waiting for their checks.

It means that 36,000 farm workers—who voted to be represented by the United Farm Workers in free elections—are still waiting for contracts from growers who refuse to bargain in good faith.

It means that, for farm workers, child labor will continue. It means that infant mortality will continue. It means malnutrition among our children will continue. It means the short life expectancy and the inhuman living and working conditions will continue.

Are these make-believe threats? Are they exaggerations?

Ask the farm workers who are still waiting for growers to bargain in good faith and sign contracts. Ask the farm workers who've been fired from their jobs because they spoke out for the union. Ask the farm workers who've been threatened with physical violence because they support the UFW.

Ask the family of Rene Lopez, the young farm worker from Fresno who was shot to death last year because he supported the union.

These tragic events forced farm workers to declare a new international boycott of California table grapes. That's why we are asking Americans once again to join the farm workers by boycotting California grapes.

The Louis Harris poll revealed that 17 million American adults boycotted grapes. We are convinced that those people and that good will have not disappeared.

That segment of the population which makes our boycotts work are the Hispanics, the Blacks, the other minorities and our allies in labor and the church. But it is also an entire generation of young Americans who matured politically and socially in the 1960s and '70s— millions of people for whom boycotting grapes and other products became a socially accepted pattern of behavior.

If you were young, Anglo and on or near campus during the late '60s and early '70s, chances are you supported farm workers.

Fifteen years later, the men and women of that generation of are alive and well. They are in their mid-30s and '40s. They are pursuing professional careers. Their disposable income is relatively high. But they are still inclined to respond to an appeal from farm workers. The union's mission still has meaning for them.

Only today we must translate the importance of a union for farm workers into the language of the 1980s. Instead of talking about the right to organize, we must talk about protection against sexual harassment in the fields. We must speak about the right to quality food— and food that is safe to eat.

I can tell you that the new language is working; the 17 million are still there. They are responding—not to picketlines and leafletting alone, but to the high-tech boycott of today—a boycott that uses computers and direct mail and advertising techniques which have revolutionized business and politics in recent years.

We have achieved more success with the boycott in the first 11 months of 1984 that we achieved in the 14 years since 1970.

The other trend that gives us hope is the monumental growth of Hispanic influence in this country and what that means in increased population, increased social and economic clout, and increased political influence.

South of the Sacramento River in California, Hispanics now make up more than 25 percent of the population. That figure will top 30 percent by the year 2000.

There are 1.1 million Spanish-surnamed registered voters in California; 85 percent are Democrats; only 13 percent are Republicans.

In 1975, there were 200 Hispanic elected officials at all levels of government. In 1984, there are over 400 elected judges, city council members, mayors and legislators.

In light of these trends, it is absurd to believe or suggest that we are going to go back in time—as a union or as a people!

The growers often try to blame the union for their problems—to lay their sins off on us—sins for which they only have themselves to blame.

The growers only have themselves to blame as they begin to reap the harvest from decades of environmental damage they have brought upon the land—the pesticides, the herbicides, the soil fumigants, the fertilizers, the salt deposits from thoughtless irrigation—the ravages from years of unrestrained poisoning of our soil and water.

Thousands of acres of land in California have already been irrevocably damaged by this wanton abuse of nature. Thousands more will be lost unless growers understand that dumping more poisons on the soil won't solve their problems—on the short term or the long term.

Health authorities in many San Joaquin Valley towns already warn young children and pregnant women not to drink the water because of nitrates from fertilizers which have contaminated the groundwater.

The growers only have themselves to blame for an increasing demand by consumers for higher quality food—food that isn't tainted by toxics; food that doesn't result from plant mutations or chemicals which produce red, luscious-looking tomatoes—that taste like alfalfa.

The growers are making the same mistake American automakers made in the '60s and '70s when they refused to produce small economical cars—and opened the door to increased foreign competition.

Growers only have themselves to blame for increasing attacks on their publicly-financed hand-outs and government welfare: Water subsidies; mechanization research; huge subsidies for not growing crops.

These special privileges came into being before the Supreme Court's one-person, one-vote decision—at a time when rural lawmakers dominated the Legislature and the Congress. Soon, those hand-outs could be in jeopardy as government searches for more revenue and as urban taxpayers take a closer look at farm programs—and who they really benefit.

The growers only have themselves to blame for the humiliation they have brought upon succeeding waves of immigrant groups which have sweated and sacrificed for 100 years to make this industry rich. For generations, they have subjugated entire races of dark-skinned farm workers.

These are the sins of the growers, not the farm workers. We didn't poison the land. We didn't open the door to imported produce. We didn't covet billions of dollars in government hand-outs. We didn't abuse and exploit the people who work the land.

Today, the growers are like a punch-drunk old boxer who doesn't know he's past his prime. The times are changing. The political and social environment has changed. The chickens are coming home to roost—and the time to account for past sins is approaching.

I am told, these days, why farm workers should be discouraged and pessimistic: The Republicans control the governor's office and the White House. They say there is a conservative trend in the nation.

Yet we are filled with hope and encouragement. We have looked into the future and the future is ours!

History and inevitability are on our side. The farm workers and their children—and the Hispanics and their children—are the future in California. And corporate growers are the past!

Those politicians who ally themselves with the corporate growers and against the farm workers and the His-

panics are in for a big surprise. They want to make their careers in politics. They want to hold power 20 and 30 years from now.

But 20 and 30 years from now—in Modesto, in Salinas, in Fresno, in Bakersfield, in the Imperial Valley, and in many of the great cities of California—those communities will be dominated by farm workers and not by growers, by the children and grandchildren of farm workers and not by the children and grandchildren of growers.

These trends are part of the forces of history that cannot be stopped. No person and no organization can resist them for very long. They are inevitable.

Once social change begins, it cannot be reversed.

You cannot uneducate the person who has learned to read. You cannot humiliate the person who feels pride. You cannot oppress the people who are not afraid anymore.

Our opponents must understand that it's not just a union we have built. Unions, like other institutions, can come and go.

But we're more than an institution. For nearly 20 years, our union has been on the cutting edge of a people's cause—and you cannot do away with an entire people; you cannot stamp out a people's cause.

Regardless of what the future holds for the union, regardless of what the future holds for farm workers, our accomplishments cannot be undone. "La Causa"—our cause—doesn't have to be experienced twice.

The consciousness and pride that were raised by our union are alive and thriving inside millions of young Hispanics who will never work on a farm!

Like the other immigrant groups, the day will come when we win the economic and political rewards which are in keeping with our numbers in society. The day will come when the politicians do the right thing by our people out of political necessity and not out of charity or idealism.

That day may not come this year. That day may not come during this decade. But it will come, someday!

And when that day comes, we shall see the fulfillment of that passage from the Book of Matthew in the New Testament, "That the last shall be first and the first shall be last."

And on that day, our nation shall fulfill its creed—and that fulfillment shall enrich us all.

GLOSSARY

Anglo: A Caucasian American of non-Hispanic ancestry.

Bill of Rights: The first ten amendments to the United States Constitution. These for the most part guarantee various rights to the people, including freedom of religion, freedom of the press, free speech, and so on.

Boycott: Usually a form of protest or social activism, a boycott is when an individual or group of individuals chooses not to deal with a particular business, organization, or other entity in the hope of changing some policy. Usually this takes the form of an economic boycott designed to force a change in policy because of economic loss.

Bracero: A Spanish term signifying a manual laborer, it refers to the Bracero Program by which the United States imported farm workers from Mexico between 1942 and 1964. The term also refers to an individual in this program, or by extension is sometimes applied generically, and pejoratively, to Mexican farm workers.

Chicano: A person born in the United States of Mexican ancestry.

La Causa: A Spanish phrase meaning "The Cause," this refers to the movement to organize Mexican farm workers in the United States led by César Chávez.

Explanation and Analysis of the Document

Since Chávez's speech to the convention of the United Farm Workers had the dual purpose of stimulating membership and reinforcing the purpose of the organization, he began with a story calculated to create sympathy at the outset, the deaths of 32 farm workers in a horrible traffic accident as they rode in a vehicle that lacked government approval. It was a perfect opening as he proceeded to describe the severe conditions the workers were forced to endure in the fields and the deplorable housing provided by the growers, the latter unsanitary, lacking even rudimentary facilities including clean water, and often infested with rats and vermin. Child labor proliferated. The result of this, he informed his listeners was that children "born to migrant workers suffer 25 percent higher infant mortality than the rest of the population. Malnutrition among migrant worker children is 10 times higher than the national rate. ... Farm workers' average life expectancy is still 49 years—compared to 73 years for the average American." All of this firmly illustrated the basic rationale for the UFW's existence.

To personalize his appeal, Chávez next indulged in self-reflection, confiding to the audience the motivation for his activism on their behalf. He recalled his parents and their difficult life as migrant farm workers, his experience with racism while growing up, his dream of a better future. He spoke of his early interest in organizing, to help people become citizens, to register them to vote, to "empower" his people. It was a poignant story, one with every expectation that it would touch a sympathetic chord with the audience, which of course was exactly what the speaker hoped.

Chávez made it a point to connect his own crusade to the greater civil rights struggle. In truth, this was indeed the case. The modern African-American civil rights movement not only benefitted members of that group, it's success proved to be a stimulus to other groups who emulated its strategies in their own quests for equality. "Those who attack our union often say, 'It's not really a union. It's something else: A social movement. A civil rights movement. It's something dangerous,'" he declared. "They're half right. The United Farm Workers is first and foremost a union. A union like any other. A union that either produces for its members on the bread and butter issues or doesn't survive. But the UFW has always been something more than a union—although it's never been dangerous if you believe in the Bill of Rights." It was not just a union, it was a movement of the people, and he was not shy about rallying the support of every Hispanic who hoped for a better life, and he ascribed successes in college attendance and politics to the earlier union endeavors. "The message was clear: If it could happen in the fields, it could happen anywhere—in the cities, in the courts, in the city councils, in the state legislatures. I didn't really appreciate it at the time, but the coming of our union signaled the start of great changes among Hispanics that are only now beginning to be seen."

To those who argued that the union was really weak, Chávez had a ready answer. "How ironic it is that the same forces which argue so passionately that the union is not influential are the same forces that continue to fight us so hard." After listing a number of successes the union had already enjoyed, he launched into politics, castigating the Republican administration of Governor George Deukmejian for its hostility to the union and the farm workers, while predicting that increased political influence would change things since "There are 1.1 million Spanish-surnamed registered voters in California; 85 percent are Democrats; only 13 percent are Republicans. In 1975, there were 200 Hispanic elected officials at all levels of government. In 1984, there are over 400 elected judges, city council members, mayors and legislators. In light of these trends, it is absurd to believe or suggest that we are going to go back in time—as a union or as a people!" In this Chávez was reaffirming the traditional bond between unions and the Democratic Party which had existed since the coalition of blue collar workers, ethnics, and unions first elected Franklin Delano Roosevelt in 1932.

Next, Chávez moved on to environmental concerns, blaming the owners for "decades of environmental damage" through the use of "the pesticides, the herbicides, the soil fumigants, the fertilizers, the salt deposits from thoughtless irrigation." All of these, he asserted, resulted not only in "poisoning of our soil and water," but "irrevocably damages" wide tracts of land and have "contaminated groundwater" causing serious health concerns. The blame for all of this he placed at the feet of the growers.

Finally, he ends with a promise. "Those politicians who ally themselves with the corporate growers and against the farm workers and the Hispanics are in for a big surprise." It is the children and grandchildren of these people who will decide the political future. "The consciousness and pride that were raised by our union are alive and thriving inside millions of young Hispanics who will never work on a farm! Like the other immigrant groups, the day will come when we win the economic and political rewards which are in keeping with our numbers in society. The day will come when the politicians do the right thing by our people out of political necessity and not out of charity or idealism."

Essential Themes

There are four essential themes that emerge from Chávez's speech. This first is Chávez as ethnic leader. Emerging as one of the first nationally-known Hispanic leaders, his appeals to ethnic pride and religious values are clearly evident throughout his speech. The second theme is the traditional union approach to organization of which Chávez proved to be a master. He was the first prominent labor leader to successfully focus his primary efforts on agricultural workers, organizing the United Farm Workers which succeeded in negotiating landmark contracts with California fruit and vegetable growers. Although interested in his own ethnic group, he expanded his activism across ethnic lines which certainly strengthened both the union and his movement.

The third theme is reflective of the modern civil rights movement embodied in Martin Luther King, Jr., and that is the non-violent organization of people to achieve the equality promised in America's founding documents. Although Chávez led a union, he conceived of it as a movement that went beyond the confines of the organization or its members to embrace all agricultural workers. Like King, Chávez grounded his rhetoric in the realism of the experience of common people and their struggle for not just acceptance, but survival. Both leaders envisioned a popular movement that appealed across ethnic and racial lines for support to correct past injustices and realize the proverbial "American dream" for anyone regardless of their ancestry or cultural heritage.

Fourth, Chávez also made direct appeals to the political process. He encouraged listeners who were as yet not citizens to become naturalized and those who were citizens to vote. But not just to vote, to vote for candidates of the Democratic Party. In this respect Chávez also carried on a union tradition dating to the 1932 election of Franklin Roosevelt which created a marriage between unions and the Democrats Party which survives to this day.

Bibliography and Further Reading

Frank Bardacke, *Trampling Out the Vintage: Cesar Chavez and the Two Souls of the United Farm Workers* (London: Verso, 2011).

Roger A. Bruns, *Cesar Chavez and the United Farm Workers Movement* (Santa Barbara, CA: Greenwood, 2011).

Susan Ferriss, Ricardo Sandoval, and Diana Hembree, eds., *The Fight in the Fields: Cesar Chavez and the Farmworkers Movement* (New York: Harcourt Brace, 1997).

Richard Griswold del Castillo and Richard A. Garcia. *César Chávez: A Triumph of Spirit* (Norman: University of Oklahoma Press, 1995).

Peter Matthiessen, *Sal si puedes; Cesar Chavez and the New American Revolution* (New York: Random House, 1969).

Ronald B. Taylor, *Chavez and the Farm*. Boston: Beacon Press, 1975. Print.

ANTI-IMMIGRANT RHETORIC

Immigration has had a continuous influence on American history from the earliest years of settlement through today. Along with it has also come opposition. Early in the colonial era it was based on differences between national groups influenced by the international wars—the Dutch, the English, the French, the Spanish—each wishing to preserve its own colonies for the benefit only of its own citizens. Within the colonies, religious differences between the various groups worked to generate opposition by some groups to the arrival of others and non-English people including especially the Irish, Scots-Irish, Germans, Dutch, French, and smaller groups began to establish settlements of their own where they could speak their languages, maintain their cultural traditions, and worship as they pleased. Naturally, animosities between groups arose and there were times when the English began to wonder if the continued arrival of non-English would not permanently change the nature of the colonies. Most famously, Benjamin Franklin was on record opposing continued German settlement in Pennsylvania since it threatened to overwhelm the English-speaking population.

Following the American Revolution, as Irish and German immigration reached new levels every decade, a largely English Protestant backlash stirred nativist feelings in support of longer naturalization periods and the exclusion of immigrants and Catholics from office. Platform of the American Party reproduces the political platform of the American Party, sometimes known as the Know-Nothings, an anti-immigrant, anti-Catholic movement that actually succeeded in electing several Senators and Representatives in the 1850s, as well as numerous governors and state legislators. This is the first really "national" statement of the political philosophy and aims of the early 19th century nativist movement. As such, it reflects the deeply religious tones of the faction and the prevailing concerns and nativ-

ist rhetoric of the times, especially as it opposed Irish Catholics.

Following the Civil War immigration began to rise to even more unprecedented levels, but perhaps more importantly the sources of the immigration changed. Whereas earlier European emigration to the U.S. came mainly from Northern and Western Europe, between 1880 and 1920 the overwhelming majority were from Southern and Eastern Europe bringing new languages, new cultures, and new religions. Just as in earlier years, nativism rose in rough proportion to the perceived threat. One result was the establishment of the United States Immigration Commission formed in 1906 by opponents of the nativists in the hopes of stalling any restrictionist legislation. The Dillingham Commission Report excerpts a portion of the summary of the Commission's reports. Although a massive 41-volume study that was seemingly based on exceptionally detailed research, scholars have since shown that its methodology was flawed and its conclusions often unwarranted. Nevertheless, the Commission's conclusions played an influential role in shaping public and political opinion in favor of limiting not only overall immigration, but admission from the specific area of Eastern and Southern Europe that members of the Commission had predetermined to be unworthy of entering America. In many ways it formed the rationale for the discriminatory Immigration Acts of 1921 and 1924.

An example of the political rhetoric of the day, influenced by the Dillingham reports, was a speech by U.S. Senator Ellison "Cotton Ed" Smith of South Carolina. Reproduced as "Shut the Door", Smith called into question the loyalty of immigrants to the United States during World War I, a popular but unsubstantiated belief circulating in the aftermath of the conflict and also reinforced by none other than President Woodrow Wilson in his Third Annual Message to Congress. The basis of the balance of his argument rested on the familiar racist attacks of inferiority leveled against Southern and Eastern Europeans by the Dillingham Commission and others, as well as the assertion that they could not be assimilated. In some respects Smith's arguments synthesize the prevailing restrictionist arguments of any era, whether leveled against the Irish and Germans in the antebellum years, the Chinese following the Civil War, Southern and Eastern Europeans between 1880 and 1920, or later Mexican and Hispanic immigrants.

Although the immigration acts of the early 1920s did not place any limits on the entry of people from the Western Hemisphere, there were those in Congress and in the general public who also believed that the limita-tions should be extended to include these regions. Particularly vocal were people in the states bordering Mexico once immigration from the south began to rise during the 1920s. Speech on Mexican Immigration by Representative John Calvin Box of Texas argues that all of the reasons for the earlier reduction in immigration, and the exclusion of specific groups, applied equally to Mexicans and ought therefore to be similarly written into law. If nothing else, Box's speech, when compared to similar speeches and publications both before and after, illustrates the continuous resurfacing of the same arguments against one group after another depending upon which is seen as the largest "threat" in any given era.

■ Platform of the American Party

Date: June 15, 1855
Author: E. B. Bartlett, C. D. Deshler, James M. Stephens
Genre: Political Platform

Summary Overview

Immigration was an issue in the United States even before it became an independent nation. During the colonial era the fear of French encirclement, reinforced by the religious divide between Catholic France and the largely Protestant English colonies, led to suspicion and restriction of French migration in the same way that it did with the Catholic Spanish areas to the south. During the American revolution, the British use of Hessian mercenaries likewise fueled anti-German feelings that survived for decades.

With independence, the United States became a magnet for poor Irish emigrants seeking refuge from the English domination of their homeland. The vast majority of these were Catholic, raising fears among resident Protestants that "their" country would be corrupted by thousands of Catholics whom they believed would not only rival their own religion for prominence but also would readily give their allegiance to the Pope rather than the United States government. The waves of Irish were followed by even larger numbers of Germans, many of whom were also Catholics and who, in addition to speaking a different language, brought customs such as Sunday picnics that horrified the conservative Protestant majority. The result was the growth of "nativism"; a movement to restrict or deny entry into the United States of immigrants of which native-born citizens disapproved and to prohibit those already in the country from having any influence in the political process.

Defining Moment

As immigration increased in the 1830s and 1840s, nativism kept pace resulting in ugly incidents including the wanton burning of a Catholic convent and school near Boston in 1834 and the creation, in the following year, of the Native American Democratic Association, a New York political party dedicated to opposition to Catholics and immigrants. The new organization, which enjoyed the support of much of the state's Whigs, showed sur-

prising strength polling about forty percent of the vote in the fall canvass. Over the next decade similar groups appeared in Maryland, Pennsylvania, and other places. These movements began to crystallize into a national organization with the founding of the American Republican Party in 1843. No relation to the modern Republican Party, it soon changed its name to the Native American Party and in 1855 to simply the American Party. Because of its early secretiveness its opponents took to calling its members "Know-Nothings" because of their reluctance to speak about their beliefs or activities.

The new party was virulently anti-Irish, anti-Catholic, and anti-foreign. It sought to exclude all of these groups from the country as much as possible, advocating a twenty-year residency requirement for those who did arrive before they could become citizens and vote. The movement reached its peak in the early 1850s when it elected five U.S. Senators, 43 U.S. Representatives, and enjoyed great success in some state elections claiming eight governorships and thousands of state and local elected officials. In 1854 it gained control of the governorship and the legislature in Massachusetts and polled about forty percent of the popular vote in Pennsylvania. Massachusetts's legislature immediately enacted laws requiring the reading of passages from the Protestant Bible in public schools, replacing Irish holding jobs on the public payroll, and in other ways infringing on the civil rights of Irish Catholics.

In 1856 the American Party met in Philadelphia for what would be its only national convention. Although a number of anti-slavery delegates walked out when the group approved a position statement endorsing the status quo on slavery, the convention did manage to endorse Millard Fillmore of New York for president and to adopt a platform statement outlining its political beliefs. Amazingly, in a time when the nation was on the verge of being torn apart over the slavery issue, the anti-foreign, anti-Catholic "Know-Nothings" managed to garner 21.5 percent of the popular vote and eight electoral votes from Maryland. Fatally split over the slavery issue, the party ceased to exist for all practical purposes before the next presidential election in 1860.

Author Biography

Little is known of those whose names appear at the bottom of the American Party platform. E. B. Bartlett lived in Covington, Kentucky, was a conservative Baptist elder, used the title "major," and was a former Democratic clerk of the Kenton Circuit Court. In addition to being elected president of the American Party National Council on June 5, 1855, he was also elected president of the Kentucky State Council on August 16 of the same year. As national president, he presided over the last National Council meeting held in Louisville, Kentucky, in 1857. He died about 1863.

Charles D. Deshler was born in Williamsport, Pennsylvania, in 1819. Moving to New Jersey, during his lifetime he was a reader for *Harper's Magazine*, a lay judge of Middlesex County, superintendent of the New Brunswick County schools, and the local postmaster. A member of Christ Episcopal Church, he died at age 91 in 1909. He was the corresponding secretary of the National Council. James M. Stephens was born in Maryland in 1829. A resident of Baltimore, he died in 1908. His name appears on the document as the recording secretary

HISTORICAL DOCUMENT

I. The acknowledgement of that Almighty Being, who rules over the Universe—who presides over the councils of nations—who conducts the affairs of men, and who, in every step by which we have advanced to the character of an independent nation, has distinguished us by some token of Providential agency.

II. The cultivation and development of a sentiment of profoundly intense American feeling; of passionate attachment to our country, its history, and its institutions; of admiration for the purer days of our national existence; of veneration for the heroism that precipitated our revolution; and of emulation of the virtue, wisdom, and patriotism that framed our Constitution and first successfully applied its provisions.

III. The maintenance of the union of these United States as the paramount political good; or, to use the language of Washington, "the primary object of patriotic desire." And hence—

1st. Opposition to all attempts to weaken or subvert it.
2nd. Uncompromising antagonism to every principle of policy that endangers it.

3rd. The advocacy of an equitable adjustment of all political differences which threaten its integrity or perpetuity.
4th. The suppression of all tendencies to political division, founded on "geographical discriminations, or on the belief that there is a real difference of interests and views" between the various sections of the Union.
5th. The full recognition of the rights of the several States, as expressed and reserved in the Constitution; and a careful avoidance, by the General Government, of all interferences with their rights by legislative or executive action.

IV. Obedience to the Constitution of these U. States, as the supreme law of the land, sacredly obligatory upon all its parts and members; and steadfast resistance to the spirit of innovation upon its principles, however specious the pretexts, Avowing that in all doubtful or disputed points it may only be legally ascertained and expounded by the judicial powers of the U. States.

And, as a corollary to the above—

1. A habit of reverential obedience to the laws,

whether National, State, or Municipal, until they are either repealed or declared unconstitutional by the proper authority.

2. A tender and sacred regard for those acts of statesmanship, which are to be distinguished from acts of ordinary legislation, by the fact of their being of the nature of compacts and agreements; and so, to be considered a fixed and settled national policy.

V. A radical revision and modification of the laws regulating immigration, and the settlement of immigrants. Offering to the honest immigrant, who, from love of liberty or hatred of oppression, seeks an asylum in the U. States, a friendly reception and protection. But unqualifiedly condemning the transmission to our shores of felons and paupers.

VI. The essential modification of the Naturalization Laws.

The repeal by the Legislatures of the respective States of all State laws allowing foreigners not naturalized to vote.

The repeal, without retroactive operation, of all acts of Congress making grants of land to unnaturalized foreigners, and allowing them to vote in the Territories.

VII. Hostility to the corrupt means by which the leaders of party have hitherto forced upon us our rulers and our political creeds.

Implacable enmity against the prevalent demoralizing system of rewards for political subserviency, and of punishments for political independence.

Disgust for the wild hunt after office which characterizes the age.

Imitation of the practice of the purer days of the Republic; and admiration of the maxim that "office should seek the man, and not man the office," and of the rule that, the just mode of ascertaining fitness for office is the capability, the faithfulness, and the honesty of the incumbent or candidate.

VIII. Resistance to the aggressive policy and corrupting tendencies of the Roman Catholic Church in our country by the advancement to all political stations—executive, legislative, judicial, or diplomatic—of those only who do not hold civil allegiance, directly or indirectly, to any foreign power whether civil or ecclesiastical, and who are Americans by birth, education, and training—thus fulfilling the maxim "Americans only shall govern America."

The protection of all citizens in the legal and proper exercise of their civil and religious rights and privileges; the maintenance of the right of every man to the full, unrestrained, and peaceful enjoyment of his own religious opinions and worship and a jealous resistance of all attempts by any sect, denominations, or church to obtain an ascendancy over any other in the State, by means of any special privileges or exemption, by any political combination of its members, or by a division of their civil allegiances with any foreign power, potentate, or ecclesiastic.

IX. The reformation of the character of our National Legislature, by elevating to that dignified and responsible position men of higher qualifications, purer morals, and more unselfish patriotism.

X. The restriction of executive patronage, especially in the matter of appointments to office, so far as it may be permitted by the Constitution, and consistent with the public good.

XI. The education of the youth of our country in schools provided by the State; which schools shall be common to all, without distinction of creed or party, and free from any influence or direction of a denominational or partisan character.

And, inasmuch as Christianity by the Constitutions of nearly all the States, by the decisions of the most eminent judicial authorities, and by the consent of the people of America, is considered an element of our political system, and as the Holy Bible is at once the source of Christianity, and the depository and fountain of all civil and religious freedom, we oppose every attempt to exclude it from the schools thus established in the States.

XII. The American party, having arisen upon the ruins and in spite of the opposition of the Whig and Democratic parties, cannot be held in any manner responsible for the obnoxious acts or violated pledges of either. And the systematic agitation of the slavery question by those parties having elevated sectional hostility into a positive element of political power, and brought our institutions into peril, it has therefore become the imperative duty of the American party to interpose for the purpose of giving peace to the country and perpetuity to the Union. And as experience has shown it impossible to reconcile opinions so extreme as those which separate the disputants, and as there can be no dishonor in submitting to the laws, the National Council has deemed it the best guarantee of common justice and of future peace, to abide by and maintain the existing laws upon the subject of slavery, as a final and conclusive settlement of that subject, in spirit and in substance:

And regarding it in the highest duty to avow their opinions upon a subject so important, in distinct and unequivocal terms, it is hereby declared as the sense of this National Council, that Congress possesses no power, under the Constitution, to legislate upon the subject of slavery in the States where it does or may exist, or to exclude any State from admission into the Union because its constitution does or does not recognize the institution of slavery as a part of its social system, and expressly pretermitting any expression of opinion upon the power of Congress to establish or prohibit slavery in any Territory, it is the sense of the National Council that Congress ought not to legislate upon the subject of slavery within the territory of the United States, and that any interference by Congress with slavery as it exists in the District of Columbia would be a violation of the spirit and intention of the compact by which the State of Maryland ceded the District to the United States, and a breach of the National faith.

XIII. The policy of the Government of the United States, in its relations with foreign governments, is to exact justice from the strongest, and do justice to the weakest, restraining, by all the power of the government, all its citizens from interference with the internal concerns of nations with whom we are at peace.

XIV. This National Council declares that all the principles of the Order shall be henceforward everywhere openly avowed, and that each member shall be at liberty to make known the existence of the Order, and the fact that he himself is a member; and it recommends that there be no concealment of the places of meeting or subordinate councils.

GLOSSARY

Agency: In the sense that it is used in the documents, "agency" refers to the action of intervening or exerting influence.

Corollary: A proposition that follows naturally from one already stated or proved.

Ecclesiastic: A member of the clergy or a reference to the clerical hierarchy.

Potentate: A monarch or other sovereign, often used when referring to an autocratic leader.

Document Analysis

The Protestant religious roots of much of the Know-Nothing movement can be seen in the opening sections where the platform links the importance of the "Almighty Being" in the creation of the United States with the value of "passionate attachment to our country, its history, and its institutions." Nativists in the American Party unmistakably imagined themselves as divinely inspired and possessed of a true American spirit unlike immigrants from almost anywhere else. The maintenance of an undivided nation, to them, was "the primary object of patriotic desire," thus they must always support its laws and be ever vigilant and oppose anything that might weaken or divide the country.

To these ends, party members believed it was especially important to revise the immigration and naturalization laws to eliminate the ability of alien immigrants to vote in those states that allowed it, abolish existing legislation allowing aliens to obtain Congressional land grants, and prohibit them from being able to vote in the territories. To be sure, the platform distinguishes between "honest" immigrants who came to American because of their love for liberty and others who it labels "felons and paupers," but of course the unspoken detail here is *who* would decide which immigrants fit into which category. Without doubt, the "honest" immigrants would be Protestants from the same countries of Northwestern Europe that had already populated most of the states.

Not coincidentally, the platform specifically calls for action against the "corrupting tendencies of the Roman Catholic Church" through all means possible, "executive, legislative, judicial, or diplomatic." The only exceptions were to be those of American birth and education and owe allegiance only to the United States, the goal being that "Americans only shall govern America." Since the nativists believed that Catholics owed their primary loyalty to the Vatican rather than to the nation's capital in Washington, they would naturally be excluded as people who owed their allegiance to a foreign power. Although the platform pledges to protect the "civil and religious rights" of all citizens, this is at odds with the rest of the document which consistently seeks to limit or eliminate these exact rights. A case in point is the provision that children should be educated in public schools where Christianity would be linked with the national "political system" and the "Holy Bible"—no doubt the Protestant version—would be present in every school.

The section bemoaning the "corrupt means" by which political leaders maintain power alludes to "the prevalent demoralizing system of rewards for political subserviency," which is not only a general condemnation of the political spoils system rampant in the era, but most likely also an allusion to the belief that immigrants in the cities willingly sold their votes for jobs on the public payroll or other favors. The authors bemoan the loss of "purer days" when honesty and the call to service reigned, an imagined time that did not in reality exist as the colonial and early national politics were as laden with ambitious office-seekers as any other.

Since virtually all Know-Nothings were members of some other political faction before associating themselves with the American Party, the platform makes an attempt to disassociate them from the ills of society that they condemn by noting that the American Party rose "upon the ruins and in spite of the opposition of the Whig and Democratic parties" and "cannot be held in any manner responsible for the obnoxious acts or violated pledges of either." Having said that, the platform moves on to the major issue dividing the nation in 1856—slavery. By its own assertion it is not responsible for the trouble then besetting the nation. It can only look upon the situation as unfortunate and propose as a solution to the national dilemma the maintenance of the status quo. Finally, to overcome the "know-nothing" image of secretiveness, it commits itself to open meetings, an honest assertion of its principles, and urges members to publicly identify themselves with the party.

Essential Themes

This is the first really "national" statement of the political philosophy and aims of the early 19th century nativist movement. As such, it codifies the prevalent anti-foreign feeling, particularly at that time against the Irish Catholics. It was also supported by some of the early Protestant social activists who promoted temperance, opposed slavery, and participated in other reform movements of the era. Its most prominent members were President Millard Fillmore of New York (who was elected vice president as a Whig), Representative Nathaniel Banks of Massachusetts who would later lead thousands of immigrant soldiers as a Union general in the Civil War, and Lewis C. Levin a leading temperance supporter and member of the House of Representatives from Pennsylvania. Ironically, though born in the United States, Levin was Jewish, a group the nativists also sought to exclude. The Know-Nothings were also very active in California where they were among the early advocates of Chinese exclusion.

The American Party was an example of the early fragmentation of American politics into what we might call today "special interest" groups. The factional division between the Federalists, led by John Adams and Alexander Hamilton, and the Democratic-Republicans led by James Madison and Thomas Jefferson, was the first major division on the road to the creation of modern political parties. These were followed by the Democratic Party, the first really modern political party, led by Andrew Jackson, and the Whigs who in some ways were the heirs to the Federalists. The American Party emerged as a third, though short-lived, alternative with its major focus on promoting anti-foreign and anti-Catholic policies. As such it was a part of the political maturation of the nation which later saw the rise of the Republican Party as an anti-slavery alternative, followed by attempts to form other political parties such as the Populists of the late 19th century, Progressives in the early 20th century, and Dixiecrats in the post-World War II era.

Bibliography and Additional Reading

Tyler Anbinder, "Nativism and Prejudice Against Immigrants," in Reed Ueda, ed., *A Companion to American Immigration* (Malden, MA: Blackwell Pub., 2006), 177-201.

Tyler Anbinder, *Nativism and Slavery: The Northern Know Nothings and the Politics of the 1850s* (New York: Oxford University Press, 1992).

Ray Allen Billington, *The Protestant Crusade, 1800–1860: A Study of the Origins of American Nativism* (Chicago: Quadrangle Books, 1964).

Peter Condon, "Knownothingism," *The Catholic Encyclopedia* (New York: Robert Appleton Company, 1910).

Stephen E. Maizlish, "The Meaning of Nativism and the Crisis of the Union: The Know-Nothing Movement in the Antebellum North," in William Gienapp, Stephen E. Maizlish, and John J. Kushma eds., *Essays on American Antebellum Politics, 1840–1860* (College Station, TX: Texas A & M University Press, 1982), 166–98.

■ Dillingham Commission Report

Date: 1911
Author: William P. Dillingham
Genre: Committee Report

Summary Overview

The years 1870-1914 witnessed a period of unprecedented immigration, the most numerous in American history to that time. Along with this influx came growing demands for restriction of the new arrivals. In response, in 1888 the House of Representatives formed a Select Committee to investigate the effects of this rising tide. The committee published its findings as the "Ford Committee Report" in 1889, concluding that it was time not only to reduce immigration but "to select the good from the bad, and to sift the wheat from the chaff." It is apparent, the Committee concluded, "that this country cannot properly assimilate the immigration now coming to our shores."

Nativist calls for the reduction in immigration were so prevalent that by 1892 both the Democratic and Republican Party platforms contained planks supporting restriction. During the decade organized labor made a concerted effort to not only support but lead the restrictionist movement, which began to crystallize around the proposal for a literacy test that, it was hoped, would allow in people from the traditional areas of Northern and Western Europe while excluding people from other regions of the continent. This idea was enthusiastically endorsed by Henry Cabot Lodge who, at great expense to himself, conducted a study designed to demonstrate the superiority of the "English racial strain" over all other groups within the United States. It was no longer sheer numbers that fueled the nativist backlash against immigration, the issue of "race," what we today would call ethnicity, began to shape thinking on the issue. As the new century dawned, the clamor for restriction continued to stir emotions with the result that some political action appeared more and more likely.

Defining Moment

By the first decade in the 20th century efforts of the Immigration Restriction League and its Congressional supporters renewed attempts to limit the influx of peoples into the United States. In 1906 they introduced into Congress a bill to establish a literacy text requirement for entry, a move that opponents feared might gain momentum. To counter this, those who resisted attempts to impose new regulations called for the establishment of a commission to study the immigration question in the hope that this would at least delay any precipitate action. The result was creation of the United States Immigration Commission, often referred to as the Dillingham Commission after its chair, Senator William P. Dillingham of Vermont.

The Commission consisted of three Senators, three members of the House of Representatives, and three statisticians. Of the six politicians, five were already on record favoring immigration restriction. The statisticians included Jeremiah Jenks, a well-known advocate of restriction, and William R. Wheeler who, as the California Commissioner of Immigration, also had documented restrictionist views. With this composition, the Commission could hardly be considered objective. It conducted intensive investigations between 1907 and 1911 employing over 300 staff members to sift through a mass of data on crime, education, labor, living conditions, and various other then-current topics of interest.

Author Biography

The Commission's chair, William P. Dillingham, was a native of Waterbury, Vermont, where he was born in 1843. Educated in local schools, he studied law and was admitted to the bar in 1867. Pursuing a political career, he gained election to the Vermont House of Representatives in 1876, the state Senate in 1878, and the governor's office in 1888. In 1900 he was elected to fill the United States Senate seat that became vacant with the death of Justin Morrill, being re-elected continuously until his own death in Montpelier in 1923. Among his Senate duties was chairmanship of the Committee on Immigration.

Dillingham quickly developed a reputation for his opposition to open immigration, arguing that peoples from Southern and Eastern Europe posed a serious threat to American culture and tradition since they could not be readily assimilated. As governor of Vermont, he established a state commission on immigration and strongly advocated the recruitment of people from Sweden as the best stock available to populate the state. A promoter of hereditary societies, he was president of the Vermont Society of the Sons of the American Revolution which believed that Anglo-Saxon Protestants were the true backbone of the American republic. In his very first speech in the U.S. Senate he admitted that he had never met anyone from China, but nevertheless was certain that they ought to be barred as a class from entry into the country. Throughout his service in the Senate he supported every effort at further immigration regulation presented to that body.

HISTORICAL DOCUMENT

During the fiscal year 1907, in which the Commission was created, a total of 1,285,349 immigrants were admitted to the United States. Of this number 1,207,619 were from Europe, including Turkey in Asia, and of these 979,661, or 81 per cent, came from the southern and eastern countries, comprising Austria-Hungary, Bulgaria, Greece, Italy, Montenegro, Poland, Portugal, Roumania, Russia, Servia, Spain, Turkey in Europe, and Turkey in Asia.

Twenty-five years earlier, in the fiscal year 1882, 648,186 European immigrants came to the United States, and of these only 84,973, or 13.1 per cent, came from the countries above enumerated, while 563,213, or 86.9 per cent, were from Belgium, Great Britain and Ireland, France, Germany, the Netherlands, Scandinavia, and Switzerland, which countries furnished about 95 per cent of the immigration movement from Europe to the United States between 1819 and 1883.

During the entire period for which statistics are available—July 1, 1819, to June 30, 1910—a total of 25,528,410 European immigrants, including 106,481 from Turkey in Asia, were admitted to the United States." Of these, 16,052,900, or 62.9 per cent, came from the northern and western countries enumerated, and 9,475,510, or 37.1 per cent, from southern and eastern Europe and Turkey in Asia. For convenience the former movement will be referred to in the Commission's reports as the "old immigration" and the latter as the "new immigration." The old and the new immigration differ in many essentials. The former was, from the beginning, largely a movement of settlers who came from the most progressive sections of Europe for the purpose of making for themselves homes in the New World. They entered practically every line of activity in nearly every part of the country. Coming during a period of agricultural development, many of them entered agricultural pursuits, sometimes as independent farmers, but more often as farm laborers, who, nevertheless, as a rule soon became landowners. They formed an important part of the great movement toward the West during the last century, and as pioneers were most potent factors in the development of the territory between the Allegheny Mountains and the Pacific coast. They mingled freely with the native Americans and were quickly assimilated, although a large proportion of them, particularly in later years, belonged to non-English-speaking races. This natural bar to assimilation, however, was soon overcome by them, while the racial identity of their children was almost entirely lost and forgotten.

On the other hand, the new immigration has been largely a movement of unskilled laboring men who have come, in large part temporarily, from the less progressive and advanced countries of Europe in response to the call for industrial workers in the eastern and middle western States. They have almost entirely avoided agricultural pursuits, and in cities and industrial communities have congregated together in sections apart from native Americans and the older immigrants to such an extent that assimilation has been slow as compared to that of the earlier non-English-speaking races.

The new immigration as a class is far less intelligent than the old, approximately one-third of all those over 14 years of age when admitted being illiterate. Racially they are for the most part essentially unlike the British, German, and other peoples who came during the period prior to 1880, and generally speaking they are actuated in coming by different ideals, for the old immigration came to be a part of the country, while the new, in a large measure, comes with the intention of profiting, in a pecuniary way, by the superior advantages of the new world and then returning to the old country.

The old immigration movement, which in earlier days was the subject of much discussion and the cause of no little apprehension among the people of the country, long ago became thoroughly merged into the population, and the old sources have contributed a comparatively small part of the recent immigrant tide. Consequently the Commission paid but little attention to the foreign-born element of the old immigrant class and directed its efforts almost entirely to an inquiry relative to the general status of the newer immigrants as residents of the United States. ...

In the United States, until the Bureau of Immigration departed from the custom, practically all statistics dealing with the population had been recorded by country of birth. For immigration purposes prior to 1880 this system was in the main satisfactory, for in the case of immigrants from northern and western Europe the country of birth as a usual thing also fairly established the racial status. With the development of the immigration movement from eastern and southern Europe, however, data based on a knowledge of the country of birth alone indicated practically nothing of the racial status of persons coming from such country to the United States. This may be illustrated by the fact that, according to Bureau of Immigration statistics, as many as 12 different races, all indigenous to the country, are represented among immigrants from Austria-Hungary, while people of 7 distinct races come from Russia. In the case of both countries the distinctions are even greater than those indicated merely by language, for among the immigrants the Teutonic, Slavic, Semitic, and even the Mongolian races are all largely represented. The immigration movement from Turkey also furnishes a most striking illustration of the mingling of emigrating races in a single political division, for in the fiscal year 1907 there came from that country to the United States 9,412 Bulgarians, Servians, and Montenegrins, 7,060 Greeks, 952 Syrians, 588 Hebrews, 194 Roumanians,1,124 Turks, and 1,437 persons of other races. It is not probable that all of these immigrants were born in Turkey, but nevertheless the figures show the uncertain value of a classification by

nativity, for while in the absence of other data it might be necessary to assume that all persons of the above group born in Turkey were Turks, as a matter of fact only 1 in about 18 was really of that race.

In most European countries population statistics, including censuses, are recorded by the racial or language classification, and this method has also been followed in Canada for many years. The practice of recording the population of the United States by country or place of birth has been in force since the census of 1850. When the bill providing for the census of 1910 was under consideration in Congress, the Senate, at the instance of the Immigration Commission, inserted an amendment requiring that the foreign-born should be recorded by race as well as by place of birth, but the provision was eliminated from the bill in conference. Later, however, the census act was amended to provide for the enumeration of the foreign-born in the United States according to their "nationality or mother tongue." By this amendment the result desired by the Commission will be essentially attained, except in the case of certain races or peoples whose original language is not in general use and who speak the language of the country where they reside, and both the scientific and practical value of the census undoubtedly will be greatly enhanced.

In recommending the enactment of the above-mentioned amendment Dr. E. Dana Durand, Director of the Census, stated in part as follows:

It is a well-known fact that in several of the leading foreign countries, notably in Russia, Austria, and Turkey, the population is far from being homogeneous, but is made up of a number of decidedly distinct nationalities, sometimes referred to as races. The differences in racial characteristics, language, and habits of life, as between these different sections of the population, are often very marked, and unless they are recognized in enumerating the population from these countries the census will fail to disclose facts which are of much importance from the practical as well as the scientific standpoint. In considering legislation relating to immigration particularly, information with regard to the nationality of the foreign-born population is of great importance.

No adequate statistics of the number of the different leading nationalities among our foreign-born population can be secured, even by the most elaborate method of returning the place of birth. It is true that the census act does not confine the inquiry to country of birth, but reads "place of birth," so that provinces or well-recognized sections within any country can be reported as places of birth. With this in view, the instructions for the population schedule have provided for reporting persons born in Bohemia, Poland, and Lithuania. The number of Bohemians, Poles, and Lithuanians, however, does not correspond at all precisely with the number born in those sections respectively, and the same is still more true with regard to many other provinces and nationalities.

Aside from the scientific value of a report of nationality, it appears that the members of some of the nationalities which are now largely represented in our population feel strongly opposed to a disregard of nationality in the census reports. The various Slavic nationalities coming from Austria-Hungary appear almost unanimously to object to being reported as born in Austria or Hungary, unless the additional information showing their nationality is presented, so that they will not be supposed to be Austrians or Hungarians. This strong feeling on the part of a large number of the population is likely to render it difficult for the enumerators to do their work, and may endanger the accuracy of the returns of these classes.

As far as ascertained by the Commission, the practice of classifying the foreign-born by race or people, rather than by country of birth, is acceptable to the people of such races in the United States with one exception. Indeed, as stated by Doctor Durand, many of them appear to prefer the racial classification to one of nativity, which is only natural, because as a rule they are, both here and in their native countries, more accustomed to the former.

The objection to the racial classification adopted by the Commission, referred to above, was specifically directed against the use of the word "Hebrew" or "Jewish" to designate a race. This objection was voiced by several prominent Hebrews, who contended that the Jews are not a distinct race in an ethnological sense, and that the terms "Hebrew" and "Jewish" rightly refer to a religious sect and not to a race. The alternative suggested was that Hebrews be classed according to the country in which they were born. At a hearing before the Commission December 4, 1909, Hon. Simon Wolf, of Washington, D. C, representing the executive committee of the board of delegates on civil rights of the Union of American Hebrew Congregations, appeared in opposition to the use by the Commission of the word "Hebrew" in a racial sense. Hon. Julian W. Mack, of Chicago, also made a similar argument. Mr. Wolf's argument may be briefly summarized by quoting the following extract from his remarks:

> The point we make is this: A Jew coming from Russia is a Russian; from Roumania, a Roumanian; from France, a Frenchman; from England, an Englishman; and from Germany, a German; that Hebrew or Jewish is simply a religion.

Mr. Wolf explained, however, that the Jews are not a unit in denying a racial status, but that a certain portion of the Jewish people, especially the Zionists, claim that the Jews are a race.

Subsequent to the hearing above referred to the Commission received several communications from Hebrew organizations urging the continued use of the word "Jew" or "Hebrew" to designate a race or people, one of these petitions being in the form of a special resolution adopted by the federated Jewish organizations of one of the largest cities.

While appreciating the motive which actuated the protest against the designation of the Hebrews as a race or people, the Commission is convinced that such usage is entirely justified. Unfortunately, both the terms in question are used interchangeably to designate a religion as well as a race or people, but the Commission has employed them only in the latter sense in collecting and compiling data respecting immigrants of the various races. As a matter of fact, the terms "Jewish race" and "Hebrew race" are in common and constant use, even among Hebrews themselves. Many instances of this usage are to be found in the Jewish Encyclopedia, which, in fact, treats of the Jews as a race rather than a religious sect, as appears in the following quotation taken from the introduction to that work:

> An even more delicate problem that presented itself at the very outset was the attitude to be observed by the encyclopedia in regard to those Jews who, while born within the Jewish community, have, for one reason or another, abandoned it. As the present work deals with Jews as a race, it was found impossible to exclude those who were of that race, whatever their religious affiliations may have been.

GLOSSARY

Assimilation: The process by which people (either individuals or groups) of different cultures acquire the basic cultural traits of a culture into which they are moving or being incorporated.

Ethnological: Ethnology is a science that studies the division of humans into races, their origin, dispersion, and characteristics.

Indigenous: This signifies something that is native to a particular area and is often used in reference to the original inhabitants of an area.

Zionist: A term coined by Nathan Birnbaum in 1890, it refers to the nationalist movement for the return of the Jewish people to the Land of Israel.

Explanation and Analysis of the Document

Taken from the first volume of the massive Dillingham Commission reports, this excerpt begins by reviewing immigration data from 1907 and comparing it to similar information from 1882, a quarter century earlier. Two points clearly emerge. The first is the great increase on overall European immigration numbers from 648,186 to 1,207,619 or an escalation of 86.3 percent. The second is the Commission's concentration on the European origins of those entering in each sample year. In the earlier year, 86.9 percent came from the traditional regions of Northern and Western Europe which had accounted for some 95 percent of arrivals from Europe between 1819 an 1883. This was dramatically different in 1907 when 81 percent came from areas in Southern and Eastern Europe including the Ottoman Empire. This proved to be an important point of interest to the Commission which explained that for "convenience" it would refer to the groups arriving before 1882 as the "old immigration" and those after that year as the "new immigration." Far from being a mere matter of convenience, most of the 41 volumes of published statistics and conclusions aimed to compare the "old" and the "new" immigrations in an effort to deduce differences between the two. The point

of the comparison was not long in becoming apparent.

In the very next paragraph, before any information was presented, the Commission declared that two groups were in many "essentials" different. The "old" group is described as "settlers" from the "progressive sections" of Europe who readily assimilated into the American society and economy, including the great 19th century westward movement. Conversely, the Commission described the "new" immigrants as mostly "unskilled laboring men" from "less progressive" nations who "congregated together in sections apart from native Americans and the older immigrants to such an extent that assimilation has been slow as compared to that of the earlier non-English-speaking races." Further, it described the "new" immigrants as "far less intelligent" and motivated only by economic gain, not permanent settlement. This was a very gross misrepresenting generality that did not take into consideration the relative length of time the two categories of people had been in the United States, their previous opportunities, or any other factor that made the two experiences quite different when considered outside the bounds of equal time frames. The Commission admitted this when it said that it "paid but little attention to the foreign-born element of the old immigrant class and directed its efforts almost entirely to an

General nativity and race of head of family.	Number of selected families.a	Average family income.	Number of families having a total income—					
			Under $300.b	$300 and under $500.	$500 and under $750.	$750 and under $1,000.	$1,000 and under $1,500.	$1,500 or over.
Native-born of native father:								
White	1,070	$865	24	120	339	295	223	69
Negro	124	517	5	64	41	11	2	1
Native-born of foreign father, by race of father:								
Bohemian and Moravian	24	621	......	8	10	6	......	......
Canadian, French	27	892	1	3	10	6	3	4
Canadian, Other	7	(c)	......	......	1	4	1	1
Cuban	1	(c)	......	......	......	......	1	......
Dutch	15	698	......	2	8	4	1	......
English	42	842	......	10	10	9	10	3
German	213	894	4	21	73	59	34	22
Irish	292	926	5	41	76	65	75	30
Lithuanian	1	(c)	......	......	......	1	......	......
Norwegian	1	(c)	......	......	1	......	......	......
Polish	77	681	1	22	27	16	11	......
Scotch	3	(c)	1	......	1	1	......	......
Slovak	1	(c)	......	......	1	......	......	......
Welsh	3	(c)	......	2	......	......	1	......
Total	707	866	12	110	217	171	137	60
Total native-born	1,901	843	41	294	597	477	362	130
Foreign-born:								
Armenian	101	730	9	19	30	27	11	......
Bohemian and Moravian	437	773	16	82	165	90	58	26
Brava	29	562	......	13	13	2	1	......
Bulgarian	7	(c)	1	2	4	......	......	......
Canadian, French	477	903	9	43	159	133	90	43
Croatian	560	702	58	154	174	85	54	35
Cuban	43	881	1	1	8	19	13	1
Danish	19	830	1	1	6	5	6	......
Dutch	129	772	2	19	52	30	19	7
English	425	956	8	42	111	104	113	47
Finnish	137	781	3	6	51	64	7	6
Flemish	79	798	6	8	26	25	9	5
French	130	757	5	30	38	31	21	5
German	887	878	21	113	264	231	183	75
Greek	49	632	8	17	12	3	6	3
Hebrew	660	685	60	161	237	116	66	20
Irish	675	999	14	68	177	153	156	107
Italian, North	583	657	53	159	201	104	47	19
Italian, South	1,350	569	229	474	394	165	97	21
Japanese	1	(c)	......	......	......	......	1	......
Lithuanian	763	636	53	200	311	129	52	18
Magyar	880	611	111	235	303	131	63	17
Mexican	39	472	3	24	9	2	1	......
Norwegian	26	1,015	......	1	2	10	12	1
Polish	2,038	595	215	682	713	252	132	44
Portuguese	258	790	6	66	85	49	28	24
Roumanian	69	805	7	13	23	10	8	8
Russian	76	494	5	39	24	7	1	......
Ruthenian	571	569	57	190	222	70	26	6
Scotch	123	1,142	......	12	27	19	37	28
Servian	59	465	19	20	12	4	3	1
Slovak	1,243	582	135	410	423	176	85	14
Slovenian	163	684	10	51	57	25	12	8
Spanish	37	1,099	......	1	4	9	20	3
Swedish	460	974	4	25	131	147	103	50
Syrian	142	594	25	42	41	17	13	4
Welsh	90	893	6	10	25	13	27	9
Total	13,825	704	1,160	3,433	4,534	2,457	1,581	660
Grand total	15,726	721	1,201	3,727	5,131	2,934	1,943	790

Immigrants in industries. (In twenty-five parts) (1911)

inquiry relative to the general status of the newer immigrants." Yet the Commission's perception colored the entire balance of its study and conclusions.

In the following paragraphs the Commission explains that in order to better segregate the "old" and "new" populations it is going to discontinue the practice of listing immigrants by their "country of birth" and replace this with recording their "racial status" because, for example, the Commission recognized twelve different "races" whose place of birth was the Austro-Hungarian Empire and seven in Russia. Since the Commission's whole schematic was comparing "old" and "new," and Germans and Austrians were included in the "old," then it was important to identify Hungarians, Poles, Slovaks, and others who might by birth be considered "German" or "Austrian" so they could be categorized among the "new" groups. This could often be done by recording the arrival's native language or their European racial classification.

Recognizing the ethnic self-awareness of many of the immigrants, the Commission argued that classifying people by "race" would also satisfy many of the minority populations of nations like Russia or Austria-Hungary who preferred to be listed as members of their own group rather than as "Russian" or "Austrian." Yet, the Commission itself recognized that not all groups felt this way. A case in point was Jewish immigrants. While the Commission wished to list them all as Jews, or in the nomenclature of the day, "Hebrews," it acknowledged that some prominent members of the group objected that Judaism was a religion, not a race. They preferred that Jewish arrivals be classified as members of the nation from which they derived. As one of the Jewish representatives explained, "A Jew coming from Russia is a Russian; from Roumania, a Roumanian; from France, a Frenchman; from England, an Englishman; and from Germany, a German." Since the Commission wished to categorize Jews as a separate "race" for its own comparative purposes, it noted that there was dissention on this topic within the Jewish community with some, notably Zionists, claiming that Jews were indeed a racial group. By doing this it could isolate the Jewish population which it could then use for some comparisons, but not others, depending on what it hoped to prove by the specific appraisal.

What this excerpt clearly shows is the construction of a dichotomy wherein groups with large numbers of members of lengthy residence in the United States, including often second and third generations, can be compared with groups whose members have arrived only recently in the country as immigrants or juvenile members of the second generation. This consciously sets up an inequitable comparison between groups whose composition is fundamentally different.

Essential Themes
During the last quarter of the 19th century much of the debate swirling around immigration was driven by those who wished to reduce the number of people entering the country and to restrict admission based increasingly on the grounds of race and nationality. In this same era, Social Darwinism reinforced the idea that some groups of people were more "fit" than others through a misapplication of Charles Darwin's biological principles to society, something that he never intended. Nevertheless, this faulty interpretation was used in support of restricting U.S. immigration policy and other discriminatory political and social boundaries. Similarly, the popularity of eugenics, Sir Francis Galton's theory about improving human beings through selective breeding, played a role in the immigration debates, especially after being officially approved by the Immigration Restriction League that was founded by three Harvard graduates in 1894.

The Dillingham Commission's flawed studies played a significant role in continuing the movement toward restriction, forming the basis for the Immigration Acts of 1921 and 1924 which placed severe quota restrictions on European immigration in general and the target "races" of Southern and Eastern Europe in specific. The 1921 legislation, sometimes referred to as the First Quota Act, reduced immigration from outside the Western Hemisphere 57.2 percent per year while the nationality quotas discriminated directly against those from Southern and Eastern European. In 1924, Congress made the quotas permanent with the National Origins Act, which reduced the total number to only 26.3 percent of the previous average, while the nationality quotas greatly reduced for the regions targeted for restriction. The Dillingham Commission led directly to a serious and discriminatory reduction in immigration that remained in effect until 1965.

Bibliography and Further Reading

Katherine Benton-Cohen, "Other Immigrants: Mexicans and the Dillingham Commission of 1907-1911," *Journal of American Ethnic History*, Vol. 30, no. 2 (Winter 2011), 33-57.

Barry R. Chiswick, "Jewish Immigrant Wages in America in 1909: An Analysis of the Dillingham Commission Data," *Explorations in Economic History*, Vol. 29, no. 3 (June 1992), 274-89.

James S. Pula, "United States Immigration Policy and the Dillingham Commission," *Polish American Studies*, XXXVII, No. 1 (1980), 5-31.

Reports of the Immigration Commission (Washington: Government Printing Office, 1911). 41 volumes.

Robert F. Zeidel, *Immigrants, Progressives, and Exclusion Politics: the Dillingham Commission, 1900-1927* (DeKalb, IL: Northern Illinois University Press, 2004).

◼ "Shut the Door"

Date: April 9, 1924
Author: Ellison DuRant Smith
Genre: Speech

Summary Overview

By 1924 calls for immigration restriction were not new. Over the preceding five decades they had grown progressively in number and forcefulness. The Chinese were but the first group to bear the brunt of the new political clout of the nativists, being excluded from entry in 1882. Before World War I the list of those prohibited from entry included the mentally handicapped, contract laborers, polygamists, political radicals, Japanese, prostitutes, illiterates, alcoholics, and others. A Bureau of Immigration was established under the Treasury Department to oversee immigration in 1885.

Added impetus to the nativist crusade came from the United States Immigration Commission, better known as the Dillingham Commission. Its findings added fuel to the restrictionists' cause, providing material for many popular writers including Madison Grant. An attorney and noted conservationist with degrees from Yale and Columbia Universities, he also promoted eugenics which sought to create a better form of human being through selective breeding and forced sterilization of those found unworthy. Grant combined this with his support for immigration restriction to pen *The Passing of the Great Race* which gained exceptional popularity among like-minded people. Preaching a message of Nordic superiority, Grant's writings, along with others of similar message, added a strong element of racism to the already charged nativist drive for further restriction.

Defining Moment

Often labeled the "Roaring Twenties," thoughts of the 1920s usually brings forth images of the new silent movies sweeping the country, Babe Ruth, Cole Porter, Ernest Hemingway, Ezra Pound, John Dos Passos, flappers, the jazz age, and bathtub gin. As the decade opened, optimism abounded, prosperity swept the nation, and the Nineteenth Amendment promised women the right to vote in the national election of 1920. But there were other, more ominous forces also at work.

A wave or racism and xenophobia swept the nation. The Ku Klux Klan enjoyed a resurgence, peaking in membership at some three million during the decade and sponsoring a parade down Pennsylvania Avenue in the nation's capital that drew 40,000 participants and another 500,000 to 750,000 spectators in 1928. Its message was anti-black, anti-Catholic, anti-Jewish, and anti-foreign. Prewar anti-immigrant feelings heightened in the wake of the Dillingham reports, the postwar Red Scare, and especially with the series of bombings aimed at leaders of government and industry by the anarchist followers of radical Luigi Galleani. All of these events combined to produce an exceptional intolerance that further fed anti-immigrant and pro-restriction feelings.

Events crystallized in 1921 with passage of a new immigration act. Sometimes referred to as the Emergency Quota Act, it severely restricted the total number of people who could enter the country to three percent of the whole number of immigrants living in the country in 1910 and also established, for the first time, maximum quota limitations on European nationalities. President Warren G. Harding signed the legislation the same day that Congress adopted it. Originally envisioned as a temporary measure until something more permanent could be devised, by 1924 a new bill had been introduced which promised to restrict immigration even further, especially from the target regions of Southern and Eastern Europe. Introduction of the bill spurred intense debate, both inside Congress and out, with Senator Ellison Du-Rant Smith of South Carolina taking a leading role.

Author Biography

A native of Lynchburg, South Carolina, where he was born on Tanglewood Plantation in 1864, Ellison DuRant "Cotton Ed" Smith was raised in an era of venomous racism and bigotry which he never overcame, being noted throughout his career as a white supremacist and opponent of women's rights and other liberal causes. After graduating from Wofford College he gained election to the South Carolina House of Representatives where he served from 1896 to 1900. After losing a run for the U.S. House of Representatives he was one of the organizers of the Farmer's Protective Association and the Southern Cotton Association, the latter of which gave him his nickname. In 1906 he was elected as a Democrat to the first of six consecutive terms in the U.S. Senate (1909-44).

A champion of cotton agriculture and white supremacy, he was a leader in the unsuccessful fight to defeat the 19th Amendment and most of Franklin Roosevelt's New Deal legislation including a filibuster he led against the minimum wage portions of the Fair Labor Standards Act, and opposed many of the wartime emergency measures between 1941 and 1944 when he was defeated in a primary for reelection. He died at Tanglewood Plantation on November 17, 1944. With a strong record opposing any extension of individual civil rights, it is little wonder that Cotton Ed was also in the forefront of arguing for immigration restriction during the period of the mass migration from 1870 through 1920. His speech in favor of the restrictions contained in the 1924 immigration bill is a classic of that era's opposition to open immigration.

HISTORICAL DOCUMENT

It seems to me the point as to this measure—and I have been so impressed for several years—is that the time has arrived when we should shut the door. We have been called the melting pot of the world. We had an experience just a few years ago, during the great World War, when it looked as though we had allowed influences to enter our borders that were about to melt the pot in place of us being the melting pot.

I think that we have sufficient stock in America now for us to shut the door, Americanize what we have, and save the resources of America for the natural increase of our population. We all know that one of the most prolific causes of war is the desire for increased land ownership for the overflow of a congested population. We are increasing at such a rate that in the natural course of things in a comparatively few years the landed resources, the natural resources of the country, shall be taken up by the natural increase of our population. It seems to me the part of wisdom now that we have throughout the length and breadth of continental America a population which is beginning to encroach upon the reserve and virgin resources of the country to keep it in trust for the multiplying population of the country.

I do not believe that political reasons should enter into the discussion of this very vital question. It is of greater concern to us to maintain the institutions of America, to maintain the principles upon which this Government is founded, than to develop and exploit the underdeveloped resources of the country. There are some things that are dearer to us, fraught with more benefit to us, than the immediate development of the undeveloped resources of the country. I believe that our particular ideas, social, moral, religious, and political, have demonstrated, by virtue of the progress we have made and the character of people that we are, that we have the highest ideals of any member of the human family or any nation. We have demonstrated the fact that the human family, certainty the predominant breed in America, can govern themselves by a direct government of the people. If this Government shall fail, it shall fail by virtue of the terrible law of inherited tendency. Those who come from the nations which from time immemorial have been under the dictation of a master fall more easily by the law of inheritance and the inertia of habit into a condition of political servitude than the descendants of those who cleared the forests, conquered the savage, stood at arms and won their liberty from their mother country, England.

I think we now have sufficient population in our country for us to shut the door and to breed up a pure, unadulterated American citizenship. I recognize that there is a dangerous lack of distinction between people of a certain nationality and the breed of the dog. Who is an American? Is he an immigrant from Italy? Is he an immigrant from Germany? If you were to go abroad and some one were to meet you and say, "I met a typical American," what would flash into your mind as a typical American, the typical representative of that new Nation? Would it be the son of an Italian immigrant, the son of a German immigrant, the son of any of the breeds from the Orient, the son of the denizens of Africa? We must not get our ethnological distinctions mixed up with out anthropological distinctions. It is the breed of the dog in which I am interested. I would like for the Members of the Senate to read that book just recently published by Madison Grant, *The Passing of a Great Race*. Thank God we have in America perhaps the largest percentage of any country in the world of the pure, unadulterated Anglo-Saxon stock; certainly the greatest of any nation in the Nordic breed. It is for the preservation of that splendid stock that has characterized us that I would make this not an asylum for the oppressed of all countries, but a country to assimilate and perfect that splendid type of manhood that has made America the foremost Nation in her progress and in her power, and yet the youngest of all the nations. I myself believe that the preservation of her institutions depends upon us now taking counsel with our condition and our experience during the last World War.

Without offense, but with regard to the salvation of our own, let us shut the door and assimilate what we have, and let us breed pure American citizens and develop our own American resources. I am more in favor of that than I am of our quota proposition. Of course, it may not meet the approbation of the Senate that we shall shut the door—which I unqualifiedly and unreservedly believe to be our duty—and develop what we have, assimilate and digest what we have into pure Americans, with American aspirations, and thoroughly familiar with the love of American institutions, rather than the importation of any number of men from other countries. If we may not have that, then I am in favor of putting the quota down to the lowest possible point, with every selective element in it that may be.

The great desideratum of modern times has been education not alone book knowledge, but that education which enables men to think right, to think logically, to think truthfully, men equipped with power to appreciate the rapidly developing conditions that are all about us, that have converted the world in the last 50 years into a brand new world and made us masters of forces that are revolutionizing production. We want men not like dumb, driven cattle from those nations where the progressive thought of the times has scarcely made a beginning and where they see men as mere machines; we want men who have an appreciation of the responsibility brought about by the manifestation of the power of that individual. We

have not that in this country to-day. We have men here to-day who are selfishly utilizing the enormous forces discovered by genius, and if we are not careful as statesmen, if we are not careful in our legislation, these very masters of the tremendous forces that have been made available to us will bring us under their domination and control by virtue of the power they have in multiplying their wealth.

We are struggling to-day against the organized forces of man's brain multiplied a million times by materialized thought in the form of steam and electricity as applied in the everyday affairs of man. We have enough in this country to engage the brain of every lover of his country in solving the problems of a democratic government in the midst of the imperial power that genius is discovering and placing in the hands of man. We have population enough to-day without throwing wide our doors and jeopardizing the interests of this country by pouring into it men who willingly become the slaves of those who employ them in manipulating these forces of nature, and they few reap the enormous benefits that accrue therefrom.

We ought to Americanize not only our population but our forces. We ought to Americanize our factories and our vast material resources, so that we can make each contribute to the other and have an abundance for us under the form of the government laid down by our fathers.

The Senator from Georgia [William J. Harris] has introduced an amendment to shut the door. It is not a question of politics. It is a question of maintaining that which has made you and me the beneficiaries of the greatest hope that ever burned in the human breast for the most splendid future that ever stood before mankind, where the boy in the gutter can look with confidence to the seat of the Presidency of the United States; where the boy in the gutter can look forward to the time when, paying the price of a proper citizen, he may fill a seat in this hall; where the boy to-day poverty-stricken, standing in the midst of all the splendid opportunities of America, should have and, please God, if we do our duty, will have an opportunity to enjoy the marvelous wealth that the genius and brain of our country is making possible for us all.

We do not want to tangle the skein of America's progress by those who imperfectly understand the genius of our Government and the opportunities that lie about us. Let us keep what we have, protect what we have, make what we have the realization of the dream of those who wrote the Constitution.

I am more concerned about that than I am about whether a new railroad shall be built or whether there shall be diversified farming next year or whether a certain coal mine shall be mined. I would rather see American citizenship refined to the last degree in all that makes America what we hope it will be than to develop the resources of America at the expense of the citizenship of our country. The time has come when we should shut the door and keep what we have for what we hope our own people to be.

GLOSSARY

Desideratum: Something which is needed, wanted, or essential.

Melting Pot: Derived from the "smelting pot" in which metals and other materials were melted and mixed together, the term was sometimes used as a metaphor during the 18th and 19th centuries to describe two peoples and cultures mixing together. The term was popularized in the United States by Israel Zangwill's play *The Melting Pot* (1908).

Skein: A length of thread or knitting yarn that is loosely twisted and knotted. The term is often used to describe something that is tangled or complicated.

Document Analysis

Senator Smith begins by alluding to the fears during World War I that immigrants from nations aligned against the United States might be disloyal, or even commit belligerent acts such as espionage and sabotage. Although this did not happen, the fears of immigrant disloyalty persisted.

His argument for restriction begins with the statement that sufficient "stock" was already present in the country and it was now time to "Americanize what we have, and save the resources of America for the natural increase of our population." Although he claims to believe that "political reasons" should not be brought into the debates, Smith then proceeds to do just that, arguing that it "is of greater concern to us to maintain the institutions of America, to maintain the principles upon which this Government is founded." He argues that American "social, moral, religious, and political" ideas have given citizens the "highest ideals of any member of the human family or any nation." To preserve this, he concludes, Congress must protect it from people "who come from the nations which from time immemorial have been under the dictation of a master" which inclines them more to "a condition of political servitude." It was now time to "shut the door and to breed up a pure, unadulterated American citizenship." This was consistent with the eugenics movement of that era and, of course, ignores the fact that a great number of those immigrants were com-

ing to the United States exactly *for* the freedoms it offered and to *escape* monarchical governments.

Smith follows with a lengthy discussion of what an American is *not*, which is to say not an immigrant. In case anyone is still uncertain following his explanation he suggests that the Senators ought to read Madison Grant's *The Passing of a Great Race*, a pseudo-scientific book incorporating eugenics that argues in favor of the purity of the Nordic/Anglo-Saxon race over all others and advocates the creation of a dictatorship, the segregation of "inferior races" into ghettos, and the elimination of "undesirable" traits and "worthless race types." In the early 1930s Grant received a complimentary letter from Adolf Hitler who referred to the book as his "Bible."

It was, Smith argued further, the Senate's "duty" to close the door so that Americans could develop on their own. If closing the door completely was not possible, then he proposed "putting the quota down to the lowest possible point." He explained, continuing his racist line of thought: "We want men not like dumb, driven cattle from those nations where the progressive thought of the times has scarcely made a beginning and where they see men as mere machines; we want men who have an appreciation of the responsibility brought about by the manifestation of the power of that individual." He wants an America where "the boy to-day poverty-stricken, standing in the midst of all the splendid opportunities of America, should have and, please God, if we do our duty, will have an opportunity to enjoy the marvelous wealth that the genius and brain of our country is making possible for us all." That, of course, is exactly what the immigrants he sought to exclude also wanted.

Essential Themes

Initially, support for immigration restriction was largely based on economic arguments including the backing of the American Federation of Labor which was attempting to preserve the status and economic bargaining power of skilled workers faced with the competition of the factory system employing unskilled, largely immigrant labor. Argument for restriction soon expanded to include the literacy test as the exclusion movement began to concentrate more on reducing aliens from Southern and Eastern Europe. The third phase, influenced greatly by the Dillingham Commission and the genre of literature epitomized by Madison Grant, began emphasizing the idea that inherent racial characteristics made some "races" unable to fully assimilate—the word "race" meaning what we would think of today as nationality. This was the basis of much of the racism, anti-Semitism, anti-Catholicism, and anti-foreign sentiment of the 1920s, as it was Smith's speech.

Smith's arguments also paralleled those of the developing restrictionist movement which had gone beyond the early attempt to restrict specific categories of people to argue increasingly for strict overall numerical limits if not a complete closure of the "door." In the end, the quotas from 1921 were reduced to lower levels, but the door remained open this small sliver. The Senate approved the legislation with only six negative votes, clearly indicating the sense of the group. In this, the action is a repudiation of the earlier "melting pot" ideal seen in Emma Lazarus's poem "The New Colossus" (1883) and more directly in Israel Zangwill's play *The Melting Pot* (1908). Smith's argument suggests this shift very clearly by linking the two ideas—the melting pot and closing the door.

Bibliography and Additional Reading

Roger Daniels, *Not Like Us: Immigrants and Minorities in America, 1890-1924* (Chicago: Ivan R. Dee, 1997).

Tibor Frank, "From Nativism to the Quota Laws: Restrictionist Pressure Groups and the US Congress 1879-1924," *Parliaments, Estates and Representation,* November 15, 1995, 143-157.

David Goldberg, *Discontented America: the United States in the 1920s* (Baltimore: The Johns Hopkins University Press, 1999).

Daniel W. Hollis, "'Cotton Ed Smith': Showman or Statesman?" *The South Carolina Historical Magazine,* Vol. 71, no. 4 (October 1970), 235-56.

Kenneth M. Ludmerer, "Genetics, Eugenics and the Immigration Restriction Act of 1924," *Bulletin of the History of Medicine,* Vol. 46, no. 1 (January/February 1972), 59-81.

■ Speech on Mexican Immigration

Date: 1928
Author: John C. Box
Genre: Speech

Summary Overview

Although the English-speaking colonies shared, from the earliest times, a border with Spanish and later Mexican territory, there was remarkably little migration from those lands into colonial America or the later United States. In fact, the largest "migrations," if someone who does not move can be said to have "migrated," were the residents of the Louisiana Territory who became United States citizens following the Louisiana Purchase in 1803 and those Mexicans living in the lands taken from Mexico after the hostilities of the 1840s. The discovery of gold in California in 1849 brought some north into the state and the adjoining areas, but by 1900 only an estimated 100,000 Mexicans entered the United States, an average of only 1,923 per year since the Treaty of Guadalupe-Hidalgo in 1848. Nearly all of these settled in the former Mexican areas of California, Texas, and the intervening territories that became New Mexico, Arizona, and Nevada.

The magnitude of Mexican immigration began to change in the first two decades of the new century when new irrigation projects undertaken in response to Republican President Theodore Roosevelt's conservation programs opened large new tracts to agriculture, providing jobs for agricultural workers. Though low by American standards, pay for these jobs was appreciably higher than that in Mexico. The beginning of World War I in 1914, and later U.S. entry in 1917, increased the demand for farm products and thus the demand for agrarian labor.

Defining Moment

An estimated 31,000 Mexicans entered the United States between 1901 and 1910, only 3,100 per year, but that was a third more than the previous average. The major influx began after the outbreak of the Mexican Revolution in 1910 that dragged on for the next decade. The availability of better paying jobs north of the border combined with those attempting to escape the lengthy violence of the revolution to increase Mexican immigration

to nearly 500,000 between 1920 and 1929, an average of 46,900 per year or more than fifteen times the annual average for the previous decade.

The rising tide from south of the border led to creation within the Department of Labor of the United States Border Patrol in 1924 charged with preventing illegal entry along the Canadian and Mexican borders. Despite this official interest in border security, American immigration policy remained open to Mexicans. The Immigration Act of 1917 required that all immigrants pass a literacy test and pay a head tax before being admitted, but these were waived for people from Mexico. In the same year Congress established a Guest Worker Program. The immigration acts adopted in 1921 and 1924, though enacting serious restrictions on Southern and Eastern European immigration, placed no such limitation on those from Mexico or any other portion of the Western Hemisphere other than implementing an $8 head tax and a $10 visa fee. No doubt the stereotypical view of Mexican immigrants as docile and the belief that most would eventually return to their native country contributed to this more open attitude despite the prevalent theories of eugenics and Social Darwinism notwithstanding. Yet some of this good feeling began to fade with the Cristero War pitting Catholics against the Mexican government from 1926 to 1929. The war prompted a new movement of Mexicans north, but this time a large number were politically motivated and began to organize protests in the United States against Mexico. Some even accused them of running guns across the border. American openness to Mexican immigration, especially in Texas and the other states sharing a border with Mexico, began to dim leading to calls for closing the southern border.

Author Biography

John Calvin Box was born in northern Houston County, Texas, in 1871. After attending an institute aligned with the United Methodist Church and becoming a Methodist lay minister at age eighteen, he later joined the Freemasons and read law with E. J. Mantooth, being admitted to the Texas bar in 1893. Pursuing a career in politics, he became a judge (1896-1901), was elected mayor of Jacksonville as a Democrat (1902-05), and served as a member of the Democratic state committee (1908-10). One of the original foundering trustees of Southern Methodist University in Dallas, he served as the chair of its Board from 1913 to 1918.

Box gained election to the United States House of Representatives in which he served from 1919 through 1931 where he was known for his interest in immigration issues, publishing *Selection of Immigrants at the Source. A Brief Submitted by Hon. John C. Box. Printed for the Use of the Committee on Immigration and Naturalization, House of Representatives* (Washington: Government Printing Office, 1923). Becoming increasingly concerned with the naturalization of Mexicans in Texas which gave them the right to vote, Box warned his fellow-representatives that because Mexicans were often of mixed racial ancestry they would most likely intermarry quite readily in the United States leading to a "distressing process of mongrelization." After failing to be re-nominated in 1930, he practiced law in Jacksonville until his death in 1941.

HISTORICAL DOCUMENT

Every reason which calls for the exclusion of the most wretched, ignorant, dirty, diseased, and degraded people of Europe or Asia demands that the illiterate, unclean, peonized masses moving this way from Mexico be stopped at the border....

The admission of a large and increasing number of Mexican peons to engage in all kinds of work is at variance with the American purpose to protect the wages of its working people and maintain their standard of living. Mexican labor is not free; it is not well paid; its standard of living is low. The yearly admission of several scores of thousands from just across the Mexican border tends constantly to lower the wages and conditions of men and women of America who labor with their hands in industry, in transportation, and in agriculture. One who has been in Mexico or in Mexican sections of cities and towns of the southwestern United States enough to make general observation needs no evidence or argument to convince him of the truth of the statement that Mexican peon labor is poorly paid and lives miserably in the midst of want, dirt, and disease.

In industry and transportation they displace great numbers of Americans who are left without employment and drift into poverty, even vagrancy, unable to maintain families or to help sustain American communities....

The importers of such Mexican laborers as go to farms all want them to increase farm production, not by the labor of American farmers, for the sustenance of families and the support of American farm life, but by serf labor working mainly for absentee landlords on millions of acres of semiarid lands. Many of these lands have heretofore been profitably used for grazing cattle, sheep, and goats. Many of them are held by speculative owners.

A great part of these areas can not be cultivated until the Government has spent vast sums in reclaiming them.... Their occupation and cultivation by serfs should not be encouraged....

Another purpose of the immigration laws is the protection of American racial stock from further degradation or change through mongrelization. The Mexican peon is a mixture of Mediterranean-blooded Spanish peasant with low-grade Indians who did not fight to extinction but submitted and multiplied as serfs. Into that was fused much Negro slave blood. This blend of low-grade Spaniard, peonized Indian, and Negro slave mixes with Negroes, mulattoes, and other mongrels, and some sorry whites, already here. The prevention of such mongrelization and the degradation it causes is one of the purposes of our laws which the admission of these people will tend to defeat....

To keep out the illiterate and the diseased is another essential part of the Nation's immigration policy. The Mexican peons are illiterate and ignorant. Because of their unsanitary habits and living conditions and their vices they are especially subject to smallpox, venereal diseases, tuberculosis, and other dangerous contagions. Their admission is inconsistent with this phase of our policy.

The protection of American society against the importation of crime and pauperism is yet another object of these laws. Few, if any, other immigrants have brought us so large a proportion of criminals and paupers as have the Mexican peons.

GLOSSARY

Absentee landlord: A person who owns land but does not live upon it; a person who rents out land or hires someone else to manage it.

Mongrelization: The interbreeding of differing strains; a person of mixed or uncertain ancestry.

Peonized: Being reduced to the status of a peon; that is, an unskilled agricultural worker. Colloquially, a person of low status.

Semiarid: A region characterized by light annual rainfall, between ten and twenty inches by scientific definition.

Serf: In a feudal society, an agricultural laborer who is bound to the land and subject to the will of the owner of the estate.

Vagrancy: Literally, the habit of moving about from place to place. As a legal term it refers to moving about with no means of employment or financial support.

Document Analysis

Representative Box begins his speech by immediately equating Mexican immigration with the recently restricted groups from Southern and Eastern Europe. The tactic was of course aimed to convince his Congressional colleagues that if the latter had been restricted for the same reasons then the former ought to also be regulated.

Chief among his reasoning are economic arguments. Just as the circumscribed groups of the New Immigration from Europe had been painted as unskilled masses who drove down wages, Box argued that Mexicans similarly lowered the wage scale for labor in America, and consequently the standard of living of working Americans. In making the argument he provides no data or other supporting evidence and appears, similarly to the arguments for the earlier restrictions, to reason that if people live in poverty they do so by choice rather than of necessity.

The economic argument continues with the familiar refrain, heard before and since, that immigrants were taking jobs away from Americans who are then left in dire circumstances unable to support their families. In this same manner Box claims that Mexican agricultural laborers are harming independent American farmers and using land that was previously available for the grazing of livestock. In all of this he blames the immigrants, not the owners of the land and the commercial farming enterprises except to note that many of them are absentee owners. Interestingly, in view of President Theodore Roosevelt's support for irrigation projects to reclaim the land for agriculture, Box asserts that the government has spent "vast sums" to reclaim the land only to see it used by "serfs." Could it be that Box, a Democrat, was also using the opportunity provided by his speech to criticize the Republican Roosevelt?

From economics Box turns to racism, arguing that Mexican immigration must be restricted to protect the "American racial stock from further degradation or change through mongrelization." With a decidedly unChristian spirit, the Methodist minister proceeds to denigrate Spaniards, indigenous people, and those of African heritage as "low-grade" people whose intermixture results in "mongrelization" that is a threat to the purity of the American race. This threat, he further argues, is only multiplied by his view of these immigrants as illiterate, ignorant, unsanitary, diseased, and otherwise undesirable.

Essential Themes

In his speech, Representative Box echoed all of the primary arguments used to establish the earlier restriction of Southern and Eastern Europeans—illiteracy, disease, lack of cleanliness, unfamiliarity with democracy, and a negative impact on the U.S. economy and working people. All of these arguments were used to great effect by supporters of the Immigration Acts of 1921 and 1924 that greatly restricted arrivals from Southern and Eastern Europe. Based largely on the flawed reports of the Dillingham Commission, the stereotypes of poor, illiterate, diseased masses threatening American purity was a frequent topic in popular literature of the era.

Box's two major themes are economics and racism. The former was an early argument used against immigration from Europe throughout the 19th century, and especially in the last two decades of that century when promoted nationally by the American Federation of Labor and the Immigration Restriction League. The latter became increasingly important with the rise of the eugenics movement and Social Darwinism, both of which promoted the idea that some people were more "fit" than others and led inevitably to the argument that the "unfit" must be prevented from coming in contact with the superior people less these be degraded.

In its essence, Representative Box's speech against unrestricted Mexican immigration only restates the same arguments used successfully earlier in the decade to control immigration from specific regions of Europe.

Bibliography and Additional Reading

Richard Griswold del Castillo and Arnoldo de León, *North to Aztlán: A History of Mexican Americans in the United States* (New York: Twayne Publishers, 1996).

Harvey A. Levenstein, "The AFL and Mexican Immigration in the 1920s: An Experiment in Labor Diplomacy," *Hispanic American Historical Review*, Vol. 48, no. 2 (May 1968), 206-19.

Carey McWilliams and Matt S. Meier, *North from Mexico: The Spanish-Speaking People of the United States* (New York: Praeger, 1990).

Matt Meier and Feliciano Rivera, *Mexican Americans/American Mexicans* (New York: Hill and Wang, 1993)

Julia Young, *Mexican Exodus: Emigrants, Exiles, and Refugees of the Cristero War* (New York: Oxford University Press, 2015).

FEDERAL LEGISLATION

With a diverse population from the earliest of co-lonial times, it was unlikely that the government that convened under the new Constitution in 1789 would erect strict barriers to the arrival of further newcomers, especially with abundant land that needed settling. The First Congress did the expected and established a very open immigration policy in 1790 (see Naturalization Act of 1790) when it determined that anyone could enter the country and, provided the person was "white," become a naturalized citizen after only two years of residence. In the more than two and one-quarter centuries that have elapsed since then, Congress has almost continu-ally eroded that openness in response to public pres-sure, much of which was animated by fears of people who were somehow different or were perceived, rightly or wrongly, to pose some sort of threat. This section pro-vides excerpts from the key documents through which these changes were enacted.

One of the factors that brought an early change was the westward movement. Coupled with rising fears of the thousands of Irish and Germans entering the coun-try, the Homestead Act was to some extent a compro-mise between those who wished to attract immigrants to populate what was then the west and nativists who opposed keeping the door open to all new arrivals. The Homestead Act presents the pertinent portion of the act along with an explanation of the forces that shaped it. Of course, just like the Homestead Act, not all of the legislation effecting immigration began with that intent. Another example is the Fourteenth Amendment which defined citizenship to include not only those who were naturalized, but anyone born within the jurisdiction of the United States. By doing this, thousands of people who might not have been citizens under the previous laws of the various states were made citizens of both the country and the states in which they lived.

A series of serious epidemics brought the next major shift effecting immigration when the National Quar-antine Act began to place restrictions on entry into the United States by excluding or quarantining those with diseases. Beyond this, the documents in this section were all created specifically to address immigration is-sues, beginning with the Chinese Exclusion Act. This resulted from a recession during which American work-ers on the Pacific coast sought protection from competi-tion by Asian immigrants who sought employment in the mining industry and construction of the developing rail-roads. It was the first time in U.S. history that Congress determined to exclude an entire people based on their national origin.

By the 1890s calls multiplied for restricting overall immigration. In the following year new Congressional action (Immigration Act of 1891) excluded people in a long list of categories that were believed to be unde-sirable including such things a paupers, polygamists, criminals, and those with mental diseases. In addition, the law once and for all asserted federal prerogative in immigration matters. With this established, the focus of nativist concern turned to the new wave of arrivals from the nations of Southern and Eastern Europe. The first attempt to restrict these peoples was through requir-ing a literacy test which its promoters unabashedly said would fall more on these groups and less on the arrivals from Northern and Western Europe (Immigration Act of 1917). Although passed by Congress three times only to meet with presidential veto, it finally became law in 1917.

With this success, restrictionists determined to target more specifically the people they sought to exclude. They achieved this in the Immigration Act of 1924, which not only greatly restricted overall immigration, but specifi-cally assigned quotas to each nationality that were de-signed to limit the groups intended for banning. These restrictions lasted for 28 years until the numbers were amended in 1952 (McCarran-Walter Act), although the nationality quotas were retained over the veto of President Harry Truman largely because of the fear of communist influences arriving along with immigrants from Eastern Europe. The McCarran-Walter Act of 1952 also codified previously existing immigration law into new legislation and defined a system of priorities for future admission: (1) those with special education or training or spouse and accompanying children of citizens, (2) parents of citizens, and (3) the spouses or children of aliens legally residing in the U.S.

Finally, with the new public interest in equality that accompanied the successes of the modern Civil Rights Movement, the nationality quotas were dropped in favor of general quotas on immigrants contained in the Immigration and Nationality Act of 1965. Overall, the act eliminated many of the previous inequities and also revised the list of preferences to privilege the children of citizens and permanent residents over other categories. Elimination of the previous restrictions eventually led to an increase in arrivals and to more diversity in immigrants' origins over the succeeding decades.

■ Naturalization Act of 1790

Date: March 26, 1790
Author: U.S. Congress
Genre: Act of Congress

Summary Overview

From the earliest colonial settlements in America what would become the United States developed as a multicultural society. Poles, Swiss, Dutch/Germans, Italians, and others resided in 17th century Jamestown alongside its English residents. Eighteen different languages were said to have been spoken in Dutch New Amsterdam (later New York) while Swedes established a colony near modern Philadelphia and large numbers of Germans settled in Pennsylvania and in New York's Mohawk Valley. Irish immigrants spread throughout the colonies, while Scots-Irish were found mostly in New Jersey and along the frontier regions. A study of religious organization in 1775 identified 668 Congregational Churches, 558 Presbyterian, 495 Anglican, 494 Baptist, 310 Quaker, 159 German Reformed, 150 Lutheran, 120 Dutch Reformed, 65 Methodist, 56 Catholic, and 6 Jewish congregations.

By the beginning of the American Revolution in 1775 estimates place the population of the thirteen colonies at about three million. Of these, approximately 85 percent traced their ancestry to the British Isles—English, Irish, Welsh, Scots, and Scots-Irish—8.8 percent were of German ancestry, and 3.5 percent of Dutch descent. Eventually, when the first United States census was undertaken in 1790, the enumeration included 3,929,214 people. Of these, some 2.1 million were of English ancestry, along with 757,000 African, 300,000 Scots-Irish, 270,000 German, 150,000 Scots, 100,000 Dutch, 15,000 French, 10,000 Welsh, 2,000 Jews, 2,000 Swedes, and about 200,000 total of various other ancestries. Clearly, the history of the nation was already the history of immigration, thus some means had to be established for newcomers to gain official citizenship.

Defining Moment

Each of the colonies which the Declaration of Independence transformed into states had their own requirements for political participation. These varied considerably from state to state but in most cases required some form of property ownership as a qualification for voting and holding elective office. Often, especially in the southern states, property qualifications could be significant thus limiting the franchise considerably. It has been estimated that at the time of George Washington's election as the first president only about six percent of the population was eligible to vote. With the creation of a national government it became important to clearly define national citizenship before the voting rights issue could be clarified. And to define citizenship also required clarification whether, and under what circumstances, an immigrant, the subject of a different sovereignty, might be granted citizenship.

The Constitution adopted in 1787 outlined the form of government and the responsibilities of each of its three branches. Article I, section 8, clause 4 explicitly conferred on Congress the authority and responsibility "To establish an uniform Rule of Naturalization."

Author Biography

There was no single author for the first immigration and nationalization law adopted by Congress; rather, it was loosely based on British precedents with some modification to fit the prevailing preferences. In 1740 Parliament had adopted "An Act for naturalizing such foreign Protestants, and others therein mentioned, as are settled, or shall settle in any of His Majesty's colonies in America." This act stipulated that anyone who had lived in any of the English colonies in North America for a minimum of seven years could make application for naturalization as a British subject provided that the person was not absent from the colony for more than two months and that the applicant take an oath of allegiance to the crown and be a member of a Protestant or Reformed congregation.

Aside from the religious provisions, the law provided an easy avenue to citizenship. As such, it was designed to promote immigration to the colonies not only through its liberal provisions but by effectively placing the issue under the direct control of Parliament rather than the individual colonies, although the colonial courts were authorized to determine when applicants had successfully met the required conditions. Despite this attempt, many of the colonial courts acted on their own responsibility so that the intent of the law was not uniformly applied. This resulted in the withdrawal of authority for colonial courts to rule in these cases in 1773. Nevertheless, this act served as the initial basis for the legislation adopted by the First Congress in 1790.

HISTORICAL DOCUMENT

Be it enacted by the Senate and House of Representatives of the United States of America, in Congress assembled, That any Alien being a free white person, who shall have resided within the limits and under the jurisdiction of the United States for the term of two years, may be admitted to become a citizen thereof on application to any common law Court of record in any one of the States wherein he shall have resided for the term of one year at least, and making proof to the satisfaction of such Court that he is a person of good character, and taking the oath or affirmation prescribed by law to support the Constitution of the United States, which Oath or Affirmation such Court shall administer, and the Clerk of such Court shall record such Application, and the proceedings thereon; and thereupon such person shall be considered as a Citizen of the United States. And the children of such person so naturalized, dwelling within the United States, being under the age of twenty one years at the time of such naturalization, shall also be considered as citizens of the United States. And the children of citizens of the United States that may be born beyond Sea, or out of the limits of the United States, shall be considered as natural born Citizens: Provided, that the right of citizenship shall not descend to persons whose fathers have never been resident in the United States: Provided also, that no person heretofore proscribed by any States, shall be admitted a citizen as aforesaid, except by an Act of the Legislature of the State in which such person was proscribed.

GLOSSARY

Alien: An alien is someone who is not a citizen, someone whose political allegiance is to a different nation.

Common Law Court: A court in which decisions are based on judicial precedents established by judges or courts and which can also serve as precedents for future cases.

Naturalization: A process by which someone who is not a citizen achieves citizenship.

Document Analysis

Given the existing ethnic and religious diversity of the states at the time the Constitution was adopted, and the perceived need to attract new immigrants to boost the national economy, one of the priorities for the First Congress was establishing some national regulation of the naturalization process. Inasmuch as some of the more divisive arguments during the Constitutional Convention involved the issue of slavery, the first thing that this short legislation did was to establish that the only individual eligible for citizenship was a "free white person." This provided a legal basis for denying citizenship not only to those of African ancestry, but to Asians, indigenous people, and anyone else deemed to be anything except "white."

If the applicant met the initial criteria, the remaining requirements were quite liberal in keeping with the desire to attract new immigrants. One could apply for naturalization to any common court in any state after a residence in the country of only two years and in the state of just one year. The aspiring citizen need only prove that s/he was of "good character," which could be done by a sworn witness, and take an oath of allegiance to the United States. The act also specifies that any children under the age of 21 who are living in the country when a person is naturalized are also automatically naturalized and that any child born to U.S. citizens while the parents are abroad will also be considered a citizen. The only restrictions were that the child of a female citizen born abroad to a father who had never resided in the U.S. would *not* be considered a citizen, nor would anyone be eligible who had already been rejected for citizenship by any of the states.

To implement the new policy, the law required the clerk of the court in which the naturalization oath was taken and the person approved to record the proceeding and the approval of the person so naturalized. However, the legislation did not specify the exact oath to be administered so in practice this varied across the country.

Essential Themes

In large part the 1790 legislation continued the relatively easy naturalization process adopted by the British government in 1740 with some significant differences. The most important of these was the elimination of the religious provisions of the earlier law, a change that was in accord with the Constitutional provision for freedom of religion in the First Amendment. It also reduced the residency requirement from the seven years required in the 1740 statue to only two years in keeping with the general desire to attract immigrants to the country. As James Madison stated, the purpose of the legislation was to "hold out as many inducements as possible, for the worthy part of mankind to come and settle amongst us ... to increase the wealth and strength of the community."

One of the stated reasons for the residency requirement was to discourage absentee landlords who might acquire land without actually living in the country. At the time, this was an important consideration because citizenship and land ownership were usually linked. One had to be a citizen to own land. Thus, the residency requirement prevented people from applying for

citizenship only to purchase land but with no intention of actually residing in the country.

With the growth of anti-immigrant sentiment during the Federalist administrations of George Washington and John Adams, immigration policy quickly became a political weapon. When it became obvious that recent immigrants were tending to vote for the rival Republican political faction led by Thomas Jefferson and James Madison, the Federalist-controlled Congress adopted the Alien and Sedition Acts, which were largely designed to eliminate any immigrant political influence. One result was the Immigration Act of 1795 which increased the residency requirement to five years and the Naturalization Act of 1798 which further increased it to fourteen years. When Jefferson gained the presidency his Republican followers reduced the residency requirement back to five years in 1802. Periodically, whenever nativism resurfaced, manipulation of the residency requirement once again became a political issue.

Bibliography and Additional Reading

Frank G. Franklin, *The Legislative History of Naturalization in the United States* (New York: Arno Press, 1969).

Margaret C. Jasper, *The Law of Immigration* (Dobbs Ferry, NY: Oceana Publications, 2000).

James H. Kettner, *The Development of American Citizenship, 1608–1870* (Chapel Hill: University of North Carolina Press, 1978).

Michael LeMay and Elliott Robert Barkan, eds., *U.S. Immigration and Naturalization Laws and Issues: A Documentary History* (Westport, CT: Greenwood Press, 1999).

James E. Pfander and Theresa R. Wardon, "Reclaiming the Immigration Constitution of the Early Republic: Prospectivity, Uniformity, and Transparency," *Virginia Law Review*, Vol. 96, no. 1 (2010), 359-411.

HOMESTEAD.

Land Office at *Brownville Neb*
January 20th 1868.

CERTIFICATE, } No. *1*

{ APPLICATION, No. *1*

It is hereby certified, That pursuant to the provisions of the act of Congress, approved May 20, 1862, entitled "*An act to secure homesteads to actual settlers on the public domain,*"

Daniel Freeman has

made payment in full for *S½ of NW¼ & W½ of NW¼ and SW¼ of NE¼* of

Section *twenty six (26)* in Township *four (4) N*

of Range *five (5) E* containing *160* acres.

Now, therefore, be it known, That on presentation of this Certificate to the

COMMISSIONER OF THE GENERAL LAND OFFICE, the said *Daniel Freeman* shall be entitled to a Patent for the Tract of Land above described.

Henry M. Atkinson

Register.

Certificate of homestead in Nebraska given under the Homestead Act, 1862.

■ Homestead Act

Date: May 20, 1862
Author: Aaron Galusha Grow
Genre: Act of Congress

Summary Overview

From the earliest colonial settlements in North America land was both a tangible economic asset and a draw to new settlers. It was also a source of contention between colonies, and later states, some of which asserted land claims west of the Appalachian Mountains that overlapped. A very practical problem of this ambiguity was that two states might sell the same parcel of land to different individuals who then each possessed a claim validated by a state, yet without clear title to the land. Congress moved to solve this dilemma by convincing the individual states to give up their claims and then, through a series of land acts, prescribing how the land would be settled. This legislation culminated in the Northwest Ordinance which established a pathway to statehood for the territories north of the Ohio and east of the Mississippi Rivers.

The Louisiana Purchase of 1803, which virtually doubled the size of the country, provided vast new tracts for settlement. However, land policy soon became enmeshed in the politics of the North-South divide. Northerners wanted to extend federal land grants to individual settlers, what came to be called the "Free Soil" movement. Southerners wished to make the land available for large-scale commercial agriculture based on slave labor. Frictions mounted over time as it became clear that the admission of new states might upset the even balance of political power in the Senate, thus inextricably linking land policy with the politics of the growing national chasm.

Defining Moment

By the beginning of the 1850s almost every new proposed legislation, baring occasional compromise, fell victim to the intransigence of sectional politics. With the nation beginning its inexorable decline into disintegration over the slavery issue, the Whig Party began a split along sectional lines that would lead to its extinction by the end of the decade. The new Republican Party began largely as an anti-slavery coalition, but also championed immigrant rights, internal improvements, and homestead legislation based on the free soil concept. An alliance of Southern Democrats and Northern pro-compromise Democrats prevented legislation relating to these concerns from coming to a vote in the Senate. Finally, in 1860 homestead legislation based on the Northern preference managed to make it through a Congress once the addition of new free states gave the North a majority in the Senate, only to be vetoed by Democratic President James Buchanan. All of this changed on April 12, 1861, with the firing on Fort Sumter.

Southern members of the House of Representatives and the Senate left Washington to return to their home states as each voted to leave the Union. Their absence in the coming years left the Republicans, aligned with some so-called War Democrats who supported the Lincoln administration, in a commanding position in the Congress. Lacking Southern opposition, bills which would normally never have been brought to vote not only emerged from committee but were quickly adopted. The homestead legislation owed a debt of gratitude to the English-born reformer George Henry Evans who lobbied hard for the act but passed away before it came to fruition, but its chief backers in 1862 were the prominent Republican editor of the *New York Tribune*, Horace Greeley, Democratic Senator Andrew Johnson of Tennessee, and Republican Speaker of the House of Representatives Galusha Grow from Pennsylvania who authored the original version upon which the final act was constructed. President Abraham Lincoln signed the Homestead Act into law on May 20, 1862.

Author Biography

A graduate of Amherst College in Massachusetts, Aaron Galusha Grow was born in Ashford, Connecticut, on August 31, 1823. After college he settled in Pennsylvania where he read law and gained admittance to the bar in November 1847. Taking an interest in politics, he was elected to the House of Representatives as a Democrat, but after three terms his opposition to the spread of slavery into the territories caused him to switch his allegiance to the new Republican Party over the Kansas-Nebraska controversy. He served from 1851 to 1863 including terms as chair of the Committee on Territories and Speaker of the House from 1861 to 1863.

In 1858 Grow was physically assaulted on the floor of the House by Democrat Laurence M. Keitt from South Carolina that led to a major free-for-all. With the beginning of the Civil War, Grow assumed the Speakership amid the crisis of national fragmentation. Although urgent military and economic issues naturally took precedence, Grow nevertheless found time to promote some of the internal improvement projects long supported by Republicans but blocked by Democrats—the Morrill Land Grant Act providing federal financial support for state agricultural and mechanical colleges, the Pacific Railway Act offering federal land grants for the construction of the transcontinental railroad, and the Homestead Act, which codified the Republican free soil principles into federal law. The final form of the homestead bill was based on Grow's original draft. Over the century after it was adopted, about 1.6 million homesteads were established under the legislation.

Following his service in Congress he became president of the Houston & Great Northern Railroad in Texas before returning to Pennsylvania to go into business. He later returned to the House of Representatives (1894-1903) before passing away in Glenwood, Pennsylvania, on March 31, 1907.

HISTORICAL DOCUMENT

Be it enacted by the Senate and House of Representatives of the United States of America in Congress assembled, That any person who is the head of a family, or who has arrived at the age of twenty-one years, and is a citizen of the United States, or who shall have filed his declaration of intention to become such, as required by the naturalization laws of the United States, and who has never borne arms against the United States Government or given aid and comfort to its enemies, shall, from and after the first January, eighteen hundred and. sixty-three, be entitled to enter one quarter section or a less quantity of unappropriated public lands, upon which said person may have filed a preemption claim, or which may, at the time the application is made, be subject to preemption at one dollar and twenty-five cents, or less, per acre; or eighty acres or less of such unappropriated lands, at two dollars and fifty cents per acre, to be located in a body, in conformity to the legal subdivisions of the public lands, and after the same shall have been surveyed: Provided, That any person owning and residing on land may, under the provisions of this act, enter other land lying contiguous to his or her said land, which shall not, with the land so already owned and occupied, exceed in the aggregate one hundred and sixty acres.

SEC. 2. And be it further enacted, That the person applying for the benefit of this act shall, upon application to the register of the land office in which he or she is about to make such entry, make affidavit before the said register or receiver that he or she is the head of a family, or is twenty-one years or more of age, or shall have performed service in the army or navy of the United States, and that he has never borne arms against the Government of the United States or given aid and comfort to its enemies, and that such application is made for his or her exclusive use and benefit, and that said entry is made for the purpose of actual settlement and cultivation, and not either directly or indirectly for the use or benefit of any other person or persons whomsoever; and upon filing the said affidavit with the register or receiver, and on payment of ten dollars, he or she shall thereupon be permitted to enter the quantity of land specified: Provided, however, That no certificate shall be given or patent issued therefor until the expiration of five years from the date of such entry; and if, at the expiration of such time, or at any time within two years thereafter, the person making such entry; or, if he be dead, his widow; or in case of her death, his heirs or devisee; or in case of a widow making such entry, her heirs or devisee, in case of her death; shall. prove by two credible witnesses that he, she, or they have resided upon or cultivated the same for the term of five years immediately succeeding the time of filing the affidavit aforesaid, and shall make affidavit that no part of said land has been alienated, and that he has borne rue allegiance to the Government of the United States; then, in such case, he, she, or they, if at that time a citizen of the United States, shall be entitled to a patent, as in other cases provided for by law: And provided, further, That in case of the death of both father and mother, leaving an Infant child, or children, under twenty-one years of age, the right and fee shall ensure to the benefit of said infant child or children; and the executor, administrator, or guardian may, at any time within two years after the death of the surviving parent, and in accordance with the laws of the State in which such children for the time being have their domicil, sell said land for the benefit of said infants, but for no other purpose; and the purchaser shall acquire the absolute title by the purchase, and be entitled to a patent from the United States, on payment of the office fees and sum of money herein specified.

SEC. 3. And be it further enacted, That the register of the land office shall note all such applications on the tract books and plats of, his office, and keep a register of all such entries, and make return thereof to the General Land Office, together with the proof upon which they have been founded.

SEC. 4. And be it further enacted, That no lands acquired under the provisions of this act shall in any event become liable to the satisfaction of any debt or debts contracted prior to the issuing of the patent therefor.

SEC. 5. And be it further enacted, That if, at any time after the filing of the affidavit, as required in the second section of this act, and before the expiration of the five years aforesaid, it shall be proven, after due notice to the settler, to the satisfaction of the register of the land office, that the person having filed such affidavit shall have actually changed his or her residence, or abandoned the said land for more than six months at any time, then and in that event the land so entered shall revert to the government.

SEC. 6. And be it further enacted, That no individual shall be permitted to acquire title to more than one quarter section under the provisions of this act; and that the Commissioner of the General Land Office is hereby required to prepare and issue such rules and regulations, consistent with this act, as shall be necessary and proper to carry its provisions into effect; and that the registers and receivers of the several land offices shall be entitled to receive the same compensation for any lands entered under the provisions of this act that they are now entitled to receive when the same quantity of land is entered with money, one half to be paid by the person making the application at the time of so doing, and the other half on the issue of the certificate by the person to whom it may be issued; but this shall not be construed to enlarge the maximum of compensation now prescribed by law for any register or receiver: Provided, That nothing contained in this act shall be so construed as to impair or interfere in any manner whatever with existing preemption rights : And provided, further, That all persons who may have filed their applications for a preemption right prior to the passage of this act, shall be entitled to all privileges of this act: Provided, further, That no person who has served, or may hereafter serve, for a period of not less than fourteen days in the army or navy of the United States, either regular or volunteer, under the laws thereof, during the existence of an actual war, domestic or foreign, shall be deprived of the benefits of this act on account of not having attained the age of twenty-one years.

SEC. 7. And be it further enacted, That the fifth section of the act entitled "An act in addition to an act more effectually to provide for the punishment of certain crimes against the United States, and for other purposes," approved the third of March, in the year eighteen hundred and fifty-seven, shall extend to all oaths, affirmations, and affidavits, required or authorized by this act.

SEC. 8. And be it further enacted, That nothing in this act shall be so construed as to prevent any person who has availed him or herself of the benefits of the first section of this act, from paying the minimum price, or the price to which the same may have graduated, for the quantity of land so entered at any time before the expiration of the five years, and obtaining a patent therefor from the government, as in other cases provided by law, on making proof of settlement and cultivation as provided by existing laws granting preemption rights.

GLOSSARY

Affidavit: A written statement the accuracy of which has been sworn to and signed before a notary public or other authorized official for use in a court of law.

Alienated: In property law, to be alienated means that a piece of property or a property right may be sold or transferred between parties. If there is a "restraint" on alienation it means that there is some restriction on the sale or transfer of the property.

Preemption: Preemption is a legal concept in which a law enacted by a higher authority takes precedence over one adopted by a lower authority. Federal preemption is based on Article VI, Clause 2, of the Constitution which provides that "This Constitution, and the Laws of the United States which shall be made in Pursuance thereof … shall be the supreme Law of the Land."

Tract Books and Plats: Tract books came into existence in the United States around 1800 to preserve a permanent record of transactions involving public lands. A plat is a map of a piece of property, drawn to scale, that serves as an official record used to determine ownership and in the transfer of ownership.

Explanation and Analysis of the Document

The act begins by defining to whom it applies—a citizen, or a person applying for citizenship, who is the head of a family or at least 21 years of age. Since Congress adopted the legislation in the early stages of the Civil War it also specifically excluded anyone supporting the Confederacy. The law would go into effect on the following January 1, after which any qualified person could claim up to one-quarter section of public land (160 acres) at a maximum of $1.25 per acre subject to any specific laws regarding the selected parcel. If a lesser amount of land was claimed, the person could file an additional claim provided that any individual could claim no more than 160 acres, a provision designed to restrict land to small farmers as was the intent of the Republican lawmakers. Given the influence of the anti-immigrant movement of the previous decade, it is noteworthy that the first section includes non-citizens so long as they have begun the process of becoming naturalized. It is also significant that the act specifies that "any person" may apply, not limiting the applicant by either gender or race. However, the latter did not mean that those of African ancestry were eligible since the Supreme Court had declared in the *Dred Scott* decision that they were ineligible for citizenship. That would later change once the Fourteenth Amendment was adopted.

Section 2 appears to include a qualification to the requirements set forth in the first section when it asserts that a person must be 21 years old "or" have served in the U.S. army or navy. It also specifies that the person obtaining the land must settle on it and farm it, a further requirement to guarantee that the land would be reserved for small farmers. Once the claimant paid a $10 registration fee s/he could occupy the land and, once the person could prove s/he had lived on the parcel and farmed it for five years the person could apply for a certificate of ownership. If the person died, the land would be transferred to the person's heir, or to the guardian, if the heir was not of legal age, to be held or sold for the benefit of the child.

Sections 3 to 5 require the register of land to make the proper entry into the land office books to legalize the claim, prohibit the use of the land to settle a previous debt, and stipulate that if a claim is abandoned before five years the land reverts to government ownership. Section 6 requires the Commissioner of the General Land Office to adopt policies and procedures to implement the Homestead Act and to guarantee that no individual acquired more than 160 acres and that the Commissioner be paid for this service in accordance with other such land transfers. It also reaffirms the right of those who have served in the armed forces to claim land even if they have not reached the minimum age. The final two sections also deal with administrative details, requiring of claimants an oath of allegiance to the United States and stipulating that a claimant may pay the full price of the land before the end of the five year period in order to obtain full title to the land before that time has elapsed.

Essential Themes

Passage of the Homestead Act was the largest land distribution adopted in the nineteenth century. It was a significant extension of federal law to provide for the organized settlement of the territory within the Louisiana Purchase, much as the earlier land ordinances had done for the land between the Appalachian Mountains and the Mississippi River. The legislation also carried forward the Republican Party view that the land ought to be restricted to small farmers rather than being opened to commercial agriculture. In this respect it also mirrored in a general sense the earlier thinking of Thomas Jefferson who viewed the United States as a nation of independent farmers. Eventually, some 1.6 million individual claims would be entered into the books totaling 420,000 square miles of land or 268,800,000 acres.

The act also cast into law the opportunity for immigrants to own land which was a significant issue for the nation's large German element that also formed an influential bloc within Republican ranks. In a larger sense, this also proved to be not only a stimulus to the post-Civil War westward movement, but also an incentive that attracted increasing numbers of Europeans to the United States. Although the Supreme Court had determined in 1857 that people of African heritage were not citizens, and federal law prevented them from becoming naturalized, once the Thirteenth and Fourteenth Amendments was adopted they also became eligible for land grants which proved a motivation for some to move west.

Bibliography and Further Reading

Eric Foner, *Free Soil, Free Labor, Free Men: The Ideology of the Republican Party Before the Civil War* (New York: Oxford University Press, 1970).

Jacob Freund, "The Homestead Act of 1862," *Journal of the West*, Vol. 52, no. 2 (Spring 2013), 16-21.

Grant Dinehart Langdon, "The Origins of the Homestead Act of 1862," *Journal of the West*, Vol. 51, no. 3 (Summer 2012), 56-61.

Lee Ann Potter and Wynell Schamel, "The Homestead Act of 1862," Social Education, Vol. 61, no. 6 (October 1997), 359-364.

Trina R. W. Shanks, "The Homestead Act: A Major Asset-building Policy in American History," in Michael Sherraden, ed., *Inclusion in the American Dream: Assets, Poverty, and Public Policy* (New York: Oxford University Press, 2005), 20-41.

■ Fourteenth Amendment to the U.S. Constitution

Date: July 28, 1868
Author: John A. Bingham
Genre: Constitutional Amendment

Summary Overview

In 1861 President Abraham Lincoln led the North into the bloodiest war in American history to preserve the Union. By 1864 this singular goal had been joined by the drive to eliminate slavery. The president's Emancipation Proclamation eliminated slavery in most of the nation, but it only applied to those areas in rebellion against the United States on January 1, 1863. If one lived in a loyal slave state—Delaware, Kentucky, Maryland, and Missouri—or in an area of the Confederacy already occupied by federal troops then slavery was still permissible. Something else was needed to extend freedom to the rest of the nation. Republicans in Congress were determined to make it happen.

In April 1864 the Senate adopted a proposed Thirteenth Amendment to make slavery illegal nationwide by a vote of 38-6, but two months later the House failed to obtain the required two-thirds majority vote with Democrats opposing the measure. In the wake of the failure, Lincoln began to exert all of the political pressure at his disposal, including the extensive patronage system of federal employment, to cajole and bribe enough negative votes to craft a favorable majority. After months of this horse-trading, the bill again came up for vote in the House, this time achieving the required margin by 119-56. In its final form it read: "Neither slavery nor involuntary servitude, except as a punishment for crime whereof the party shall have been duly convicted, shall exist within the United States, or any place subject to their jurisdiction."

Republicans rejoiced. The blight of slavery had finally been erased from the land forever.

Defining Moment

Although the Thirteenth Amendment eliminated slavery, it did not solve many of the issues that remained regarding people newly freed from bondage. Immediately after the conclusion of the Civil War the all-white governments of the defeated Southern states, reconciled to the fact that slavery would no longer be allowed, began thinking of ways to restrict ex-slaves so that, for all practical purposes, they would remain little better than the slaves they had been. Written into legislation, these new laws came to be known as "Black Codes" since they were designed to place limits on the freedom of the states' black population. In South Carolina, for example, the new state constitution failed to grant those of African ancestry the right to vote and included racial qualifications for serving in the state legislature. Other Black Codes provided that "no person of color shall migrate into and reside in this state, unless, within twenty days after his arrival within the same, he shall enter into a bond with two freeholders as sureties." Servants "shall not be absent from the premises without the permission of the master and must assist their masters in the defense of his own person, family, premises, or property." Africans who were unemployed or without a permanent address or who were stopped on the street and found to be without $10 on their person could be classified as vagrants. Vagrants were liable to fine or imprisonment, and if the fine could not be paid the person could be bound to a term of labor. The words "master" and "servant" were openly used, and Africans were legally prohibited from any employment other than in farming unless they obtained a special permit. Clearly, the Black Codes were designed to retain a system as close to slavery as possible.

Northern Republicans were infuriated. Congress refused to seat the new Southern delegations and adopted the Civil Rights Act of 1866 which sought to protect freedmen's rights by bringing them under federal protection. Despite the legislation, even some of its supporters believed it might be declared unconstitutional in view of previous court decisions. Northern anger was intensified when a series of racial riots swept through Memphis, New Orleans, and other Southern cities in the summer of 1866. Convinced that stricter measures were needed to protect the rights of the black population in the

South, and fearing that anything less than a constitutional amendment might be rejected by the Supreme Court, Northern Republicans acted to construct the Fourteenth Amendment.

Author Biography

There were several people who added substantively to crafting the Fourteenth Amendment, notably members of the Joint Committee on Reconstruction, but its primary architect was John A. Bingham. A Republican member of the House of Representatives from Ohio, he was born in Pennsylvania in 1815 but relocated to Ohio at the age of twelve to live with his uncle following his mother's death. His family were early abolitionists and he studied law at Franklin College where he met and became friends with Titus Basfield, the first person of African ancestry to graduate from college in Ohio. Returning to Pennsylvania, he was admitted to the bar in spring 1840 and to the Ohio bar later that year. He won his first election as district attorney as a Whig in Ohio in 1846.

Elected to the House of Representatives, he served from 1855 to 1863 when he was defeated running in a reorganized district. Most likely he lost because of the large number of soldiers who could not vote since they were away from home. This led to the introduction of the absentee ballot. Bingham was elected again in 1865, serving until 1873. During his entire service he was known for this abolitionist views and, throughout the Civil War and its aftermath, as a Radical Republican. In the spring of 1865 he served as judge advocate during the trail of the assassins of President Lincoln after which he was a leading figure on the Joint Committee on Reconstruction and played a key part in the impeachment proceedings commenced against President Andrew Johnson. President Ulysses Grant later appointed him minister to Japan. He died in Cadiz, Ohio, March 19, 1900.

HISTORICAL DOCUMENT

Section 1.

All persons born or naturalized in the United States, and subject to the jurisdiction thereof, are citizens of the United States and of the State wherein they reside. No State shall make or enforce any law which shall abridge the privileges or immunities of citizens of the United States; nor shall any State deprive any person of life, liberty, or property, without due process of law; nor deny to any person within its jurisdiction the equal protection of the laws.

Section 2.

Representatives shall be apportioned among the several States according to their respective numbers, counting the whole number of persons in each State, excluding Indians not taxed. But when the right to vote at any election for the choice of electors for President and Vice-President of the United States, Representatives in Congress, the Executive and Judicial officers of a State, or the members of the Legislature thereof, is denied to any of the male inhabitants of such State, being twenty-one years of age, and citizens of the United States, or in any way abridged, except for par-ticipation in rebellion, or other crime, the basis of representation therein shall be reduced in the proportion which the number of such male citizens shall bear to the whole number of male citizens twenty-one years of age in such State.

Section 3.

No person shall be a Senator or Representative in Congress, or elector of President and Vice-President, or hold any office, civil or military, under the United States, or under any State, who, having previously taken an oath, as a member of Congress, or as an officer of the United States, or as a member of any State legislature, or as an executive or judicial officer of any State, to support the Constitution of the United States, shall have engaged in insurrection or rebellion against the same, or given aid or comfort to the enemies thereof. But Congress may by a vote of two-thirds of each House, remove such disability.

Section 4.

The validity of the public debt of the United States, authorized by law, including debts incurred for payment of pensions and bounties for services in suppressing insurrection or rebellion, shall not be questioned. But neither the United States nor any State shall assume or pay any debt or obligation incurred in aid of insurrection or rebellion against the United States, or any claim for the loss or emancipation of any slave; but all such debts, obligations and claims shall be held illegal and void.

Section 5.

The Congress shall have the power to enforce, by appropriate legislation, the provisions of this article.

GLOSSARY

Abridge: In law, to abridge means to restrict or to reduce as in abridging a person's rights or privileges.

Bounties: During the Civil War, to which this refers, a "bounty" was a payment made to soldiers for voluntarily enlistment.

Due process of law: The principle that a person is entitled to fair and equal treatment within the legal system. This is guaranteed by the Fifth Amendment to the Constitution and by the Section 1 of the Fourteenth Amendment.

Immunities: Article IV, Section 2 of the Constitution states, in part, that "the citizens of each state shall be entitled to all privileges and immunities of citizens in the several states." In this sense "immunities" means that states may not discriminate against citizens from another state in the application of their fundamental rights.

Jurisdiction: Before a trial begins it is necessary to determine if the given court has the authority to hear the case; that is, whether it has jurisdiction. A court possesses jurisdiction over matters only to the extent granted to it by the Constitution or the legislation that governs it. Jurisdiction may take three forms: jurisdiction over the person, the subject matter, or to make the determination sought.

Explanation and Analysis of the Document

The Fourteenth Amendment was in some respects an attempt to codify the purposes of the earlier Civil Right Act of 1866 so that it would become part of the Constitution and thus unable to be ruled unconstitutional. Section 1 clarifies the status of people of African ancestry by stating unequivocally that anyone born in the United States, "and subject to the jurisdiction thereof," was a citizen of the nation and the state in which the person resided. It went on to further declare that "No State shall make or enforce any law which shall abridge the privileges or immunities of citizens of the United States; nor shall any State deprive any person of life, liberty, or property, without due process of law; nor deny to any person within its jurisdiction the equal protection of the laws." This clarity was necessary in light of the *Dred Scott* decision, which was still in effect, in which the Supreme Court found that Africans could not be citizens. Section 1 unambiguously asserts that they are, and furthermore that no state has the right to abridge the rights of citizens which also served to place the Civil Rights Act of 1866 on firm constitutional grounding and to counteract the Black Codes by making such discrimination illegal. The phrase "privileges and immunities" was taken directly from Article IV, Section 2, Clause 1 of the Constitution and "due process" from the Fifth Amendment.

Section 2 deals with representation in Congress, the purpose of which is to confirm that it will be based on the total population of each state counting the whole number of those people. This is obviously designed to eliminate the earlier Three-Fifths Compromise. One purpose of the first two sections is to make sure that Africans will be able to vote. Yet Section 2 goes on to contain a significant "but." The next sentence begins "But when the right to vote at any election … is denied … or in any way abridged, except for participation in rebellion," then the state in question would lose representation in proportion to the potential voters disqualified. This is why Radical Republicans considered this to be a compromise, one made essential by the need for Southern votes to adopt the amendment. They assumed that Southern states might devise some mechanism to restrict the rights of Africans so they gave Southern states an alternative. Accept the Fourteenth Amendment and be readmitted into the Union or reject it and remain a conquered territory with no Congressional representation. The compromise was that if the South accepted the amendment and found some way to disenfranchise black residents, the only penalty they would suffer was a reduction in representation in the House. Of course, Congressional Republicans planned to do exactly the same by disenfranchising former Confederates, but this is taken care of with the provision excluding that exception from the loss of representation provision.

Section 3 centers on those who have "engaged in insurrection or rebellion" or "given aid or comfort" to the enemies of the United States after "having previously taken an oath … to support the Constitution of the United States." Anyone who has done so will be precluded from holding the office of President, Senator, Representative, "or hold any office, civil or military, under the United States, or under any State." Authority to make exceptions was specifically given to Congress. This section was the result of two previous occurrences. The first was that when President Andrew Johnson attempted to welcome the former Confederate states back into the Union by presidential decree, some of the newly elected Southern Senators and Representatives had not only been Confederate civil and military officials, but some of the latter actually appeared to take their seats wearing their Confederate military uniforms. Outraged Republicans refused to either seat them or to recognize the legitimacy of their states' reentry into the Union. The second was that Johnson took upon himself authority for granting pardons to ex-rebels. This section was designed to undo all of that and place control of any exceptions in the hands of Congress.

Section 4 also dealt with the aftermath of the Civil War by declaring that the United States will honor its financial obligations but would *not* be liable for payment of any debts incurred by the Confederacy or by the emancipations of slaves. Enforcement of the amendment was placed in the hands of Congress through Section 5.

Essential Themes
Ratified on July 28, 1868, the Fourteenth Amendment was one of a series of Republican Civil War and Reconstruction era attempts to first eliminate slavery (the Emancipation Proclamation and the Thirteenth Amendment) and then to protect the rights of people of African

descent (Freedmen's Bureau, Civil Rights Act of 1866, Fourteenth Amendment, and Fifteenth Amendment). It was also consistent with Radical Republican efforts to punish the South for starting the Civil War and for the death of President Lincoln which many people blamed on Southern influence if not direct action (Wade-Davis Bill, some sections of the Fourteenth Amendment, First Reconstruction Act, and others).

The reference to "excluding Indians not taxed" in Section 2 was also consistent with usage at the time. Indigenous people living within the organized states, such as the Oneida in central New York, who lived as part of their surrounding communities were generally counted for representation and subject to the laws of the federal government and the various states within which they lived. Those who resided separately in tribal organizations were considered to be separate nations and treated as such. Congress signed treaties with them as it did with other foreign nations and, since they were not citizens, they were not subject to taxation or other requirements of citizenship. It was not until 1924 that Congress eventually voted citizenship to all indigenous people within the country. While the Fourteenth Amendment was being debated, women's rights advocates led by Elizabeth Cady Stanton, Susan B. Anthony, and others made an attempt to include wording specifically giving women the right to vote but they were unsuccessful.

The Fourteenth Amendment forms the basis for most modern civil rights legislation including the critically important *Brown v. the Board of Education* decision in 1954.

Bibliography and Further Reading
Joseph B. James, *The Ratification of the Fourteenth Amendment* (Macon, GA: Mercer University Press, 1984).

William Nelson, *The Fourteenth Amendment: From Political Principle to Judicial Doctrine* (Cambridge, MA: Harvard University Press, 1988).

William J. Perry, *We the People: The Fourteenth Amendment and the Supreme Court* (New York: Oxford University Press, 1999).

Jacobus tenBroek, *The Antislavery Origins of the Fourteenth Amendment* (Berkeley: University of California Press, 1951).

Robin West, "Toward an Abolitionist Interpretation of the Fourteenth Amendment," *West Virginia Law Review*, Vol. 94 (Fall 1991), 111–55.

■ National Quarantine Act

Date: April 29, 1878
Authors: Julian Hartridge and Roscoe Conkling
Genre: Act of Congress

Summary Overview

In 1800 the average life expectancy was about 37 years. Infant mortality was especially heavy, with 21.7 percent not living past the age of four. In large part this was due to the spread of communicable diseases such as measles, cholera, malaria, whooping cough, tuberculosis, and yellow fever. By mid-century, attempts were beginning to address these deadly threats at the national level. Between 1857 and 1860 four national meetings were held, all of which discussed in one form or another the possibility of establishing a national quarantine policy that would not only apply to those infected with communicable diseases inside the country, but to those attempting to enter the country. Yet, despite these efforts authority for health services continued to be decentralized among the states and individual cities.

Efforts to create a national health policy organization were revitalized in the early 1870s, but were soon sidetracked by a conflict between two of the movement's leaders, Dr. John S. Billings and Dr. John M. Woodworth. Secretary of the Treasury George S. Boutwell attempted to appoint Billings, an army major who believed that public health policy ought to be under the purview of the individual states, as the head of a federal public health effort, but the move was blocked by a U.S. Senate committee. When this failed, Boutwell appointed Woolworth as the Supervising Surgeon of the new Marine Hospital Service. Woolworth advocated the screening of immigrants as they arrived as a preventive measure to halt the entry of diseases into the country. He also believed that the Constitution provided the basis for federal supremacy in the establishment of public health policies to "promote the general welfare." To this end, a meeting in 1875 discussed the possibility of forming a federal health department but failed to agree on a specific recommendation.

Defining Moment

The early 1870s saw a number of major epidemics that took the lives of thousands of people. Especially hard-hit were the southern states, but a yellow fever epidemic traced to ships arriving from Cuba spread sickness and death throughout the eastern United States beginning in the summer of 1877. More than 27,000 were infected in New Orleans alone, with 4,000 succumbing to the illness. An estimated ten percent of the entire populations of Memphis and Vicksburg died. Panic spread, causing major population dislocations as people fled the infected regions. Trade and commerce suffered. The seriousness of the health crisis caused a public reaction in favor of government action.

President Rutherford B. Hayes appointed his former campaign manager, Senator John Sherman, as the new Secretary of the Treasury. Sherman was the brother of the famous Civil War general William Tecumseh Sherman whose personal medical officer during the March to the Sea was Dr. John M. Woodworth. Naturally, Woodworth's views on federal control of national health policy received official support. With this boost, a bill to address the issue, including protection against the arrival of infectious diseases in American ports, was introduced into the House of Representatives where Julian Hartridge, chair of the Committee on Interstate and Foreign Commerce, presented it for vote. In the Senate, Roscoe Conkling of New York introduced the same bill which became the National Quarantine Act when adopted on April 29, 1878.

Author Biography

Julian Hartridge was born in Beaufort, South Carolina, in 1829. He graduated from Brown University in 1848 and Harvard Law School in 1850, being admitted to the bar in Savannah, Georgia a year later. When the Civil War erupted he served for a year in the Southern army before being elected to represent Georgia in the Confederate Congress. Following the war he gained election to the U.S. Congress as a Democrat in 1874. He died in Washington, DC, in 1879.

A native of Albany, New York, where he was born in 1829, Roscoe Conkling grew up in a political family. After obtaining a basic education he passed up college to read law in Utica and was admitted to the bar in 1850, the same year the governor appointed him Oneida County District Attorney. Originally a Whig, he switched to the new Republican Party in time to campaign in the 1856 canvass. He was elected to the U.S. House of Representatives, serving from 1859 to 1863, quickly becoming associated with the anti-slavery leader Thaddeus Stevens and supporting both emancipation and the Lincoln Administration's war effort. After acting a Judge Advocate in the War Department, he was reelected to the House in 1864. As a leading radical who supported civil rights for African Americans, he was elected to the Senate in 1867 where he helped draft the Fourteenth and Fifteenth Amendments and the Civil Rights Act of 1875. He died in New York in 1888.

HISTORICAL DOCUMENT

Be it enacted by the Senate and House of Representatives of the United States of America in Congress assembled, That no vessel or vehicle coming from any foreign port or country where any contagious or infectious disease may exist, and no vessel or vehicle conveying any person or persons, merchandise or animals, affected with any infectious or contagious disease, shall enter any port of the United States or pass the boundary line between the United States and any foreign country, contrary to the quarantine laws of any one of said United States, into or through the jurisdiction of which said vessel or vehicle may pass, or to which it is destined, or except in the manner and subject to the regulations to be prescribed as hereinafter provided.

SEC. 2. That whenever any infectious or contagious disease shall appear in any foreign port or country, and whenever any vessel shall leave any infected foreign port, or, having on board goods or passengers coming from any place or district infected with cholera or yellow fever, shall leave any foreign port, bound for any port in the United States, the consular officer, or other representative of the United States at or nearest such foreign port shall immediately give information thereof to the Supervising Surgeon-General of the Marine Hospital Service, and shall report to him the name, the date of departure, and the port of destination of such vessel; and shall also make the same report to the health officer of the port of destination in the United States, and the consular officers of the United States shall make weekly reports to him of the sanitary condition of the ports at which they are respectively stationed;

and the said Surgeon-General of the Marine-Hospital Service shall, under the direction of the Secretary of the Treasury, be charged with the execution of the provisions of this act, and shall frame all needful rules and regulations for that purpose, which rules and regulations, shall be subject to the approval of the President, but such rules and regulations shall not conflict with or impair any sanitary or quarantine laws or regulations of any State or municipal authorities now existing or which may hereafter be enacted.

SEC. 3. That it shall be the duty of the medical officers of the Marine Hospital Service and of customs-officers to aid in the enforcement of the national quarantine rules and regulations established under the preceding section; but no additional compensation shall be allowed said officers by reason of such services as they may be required to perform under this act, except actual and necessary traveling expenses.

SEC. 4. That the Surgeon-General of the Marine-Hospital Service shall, upon receipt of information of the departure of any vessel, goods, or passengers from infected places to any port in the United States, immediately notify the proper State or municipal and United States officer or officers at the threatened port of destination of the vessel, and shall prepare and transmit to the medical officers of the Marine Hospital Service, to collectors of customs, and to the State and municipal health authorities in the United States, weekly abstracts of the consular sanitary reports and other pertinent information received by him.

SEC. 5. That wherever, at any port of the United States, any State or municipal quarantine system may now, or may hereafter exist, the officers or agents of such system shall, upon the application of the respective State or municipal authorities, be authorized and empowered to act as officers or agents of the national quarantine system, and shall be clothed with all the powers of United States officers for quarantine purposes, but shall receive no pay or emoluments from the United States. At all other ports where, in the opinion of the Secretary of the Treasury, it shall be deemed necessary to establish quarantine, the medical officers or other agents of the Marine-Hospital Service shall perform such duties in the enforcement of the quarantine rules and regulations as may be assigned them by the Surgeon-General of that service under this act: *Provided*, That there shall be no interference in any manner with any quarantine laws or regulations as they now exist or may hereafter be adopted under State laws.

SEC. 6. That all acts or parts of acts inconsistent with this act be, and the same are hereby, repealed.

GLOSSARY

Cholera: A sometimes fatal infection of the small intestine causing vomiting, diarrhea, and muscle cramps.

Marine: Something which relates to the sea. In the sense used in this document, it refers to shipping and seafaring.

Surgeon-General: The head of the U.S. Public Health Service.

Yellow fever: An acute and sometimes fatal viral disease characterized by alternating fever, chills, nausea, muscle pains, and loss of appetite.

Explanation and Analysis of the Document
In order to prevent contagious diseases from entering the United States, the National Quarantine Act required that no ship carrying passengers or animals inflicted with such a disease, and no ship arriving from any region infected with such diseases whether or not the diseases appeared among the passengers or animals at the time of arrival, could enter the United States. Any such ships or passengers were subject to exclusion not only under federal law, but under any existing state law as well. To assist in the enforcement of this, Section 2 required that consular officials or other designated representatives of the United States report the name of the ship, the date of departure, and the intended port of entry in the United States to both the Supervising Surgeon General of the Marine Hospital Service and the health officials in the anticipated port of arrival. Consular officials were further required to report the health status of the ports where they were located on a weekly basis, and charged the Surgeon General of the Marine Hospital Service with responsibility for enforcing the law. These provisions clearly placed oversight and enforcement of the public health laws as they applied to immigrants to federal rather than

state officials, thus ending that era of state control.

Once immigrants arrived, Section 3 specified that medical officers in each of the Marine Hospitals, assisted by the customs officers, were to be responsible for enforcement of the provisions of the National Quarantine Act. The Surgeon General of the Marine Hospital Service was to provide to state and local authorities advanced notice of the arrival of ships from infected areas, as well as "weekly abstracts of the consular sanitary reports and other pertinent information." Section 5 provided for enforcement, stipulating that it must be done in accordance with federal and state laws. In the absence of an existing federal system, this allowed for enforcement by personal from other agencies.

Essential Themes
The National Quarantine Act was the result of a gradual movement to bring public health policy under federal control. The legislation settled the ongoing difference of opinion on whether public health policy ought to reside with the states or the federal government and paved the way for creation of the National Board of Health in 1879 with one of its responsibilities being the determination

of when to enact a quarantine. Unfortunately for those supporting the active participation of the federal government in disease research and control, the National Board of Health authorization expired after only four years, on March 2, 1883. The National Quarantine Act did not change existing federal or state quarantine laws or procedures, but it did make the refusal of entry of an infected vessels, passengers, and animals a national policy that could be enforced by federal officials, policies that outlasted the existence of the short-lived National Board of Health.

At the same time the new law was also part of a natural progression in American immigration policy that was moving away from the virtual open admission policy established by the Naturalization Act of 1790 to more restrictive entry policies. This was the first stage in a series of Congressional actions linking health issues to immigration policies. The Immigration Act of 1891 denied entry into the United States of persons with "dangerous contagious disease" and medical examinations began on Ellis Island on January 1 of the following year. In 1893 another quarantine act required U.S. consular officers in foreign ports to verify that ships bound for the U.S. was free of disease. What these acts in effect did was to create an amalgam system of state and federal laws and enforcement mechanisms but backed by the authority and financial resources of the federal government.

Bibliography and Further Reading

Fitzhugh Mullan, *Plagues and Politics: The Story of the United States Public Health Service* (New York: Basic Books, 1989).

David Rosner, Ronald H. Lauterstein, Jerold M. Michael, "The National Board of Health: 1879–1883," *Public Health Reports*, Vol.126, no 1 (2011), 123-29.

Ralph Chester Williams, *The United States Public Health Service, 1798-1950* (Washington, DC: Commissioned Officers Association of the United States Public Health Service, 1951).

PRESIDENT WILL URGE RE-ENACTMENT OF EXCLUSION LAW.

WASHINGTON, D. C., Nov. 21, 1901.---Hon. James D. Phelan, San Francisco, Cal.; I have seen the President. I have the best authority for saying that he will not only recommend in his message the re-enactment of the Geary law, but will go further and urge that it be made stronger.

J. C. NEEDHAM.

CHINESE QUESTION ONE OF RACE

WE are the warders of the Golden Gate; we must stand here forever in the pathway of the Orient, and if there is any danger or trial it is for us to sound the alarm. I regard the Chinese question as a race question. I regard it as an international question; and above and over all, a question insulting the preservation of our civilization. The State of California, with its seven hundred miles of seaboard facing the Orient, is entitled to speak on this question for the people of the United States.—Excerpt from Mayor James D. Phelan's address at the Chinese Exclusion Convention.

WILL REMOVE ERRONEOUS IDEAS

THIS convention, meeting at this peculiar time, is to my mind the most potent instrument that could have been chosen to manifest to the people of the East that the story that California has changed her mind upon the question of Asiatic immigration is at least erroneous, if not absolutely false. California, through this convention, will tell the people of the East that she is as loyal as she ever was to her laboring population, and as determined as ever to protect them against the cheap man from the East.—Excerpt from Chairman Thomas J. Geary's address at the Chinese Exclusion Convention.

MAYOR JAMES D. PHELAN ADDRESSING THE DELEGATES TO THE BIG CHINESE EXCLUSION CONVENTION, WHICH HELD ITS INITIAL SESSION YESTERDAY AFTERNOON.

Leading Citizens Gather to Urge Re-enactment of the Geary Law.

CHINATOWN'S REMOVAL IS ADVOCATED

THE taxpayers of this city will soon be called upon to vote millions of dollars for schools, hospitals and other improvements. Gentlemen, there is no betterment that this city can procure which is more an urgent necessity than the removal of Chinatown to the southern end of San Francisco.—Excerpt from B. Sbarboro's address before the Chinese Exclusion Convention.

Strong Addresses in Behalf of the Laboring People of the Coast.

SENATOR PERKINS WOULD GO FURTHER.

IT is our people who pay the taxes that have built up our splendid institutions, and we should draw the line further, only this is not the time nor occasion. I would permit no one to come into this country unless he felt as he approaches these shores as Moses did when he approached the burning bush—that he stood upon sacred ground; and the voice coming out of that bush from the burning bush should be to the American people is "Unless you love freedom, unless you believe in republican institutions, unless you believe in the free public schools, you cannot come into this country."—Excerpt from Senator Perkins' address before the Chinese Exclusion Convention.

FRANK L. COOMBS VOICES HIS PROTEST.

AS I understand it, it is because we have thought that there might prevail in the East some idea or suspicion that the people of this country were not united as they were ten years ago that we have called this convention. And it is your office now, echoing the voice, the sentiment and the majesty of the people of this State, to send in clarion voices to the capital of the nation your protest, as it was your protest of old, against the admission of Chinese further into the State of California and into the nation.—Excerpt from Congressman Frank L. Coombs' address before the Chinese Exclusion Convention.

Front page of *The San Francisco Call* - November 20th 1911, Chinese Exclusion Convention

■ Chinese Exclusion Act

Date: May 6, 1882
Author: John F. Miller and Others
Genre: Federal Law

Summary Overview

Large-scale Chinese migration to the United States began with the "Gold Rush" in 1848. Most frequently, those seeking riches would use the "credit-ticket" system by which an agent arranged for passage on credit with the traveler agreeing to repay the loan with interest that was often substantial. As early as 1849, 325 Chinese entered California with 450 arriving in 1850, 2,716 in 1851 and 20,026 in 1852. By 1860 the U.S. census recorded 34,933 Chinese living in the U.S., more than 85 percent of whom resided on the Pacific coast.

With the rapid growth of the Chinese presence, reaction against the newcomers soon set in. As early as 1850 California enacted a Foreign Miners' License Tax of $20 per month, no doubt aimed at Chinese and Hispanic immigrants. In April 1852 Governor John Bigler clearly stated his opposition to the further arrival of Asians whom he claimed took precious metals from American soil without being liable to taxation or any of the other requirements of citizenship (A Chinese Letter to Governor John Bigler). This political sanction led to increasing restrictions on Asians over the following decade including "An Act to Prevent the Further Immigration of Chinese or Mongolians to This State" adopted by the California legislature in 1855. The law subjected new Asian immigrants to a fine of $400 to $600 and imprisonment for three months to twelve months. By 1860 Chinese had been excluded from most of the mines, while legal limitations also began to be imposed on those residing in San Francisco and other urban communities.

Defining Moment

In 1873 the United States was gripped with the beginning of an economic recession that would last for six long years. Although the full effect was not felt on the west coast for another year, when it was the crisis proved more severe because of the adoption by Congress of the Coinage Act of 1873. Sometimes referred to by detractors as the "Crime of '73," it changed U.S. monetary policy so that coins were no longer made from silver resulting in a downturn in the value of silver which exacerbated the recession on the west coast. With employment more difficult to find, calls for further regulation of Asian immigration intensified.

The movement for anti-Asian legislation was fueled not only by Gov. Bigler, but also by Denis Kearney, leader of the Workingmen's Party of California. With clearly racist motivations, Kearney is said to have ended every speech with the words "and the Chinese must go." Throughout the decade of the 1870s there were continual attempts to impose discriminatory regulations on the Chinese. San Francisco banned the use of poles for carrying merchandise since this was a typically Chinese custom, then placed a $60 tax on laundries that did not use a horse-drawn cart, again obviously aimed at Chinese businesses. The city also banned the use of firecrackers and gongs used in Chinese ceremonies and required the shaving off of all hair queues from Chinese who were arrested. In 1879 California attempted to change its state constitution to prohibit municipal hiring of Chinese and authorize cities to require them to live outside the city limits. This was declared unconstitutional as a violation of the Fourteenth Amendment. When California responded by attempting to make it illegal to grant fishing licenses to Chinese, the courts again found the legislation unconstitutional.

Calling upon supporters in the Democratic Party, anti-Chinese forces were able to get the U.S. Congress to pass legislation restricting the number of Chinese who could arrive in any single ship, but Republican President Rutherford B. Hayes vetoed the bill as a violation of the 1868 Burlingame Treaty with China. Rebuffed in their efforts, Democratic leaders in Congress determined to press on with attempts to completely eliminate Chinese immigration.

Author Biography

There was no single "author" of the Chinese Exclusion Act; rather, there were several key players. The first of these was Aaron A. Sargent, a member of the U.S. Senate from California, who in 1876 wrote the report of a committee sent to his home state to study the "Chinese question." A noted advocate of exclusion, it is not surprising that the final report argued in favor of prohibiting any further Chinese immigration into the country. The report, together with rising demands that something be done, brought into play the next characters when James B. Angell, president of the University of Michigan, was tapped by President Hayes to lead a mission to China to renegotiate the Burlingame Treaty. Angell was inclined to support anti-Chinese legislation, as was another member of the commission, John Franklin Swift, who had been a member of the California state assembly representing the County of San Francisco. The two, supported by the third member of the trio, William Henry Trescot of South Carolina, managed to push the reluctant Chinese government to sign the Angell Treaty which altered the Burlingame Agreement to allow the United States to restrict the number of Chinese laborers entering its borders.

The other major player was California Senator John F. Miller, chair of the Committee to Revise the Laws of the United States in the Forty-Seventh Congress (1881-83). A prominent active supporter of anti-Chinese measures, including the state's attempted constitutional revisions overturned by the federal courts, he viewed Asians as "barbarians" and once asserted "I believe that one such man as Newton, or Franklin, or Lincoln, glorifies the creator of the world and benefits mankind more than all the Chinese who have lived, struggled and died on the banks of the Hoang Ho." With the legal impediment of the Burlingame Treaty removed, Miller introduced into Congress what would become the Chinese Exclusion Act.

HISTORICAL DOCUMENT

Whereas in the opinion of the Government of the United States the coming of Chinese laborers to this country endangers the good order of certain localities within the territory thereof: Therefore,

Be it enacted by the Senate and House of Representatives of the United States of America in Congress assembled, That from and after the expiration of ninety days next after the passage of this act, and until the expiration of ten years next after the passage of this act, the coming of Chinese laborers to the United States be, and the same is hereby, suspended; and during such suspension it shall not be lawful for any Chinese laborer to come, or having so come after the expiration of said ninety days to remain within the United States.

SEC. 2. That the master of any vessel who shall knowingly bring within the United States on such vessel, and land or permit to be landed, any Chinese laborer, from any foreign port or place, shall be deemed guilty of a misdemeanor, and on conviction thereof shall be punished by a fine of not more than five hundred dollars for each and every such Chinese laborer so brought, and maybe also imprisoned for a term not exceeding one year.

SEC. 3. That the two foregoing sections shall not apply to Chinese laborers who were in the United States on the seventeenth day of November, eighteen hundred and eighty, or who shall have come into the same before the expiration of ninety days next after the passage of this act, and who shall produce to such master before going on board such vessel, and shall produce to the collector of the port in the United States at which such vessel shall arrive, the evidence hereinafter in this act required of his being one of the laborers in this section mentioned; nor shall the two foregoing sections apply to the case of any master whose vessel, being bound to a port not within the United States, shall come within the jurisdiction of the United States by reason of being in distress or in stress of weather, or touching at any port of the United States on its voyage to any foreign port or place: Provided, That all Chinese laborers brought on such vessel shall depart with the vessel on leaving port.

SEC. 4. That for the purpose of properly identifying Chinese laborers who were in the United States on the seventeenth day of November eighteen hundred and eighty, or who shall have come into the same before the expiration of ninety days next after the passage of this act, and in order to furnish them with the proper evidence of their right to go from and come to the United States of their free will and accord, as provided by the treaty between the United States and China dated November seventeenth, eighteen hundred and eighty, the collector of customs of the district from which any such Chinese laborer shall depart from the United States shall, in person or by deputy, go on board each vessel having on board any such Chinese laborers and cleared or about to sail from his district for a foreign port, and on such vessel make a list of all such Chinese laborers, which shall be entered in registry-books to be kept for that purpose, in which shall be stated the name, age, occupation, last place of residence, physical marks of peculiarities, and all facts necessary for the identification of each of such Chinese laborers, which books shall be safely kept in the custom-house; and every such Chinese laborer so departing from the United States shall be entitled to, and shall receive, free of any charge or cost upon application therefor, from the collector or his deputy, at the time such list is taken, a certificate, signed by the collector or his deputy and attested by his seal of office, in such form as the Secretary of the Treasury shall prescribe, which certificate shall contain a statement of the name, age, occupation, last place of residence, persona description, and facts of identification of the Chinese laborer to whom the certificate is issued, corresponding with the said list and registry in all particulars. In case any Chinese laborer after having received such certificate shall leave such vessel before her departure he shall deliver his certificate to the master of the vessel, and if such Chinese laborer shall fail to return to such vessel before her departure from port the certificate shall be delivered by the master to the collector of customs for cancellation. The certificate herein provided for shall entitle the Chinese laborer to whom the same is issued to return to and re-enter the United States upon producing and delivering the same to the collector of customs of the district at which such Chinese laborer shall seek to re-enter; and upon delivery of such certificate by such Chinese laborer to the collector of customs at the time of re-entry in the United States said collector shall cause the same to be filed in the custom-house anti duly canceled.

SEC. 5. That any Chinese laborer mentioned in section four of this act being in the United States, and desiring to depart from the United States by land, shall have the right to demand and receive, free of charge or cost, a certificate of identification similar to that provided for in section four of this act to be issued to such Chinese laborers as may desire to leave the United States by water; and it is hereby made the duty of the collector of customs of the district next adjoining the foreign country to which said Chinese laborer desires to go to issue such certificate, free of charge or cost, upon application by such Chinese laborer, and to enter the same upon registry-books to be kept by him for the purpose, as provided for in section four of this act.

SEC. 6. That in order to the faithful execution of articles one and two of the treaty in this act before mentioned, every Chinese person other than a laborer who may be entitled by said treaty and this act to come within the United States, and who shall be about to come to the United States, shall be identified as so entitled by the Chinese Government in each case, such identity to be evidenced by a certificate issued under the authority of said government, which certificate shall be in the English language or (if not in the English language) accompanied by a translation into English, stating such right to come, and which certificate shall state the name, title or official rank, if any, the age, height, and all physical peculiarities, former and present occupation or profession, and place of residence in China of the person to whom the certificate is issued and that such person is entitled, conformably to the treaty in this act mentioned to come within the United States. Such certificate shall be prima-facie evidence of the fact set forth therein, and shall be produced to the collector of customs, or his deputy, of the port in the district in the United States at which the person named therein shall arrive.

SEC. 7. That any person who shall knowingly and falsely alter or substitute any name for the name written in such certificate or forge any such certificate, or knowingly utter any forged or fraudulent certificate, or falsely personate any person named in any such certificate, shall be deemed guilty of a misdemeanor; and upon conviction thereof shall be fined in a sum not exceeding one thousand dollars, and imprisoned in a penitentiary for a term of not more than five years.

SEC. 8. That the master of any vessel arriving in the United States from any foreign port or place shall, at the same time he delivers a manifest of the cargo, and if there be no cargo, then at the time of making a report of the entry of the vessel pursuant to law, in addition to the other matter required to be reported, and before landing, or permitting to land, any Chinese passengers, deliver and report to the collector of customs of the district in which such vessels shall have arrived a separate list of all Chinese passengers taken on board his vessel at any foreign port or place, and all such passengers on board the vessel at that time. Such list shall show the names of such passengers (and if accredited officers of the Chinese Government traveling on the business of that government, or their servants, with a note of such facts), and the names and other particulars, as shown by their respective certificates; and such list shall be sworn to by the master in the manner required by law in relation to the manifest of the cargo. Any willful refusal or neglect of any such master to comply with the provisions of this section shall incur the same penalties and forfeiture as are provided for a refusal or neglect to report and deliver a manifest of the cargo.

SEC. 9. That before any Chinese passengers are landed from any such line vessel, the collector, or his deputy, shall proceed to examine such passenger, comparing the certificate with the list and with the passengers; and no passenger shall be allowed to land in the United States from such vessel in violation of law.

SEC. 10. That every vessel whose master shall knowingly violate any of the provisions of this act shall be deemed forfeited to the United States, and shall be liable to seizure and condemnation in any district of the United States into which such vessel may enter or in which she may be found.

SEC. 11. That any person who shall knowingly bring into or cause to be brought into the United States by land, or who shall knowingly aid or abet the same, or aid or abet the landing in the United States from any vessel of any Chinese person not lawfully entitled to enter the United States, shall be deemed guilty of a misdemeanor, and shall, on conviction thereof, be fined in a sum not exceeding one thousand dollars, and imprisoned for a term not exceeding one year.

SEC. 12. That no Chinese person shall be permitted to enter the United States by land without producing to the proper officer of customs the certificate in this act required of Chinese persons seeking to land from a vessel. And any Chinese person found unlawfully within the United States shall be caused to be removed therefrom to the country from whence he came, by direction of the President of the United States, and at the cost of the United States, after being brought before some justice, judge, or commissioner of a court of the United States and found to be one not lawfully entitled to be or remain in the United States.

SEC. 13. That this act shall not apply to diplomatic and other officers of the Chinese Government traveling upon the business of that government, whose credentials shall be taken as equivalent to the certificate in this act mentioned, and shall exempt them and their body and household servants from the provisions of this act as to other Chinese persons.

SEC. 14. That hereafter no State court or court of the United States shall admit Chinese to citizenship; and all laws in conflict with this act are hereby repealed.

SEC. 15. That the words "Chinese laborers", wherever used in this act shall be construed to mean both skilled and unskilled laborers and Chinese employed in mining. Approved, May 6, 1882.

GLOSSARY

Abet: A verb meaning to assist or encourage a person. It is usually used with someone aiding in the commission of a crime or other misconduct.

Customs: As used in this document, it refers to the government agency responsible for the collection of export or import taxes and enforcement of commercial and immigration regulations.

Master: The phrase "master of a vessel" refers to the commanding officer or captain of any ship.

Misdemeanor: As a legal term this refers to an offense against law that does not rise to the seriousness of a felony. Such transgressions are usually punishable by a fine, restitution, probation or imprisonment for a year or less.

Prima-facie: In legal proceedings a "prima-facie" case, literally meaning "at first face," is one that appears evident or correct until proof to the contrary is offered.

Explanation and Analysis of the Document

The Chinese Exclusion Bill passed the House of Representatives by a vote of 202-37 on April 12, 1882 and, in an amended form, the Senate by 32-15 on April 28. After the House agreed to the Senate amendments on May 3, President Chester A. Arthur signed it into law three days later. The act stipulated that it would be valid for ten years.

Under Article I of the Angell Treaty, the United States claimed the right to "regulate, limit, or suspend such coming or residence" of Chinese in America "but may not absolutely prohibit it." This was to apply "only to Chinese who may go to the United States as laborers, other classes not being included in the limitation." In return, the U.S. agreed to take action to see that those Chinese in the United States would not be "subject to personal maltreatment or abuse." To make the intent perfectly clear, Article II of the treaty stipulated that "Chinese subjects, whether proceeding to the United States as teachers, students, merchants or from curiosity, together with their body and household servants" would be able to travel freely to America and would enjoy "all the rights, privileges, immunities, and exemptions which are accorded to the citizens and subjects of the most favored nation." Because of these earlier treaty requirements the 1882 act limited its application to "Chinese laborers."

To comply with the requirements of the Angell Treaty, the act exempted Chinese laborers who were in the U.S. on November 17, 1880, the date that treaty was signed. It also restricted enforcement only to those who arrived after it went into effect with a ninety-day grace period before implementation. As an enforcement mechanism, ship captains who "knowingly" brought restricted persons into the country could be penalized by a fine of up to $500, a considerable sum at that time, and up to a year in prison *for each person* they landed.

Sections 4 and 5 addressed the issue of whether laborers already in the United States could legally return if they left for any reason. The answer was that they could, provided they obtain from the collector of customs a certificate of identity and intention. Similarly, Section 6 provided that the Chinese government make available to travelers who were not in the excluded class of laborers similar certificates, with English translations, which would be accepted by U.S. customs officials as "prima-facie evidence" of the person's eligibility for entrance.

As enforcement, Section 7 stipulated a fine of up to $1,000 and incarceration for up to five years for anyone falsifying one of these certificates in any way, including changing the original name of the person to whom it was issued. Again, ship captains were made responsible for providing required information on their passengers. In 1884 new legislation added supplementary requirements, as well as new conditions of the issuing of Chinese certificates to non-laborers, but because of the difficulty in administering this system Congress adopted the Scott Act in 1888 prohibiting the return of any Chinese laborers who left the country. In a further attempt to eliminate those already in the country, the Geary Act, which extended the original 1882 act for another ten years, also required that those Chinese legally residing in the United States had to obtain a certificate so stating and that any

Chinese who might be arrested were required to prove their legal presence in the United States; thus, rather than the government having to prove guilt the accused was required to prove innocence.

In accordance with the Treaty of Tientsin which established diplomatic relations with China in 1858, diplomats and their servants were specifically exempted from the provisions of the act. Finally, the act defined "laborers" as "both skilled and unskilled laborers and Chinese employed in mining" and specifically ordered that no Chinese were to be admitted to U.S.citizenship by any state or federal court. The latter provision applied to those seeking naturalization. This would lead to legal actions challenging the constitutionality of the provision.

Essential Themes

Although there had previously been racial limitations on who could become a citizen of the United States, the Chinese Exclusion Act was the first time in American history that members of a specific ethnic group were excluded from entry into the country. As such, this was a precursor of further racial and ethnic limitations to come such as the Immigration Acts of 1921 and 1924 which placed severe limits on people of Southern and Eastern European origin.

Since it established a new precedent, the law resulted in numerous legal challenges. In 1889 the U.S.Supreme Court sustained the constitutionality of the act in *Chae Chan Ping v. United States* and four years later it upheld the right of Congress to expel Chinese in *Fong Yue Ting v. United States*. However, in 1898 it found that Wong Kim Ark could not be denied entry into the country because he had been born and raised in the United States and could not therefore be deprived of his rights as a U.S. citizen.

The restriction on Chinese continued in effect until 1943 when, under the pressures of the wartime alliance with China, the Magnuson Act rescinded the prohibition against Chinese immigration and allowed for at least limited Chinese naturalization as citizens for the first time. However, it also prohibited Chinese from owning businesses or property, provisions that remained in force until the Immigration Act in 1965.

Bibliography and Further Reading

Andrew Gyory, *Closing the Gate: Race, Politics, and the Chinese Exclusion Act* (Chapel Hill: University of North Carolina Press, 1998).

Erika Lee, *At America's Gate: Chinese Exclusion During the Exclusion Era, 1882–1943* (Chapel Hill: University of North Carolina Press, 2003).

Charles J. McClain, *In Search of Equality: The Chinese Struggle against Discrimination in Nineteenth-Century America* (Berkeley: University of California Press, 1994).

Stuart Creighton Miller, *The Unwelcome Immigrant; the American Image of the Chinese, 1785-1882* (Berkeley: University of California Press, 1969).

John Robert Soennichsen, *The Chinese Exclusion Act of 1882* (Santa Barbara, CA: Greenwood, 2011).

■ Immigration Act of 1891

Date: March 3, 1891
Author: William D. Owen
Genre: Act of Congress

Summary Overview

Following the Civil War immigration was on the rise and becoming an important national issue. The Page Act of 1875 identified for the first time a class of "undesirable" immigrants that would be denied entry, specifically naming any Asians arriving as contract laborers and imposing fines and prison sentences for anyone forcing Asians, without their consent, to be held "to a term of service." This set the stage for both the Chinese Exclusion Act of 1882 and the Alien Contract Labor Law of 1885. The former prohibited the entry of Chinese laborers, forbade the naturalization of Chinese, and provided for the deportation of those who entered illegally. The latter extended the ban on Asian contract laborers to all alien contract laborers.

By the end of the 1880s it was becoming clear that the origins of European immigration were changing dramatically. During the decade of the 1870s, 2,812,191 aliens entered the United States, a figure that rose by a massive 86.6 percent to 5,246,613 during the 1880s. Additionally, it was apparent by the end of the latter decade that the origin of arrivals from Europe was experiencing a similar dramatic shift. Prior to 1870, Europeans came predominantly from the nations of Northern and Western Europe—Germany, France, Scandinavia and the British Isles. The new arrivals were increasingly dominated by peoples from Southern and Eastern Europe. The most numerous among these were Italians, Poles and Jews. These new peoples (new in the sense of the large numbers, since there were representatives of these groups in America long before the American Revolution) brought with them non-English languages, a multitude of non-Protestant religions (Catholic, Jewish, Orthodox, and others), and many other customs and traditions that differed from the dominant culture imported from the British Isles and Northwestern Europe. Both the numbers and the cultural differences fed into the rising nativist movement.

Defining Moment

In the last two decades of the nineteenth century the United States emerged as the largest and most rapidly growing economy in the world, producing a demand for new labor sources, a need that was fulfilled by immigrants. Yet, the marriage between American industry and immigrant labor was not universally accepted. A recession that ran from 1882 to 1885, with its high rate of unemployment, increasingly convinced the Knights of Labor and the American Federation of Labor to argue that the introduction of large numbers of unskilled European workers would decrease the price labor could command in the marketplace. Largely through the lobbying efforts of organized labor, the bill to exclude contract labor became law in February 1885.

In 1883 the American Economic Association offered a prize for the best essay on "The Evil Effects of Unrestricted Immigration" and four years later economist Edward Bemis suggested the use of a literacy test as a qualification for admission to the country. Principally because of the continuing economic arguments against immigration, in 1888 the House of Representatives organized a Select Committee to investigate the effects of immigration. The following year its findings were issued as the "Ford Committee Report" which concluded that it was time "to select the good from the bad, and to sift the wheat from the chaff." It is apparent, the Committee continued, "that this country cannot properly assimilate the immigration now coming to our shores." The report lent impetus to calls for new immigration legislation.

Author Biography

The Immigration Act of 1891 was modeled on the Chinese Exclusion Act of 1882, but the substance of the legislation developed out of a report submitted to the House of Representatives by William D. Owen, chair of the House Committee on Immigration and Naturalization. Born in Bloomington, Indiana, in September 1846, he entered Indiana University in 1865 but left after three years to read law. After pursuing careers as a member of the clergy, attorney, and newspaper editor, he was elected as a Republican to Congress for the sessions from 1885 through 1891. He is generally credited with a leading role in forming the 1891 act and guiding it through Congress, for which it was at the time often referred to as the Owen Immigration Law.

Some insight into Owen's view may be gained from the opening portion of his report to Congress which states: "The intent of our immigration laws is not to restrict immigration, but to sift it, to separate the desirable from the undesirable immigrants, and to permit only those to land on our shores who have certain physical and moral qualities. The inadequacy of the laws and amended laws on this subject is confessed, but your committee [meaning the House Committee Owen chaired] believe that the testimony taken in this investigation, and herewith submitted, contains suggestions which put in operation will cure the defects in existing laws, and that with added amendments the statute will furnish regulations that will be just to the immigrant and beneficial to the country. ... The time is far in the future when we will suffer from an overcrowded population. The territory of the United States will support seven times our present inhabitants. It will be fifty years before statesmanship need apprehend a burden from the influx of desirable aliens, but the time now is, and always will be, when the undesirable should be prohibited a landing in our country."

Following his service in Congress he was appointed the first Superintendent of the United States Office of Immigration (1891-93), then served as Indiana Secretary of State from 1895 to 1899. Later he pursued private interests including investments in coffee and rubber plantations in Mexico, but when his business partner was convicted of fraud and sentenced to prison in 1906, Owen fled the country and disappeared.

HISTORICAL DOCUMENT

An act in amendment to the various acts relative to immigration and the importation of aliens under contract or agreement to perform labor.

Be it enacted by the Senate and House of Representatives of the United States of America in Congress assembled, That the following classes of aliens shall be excluded from admission into the United States, in accordance with the existing acts regulating immigration, other than those concerning Chinese laborers: All idiots, insane persons, paupers or persons likely to become a public charge, persons suffering from a loathsome or a dangerous contagious disease, persons who have been convicted of a felony or other infamous crime or misdemeanor involving moral turpitude, polygamists, and also any person whose ticket or passage is paid for with the money of another or who is assisted by others to come, unless it is affirmatively and satisfactorily shown on special inquiry that such person does not belong to one of the foregoing excluded classes, or to the class of contract laborers excluded by the act of February twenty-sixth, eighteen hundred and eighty-five, but this section shall not be held to exclude persons living in the United States from sending for a relative or friend who is not of the excluded classes under such regulations as the Secretary of the Treasury may prescribe: *Provided,* That nothing in this act shall be construed to apply to or exclude persons convicted of a political offense, notwithstanding said political offense may be designated as a "felony, crime, infamous crime, or misdemeanor, involving moral turpitude" by the laws of the land whence he came or by the court convicting.

SEC. 2. That no suit or proceeding for violations of said act of February twenty-sixth, eighteen hundred and eighty-five, prohibiting the importation and migration of foreigners under contract or agreement to perform labor, shall be settled, compromised, or discontinued without the consent of the court entered of record with reasons therefor.

SEC. 3. That it shall be deemed a violation of said act of February twenty-sixth, eighteen hundred and eighty-five, to assist or encourage the importation or migration of any alien by promise of employment through advertisements printed and published in any foreign country; and any alien coming to this country in consequence of such an advertisement shall be treated as coming under a contract as contemplated by such act; and the penalties by said act imposed shall be applicable in such a case: *Provided* This section shall not apply to States and Immigration Bureaus of States advertising the inducements they offer for immigration to such States.

SEC. 4. That no steamship or transportation company or owners of vessels shall directly, or through agents, either by writing, printing, or oral representations, solicit, invite or encourage the immigration of any alien into the United States except by ordinary commercial letters, circulars, advertisements, or oral representations, stating the sailings of their vessels and the terms and facilities of transportation therein; and for a violation of this provision any such steamship or transportation company, and any such owners of vessels, and the agents by them employed, shall be subjected to the penalties imposed by the third section of said act of February twenty-sixth, eighteen hundred and eighty-five, for violations of the provision of the first section of said act.

SEC. 5. That section five of said act of February twenty-sixth, eighteen hundred and eighty-five, shall be, and hereby is, amended by adding to the second proviso in said section the words "nor to ministers of any religious denomination, nor persons belonging to any recognized profession, nor professors for colleges and seminaries," and by excluding from the second proviso of said section the words "or any relative or personal friend."

SEC. 6. That any person who shall bring into or land in the United States by vessel or otherwise, or who shall aid to bring into or land in the United States by vessel or otherwise, any alien not lawfully entitled to enter the United States shall be deemed guilty of a misdemeanor, and shall, on conviction, be punished by a fine not exceeding one thousand dollars, or by imprisonment for a term not exceeding one year, or by both such fine and imprisonment.

SEC. 7. That the office of superintendent of immigration is hereby created and established, and the President, by and with the advice and consent of the Senate, is authorized and directed to appoint such officer, whose salary shall be four thousand dollars per annum, payable monthly. The superintendent of immigration shall be an officer in the Treasury Department, under the control and supervision of the Secretary of the Treasury, to whom he shall make annual reports in writing of the transactions of his office, together with such special reports, in writing, as the Secretary of the Treasury shall require. The Secretary shall provide the superintendent with a suitable furnished office in the city of Washington, and with such books of record and facilities for the discharge of the duties of his office as may be necessary. He shall have a chief clerk, at a salary of two thousand dollars per annum, and two first-class clerks.

SEC. 8. That upon the arrival by water at any place within the United States of any alien immigrants it shall be the duty of the commanding officer and the agents of the steam or sailing vessel by which they came to report the name, nationality, last residence, and destination of every such alien, before any of them are landed, to the proper inspection officers, who shall thereupon go or send competent assistants on board such vessel and there inspect all such aliens, or the inspection officers may order a temporary removal of such aliens for examination at a designated time and place, and then and there detain them until a thorough inspection is made. But such removal shall not be considered a landing during the pendency of such examination. The medical examination shall be made by surgeons of the Marine Hospital Service. In cases where the services of a Marine Hospital Surgeon can not be obtained without causing unreasonable delay the inspector may cause an alien to be examined by a civil surgeon and the Secretary of the Treasury shall fix the compensation for such examination. The inspection officers and their assistants shall have power to administer oaths, and to take and consider testimony touching the right of any such aliens to enter the United States, all of which shall be entered of record. During such inspection after temporary removal the superintendent shall cause such aliens to be properly housed, fed, and cared for, and also, in his discretion, such as are delayed in proceeding to their destination after inspection. All decisions made by the inspection officers or their assistants touching the right of any alien to land, when adverse to such right, shall be final unless appeal be taken to the superintendent of immigration, whose action snail be subject to review by the Secretary of the Treasury. It shall be the duty of the aforesaid officers and agents of such vessel to adopt due precautions to prevent the landing of any alien immigrant at any place or time other than that designated by the inspection officers, and any such officer or agent or person in charge of such vessel who shall either knowingly or negligently land or permit to land any alien immigrant at any place or time other than that designated by the inspection officers, shall be deemed guilty of a misdemeanor and punished by a fine not exceeding one thousand dollars, or by imprisonment for a term not exceeding one year, or by both such fine and imprisonment.

That the Secretary of the Treasury may prescribe rules for inspection along the borders of Canada, British Columbia, and Mexico so as not to obstruct or unnecessarily delay, impede, or annoy passengers in ordinary travel between said countries: *Provided*, That not exceeding one inspector shall be appointed for each customs district, and whose salary shall not exceed twelve hundred dollars per year.

All duties imposed and powers conferred by the second section of the act of August third, eighteen hundred and eighty-two, upon State commissioners, boards, or officers acting under contract with the Secretary of the Treasury shall be performed and exercised," as occasion may arise, by the inspection officers of the United States.

SEC. 9. That for the preservation of the peace and in order that arrests may be made for crimes under the laws of the States where the various United States immigrant stations are located, the officials in charge of such stations as occasion may require shall admit therein the proper State and municipal officers charged with the enforcement of such laws, and for the purposes of this section the jurisdiction of such officers and of the local courts shall extend over such stations.

SEC. 10. That all aliens who may unlawfully come to the United States shall, if practicable, be immediately sent back on the vessel by which they were brought in.

The cost of their maintenance while on land, as well as the expense of the return of such aliens, shall be borne by the owner or owners of the vessel on which such aliens came; and if any master, agent, consignee, or owner of such vessel shall refuse to receive back on board the vessel such aliens, or shall neglect to detain them thereon, or shall refuse or neglect to return them to the port from which they came, or to pay the cost of their maintenance while on land, such master, agent, consignee, or owner shall be deemed guilty of a misdemeanor, and shall be punished by a fine not less than three hundred dollars for each and every offense; and any such vessel shall not have clearance from any port of the United States while any such fine is unpaid.

SEC. 11. That any alien who shall come into the United States in violation of law may be returned as by law provided, at any time within one year thereafter, at the expense of the person or persons, vessel, transportation company, or corporation bringing such alien into the United States, and if that can not be done, then at the expense of the United States; and any alien who becomes a public charge within one year after his arrival in the United States from causes existing prior to his landing therein shall be deemed to have come in violation of law and shall be returned as aforesaid.

SEC. 12. That nothing contained in this act shall be construed to affect any prosecution or other proceeding, criminal or civil, begun under any existing act or any acts hereby amended, but such prosecution or other proceedings, criminal or civil, shall proceed as if this act had not been passed.

SEC. 13. That the circuit and district courts of the United States are hereby invested with full and concurrent jurisdiction of all causes, civil and criminal, arising under any of the provisions of this act; and this act shall go into effect on the first day of April, eighteen hundred and ninety-one.

GLOSSARY

Contract Laborer: A contract laborer is one who signs a contract to work for a specified period of time or job, as opposed to an "employee" who is hired on a permanent basis. In immigration law at the time of this document, it referred to someone who was contracted as a laborer abroad and then brought to the United States to work.

Felony: The most serious category of crime in the U.S. Felonies can be broken into different classifications with punishments ranging from a minimum of one year in jail and a maximum of death.

Pauper: A very poor or financially destitute person. Usually it has referred, historically, to a person dependent upon charity or public assistance.

Polygamy: The practice in some cultures in which a man may have multiple wives or a woman multiple husbands.

Turpitude: An act of moral turpitude is one that is considered to be particularly shameful, vile, or depraved.

Explanation and Analysis of the Document

By 1891 a majority of people in Congress were interested in updating and centralizing enforcement for immigration laws based not only on increasing anti-immigrant feelings in the country but also on several issues that arose during and after the enactment of the Chinese Exclusion Act in 1882. The first question the legislation addressed was the further restriction of aliens wishing to enter the country. Added to the exclusion list of the earlier law were "All idiots, insane persons, paupers or persons likely to become a public charge," as well as those afflicted by a "loathsome or a dangerous contagious disease" and anyone convicted of "a felony or other infamous crime or misdemeanor involving moral turpitude, polygamists." Aside from the obvious wish to exclude those who would be unable to support themselves, disease-carriers, and criminals, much of the support for this came from people increasingly concerned with the growing overcrowding of the cities. A specific exception was made for those who had been convicted of "political crimes."

The act also made an effort to restrict contract laborers, a question that had surfaced in the debate over Chinese exclusion and was strongly supported by Samuel Gompers and the American Federation of Labor. Section 2 addressed this issue by prohibiting any legal actions dealing with it from being terminated for any reason without the consent of the original court of record. The importance of this portion of the law is made evident in Sections 3 and 4 where it is made illegal for anyone to offer employment to aliens or encourage them to emigrate to the United States in consideration of such employment, while also prohibiting any transportation companies or ship owners or their agents from similarly encouraging the migration of aliens with promises of employment. Under Section 6, violation of these provisions was made punishable by a fine of up to $1,000 and/or imprisonment of up to one year.

Section 7 of the act creates an "office of superintendent of immigration," under the supervision of the Treasury Department, in an attempt to organize immigration functions into a single government agency. Section 8 specifies the information regarding aliens to be required from the captains of ships arriving in the United States and further requires the medical inspection of each alien. Violations of the law by any official would be punishable by a fine of up to $1,000 and up to a year in prison. Further, Sections 10 and 11 provided that the cost for any aliens denied entry, or for any alien entering illegally, should be borne by the steamship company including not only transportation back to their original point of departure but their expenses while being cared for prior to their return departure. The law also provided for the establishment of similar inspections along the borders with Canada, and Mexico. It was this system that the new superintendent of immigration was to oversee.

Essential Themes

The Immigration Act of 1891 built upon the growing popular support for immigration restriction by expanding the list of excludable and deportable aliens and by increasing federal authority to deport immigrants. At the same time it allowed entry of those convicted of a crime provided it was designated as "political" in nature. Ellis Island in New York Harbor opened as the largest of the immigration inspection stations the following year.

The law unambiguously asserted federal control of immigration, eliminating the previous policy of allowing states to administer the immigration process. To increase the effectiveness of immigration control it systematized federal regulation of immigration by establishing an office of superintendent of immigration with the beginnings of a bureaucratic support organization and by specifying the information to be provided for each alien on arrival and the penalties for violation of the immigration law's provisions. Whereas previous legislation focused on people arriving at the coastal ports, the 1891 law added the Canadian and Mexican borders as areas where inspections should take place. This was a clear step toward further government oversight, control, and data collection in response to the growing national sentiment in favor of further immigration restriction. In 1895 the office was renamed the Bureau of Immigration with its head being the Commissioner-general of Immigration. In 1903, the Bureau was reassigned to the jurisdiction of the new Department of Commerce and Labor. Jurisdiction over legal issues arising from the immigration laws was given to the federal courts.

Bibliography and Further Reading

Roger Daniels, *Guarding the Golden Door: American Immigration Policy and Immigrants Since 1882* (New York: Hill & Wang, 2004).

Edward Prince Hutchinson, *Legislative History of American Immigration Policy, 1798-1965* (Philadelphia: University of Pennsylvania Press, 1981).

Michael C. Lemay and Elliott R. Barkan, *U.S. Immigration and Naturalization Laws and Issues: a Documentary History* (Westport, CT: Greenwood, 1999).

■ Immigration Act of 1917

Date: February 5, 1917
Author: Henry Cabot Lodge
Genre: Act of Congress

Summary Overview

As the movement to restrict immigration gathered traction in the late 1880s one of the proposals for limiting entry into the United States was the use of a literacy test. The idea was adopted by Massachusetts Senator Henry Cabot Lodge who, in 1892, introduced into Congress a bill to require a federal literacy test for immigrants to exclude "all persons physically capable and over twelve years of age who can not read and write with reasonable facility their own language." The most prominent proponents of this option were the members of the Immigration Restriction League founded in 1894 by three Harvard University alumni—Charles Warren, Robert DeCourcy Ward, and Prescott F. Hall. Support also came from the American Federation of Labor and its president, Samuel Gompers, which advocated the requirement as a means of keeping out "undesirables." Although the bill for a literacy test was approved by both houses of Congress in 1896, it was vetoed by President Grover Cleveland as a "radical departure" from traditional American policy.

The veto did not end the effort. In 1906 Gompers testified that "Both the intelligence and the prosperity of our working people are endangered by the present immigration. Cheap labor, ignorant labor, takes our jobs and cuts our wages." The A.F.L. convention that year endorsed the literacy test by a vote of 1,858 to 352. Lobbyists for the Immigration Restriction League and the American Federation of Labor renewed their efforts for a literacy test in 1906. The continuing push for further restriction led Congress to pass a new literacy bill in 1913, only to have it vetoed by President William Howard Taft. Another literacy bill was adopted by Congress in 1915 only to be vetoed by President Woodrow Wilson who quipped that such a law would test opportunity, not intellect. Despite these defeats, advocates of restriction persisted.

Defining Moment

The push for a literacy test in 1906 led to formation of the Dillingham Commission to investigate the effect of immigration on the United States. Although there were serious problems with the way in which the Commission's studies were conducted and their conclusions, the group's judgment that immigration ought to be restricted was generally accepted. Much of the Commission reports were aimed at proving the existence of purported intrinsic racial differences that argued for the restriction of people from Southern and Eastern Europe. These stereotypes found their way into popular literature as demonstrated in a study by T. J. Woofter who looked at publications during the years 1907 through 1914. He found "a marked change in public sentiment toward immigration" with the old restrictionist arguments based upon economics giving way to a rationale based upon "the undesirability of certain racial elements." At that time "race" was understood to include what we today would refer to as nationality; that is, Italians, Irish, Germans, Poles, and so on.

This new rationale became a favorite of nativist writers like Madison Grant whose *The Passing of the Great Race*, published in 1916, argued that the pure, superior American racial stock was being diluted by the influx of "new" immigrants from the Mediterranean, the Balkans and Eastern Europe. Grant's racist diatribe gained wide popularity among the American public and greatly influenced federal immigration legislation in the months leading up to passage of the Immigration Act of 1917.

Author Biography

The Immigration Act of 1917 was first introduced into Congress by Senator Henry Cabot Lodge who had advocated for such legislation as early as the January 1891 issue of the *North American Review*. It was Lodge's original proposal, supplemented over the years by members of the Immigration Restriction League, that transformed into the 1917 act.

Lodge was born in Beverly, Massachusetts, in 1850. He graduated from Harvard Law School in 1874 and earned a doctorate in political science from Harvard University two years later. Elected as a Republican to the state House of Representatives for 1880-82, he moved on to the United States House of Representatives (1887-93) and then the Senate (1893-1824). In 1890 he co-authored an attempt to enforce voting rights for African Americans that was defeated by a Democratic filibuster. Despite this support for African Americans, when eleven Italians were lynched in New Orleans in the same year he blamed the victims and called for the restriction of Italian immigration. Like many Progressives of his era, despite some liberal tendencies he consistently tended to criticize the poor for their condition and to use this belief to advocate for the restriction of immigration.

Lodge also based his opposition to immigration on racist beliefs that some national groups, often referred to at the time as "races," were innately inferior and, if allowed continued entry to the U.S., would pollute American culture. He made very specific his intent in pursuing the literacy test requirement: "[T]he illiteracy test will bear most heavily upon the Italians, Russians, Poles, Hungarians, Greeks, and Asiatics, and very lightly, or not at all, upon English-speaking emigrants or Germans, Scandinavians, and French. In other words, the races most affected by the illiteracy test are those whose emigration to this country has begun within the last twenty years and swelled rapidly to enormous proportions, races with which the English-speaking people have never hitherto assimilated, and who are most alien to the great body of the people of the United States."

HISTORICAL DOCUMENT

Sec. 2. That there shall be levied, collected, and paid a tax of $8 for every alien, including alien seamen regularly admitted as provided in this Act, entering the United States: Provided, That children under sixteen years of age who accompany their father or their mother shall not be subject to said tax. The said tax shall be paid to the collector of customs of the port or customs district to which said alien shall come, or, if there be no collector at such port or district, then to the collector nearest thereto, by the master, agent, owner, or consignee of the vessel, transportation line, or other conveyance or vehicle bringing such alien to the United States, or by the alien himself if he does not come by a vessel, transportation line, or other conveyance or vehicle or when collection from the master, agent, owner, or consignee of the vessel, transportation line, or other conveyance, or vehicle bringing such alien to the United States is impracticable.

Sec. 3. That the following classes of aliens shall be excluded from admission into the United States: All idiots, imbeciles, feeble-minded persons, epileptics, insane persons; persons who have had one or more attacks of insanity at any time previously; persons of constitutional psychopathic inferiority; persons with chronic alcoholism; paupers; professional beggars; vagrants; persons afflicted with tuberculosis in any form or with a loathsome or dangerous contagious disease; persons not comprehended within any of the foregoing excluded classes who are found to be and are certified by the examining surgeon as being mentally or physically defective, such physical defect being of a nature which may affect the ability of such alien to earn a living; persons who have been convicted of or admit having committed a felony or other crime or misdemeanor involving moral turpitude; polygamists, or persons who practice polygamy or believe in or advocate the practice of polygamy; anarchists, or persons who believe in or advocate the overthrow by force or violence of the Government of the United States, or of all forms of law, or who disbelieve in or are opposed to organized government, or who advocate the assassination of public officials, or who advocate or teach the unlawful destruction of property; persons who are members of or affiliated with any organization entertaining and teaching disbelief in or opposition to organized government, or who advocate or teach the duty, necessity, or propriety of the unlawful assaulting or killing of any officer or officers, either of specific individuals or of officers generally, of the Government of the United States or of any other organized government, because of his or their official character, or who advocate or teach the unlawful destruction of property; prostitutes, or persons coming into the United States for the purpose of prostitution or for any other immoral purpose; persons who directly or indirectly procure or attempt to procure or import prostitutes or persons for the purpose of prostitution or for any other immoral purpose; persons who are supported by or receive in whole or in part the proceeds of prostitution; persons hereinafter called contract laborers, who have been induced, assisted, encouraged, or solicited to migrate to this country by offers or promises of employment, whether such offers or promises are true or false, or in consequence of agreements, oral, written or printed, express or implied, to per-form labor in this country of any kind, skilled or unskilled; persons who have come in consequence of advertisements for laborers printed, published, or distributed in a foreign country; persons likely to become a public charge; persons who have been deported under any of the provisions of this Act, and who may again seek admission within one year from the date of such deportation, unless prior to their reembarkation at a foreign port or their attempt to be admitted from foreign contiguous territory the Secretary of Labor shall have consented to their reapplying for admission; persons whose tickets or passage is paid for with the money of another, or who are assisted by others to come, unless it is affirmatively and satisfactorily shown that such persons do not belong to one of the foregoing excluded classes; persons whose ticket or passage is paid for by any corporation, association, society, municipality, or foreign Government, either directly or indirectly; stowaways, except that any such stowaway, if otherwise admissible, may be admitted in the discretion of the Secretary of Labor; all children under sixteen years of age, unaccompanied by or not coming to one or both of their parents, except that any such children may, in the discretion of the Secretary of Labor, be admitted if in his opinion they are not likely to become a public charge and are otherwise eligible; unless otherwise provided for by existing treaties, persons who are natives of islands not possessed by the United States adjacent to the Continent of Asia, situate south of the twentieth parallel latitude north, west of the one hundred and sixtieth meridian of longitude east from Greenwich, and north of the tenth parallel of latitude south, or who are natives of any country, province, or dependency situate on the Conti-

nent of Asia west of the one hundred and tenth meridian of longitude east from Greenwich and east of the fiftieth meridian of longitude east from Greenwich and south of the fiftieth parallel of latitude north, except that portion of said territory situate between the fiftieth and the sixty-fourth meridians of longitude east from Greenwich and the twenty-fourth and thirty-eighth parallels of latitude north, and no alien now in any way excluded from, or prevented from entering, the United States shall be admitted to the United States, the provision next foregoing, however, shall not apply to persons of the following status or occupations: Government officers, ministers or religious teachers, missionaries, lawyers, physicians, chemists, civil engineers, teachers, students, authors, artists, merchants, and travelers for curiosity or pleasure, nor to their legal wives or their children under sixteen years of age who shall accompany them or who subsequently may apply for admission to the United States, but such persons or their legal wives or foreign-born children who fail to maintain in the United States a status or occupation placing them within the excepted classes shall be deemed to be in the United States contrary to law, and shall be subject to deportation as provided in section nineteen of this Act.

That after three months from the passage of this Act, in addition to the aliens who are by law now excluded from admission into the United States, the following persons shall also be excluded from admission thereto, to wit:

All aliens over sixteen years of age, physically capable of reading, who can not read the English language, or some other language or dialect, including Hebrew or Yiddish: Provided, That any admissible alien, or any alien heretofore or hereafter legally admitted, or any citizen of the United States, may bring in or send for his father or grandfather over fifty-five years of age, his wife, his mother, his grandmother, or his unmarried or widowed daughter, if otherwise admissible, whether such relative can read or not; and such relative shall be permitted to enter. That for the purpose of ascertaining whether aliens can read the immigrant inspectors shall be furnished with slips of uniform size, prepared under the direction of the Secretary of Labor, each containing not less than thirty nor more than forty words in ordinary use, printed in plainly legible type in some one of the various languages or dialects of immigrants. Each alien may designate the particular language or dialect in which he desires the examination to be made, and shall be required to read the words printed on the slip in such language or dialect. That the following classes of persons shall be exempt from the operation of the illiteracy test, to wit: All aliens who shall prove to the satisfaction of the proper immigration officer or to the Secretary of Labor that they are seeking admission to the United States to avoid religious persecution in the country of their last permanent residence, whether such persecution be evidenced by overt acts or by laws or governmental regulations that discriminate against the alien or the race to which he belongs because of his religious faith; all aliens who have been lawfully admitted to the United States and who have resided therein continuously for five years, and who return to the United States within six months from the date of their departure therefrom; all aliens in transit through the United States; all aliens who have been lawfully admitted to the United States and who later shall go in transit from one part of the United States to another through foreign contiguous territory: Provided, That nothing in this Act shall exclude: if otherwise admissible, persons convicted, or who admit the commission, or who teach or advocate the commission, of an offense purely political: Provided further, That the provisions of this Act, relating to the payments for tickets or passage by any corporation, association, society, municipality, or foreign Government shall not apply to the tickets or passage of aliens in immediate and continuous transit through the United States to foreign contiguous territory: Provided further, That skilled labor, if otherwise admissible, may be imported if labor of like kind unemployed can not be found in this country, and the question of the necessity of importing such skilled labor in any particular instance may be determined by the Secretary of Labor upon the application of any person interested, such application to be made before such importation and such determination by the Secretary of Labor to be reached after a full hearing and an investigation into the facts of the case: Provided further, That the provisions of this law applicable to contract labor shall not be held to exclude professional actors, artists, lecturers, singers, nurses, ministers of any religious denomination, professors for colleges or seminaries, persons belonging to any recognized learned profession, or persons employed as domestic servants: Provided further, That whenever the President shall be satisfied that passports issued by any foreign Government to its citizens or subjects to go to any country other than the United States, or to any insular possession of the United States or to the Canal Zone, are being used for the purpose of enabling the holder to come to the continental territory of the United States to the detriment of labor conditions therein, the President shall refuse to permit such citizens or subjects of the country issuing such passports to enter the continental territory of the United States from such other country or from such insular possession or from the Canal Zone: Provided further, That aliens returning after a temporary absence to an unrelinquished United States domicile of seven consecutive years may be admitted in the discretion of the Secretary of Labor, and under such conditions as he may prescribe: Provided further, That nothing in the contract-labor or reading-test provisions of this Act shall be construed to prevent, hinder, or restrict any alien exhibitor, or holder of concession or privilege for any fair or exposition authorized by Act of Congress, from bringing into the United States, under contract such otherwise admissible alien mechanics, artisans, agents, or other employees, natives of his country as may be necessary for installing or conducting his exhibit or for preparing for installing or conducting any business authorized or permitted under any concession or privilege which may have been or may be granted by any such fair or exposition in connection therewith, under such rules and regulations as the Commissioner General of Immigration, with the approval of the Secretary of Labor, may prescribe both as to the admission and return of such persons: Provided further, That the Commissioner General of Immigration with the approval of the Secretary of Labor shall issue rules and prescribe conditions, including exaction of such bonds as may be necessary, to control and regulate the admission and return of otherwise inadmissible aliens applying for temporary admission: Provided further, That nothing in this Act shall be construed to apply to accredited officials of foreign Governments, nor to their suites, families, or guests. ...

Sec. 18. That all aliens brought to this country in violation of law shall be immediately sent back, in accommodations of the same class in which they arrived, to the country whence they respectively came, on the vessels bringing them, unless in the opinion of the Secretary of Labor immediate deportation is not practicable or proper. The cost of their maintenance while on land, as well as the expense of the return of such aliens, shall be borne by the owner or owners of the vessels on which they respectively came. That it shall be unlawful for any master, purser, person in charge, agent, owner, or consignee of any such vessel to refuse to receive back on board thereof, or on board of any other vessel owned or operated by the same interests, such aliens; or to fail to detain them thereon; or to refuse or fail to return them in the manner aforesaid to the foreign port from which they came; or to fail to pay the cost of their maintenance while on land or to make any charge for the return of any such alien, or to take any security for the payment of such charge; or to take any consideration to be returned in case the alien is landed; or knowingly to bring to the United States at any time within one year from the date of deportation any alien rejected or arrested and deported under any provision of this Act, unless prior to reembarkation the Secretary of Labor has consented that such alien shall reapply for admission, as required by section three hereof; and if it shall appear to the satisfaction of the Secretary of Labor that such master, purser, person in charge, agent, owner, or consignee has violated any of the foregoing provisions, or any of the provisions of section fifteen hereof, such master, purser, person in charge, agent, owner, or consignee shall pay to the collector of customs of the district in which the port of arrival is located, or in which any vessel of the line may be found, the sum of $300 for each and every violation of any provision of said sections; and no vessel shall have clearance from any port of the United States while any such fine is unpaid, nor shall such fine be remitted or refunded: Provided, That clearance may be granted prior to the determination of such question upon the deposit with the collector of customs of a sum sufficient to cover such fine. If the vessel by which any alien ordered deported came has left the United States and it is impracticable for any reason to deport the alien within a reasonable time by another vessel owned by the same interests, the cost of deportation may be paid by the Government and recovered by civil suit from any agent, owner, or consignee of the vessel: Provided further, That the Commis-

sioner General of Immigration, with the approval of the Secretary of Labor, may suspend, upon conditions to be prescribed by the Commissioner General of Immigration, the deportation of any aliens found to have come in violation of any provision of this Act if, in his judgment, the testimony of such alien is necessary on behalf of the United States Government in the prosecution of offenders against any provision of this Act or other laws of the United States; and the cost of maintenance of any person so detained resulting from such suspension of deportation, and a witness fee in the sum of $1 per day for each day such person is so detained, may be paid from the appropriation for the enforcement of this Act, or such alien may be released under bond, in the penalty of not less than $500, with security approved by the Secretary of Labor, conditioned that such alien shall be produced when required as a witness and for deportation. No alien certified, as provided in section sixteen of this Act, to be suffering from tuberculosis in any form, or from a loathsome or dangerous contagious disease other than one of quarantinable nature, shall be permitted to land for medical treatment thereof in any hospital in the United States, unless the Secretary of Labor is satisfied that to refuse treatment would be inhuman or cause unusual hardship or suffering, in which case the alien shall be treated in the hospital under the supervision of the immigration officials at the expense of the vessel transporting him: Provided further, That upon the certificate of an examining medical officer to the effect that the health or safety of an insane alien would be unduly imperiled by immediate deportation, such alien may, at the expense of the appropriation for the enforcement of this Act, be held for treatment until such time as such alien may, in the opinion of such medical officer, be safely deported: Provided further, That upon the certificate of an examining medical officer to the effect that a rejected alien is helpless from sickness, mental or physical disability, or infancy, if such alien is accompanied by another alien whose protection or guardianship is required by such rejected alien, such accompanying alien may also be excluded, and the master, agent, owner, or consignee of the vessel in which such alien and accompanying alien are brought shall be required to return said alien and accompanying alien in the same manner as vessels are required to return other rejected aliens.

GLOSSARY

Anarchist: A person who believes in the complete freedom of the individual and rejects law and government. Anarchists often advocate the overthrow of authority by violence.

Bond: In the sense used in this document, a bond is an amount of money offered as security for the appearance of a person in court or another official hearing. If the person appears as ordered, the money it returned. If the person does not appear the money is forfeited.

Moral turpitude: In immigration law, this is a general phrase that refers to any crime that, according to public morals, is deemed especially abhorrent or depraved. Normally a person charged with such a crime is believed to have committed it purposefully and with malicious intent.

Quarantine: To quarantine a person means to keep one in strict isolation. This is normally done to prevent the spread of a contagious disease with the person being released once no longer contagious.

Document Analysis

The Immigration Act of 1917 was the most comprehensive legislation on the topic up until that time. The first section of this document, not reproduced above, defined some basic terms such as "alien" and provided for the application of the act to the Philippine Islands, then under American rule. Likewise not included are Sections 4-17 which generally define administrative procedures and punishments for failure to adhere to various portion of the law, as well as Sections 19-38 which continue these provisions, explain deportation procedures, enumerate exception to the policies, and prescribe other administrative procedures.

In keeping with previous acts, Section 2 of the 1917 statute levies a tax on each alien landed in the country, except for children under the age of sixteen, to be paid by the shipping line or other agency that brings them to the country. If the person enters individually, such as arriving by foot from Canada or Mexico, the alien is personally responsible for payment. For the first time, Mexican immigrants were *not* exempted from the tax. Similarly, Section 3 continues the then recent trend toward restricting groups by defining various categories of aliens who are excluded from entry. Then a lengthy enumerated list of exclusions largely repeats and more clearly defines those who have been previously excluded by one law or another. The terms "mentally defective" and "persons with constitutional psychopathic inferiority" that were part of the excluded list were in practice used to ban homosexuals. The list also extended the Chinese Exclusion Act of 1882 by including a wide geographic definition of Asia

with the provision that "natives of any country, province, or dependency situate on the Continent of Asia" would not be allowed to enter the United States. The area in question included the Asian Pacific Islands, Southeast Asia, the Indian subcontinent, part of the Middle East (modern Afghanistan, Iran, the Arabian peninsula), and parts of the Ottoman Empire and Russia. The only exceptions to be made were for government officials, religious people, specific professionals and students, tourists, and spouses and minor children. Because of the new geographic region created by this broadening of the original 1882 legislation, the 1917 law is sometimes referred to as the "Asian Barred Zone Act."

For the first time the law contained a provision for a literacy test, something that nativists had been arguing for since the early 1880s. This was the first time that Congress had adopted a law with the expected result of specifically limiting a large number of would-be European immigrants, and especially those from Southern and Eastern Europe upon whom it was anticipated the provision would fall most heavily. The legislation required that aliens over the age of sixteen who were "physically capable of reading" were required to prove their ability to do so either in English or in the language of the alien's choice. To verify they met the standard, aliens were required to read between 30 and 40 individual words that had been printed on cards. To be admissible, an alien had to prove the ability to read those words. Exceptions were made for the immediate family of previously admitted aliens or U.S. citizens, those who the Secretary of Labor affirmed were entering the country to escape religious persecution, aliens who had already resided in the country for five years and had returned for a visit to their home country of no more than six months, and aliens who were only passing through the U.S. to another destination.

Section 18 requires that any alien "brought to this country in violation of law shall be immediately sent back" to their original country with the cost of the trip, as well as any maintenance cost before the alien's departure, to be paid by the shipping company through which the person arrived. Violations of the law were subject to a fine with a ship being prevented from leaving harbor until all such fines were paid or a sufficient bond posted with the collector of customs.

Essential Themes

The 1917 law continued the trend toward stricter immigration requirements and increased exclusions that had begun in the 1870s. It increased the existing head tax and required Mexicans to pay it for the first time. It greatly expanded the various categories of excluded peoples and applied increased enforcement and penalty provisions. Beyond these factors, the legislation created an Asiatic Barred Zone that added to the Chinese, Koreans, and Japanese who had already been barred by previous laws people from eastern Asia, the Pacific islands, Southeast Asia, the Indian subcontinent, and portions of the Middle East. Finally, it added for the first time a literacy test that applied, with some exceptions, to everyone but was expected to especially limit those from Southern and Eastern Europe. In practice, the tax on aliens from Mexico was quickly suspended to encourage needed labor for industries and agriculture during World War I. It remained deferred until 1921.

The continuing increase on restriction fit into the pattern of rising nativism as well as the growing popularity of Social Darwinism and eugenics during the decades leading up to the law's enactment. However, much to the dismay of its proponents it has been estimated that in the twelve months between July 1, 1920, and June 30, 1921, over 800,000 aliens entered the country with only 1,450 being excluded because of the literacy test. The next steps in the process of closing the door would be the Immigration Acts of 1921 and 1924 that imposed not only maximum quotas, but extended those to specific nationality groups.

Bibliography and Additional Reading

Bill Ong Hing, *Defining America Through Immigration Policy* (Philadelphia: Temple University Press, 2004,), especially Chapter 3.

Desmond King, *Making Americans: Immigration, Race, and the Origins of the Diverse Democracy* (Cambridge, MA: Harvard University Press, 2000).

Erika Lee, *At America's Gates: Chinese Immigration During the Era of Exclusion, 1882-1943* (Chapel Hill: University of North Carolina Press, 2007).

Samuel McSeveney, "Immigrants, the Literacy Test, and Quotas: Selected American History College Textbooks' Coverage of the Congressional Restriction of European Immigration, 1917-1929," *The History Teacher*, Vol. 21 (1987), 41-51.

Cheryl Shanks, *Immigration and the Politics of American Sovereignty, 1890-1990* (Ann Arbor: University of Michigan Press, 2001).

Seema Sohi, (2013). "Immigration Act of 1917 and the "Barred Zone," in Xiaojian Zhao and Edward J. W. Park, eds., *Asian Americans: An Encyclopedia of Social, Cultural, Economic, and Political History* (Santa Barbara, CA: ABC-CLIO, 2013).

■ Immigration Act of 1924

Date: May 19, 1924
Authors: Albert Johnson and David Reed
Genre: Act of Congress

Summary Overview

By the end of the nineteenth century the United States had the largest and most rapidly growing economy in the world. Favorable government legislation combined with new technological inventions and growing consumer markets to produce an economy hungry for new workers, a need that was fulfilled by immigrants from the Old World eager for fresh opportunities in the New. Yet, organized labor looked upon immigration as a tool of management to flood the market with unskilled laborers who could just as easily be enlisted as strikebreakers as they could machine operatives. By 1892 both the Democratic and Republican Party platforms contained planks calling for immigration restriction.

Efforts to restrict immigration crystallized around the proposal for a literacy test, a concept enthusiastically endorsed by Massachusetts Senator Henry Cabot Lodge who believed it would privilege the "English racial strain" over all other groups. Although a literacy test was approved by both houses of Congress in 1896, it was vetoed by President Grover Cleveland as a "radical departure" from traditional American policy. In 1894, Lodge and a number of other New Englanders formed the Immigration Restriction League in Boston to push for a literacy test as a requirement for admission to the U.S., and other immigration "reforms."

The first two decades of the twentieth century marked a period of unprecedented growth in immigration. This prompted new calls for restriction. Lobbyists for the Immigration Restriction League and the American Federation of Labor renewed their efforts for a literacy test in 1906. This led to the formation of the United States Immigration Commission, better known as the Dillingham Commission, which purported to find that immigrants had a number of negative effects on the nation, particularly those from nations in Southern and Eastern Europe. Calls for action reached new levels of immediacy.

Defining Moment

In the wake of World War I the Red Scare brought with it renewed demands by nativists for closing the door. When Warren G. Harding took the oath of office as the new president in 1921 he summoned a special session of Congress to consider new legislation. The proposed measure cleared both Houses of Congress in a matter of hours. On May 19, 1921, the president signed into law a fundamental change in traditional U.S. immigration policy, the first federal legislation in American history designed specifically to limit European immigration. Senator Albert Johnson commented that "The welfare of the United States demands that the door should be closed to immigrants for a time. We are being made a dumping-ground for the human wreckage of the war." Calvin Coolidge, later to become president, stated that "Biological law tells us that certain divergent people will not mix or blend."

Between 1901 and 1920 an average of 625,629 people entered the United States each year. The Immigration Act of 1921 was designed both to limit total immigration to America, and to alter the composition of that immigration in favor of people whose origins lay in the nations of Northwestern Europe. To accomplish the first goal, the law imposed a maximum of 357,803 people allowed to legally enter the country from outside the Western Hemisphere in any single year. In addition, each nationality group was given a separate quota based upon three percent of the number of people from that group residing in the United States in 1910. This provision addressed the second goal by discriminating directly against Southern and Eastern Europeans.

The 1921 legislation was due to expire in 1924. To maintain the new restrictions, Albert Johnson led a drive to not only make its provisions permanent but to add further restrictive conditions. The result was the Immigration Act of 1924, often referred to as the National Origins Act or the Johnson-Reed Act.

Author Biography

The Congressional sponsors of the Immigration Act of 1924 were Representative Albert Johnson and Senator David Reed. Johnson was born in Springfield, Illinois, in 1869, and worked in journalism before becoming news editor for the *Washington Post* and later editor and publisher of the *Washingtonian* in Greys Harbor, Washington. He was elected to the House of Representatives as a Republican serving from 1913 to 1933. As chair of the Committee on Immigration and Naturalization he believed that the "stream of alien blood" pouring into America needed to be stopped because the new arrivals were not familiar with democratic forms of government and thus would be destructive to American ideals. Historian Dennis Wepman has described him as "an unusually energetic and vehement racist and nativist" who also led the Eugenics Research Association that opposed interracial marriage and advocated the sterilization of the mentally challenged. A noted anti-Semite, he once described Jews as "filthy, un-American, and often dangerous in their habits."

Born in Pittsburgh in 1880, David Reed earned his B.A. degree at Princeton University and his law degree at the University of Pittsburgh. After practicing law he was appointed to the U.S. Senate as a Republican to fill a vacancy left by the death of the incumbent. As expressed in a *New York Times* article, he believed that Southern and Eastern Europeans were "wholly dissimilar to the native-born Americans ... untrained in self-government [and] want neither to learn our common speech nor to share our common life." Thus, he believed it best that "our incoming immigrants should hereafter be of the same races as those of us who are already here, so that each year's immigration should so far as possible be a miniature America, resembling in national origins the persons who are already settled in our country."

HISTORICAL DOCUMENT

Be it enacted by the Senate and House of Representatives of the United States of America in Congress assembled, That this Act may be cited as the "Immigration Act of 1924."

Section 2.

(a) A consular officer upon the application of any immigrant (as defined in section 3) may (under the conditions hereinafter prescribed and subject to the limitations prescribed in this Act or regulations made thereunder as to the number of immigration visas which may be issued by such officer) issue to such immigrant an immigration visa which shall consist of one copy of the application provided for in section 7, visaed by such consular officer. Such visa shall specify (1) the nationality of the immigrant; (2) whether he is a quota immigrant [defined in an unexcerpted passage as, simply, "any immigrant who is not a non-quota immigrant"] ... or a non-quota immigrant (as defined in section 4); (3) the date on which the validity of the immigration visa shall expire; and such additional information necessary to the proper enforcement of the immigration laws and the naturalization laws as may be by regulations prescribed.

(b) The immigrant shall furnish two copies of his photograph to the consular officer. One copy shall be permanently attached by the consular officer to the immigration visa and the other copy shall be disposed of as may be by regulations prescribed.

(c) The validity of an immigration visa shall expire at the end of such period, specified in the immigration visa, not exceeding four months, as shall be by regulations prescribed. In the case of an immigrant arriving in the United States by water, or arriving by water in foreign contiguous territory on a continuous voyage to the United States, if the vessel, before the expiration of the validity of his immigration visa, departed from the last port outside the

United States and outside foreign contiguous territory at which the immigrant embarked, and if the immigrant proceeds on a continuous voyage to the United States, then, regardless of the time of his arrival in the United States, the validity of his immigration visa shall not be considered to have expired.

(d) If an immigrant is required by any law, or regulations or orders made pursuant to law, to secure the visa of his passport by a consular officer before being permitted to enter the United States, such immigrant shall not be required to secure any other visa of his passport than the immigration visa issued under this Act, but a record of the number and date of his immigration visa shall be noted on his passport without charge therefor. This subdivision shall not apply to an immigrant who is relieved, under subdivision (b) of section 13, from obtaining an immigration visa.

(e) The manifest or list of passengers required by the immigration laws shall contain a place for entering thereon the date, place of issuance, and number of the immigration visa of each immigrant. The immigrant shall surrender his immigration visa to the immigration officer at the port of inspection, who shall at the time of inspection indorse on the immigration visa the date, the port of entry, and the name of the vessel, if any, on which the immigrant arrived. The immigration visa shall be transmitted forthwith by the immigration officer in charge at the port of inspection to the Department of Labor under regulations prescribed by the Secretary of Labor.

(f) No immigration visa shall be issued to an immigrant if it appears to the consular officer, from statements in the application, or in the papers submitted therewith, that the immigrant is inadmissible to the United States under the immigration laws, nor shall such immigration visa be issued if the application fails to comply with the provisions of this Act, nor shall such immigration visa be issued if the consular officer knows or has reason to believe that the immigrant is inadmissible to the United States under the immigration laws.

(g) Nothing in this Act shall be construed to entitle an immigrant, to whom an immigration visa has been issued, to enter the United States, if, upon arrival in the United States, he is found to be inadmissible to the United States under the immigration laws. The substance of this subdivision shall be printed conspicuously upon every immigration visa.

(h) A fee of $9 shall be charged for the issuance of each immigration visa, which shall be covered into the Treasury as miscellaneous receipts.

DEFINITION OF IMMIGRANT.

Section 3.
When used in this Act the term "immigrant" means an alien departing from any place outside the United States destined for the United States, except (1) a government official, his family, attendants, servants, and employees, (2) an alien visiting the United States temporarily as a tourist or temporarily for business or pleasure, (3) an alien in continuous transit through the United States, (4) an alien lawfully admitted to the United States who later goes in transit from one part of the United States to another through foreign contiguous territory, (5) a bona fide alien seaman serving as such on a vessel arriving at a port of the United States and seeking to enter temporarily the United States solely in the pursuit of his calling as a seaman, and (6) an alien entitled to enter the United States solely to carry on trade under and in pursuance of the provisions of a present existing treaty of commerce and navigation.

NON-QUOTA IMMIGRANTS.

Section 4.
When used in this Act the term "non-quota immigrant" means

(a) An immigrant who is the unmarried child under 18 years of age, or the wife, of a citizen of the United States who resides therein at the time of the filing of a petition under section 9;

(b) An immigrant previously lawfully admitted to the United States, who is returning from a temporary visit abroad;

(c) An immigrant who was born in the Dominion of Canada, Newfoundland, the Republic of Mexico, the Republic of Cuba, the Republic of Haiti, the Dominican Republic, the Canal Zone, or an independent country of Central or South America, and his wife, and his unmarried children under 18 years of age, if accompanying or following to join him;

(d) An immigrant who continuously for at least two years immediately preceding the time of his application for admission to the United States has been, and who seeks to enter the United States solely for the purpose of, carrying on the vocation of minister of any religious denomination, or professor of a college, academy, seminary, or university; and his wife, and his unmarried children under 18 years of age, if accompanying or following to join him; or

(e) An immigrant who is a bona fide student at least 15 years of age and who seeks to enter the United States solely for the purpose of study at an accredited school, college, academy, seminary, or university, particularly designated by him and approved by the Secretary of Labor, which shall have agreed to report to the Secretary of Labor the termination of attendance of each immigrant student, and if any such institution of learning fails to make such reports promptly the approval shall be withdrawn....

Section 11.

(a) The annual quota of any nationality shall be 2 per centum of the number of foreign-born individuals of such nationality resident in continental United States as determined by the United States census of 1890, but the minimum quota of any nationality shall be 100.

(b) The annual quota of any nationality for the fiscal year beginning July 1, 1927, and for each fiscal year thereafter, shall be a number which bears the same ratio to 150,000 as the number of inhabitants in continental United States in 1920 having that national origin (ascertained as hereinafter provided in this section) bears to the number of inhabitants in continental United States in 1920, but the minimum quota of any nationality shall be 100.

(c) For the purpose of subdivision (b) national origin shall be ascertained by determining as nearly as may be, in respect of each geographical area which under section 12 is to be treated as a separate country (except the geographical areas specified in subdivision (c) of section 4) the number of inhabitants in continental United States in 1920 whose origin by birth or ancestry is attributable to such geographical area. Such determination shall not be made by tracing the ancestors or descendants of particular individuals, but shall be based upon statistics of immigration and emigration, together with rates of increase of population as shown by successive decennial United States censuses, and such other data as may be found to be reliable.

(d) For the purpose of subdivisions (b) and (c) the term "inhabitants in continental United States in 1920" does not include (1) immigrants from the geographical areas specified in subdivision (c) of section 4 or their descendants, (2) aliens ineligible to citizenship or their descendants, (3) the descendants of slave immigrants, or (4) the descendants of American aborigines.

(e) The determination provided for in subdivision (c) of this section shall be made by the Secretary of State, the Secretary of Commerce, and the Secretary of Labor, jointly. In making such determination such officials may call for information and expert assistance from the Bureau of the Census. Such officials shall, jointly, report to the President the quota of each nationality, determined as provided in subdivision (b), and the President shall proclaim and make known the quotas so reported. Such proclamation shall be made on or before April 1, 1927.

(f) There shall be issued to quota immigrants of any nationality (1) no more immigration visas in any fiscal year than the quota for such nationality, and (2) in any calendar month of any fiscal year no more immigration visas than 10 per centum of the quota for such nationality, except that if such quota is less than 300 the number to be issued in any calendar month shall be prescribed by the Commissioner General, with the approval of the Secretary of Labor, but the total number to be issued during the fiscal year shall not be in excess of the quota for such nationality.

(g) Nothing in this Act shall prevent the issuance (without increasing the total number of immigration visas which may be issued) of an immigration visa to an immigrant as a quota immigrant even though he is a non-quota immigrant.

NATIONALITY.

Section 12.

(a) For the purposes of this Act nationality shall be determined by country of birth, treating as separate countries the colonies, dependencies, or self-governing dominions, for which separate enumeration was made in the United States census of 1890; except that (1) the nationality of a child under twenty-one years of age not born in the United States, accompanied by its alien parent not born in the United States, shall be determined by the country of birth of such parent if such parent is entitled to an immigration visa, and the nationality of a child under twenty-one years of age not born in the United States, accompanied by both alien parents not born in the United States, shall be determined by the country of birth of the father if the father is entitled to an immigration visa; and (2) if a wife is of a different nationality from her alien husband and the entire number of immigration visas which may be issued to quota immigrants of her nationality for the calendar month has already been issued, her nationality may be determined by the country of birth of her husband if she is accompanying him and he is entitled to an immigration visa, unless the total number of immigration visas which may be issued to quota immigrants of the nationality of the husband for the calendar month has already been issued. An immigrant born in the United States who has lost his United States citizenship shall be considered as having been born in the country of which he is a citizen or subject, or if he is not a citizen or subject of any country, then in the country from which he comes.

(b) The Secretary of State, the Secretary of Commerce, and the Secretary of Labor, jointly, shall, as soon as feasible after the enactment of this Act, prepare a statement showing the number of individuals of the various nationalities resident in continental United States as determined by the United States census of 1890, which statement shall be the population basis for the purposes of subdivision (a) of section 11....

EXCLUSION FROM UNITED STATES.

Section 13.

(a) No immigrant shall be admitted to the United States unless he (1) has an unexpired immigration visa or was born subsequent to the issuance of the immigration visa of the accompanying parent, (2) is of the nationality specified in the visa in the immigration visa [sic], (3) is a non-quota immigrant if specified in the visa in the immigration visa [sic] as such, and (4) is otherwise admissible under the immigration laws.

(b) In such classes of cases and under such conditions as may be by regulations prescribed immigrants who have been legally admitted to the United States and who depart therefrom temporarily may be admitted to the United States without being required to obtain an immigration visa.

(c) No alien ineligible to citizenship shall be admitted to the United States unless such alien (1) is admissible as a non-quota immigrant under the provisions of subdivision (b), (d), or (e) of section 4, or (2) is the wife, or the unmarried child under 18 years of age, of an immigrant admissible under such subdivision (d), and is accompanying or following to join him, or (3) is not an immigrant as defined in section 3.

(d) The Secretary of Labor may admit to the United States any otherwise admissible immigrant not admissible under clause (2) or (3) of subdivision (a) of this section, if satisfied that such inadmissibility was not known to, and could not have been ascertained by the exercise of reasonable diligence by, such immigrant prior to the departure of the vessel from the last port outside the United States and outside foreign contiguous territory or, in the case of an immigrant coming from foreign contiguous territory, prior to the application of the immigrant for admission.

(e) No quota immigrant shall be admitted under subdivision (d) if the entire number of immigration visas which may be issued to quota immigrants of the same nationality for the fiscal year has already been issued. If such entire number of immigration visas has not been issued, then the Secretary of State, upon the admission of a quota immigrant under subdivision (d), shall reduce by one the number of immigration visas which may be issued to quota immigrants of the same nationality during the fiscal year in which such immigrant is admitted; but if the Secretary of State finds that it will not be practicable to make such reduction before the end of such fiscal year, then such immigrant shall not be admitted.

(f) Nothing in this section shall authorize the remission or refunding of a fine, liability to which has accrued under section 16.

DEPORTATION

Section 14.

Any alien who at any time after entering the United States is found to have been at the time of entry not entitled under this Act to enter the United States, or to have remained therein for a longer time than permitted under this Act or regulations made thereunder, shall be taken into custody and deported in the same manner as provided for in sections 19 and 20 of the Immigration Act of 1917: Provided, That the Secretary of Labor may, under such conditions and restrictions as to support and care as he may deem necessary, permit permanently to remain in the United States, any alien child who, when under sixteen years of age was heretofore temporarily admitted to the United States and who is now within the United States and either of whose parents is a citizen of the United States....

GLOSSARY

Aborigines: Members of a group of people considered to be the earliest known inhabitants of a particular country or region.

Bona fide: A Latin term meaning something done in "good faith," in American legal writing it refers to something that is real, genuine, or done in good faith.

Deportation: The act of removing an alien from a country where the person's presence is either unlawful or presents some perceived danger.

Fiscal year: As opposed to the calendar year beginning January 1 and ending December 31, the fiscal year is an accounting device used for the purpose of tracking expenses, taxation, revenue flow, and other business purposes. It covers a twelve-month period whose beginning and ending dates are determined by the business, organization, or governmental agency in which it is used.

Passport: An official document issued by a government identifying a person and certifying that the person is a citizen of the issuing nation. It is necessary for exiting and reentering the issuing country and is usually required to enter other nations.

Quota: A fixed number that is used as a goal or a limit. In immigration policy it refers to the maximum number of people who may be admitted under certain conditions or in various categories established by a government agency.

Visa: An official stamp or endorsement made on a passport to certify that the bearer is allowed to enter or leave a country. Often the visa indicates other limitations as well, such as the purpose of the visit (student, tourist, work, diplomat, etc.) or the length of stay allowed in a country.

Explanation and Analysis of the Document

After explaining the administrative procedures to be followed by consular officers in issuing visas for travel to the United States, including the key provision that no visa was to be issued if the official believed the person would be inadmissible to the U.S., the act describes the categories of people who may and may not be admissible. Taking its cue from the Immigration Act of 1921, these categories were largely based on the perceived nationality of the immigrant, a concept that was at the time largely equated with what we call national or ethnic groups today.

Section 3 defined an "immigrant" as an alien attempting to enter the United States but made exceptions for diplomatic personnel (including their families and personal employees), tourists or those on temporary business, people in transit to other destinations outside the U. S., and seamen arriving temporarily as part of their employment. All others were to be considered immigrants and thus came under the applicable immigration and naturalization laws.

Within the category of immigrants, Section 4 defines those people who would not be subject to entry under the existing quotas. These were to include the wives and unmarried children under the age of eighteen of citizens, those who previously entered as immigrants and were returning from a temporary visit abroad, people from the Western Hemisphere, members of the clergy (and the spouse and unmarried children under eighteen years of age), and students. The major result of this provision was the beginning of immigration from the Spanish-speaking nations in the Western Hemisphere, especially Mexico.

Section 11 begins to deal with the major changes envisioned by the legislation's sponsors. The number of people of each "nationality" eligible to enter the country each year was not only revised downward from three percent in the 1921 law to two percent in the 1924 act, but the base year was moved back from the 1910 census to the enumeration of 1890. This effectively eliminated hundreds of thousands of Southern and Eastern Europeans who entered after 1890, along with their offspring, thereby decreasing the total admissible in the future to much less than the two percent might on the surface suggest. Each nationality subject to the quotas would have a minimum allowable allocation of 100 per year. There was also the interesting provision that "Nothing in this Act shall prevent the issuance (without increasing the total number of immigration visas which may be issued) of an immigration visa to an immigrant as a quota immigrant even though he is a non-quota immigrant." What this did was to allow a further reduction in the quotas of admissible immigrants of some nationalities by issuing immigrants not subject to the quota a visa that would nevertheless count against that quota.

A key issue in the administration of the new law was the definition of "nationality." This was to be determined, according to Section 12, by country of birth with "colonies, dependencies, or self-governing dominions" enumerated separately in the 1890 census continuing to be considered as separate nations for the purposes of this definition. Provisions were also established for determining the nationality of minor children whose parents were born in separate nations.

Having defined nationality, Section 13 described a number of categories of people that were excluded from entry. These included those without a valid visa, accompanying children born after the issuance of a visa to the parents, those whose nationality was not correctly stated on their visa, non-quota immigrants, and those "otherwise admissible under the immigration laws." No alien could be admitted if the quota for the person's nationality had already been filled for that year or, additionally, "No alien ineligible to citizenship shall be admitted to the United States unless such alien is admissible as a non-quota immigrant." This section was important because what it did was to deny entry to Asians or those from Africa since the Immigration Act of 1790 specified that only "white" people could become citizens.

As an enforcement mechanism, Section 14 of the law provided that aliens could be deported "at any time" if "found to have been at the time of entry not entitled under this Act to enter the United States, or to have remained therein for a longer time than permitted." Section 23 asserts that "the burden of proof shall be upon the alien to establish that he is not subject to exclusion under any of the provisions of the immigration laws," while Sections 24 to 32 mostly repeat provisions of earlier legislation relating to fines applicable to steamship lines and the illegal landing of

inadmissible aliens.

Essential Themes

The Immigration Act of 1924 continued the prevailing nativist theme of increasing restrictions on immigration, both in terms of overall numbers and specifically *who* could be admitted. In the first instance, the new law reduced the maximum number of people who could legally be admitted to the United States by changing the formula on which it was calculated from three percent of the 1910 census number to two percent of the 1890 figure. The effect was that the 357,803 stipulated as the legal entry number in 1921 reduced to 164,667, a decrease of 54 percent. This was also 79.5 percent below the approximately 805,000 who arrived in the United States as recently as 1921.

The 1924 legislation was unmistakably designed to discriminate against people from Southern and Eastern Europe. This can be seen in the fact that the basis for calculating the quota percentage of each group was moved back from the 1910 census to the 1890 enumeration, thus excluding the massive immigration from those regions that arrived in the two decades between these enumerations. The result was exactly what the framers of the legislation intended, some 86.5 percent of the available slots under the new quotas were reserved for people from Northern and Western Europe. Conversely, the total quota for all Southern and Eastern Europeans was only 11.2 percent. A mere 2.3 percent was allocated for people originating in Africa, the Middle East, and the Pacific region. There had been an average of about 200,000 Italians per year arriving in the United States between 1900 and 1910; under the 1924 act their maximum annual quota was 3,845, a reduction of 98.1 percent. For Poles, the second largest nationality group arriving after Italians between 1880 and 1920, the maximum allowable quota declined by more than 94 percent. As a result, the total number of Poles arriving in the U.S. between 1921 and 1940 was less than in any single year between 1900 and 1914.

Finally, the act allowed free entry to peoples from the Western Hemisphere but excluded Asians. The former led to an abrupt increase in Hispanic immigrants, especially those from Mexico. The latter further strained already taut relations with Japan which believed it was both an insult and an abrogation of the Gentlemen's Agreement reached in 1907. These discriminatory policies, against Southern and Eastern Europeans and Asians, remained in effect for more than forty years, not being abandoned until the Immigration Act of 1965.

Bibliography and Further Reading

Roger Daniels, *Guarding the Golden Door: American Immigration Policy and Immigrants since 1882* (Boston & New York: Hill and Wang, 2004).

Edward Prince Hutchinson, *Legislative History of American Immigration Policy, 1768–1965* (Philadelphia: University of Pennsylvania Press, 1981).

Michael LeMay and Elliot Robert Barkan, eds., *U.S. Immigration and Naturalization Laws and Issues: A Documentary History* (Westport, CT: Greenwood Press, 1999).

Mae M. Ngai, "The Architecture of Race in American Immigration Law: A Reexamination of the Immigration Act of 1924," *Journal of American History*, Vol. 86, no. 1 (1999), 67-92.

Dennis Wepman, *Immigration: From the Founding of Virginia to the Closing of Ellis Island* (New York: Facts on File, 2002).

■ McCarran-Walter Act

Date: June 27, 1952
Author: Patrick McCarran and Francis Walter
Genre: Federal Law

Summary Overview

The rise of nativism between 1880 and 1920 finally led in 1921 and 1924 to legislation greatly restricting the total number of people entering the country and specifically discriminating against those from Southern and Eastern Europe. Because of this the number of people entering the country fell precipitously. With the beginning of the Great Depression, President Herbert Hoover restricted entry even further so that in 1933 only some 23,000 people arrived. At the same time, hundreds of thousands of Mexican immigrants were forcibly returned to their native country. In June 1933 Franklin Roosevelt issued Executive Order 6166 consolidating the Bureau of Immigration and Bureau of Naturalization into a single Immigration and Naturalization Service charged mainly with preventing illegal entries and the deportation of aliens deemed to be criminals or subversives.

The outbreak of World War II found the United States allied with China, the Philippines, and India in the fight against Japan, leading to the repeal of the Chinese Exclusion Act in 1943 and the Luce-Celler Act of 1946 which provided for the naturalization, for the first time, of people from India and the Philippines. The war also increased the need for agricultural workers since millions of Americans were drafted into the armed forces. This brought another change in policy in the same year when the Bracero Program began to encourage the entry of seasonal agricultural workers from Mexico, Central, and South America.

Along with the war came relationships between members of the American armed forces and citizens of other nations leading to the War Brides Act of 1945 and the Fiancées Act of 1946, each of which provided expedited admission for the spouses and families of American citizens. In the postwar years, pressure to assist the hundreds of thousands of displaced persons in temporary European camps led to adoption of the Displaced Persons Act in 1948 allowing 205,000 refugees to enter the United States as exceptions to the quotas. Two years later the number was increased to 415,000. This process was further expanded by the Refugee Relief Act of 1953 designed to admit refugees who would otherwise be unable to enter the country under the existing quotas.

Defining Moment

In 1945 World War II ended only to be followed immediately by the Cold War. Mutual suspicions fueled spiraling tensions between East and West, often stemming from wartime mistrust and misunderstanding. As Americans read their daily newspapers many became alarmed at the spread of communist influence. The Red Army occupied Eastern Europe, civil war raged in China, eventually leading to the ascendency of Mao Zedong's communist government, and in Greece, Turkey, and the Philippines, communist insurgencies threatened the pro-Western governments. In response, President Harry Truman announced that the United States would provide aid to Greece and Turkey in their fight against communis. By 1948, it was clear that the U.S. and its allies were in a struggle to contain the expansion of Soviet and communist influence.

At home, Americans were appalled to read in 1948 that Whittaker Chambers, a communist agent, accused State Department official Alger Hiss of passing classified documents to the Soviet Union. A year later Justice Department employee Judith Conlon was found guilty of engaging in espionage with Soviet consular official Valentin Gubichev. In 1951 Julius and Ethel Rosenberg were convicted of espionage for their role in passing atomic secrets to the Soviets. All of this, and other similar instances, led to a "Red Scare" in which some people became increasingly suspicious of immigrants from areas now controlled by communist regimes. This feeling was only heightened by Wisconsin Senator Joseph McCarthy whose repeated accusations of communist influence in government only served to feed into the public's fears.

Because of the mounting Cold War suspicions, in

1950 aliens were required to report their addresses annually and the criteria for denial of entry and deportation of subversives expanded. Rising calls for immigration reform resulted in the McCarran-Walter Act. Approved by the House and Senate in the spring of 1952, the bill met with a presidential veto in June but was subsequently passed over his veto by the House (278-113) and Senate (57-26) to become law on June 27, 1952.

Author Biography

Patrick Anthony McCarran was born in Nevada in 1876 to Irish immigrant parents. After studying law he was admitted to the bar in 1905, then he served in several political positions. As a Democrat he was defeated twice in attempts to win election to the U.S. Senate, but the third time was the charm and he entered that body in 1933. Although part of the contingent of Congress that entered in the Franklin Roosevelt landslide, he be-

came an outspoken opponent of New Deal legislation and a noted supporter of the fascist Francisco Franco in Spain and the nationalist Chiang Kai-shek in China. Following World War II he was a leading Congressional anti-communist and active in hearings to root out communist influence in government. His fears of communism no doubt played a major part in his support for stringent immigration quotas, especially from those areas under communist control.

A native of Pennsylvania where he was born in Easton in 1894, Francis E. Walter served in both World Wars. Admitted to the bar in 1919, he was a successful corporate lawyer and banking official before being elected as a Democrat to the U.S. House of Representatives in the 1932 election. An avid anti-communist, he was a member and later chair of the House Committee on Un-American Activities where he also gained a reputation for his racist views. He died in 1963.

HISTORICAL DOCUMENT

... TITLE II-IMMIGRATION

Chapter 1-Quota System

Numerical Limitations; Annual Quota Based upon National Origin; Minimum Quotas

Sec. 201.

(a) The annual quota of any quota area shall be one-sixth of 1 per centum of the number of inhabitants in the continental United States in 1920, which number, except for the purpose of computing quotas for quota areas within the Asia-Pacific triangle, shall be the same number heretofore determined under the provisions of section 11 of the Immigration Act of 1924, attributable by national origin to such quota area: Provided, That the quota existing for Chinese persons prior to the date of enactment of this Act shall be continued, and, except as otherwise provided in section 202 (e), the minimum quota for any quota area shall be one hundred.

(b) The determination of the annual quota of any quota area shall be made by the Secretary of State, the Secretary of Commerce, and the Attorney General,

jointly. Such officials shall, jointly, report to the President the quota of each quota area, and the President shall proclaim and make known the quotas so reported. Such determination and report shall be made and such proclamation shall be issued as soon as practicable after the date of enactment of this Act. Quotas proclaimed therein shall take effect on the first day of the fiscal year, or the next fiscal half year, next following the expiration of six months after the date of the proclamation, and until such date the existing quotas proclaimed under the Immigration Act of 1924 shall remain in effect. After the making of a proclamation under this subsection the quotas proclaimed therein shall continue with the same effect as if specifically stated herein and shall be final and conclusive for every purpose, except (1) insofar as it is made to appear to the satisfaction of such officials and proclaimed by the President, that an error of fact has occurred in such determination or in such proclamation, or (2) in the case provided for in section 202 (e).

(c) There shall be issued to quota immigrants chargeable to any quota (1) no more immigrant visas in any fiscal year than the quota for such year, and (2) in any calendar month of any fiscal year, no more immigrant visas than 10 per centum of the quota for such year; except that during the last two months of any fiscal year immigrant visas may be issued without regard to the 10 per centum limitation contained herein.

(d) Nothing in this Act shall prevent the issuance (without increasing the total number of quota immigrant visas which may be issued) of an immigrant visa to an immigrant as a quota immigrant even though he is a nonquota immigrant.

(e) The quota numbers available under the annual quotas of each quota area proclaimed under this Act shall be reduced by the number of quota numbers which have been ordered to be deducted from the annual quotas authorized prior to the effective date of the annual quotas proclaimed under this Act under—(1) section 19 (c) of the Immigration Act of 1917, as amended; (2) the Displaced Persons Act of 1948, as amended; and (3) any other Act of Congress enacted prior to the effective date of the quotas proclaimed under this Act.

Determination of Quota to which an Immigrant is Chargeable

Sec. 202.

(a) Each independent country, self-governing dominion, mandated territory, and territory under the international trusteeship system of the United Nations, other than the United States and its outlying possessions and the countries specified in section 101(a) (27) (C), shall be treated as a separate quota area when approved by the Secretary of State. All other inhabited lands shall be attributed to a quota area specified by the Secretary of State. For the purposes of this Act, the annual quota to which an immigrant is chargeable shall be determined by birth within a quota area, except that—(1) an alien child, when accompanied by his alien parent or parents may be charged to the quota of the accompanying parent or of either accompanying parent if such parent has received or would be qualified for an immigrant visa, if necessary to prevent the separation of the child from the accompanying parent or parents, and if the quota to which such parent has been or would be chargeable is not exhausted for that fiscal year; (2) if an alien is chargeable to a dif-

ferent quota from that of his accompanying spouse, the quota to which such alien is chargeable may, if necessary to prevent the separation of husband and wife, be determined by the quota of the accompanying spouse, if such spouse has received or would be qualified for an immigrant visa and if the quota to which such spouse has been or would be chargeable is not exhausted for that fiscal year; (3) an alien born in the United States shall be considered as having been born in the country of which he is a citizen or subject, or if he is not a citizen or subject of any country then in the last foreign country in which he had his residence as determined by the consular officer; (4) an alien born within any quota area in which neither of his parents was born and in which neither of his parents had a residence at the time of such alien's birth may be charged to the quota area of either parent; (5) notwithstanding the provisions of paragraphs (2), (3), and (4) of this subsection, any alien who is attributable by as much as one-half of his ancestry to a people or peoples indigenous to the Asia-Pacific triangle defined in subsection (b) of this section, unless such alien is entitled to a nonquota immigrant status ... shall be chargeable to a quota as specified in subsection (b) of this section: Provided, That the child of an alien ..., if accompanying or following to join him, shall be classified under section 101 (a) (27) (C), notwithstanding the provisions of subsection (b) of this section.

(b) With reference to determination of the quota to which shall be chargeable an immigrant who is attributable by as much as one-half of his ancestry to a people or peoples indigenous to the Asia-Pacific triangle comprising all quota areas and all colonies and other dependent areas situate wholly east of the meridian sixty degrees east of Greenwich, wholly west of the meridian one hundred and sixty-five degrees west, and wholly north of the parallel twenty-five degrees south latitude—(1) there is hereby established, in addition to quotas for separate quota areas comprising independent countries, self-governing dominions, and territories under the international trusteeship system of the United Nations situate wholly within said Asia-Pacific triangle, an Asia-Pacific quota of one hundred annually, which quota shall not be subject to the provisions of subsection (e); (2) such immigrant born within a separate quota area situate wholly within such Asia-Pacific triangle shall not be chargeable to the

Asia-Pacific quota, but shall be chargeable to the quota for the separate quota area in which he was born; (3) such immigrant born within a colony or other dependent area situate wholly within said Asia- Pacific triangle shall be chargeable to the Asia-Pacific quota; (4) such immigrant born outside the Asia-Pacific triangle who is attributable by as much as one- half of his ancestry to a people or peoples indigenous to not more than one separate quota area, situate wholly within the Asia-Pacific triangle, shall be chargeable to the quota of that quota area; (5) such immigrant born outside the Asia-Pacific triangle who is attributable by as much as one- half of his ancestry to a people or peoples indigenous to one or more colonies or other dependent areas situate wholly within the Asia-Pacific triangle, shall be chargeable to the Asia-Pacific quota; (6) such immigrant born outside the Asia-Pacific triangle who is attributable by as much as one- half of his ancestry to peoples indigenous to two or more separate quota areas situate wholly within the Asia-Pacific triangle, or to a quota area or areas and one or more colonies and other dependent areas situate wholly therein, shall be chargeable to the Asia-Pacific quota.

(c) Any immigrant born in a colony or other component or dependent area of a governing country for which no separate or specific quota has been established, unless a nonquota immigrant as provided in section 101 (a) (27) of this Act, shall be chargeable to the quota of the governing country, except that (1) not more than one hundred persons born in any one such colony or other component or dependent area overseas from the governing country shall be chargeable to the quota of its governing country in any one year, and (2) any such immigrant, if attributable by as much as one-half of his ancestry to a people or peoples indigenous to the Asia-Pacific triangle, shall be chargeable to a quota as provided in subsection (b) of this section.

(d) The provision of an immigration quota for a quota area shall not constitute recognition by the United States of the political transfer of territory from one country to another, or recognition of a government not recognized by the United States.

(e) After the determination of quotas has been made as provided in section 201, revision of the quotas shall be made by the Secretary of State, the Secretary of Commerce, and the Attorney General, jointly, whenever nec-essary, to provide for any change of boundaries resulting in transfer of territory from one sovereignty to another, a change of administrative arrangements of a colony or other dependent area, or any other political change, requiring a change in the list of quota areas or of the territorial limits thereof, but any increase in the number of minimum quota areas above twenty within the Asia-Pacific triangle shall result in a proportionate decrease in each minimum quota of such area in order that the sum total of all minimum quotas within the Asia-Pacific triangle shall not exceed two thousand. In the case of any change in the territorial limits of quota areas, not requiring a change in the quotas for such areas, the Secretary of State shall, upon recognition of such change, issue appropriate instructions to all consular offices concerning the change in the territorial limits of the quota area involved.

Allocation of Immigrant Visas within Quotas

Sec. 203.

(a) Immigrant visas to quota immigrants shall be allotted in each fiscal year as follows:

(1) The first 50 per centum of the quota of each quota area for such year, plus any portion of such quota not required for the issuance of immigrant visas to the classes specified in paragraphs (2) and (3), shall be made available for the issuance of immigrant visas (A) to qualified quota immigrants whose services are determined by the Attorney General to be needed urgently in the United States because of the high education, technical training, specialized experience, or exceptional ability of such immigrants and to be substantially beneficial prospectively to the national economy, cultural interests, or welfare of the United States, and (B) to qualified quota immigrants who are the spouse or children of any immigrant described in clause (A) if accompanying him.

(2) The next 30 per centum of the quota for each quota area for such year, plus any portion of such quota not required for the issuance of immigrant visas to the classes specified in paragraphs (1) and (3), shall be made available for the issuance of immigrant visas to qualified quota immigrants who are the parents of citizens of the United States, such citizens being at least twenty-one years of age.

(3) The remaining 20 per centum of the quota for each quota area for such year, plus any portion of such quota not required for the issuance of immigrant visas to the classes specified in paragraphs (1) and (2), shall be made available for the issuance of immigrant visas to qualified quota immigrants who are the spouses or the children of aliens lawfully admitted for permanent residence.

(4) Any portion of the quota for each quota area for such year not required for the issuance of immigrant visas to the classes specified in paragraphs (1), (2), and (3) shall be made available for the issuance of immigrant visas to other qualified quota immigrants chargeable to such quota. Qualified quota immigrants of each quota area who are the brothers, sisters, sons, or daughters of citizens of the United States shall be entitled to a preference of not exceeding 25 per centum of the immigrant visas available for issuance for each quota area under this paragraph.

(b) Quota immigrant visas issued pursuant to paragraph (1) of subsection (a) shall, in the case of each quota area, be issued to eligible quota immigrants in the order in which a petition on behalf of each such immigrant is filed with the Attorney General as provided in section 204; and shall be issued in the first calendar month after receipt of notice of approval of such petition in which a quota number is available for an immigrant chargeable to such quota area.

(c) Quota immigrant visas issued to aliens in the classes designated in paragraphs (2), (3), and (4) of subsection (a) shall, in the case of each quota, be issued to qualified quota immigrants strictly in the chronological order in which such immigrants are registered in each class on quota waiting lists which shall be maintained for each quota in accordance with regulations prescribed by the Secretary of State.

(d) In determining the order for consideration of applications for quota immigrant visas under subsection (a), consideration shall be given first to applications under paragraph (1), second to applications under paragraph (2), third to applications under paragraph (3), and fourth to applications under paragraph (4).

(e) Every immigrant shall be presumed to be a quota immigrant until he establishes to the satisfaction of the consular officer, at the time of application for a visa, and to the immigration officers, at the time of application for admission, that he is a nonquota immigrant. Every quota immigrant shall be presumed to be a nonpreference quota immigrant until he establishes to the satisfaction of the consular officer and the immigration officers that he is entitled to a preference quota status under paragraph (1), (2), or (3) of subsection (a) or to a preference under paragraph (4) of such subsection.

Sec. 204. (a) In the case of any alien claiming in his application for an immigrant visa to be entitled to an immigrant status under section 101 (a) (27) (F) (i) or section 203 (a) (1) (A), the consular officer shall not grant such status until he has been authorized to do so as provided in this section.

(b) Any person, institution, firm, organization, or governmental agency desiring to have an alien classified as an immigrant under section 101 (a) (27) (F) (i) or section 203 (a) (1) (A) shall file a petition with the Attorney General for such classification of the alien. The petition shall be in such form as the Attorney General may by regulations prescribed and shall state the basis for the need of the services of such alien and contain such additional information and be supported by such documentary evidence as may be required by the Attorney General. The petition shall be made under oath administered by any individual having authority to administer oaths, if executed in the United States, but, if executed outside the United States, administered by a consular officer.

(c) After an investigation of the facts in each case, and after consultation with appropriate agencies of the Government, the Attorney General shall, if he determines that the facts stated in the petition are true and that the alien in respect of whom the petition is made is eligible for an immigrant status under section 101(a) (27) (F) (i) or section 203(a) (1) (A), approve the petition and forward one copy thereof to the Department of State. The Secretary of State shall then authorize the consular officer concerned to grant such immigrant status.

(d) Nothing in this section shall be construed to entitle an immigrant, in respect of whom a petition under this section is approved, to enter the United States as an immigrant under section 101 (a) (27) (F) (i) or section 203 (a) (1) (A) if upon his arrival at a port of entry in the United States he is found not to be entitled to such classification.

Procedure for Granting Nonquota Status or Preference by Reason or Relationship

Sec. 205.

(a) In the case of any alien claiming in his application for an immigrant visa to be entitled to a nonquota immigrant status under section 101 (a) (27) (A), or to a quota immigrant status under section 203 (a) (2) or 203 (a) (3), or to a preference under section 203 (a) (4), the consular officer shall not grant such status or preference until he has been authorized to do so provided in this section.

(b) Any citizen of the United States claiming that any immigrant is his spouse or child and that such immigrant is entitled to a nonquota immigrant status under section 101 (a) (27) (A), or any citizen of the United States claiming that any immigrant is his parent and that such immigrant is entitled to a quota immigrant status under section 203 (a) (2), or any alien lawfully admitted for permanent residence claiming that any immigrant is his spouse or child and that such immigrant is entitled to a quota immigrant status under section 203 (a) (3), or any citizen of the United States claiming that any immigrant is his brother, sister, son, or daughter and that such immigrant is entitled to a preference under section 203 (a) (4) may file a petition with the Attorney General. The petition shall be in such form and shall contain such information and be supported by such documentary evidence as the Attorney General may by regulations prescribe. The petition shall be made under oath administered by any individual having authority to administer oaths, if executed in the United States, but, if executed outside the United States, administered by a consular officer.

(c) After an investigation of the facts in each case the Attorney General shall, if he determines the facts stated in the petition are true and that the alien in respect of whom the petition is made is eligible for a nonquota immigrant status under section 101 (a) (27) (A), or for a quota immigrant status under section 203 (a) (2) or 203 (a) (3), or for a preference under section 203 (a) (4), approve the petition and forward one copy thereof to the Department of State. The Secretary of State shall then authorize the consular officer concerned to grant the nonquota immigrant status, quota immigrant status, or preference, as the case may be.

(d) Nothing in this section shall be construed to entitle an immigrant, in respect of whom a petition under this section is approved, to enter the United States as a nonquota immigrant under section 101 101 (a) (27) (A) if upon his arrival at a port of entry in the United States he is found not to be entitled to such classification, or to enter the United States as a quota immigrant under section 203 (a) (2) or 203 (a) (3) if upon his arrival at a port of entry in the United States he is found not to be entitled to such classification, or to enter the United States as a preference quota immigrant under section 203 (a) (4) if upon his arrival at a port of entry in the United States he is found not to be entitled to such preference.

Revocation of Approval of Petitions

Sec. 206.

The Attorney General may, at any time, for what he deems to be good and sufficient cause, revoke the approval of any petition approved by him under section 204, section 205, or section 214 (c) of this title. Such revocation shall be effective as of the date of approval of any such petition. In no case, however, shall such revocation have effect unless there is mailed to the petitioner's last known address a notice of the revocation and unless notice of the revocation is communicated through the Secretary of State to the beneficiary of the petition before such beneficiary commences his journey to the United States. If notice of revocation is not so given, and the beneficiary applies for admission to the United States, his admissibility shall be determined in the manner provided for by sections 235 and 236.

Unused Quota Immigrant Visas

Sec. 207.

If a quota immigrant having an immigrant visa is excluded from admission to the United States and deported, or does not apply for admission to the United States before the expiration of the validity of the immigrant visa, or if an alien having an immigrant visa issued to him as a quota immigrant is found not to be a quota immigrant, no immigrant visa shall be issued in lieu thereof to any other immigrant.

Chapter 2-Qualifications for Admission of Aliens; Travel Control of Citizens and Aliens Documentary Requirements

Sec. 211.

(a) No immigrant shall be admitted into the United States unless at the time of application for admission he (1) has a valid unexpired immigrant visa or was born subsequent to the issuance of such immigrant visa of the accompanying parent, (2) is properly chargeable to the quota specified in the immigrant visa, (3) is a non-quota immigrant if specified as such in the immigrant visa, (4) is of the proper status under the quota specified in the immigrant visa, and (5) is otherwise admissible under this Act.

(b) Notwithstanding the provisions of section 212 (a) (20) of this Act, in such cases or in such classes of cases and under such conditions as may be by regulations prescribed, otherwise admissible aliens lawfully admitted for permanent residence who depart from the United States temporarily may be readmitted to the United States by the Attorney General in his discretion without being required to obtain a passport, immigrant visa, reentry permit or other documentation.

(c) The Attorney General may in his discretion, subject to subsection (d), admit to the United States any otherwise admissible immigrant not admissible under clause (2), (3), or (4) of subsection (a), if satisfied that such inadmissibility was not known to and could not have been ascertained by the exercise of reasonable diligence by, such immigrant prior to the departure of the vessel or aircraft from the last port outside the United States and outside foreign contiguous territory, or, in the case of an immigrant coming from foreign contiguous territory, prior to the application of the immigrant for admission.

(d) No quota immigrant within clause (2) or (3) of subsection (a) shall be admitted under subsection (c) if the entire number of immigrant visas which may be issued to quota immigrants under the same quota for the fiscal year, or the next fiscal year, has already been issued. If such entire number of immigrant visas has not been issued, the Secretary of State, upon notification by the Attorney General of the admission under subsection (c) of a quota immigrant within clause (2) or (3) of subsection (a), shall reduce by one the number of immigrant visas which may be issued to quota immigrants under the same quota during the fiscal year in which such immigrant is admitted, or, if the entire number of immigrant visas which may be issued to quota immigrants under the same quota for the fiscal year has been issued, then during the next following fiscal year.

(e) Every alien making application for admission as an immigrant shall present a valid unexpired passport, or other suitable travel document, or document of identity and nationality, if such document is required under the regulations issued by the Attorney General.

General Classes of Aliens Ineligible to Receive Visas and Excluded from Admission

Sec. 212.

(a) Except as otherwise provided in this Act, the following classes of aliens shall be ineligible to receive visas and shall be excluded from admission into the United States: (1) Aliens who are feeble-minded; (2) Aliens who are insane; (3) Aliens who have had one or more attacks of insanity; (4) Aliens afflicted with psychopathic personality, epilepsy, or a mental defect; (5) Aliens who are narcotic drug addicts or chronic alcoholics; (6) Aliens who are afflicted with tuberculosis in any form, or with leprosy, or any dangerous contagious disease; (7) Aliens not comprehended within any of the foregoing classes who are certified by the examining surgeon as having a physical defect, disease, or disability, when determined by the consular or immigration officer to be of such a nature that it may affect the ability of the alien to earn a living, unless the alien affirmatively establishes that he will not have to earn a living; (8) Aliens who are paupers, professional beggars, or vagrants; (9) Aliens who have been convicted of a crime involving moral turpitude (other than a purely political offense), or aliens who admit having committed such a crime, or aliens who admit committing acts which constitute the essential elements of such a crime; except that aliens who have committed only one such crime while under the age of eighteen years may be granted a visa and admitted if the crime was committed more than five years prior to the date of the application for a visa or other documentation, and more than five years prior to date of application for admission to the United States, unless the crime resulted confinement in a prison or correctional institution, in which case such alien must have been released from such confinement more than five years prior to the date of the application for a visa or other documentation, and for admission, to the United States; (10) Aliens who have been convicted of two or more offenses (other than purely political offenses), regardless of whether the conviction was in a single trial or whether the offenses arose from a single scheme of misconduct and regardless of whether the offenses involved moral turpitude, for which the aggregate sentences to confinement actually imposed were five years or more; (11) Aliens who are polygamists or who practice polygamy or advocate the practice of polygamy; (12) Aliens who are prostitutes or who have engaged in prostitution, or aliens coming to the United States solely, principally, or incidentally to engage in prostitution; aliens who directly or indirectly procure or attempt to procure, or who have procured or attempted to procure or to import, prostitutes or persons for the purpose of prostitution or for any other immoral purpose; and aliens who are or have been supported by, or receive or have received, in whole or in part, the proceeds of prostitution or aliens coming to the United States to engage in any other unlawful commercialized vice, whether or not related to prostitution; (13) Aliens coming to the United States to engage in any immoral sexual act; (14) Aliens seeking to enter the United States for the purpose of performing skilled or unskilled labor, if the Secretary of Labor has determined and certified to the Secretary of State and to the Attorney General that (A) sufficient workers in the United States who are able, willing, and qualified are available at the time (of application for a visa and for admission to the United States) and place (to which the alien is destined) to perform such skilled or unskilled labor, or (B) the employment of such aliens will adversely affect the wages and working conditions of the workers in the United States similarly employed. The exclusion of aliens under this paragraph shall apply only to the following classes: (i) those aliens described in the nonpreference category of section 203 (a) (4), (ii) those aliens described in section 101 (a) (27) (C), (27) (D), or (27) (E) (other than the parents, spouses, or children of United States citizens or of aliens lawfully admitted to the United State for permanent residence), unless their services are deter-

mined by the Attorney General to be needed urgently in the United States because of the high education, technical training, specialized experience, or exceptional ability of such immigrants and to be substantially beneficial prospectively to the national economy, cultural interest or welfare of the United States; (15) Aliens who, in the opinion of the consular officer at the time of application for a visa, or in the opinion of the Attorney General at the time of application for admission, are likely at any time to become public charges; (16) Aliens who have been excluded from admission and deported and who again seek admission within one year from the date of such deportation, unless prior to their reembarkation at a place outside the United States or their attempt to be admitted from foreign contiguous territory the Attorney General has consented to their reapplying for admission; (17) Aliens who have been arrested and deported, or who have fallen into distress and have been removed pursuant to this or any prior act, or who have been removed as alien enemies, or who have been removed at Government expense in lieu of deportation pursuant to section 242 (b), unless prior to their embarkation or reembarkation at a place outside the United States or their attempt to be admitted from foreign contiguous territory the Attorney General has consented to their applying or reapplying for admission; (18) Aliens who are stowaways; (19) Any alien who seeks to procure, or has sought to procure, or has procured a visa or other documentation, or seeks to enter the United States, by fraud, or by willfully misrepresenting a material fact; (20) Except as otherwise specifically provided in this Act, any immigrant who at the time of application for admission is not in possession of a valid unexpired immigrant visa, reentry permit, border crossing identification card, or other valid entry document required by this Act, and a valid unexpired passport, or other suitable travel document, or document of identity and nationality, if such document Certificate of Nationality to Be Issued by the Secretary of State for a Person not a Naturalized Citizen of the United States for Use in Proceedings of a Foreign State

Sec. 359.

The Secretary of State is hereby authorized to issue, in his discretion and in accordance with rules and regulations prescribed by him, a certificate of nationality for any person not a naturalized citizen of the United States who presents satisfactory evidence that he is an American national and that such certificate is needed for use in judicial or administrative proceedings in a foreign state. Such certificate shall be solely for use in the case for

which it was issued and shall be transmitted by the Secretary of State through appropriate official channels to the judicial or administrative officers of the foreign state in which it is to be used.

GLOSSARY

Asia-Pacific Triangle: The Immigration Act of 1924 banned immigration from the "Asia–Pacific Triangle" which it defined to include China, Japan, the Philippines, Southeast Asia (French Indochina, Malaya, Siam, and Singapore), Korea, the Dutch East Indies, Burma, India, and Ceylon.

Displaced Persons Act of 1948: A law authorizing the entry into the United States of European displaced persons outside the limits imposed by the quotas established in the Immigration Act of 1924.

Mandated territory: A territory legally under the control of some other sovereign nation, usually as approved by the League of Nations or later the United Nations.

Non-quota immigrant: A person allowed to enter the country outside the restrictions of the quota system provided the person meets a certain specified legal category.

Document Analysis

Title II of the McCarran-Walter Act was designed to eliminate the former racial prohibitions which stretched back to the first Naturalization Act of 1790 that limited naturalization to "white" people. At the same time, however, Section 201 preserved the quota system that had been incorporated under the immigration acts in 1921 and 1924. It also responded to fears of communism by making it easier for the government to deport aliens, or even naturalized citizens, believed to be "subversive."

Section 201 charged the Secretary of State, the Secretary of Commerce, and the Attorney General to "jointly" establish the annual quota rates which could be flexible going forward, and also establishes rules for the issuing of quota visas. Interestingly, it also provides that an immigrant *not* subject to the quotas may nevertheless be counted toward a given quota. This approach would allow the immigration bureaucracy to fill a quota from a country they chose to limit with appropriate non-quota immigrants so as to limit the overall number of people from that nation who might enter if the quota and non-quota immigrant classifications were kept separate.

Section 202 defines the countries and regions to which quotas will apply and the people eligible to enter under those quotas. It also provides that accompanying chil-

dren be charged to the quota of their parents, and that "an alien born in the United States shall be considered as having been born in the country of which he is a citizen or subject, or if he is not a citizen or subject of any country then in the last foreign country in which he had his residence as determined by the consular officer." This is directly contradictory to the current interpretation of the Constitution which holds that *anyone* born in the United States is automatically a native-born citizen regardless of the status of the baby's parents. In cases where married individuals have different places of origin the two may both be charged to the quota of either.

Section 203 defines how visas for quota immigrants will be allocated, setting up a priority system, which favors people with special education, training, or experience "urgently" needed in the United States. These, together with the spouses and accompanying children, were to fill the first fifty percent of any annual quota. The next thirty percent was to include the parents of U.S. citizens provided the children were at least 21 years old and the parents otherwise legally admissible. Finally, the remaining twenty percent of visas were to go to "qualified quota immigrants who are the spouses or the children of aliens lawfully admitted for permanent residence." This, for the first time, established a specific priority listing that privileged those with qualifications most needed or useful to the United States.

Every immigrant was to be classified as a non-preference arrival unless the person could prove a priority status. Final determination was to be left to the Attorney General. Section 205 deals with the procedure to be followed to obtain non-quota status or a preference due to family relationship. Section 206 provides for the revocation of approved petitions and Section 207 specifies that any unused visas that are issued may not be reissued to anyone else.

Section 211 defines which aliens are legally admissible and the documents necessary to establish this status, while Section 212 identifies categories of immigrants who are to be excluded from entry. It closes by requiring that "any immigrant who at the time of application for admission is not in possession of a valid unexpired immigrant visa, reentry permit, border crossing identification card, or other valid entry document required by this Act, and a valid unexpired passport, or other suitable travel document, or document of identity and nationality."

Essential Themes
The McCarran-Walter Act brought pre-existing laws into a single document, restated the previous national origins quotas, left entry from the Western Hemisphere without restriction, and largely restated the excluded categories incorporated into previous Congressional acts, but with the added emphasis on excluding communists or those believed to be subversive. Where the legislation diverged from American tradition was in eliminating the former racial prohibitions which stretched back to the first Naturalization Act of 1790 that limited naturalization to "white" people and in establishing a priority preference for the educated, skilled workers, and relatives of U.S. citizens.

In a speech before the Senate in support of the bill that bore his name, Patrick McCarran asserted the necessity of adopting the legislation since the United States was threatened by "hard-core, indigestible blocs which have not become integrated into the American way of life, but which, on the contrary are its deadly enemies. ... The solution of the problems of Europe and Asia will not come through a transplanting of those problems en masse to the United States." The argument was largely a restatement of traditional nativist views that believed immigrant groups could not assimilate. In his veto message President Harry Truman noted the irony of trying to restrict immigration from communist nations because those people were migrating in search of freedom, not to spread communism. It was the same as in 1924, he noted. But in 1952 he saw no need to perpetuate this discrimination. "We do not need to be protected against immigrants from these countries—on the contrary we want to stretch out a helping hand, to save those who have managed to flee into Western Europe, to succor those who are brave enough to escape from barbarism, to welcome and restore them against the day when their countries will, as we hope, be free again.... These are only a few examples of the absurdity, the cruelty of carrying over into this year of 1952 the isolationist limitations of our 1924 law."

Bibliography and Additional Reading
Robert C. Alexander, "A Defense of the McCarran-Walter Act," *Law and Contemporary Problems*, Vol. 21, no. 2 (Spring, 1956), 382-400.
Robert A. Divine, *American Immigration Policy, 1924-1952* (New Haven: Yale University Press, 1957).
Maddalena Marinari, "Divided and Conquered: Immigration Reform Advocates and the Passage of the 1952 Immigration and Nationality Act," *Journal of American Ethnic History*, Vol. 35, no. 3 (Spring 2016), 9-40.
William R. Tamayo, "Asian Americans and the McCarran-Walter Act," in *Asian Americans and Congress: A Documentary History*, edited by Hyung-chan Kim (Westport, CT: Greenwood Press, 1996), 336-528.

■ Immigration and Nationality Act of 1965

Date: October 3, 1865
Author: Emanuel Celler
Genre: Act of Congress

Summary Overview

Since its founding in 1910, the National Association for the Advancement of Colored People (NAACP) began undertaking legal challenges to the Jim Crow laws that relegated those of African ancestry to a second-class citizenship by depriving them of their basic civil rights as Americans. Its unremitting efforts brought success in 1954 with the epic *Brown v. the Board of Education* decision in which the U.S. Supreme Court found the principle of "separate but equal" to be inherently unequal and thus unconstitutional. This landmark ruling finally opened the doors for dismantling the *de jure* segregation of American citizens by race.

There was still a long way to go in reversing centuries of inequity, but legal victories began to multiple. Two years after Brown *v*. the Board, the Supreme Court ruled that segregated city bus lines were illegal. In 1964 a new Civil Right Act banned discrimination based on race, color, religion, sex, or national origin, while the following year the Voting Rights Act finally guaranteed the right of qualified citizens to vote that had been promised in the Fourteenth and Fifteenth Amendments following the Civil War. All of these political successes, coupled with changes in public opinion, served to finally begin addressing issues of discrimination that had long detracted from the promise in the Declaration of Independence that in America "all men are created equal."

Defining Moment

Although beginning as a quest for African American rights and freedoms, the modern Civil Rights Movement soon reached well beyond its original intentions, inspiring other groups to pursue their own protests. In 1960 César Chávez organized the United Farm Workers Union whose successes soon brought a wave of Mexican American pride and commitment to gaining and maintaining their own equal justice. Eight years later the American Indian Movement emerged to press claims for equality for indigenous people. Joined by other groups representing Asians and various European ethnic groups, all of these groups took up the mantle of civil rights as it affected their groups.

One of the early joint victories of these groups was the Ethnic Heritage Studies Program Act of 1974 which provided federal funding for programs designed to teach school children about the various people that made up the United States. Proposals from a broad spectrum of ethnic and religious groups were approved over the next several years. All of this, the successes of the Civil Rights Movement and the renewed interest in genealogy and one's ancestral group, combined to increase interest in the story of immigration, of how America came to be America. And with this renewed interest came an upsurge in opposition to the discriminatory nationality quotas that had been in force, by 1965, for more than forty years. In the spirit of the era, it was time that something be done about this lingering inequity. The result was the Immigration Act of 1965, legislation sought by one Congressman ever since the initial quotas were enacted in 1921 and 1924.

Author Biography

Born in Brooklyn in 1888, Emanuel Celler was the son of immigrants from Germany. After graduating from Columbia Law School he was admitted to the bar and practiced his profession before being elected to the House of Representatives as a Democrat in 1922, serving there for almost fifty years. Known for his work on judicial affairs and immigration issues, he became closely associated with the latter when he made an impassioned speech before the House against the discriminatory quota system in the then-pending Immigration Act of 1924. From that point on, he continuously opposed the national origins quotas for the next four decades. Celler vigorously opposed President Franklin D. Roosevelt and his own Democratic Party in the early 1940s by advocating the admittance of people fleeing the Holocaust regardless of the quota system, labeling FDR's strict immigration policy "cruel." His advocacy of easing immigration laws brought upon him the wrath of Senator Joseph McCarthy's anti-communist witch hunt.

A champion of civil liberties, Celler participated in drafting the Civil Rights Act of 1964, the Voting Rights Act of 1965, and the Civil Rights Act of 1968. During this era of civil rights legislation, he submitted to the House what would later become the Immigration Act of 1965, also known as the Hart-Cellar Act, which finally addressed the inequities he had so long opposed. Following his lengthy service in Congress, Celler continued to speak on immigration and judicial issues. He passed away in Brooklyn in 1981.

HISTORICAL DOCUMENT

SEC. 201.

(a) Exclusive of special immigrants defined in section 101(a) (27), and of the immediate relatives of United States citizens specified in subsection (b) of this section, the number of aliens who may be issued immigrant visas or who may otherwise acquire the status of an alien lawfully admitted to the United States for permanent residence, or who may, pursuant to section 203(a) (7) enter conditionally, (i) shall not in any of the first three quarters of any fiscal year exceed a total of 45,000 and (ii) shall not in any fiscal year exceed a total of 170,000.

(b) The "immediate relatives" referred to in subsection (a) of this section shall mean the children, spouses, and parents of a citizen of the United States: *Provided*, That in the case of parents, such citizen must be at least twenty-one years of age. The immediate relatives specified in this subsection who are otherwise qualified for admission as immigrants shall be admitted as such, without regard to the numerical limitations in this Act.

(c) During the period from July 1, 1965, through June 30, 1968, the annual quota of any quota area shall be the same as that which existed for that area on June 30, 1965. The Secretary of State shall, not later than on the sixtieth day immediately following the date of enactment of this subsection and again on or before September 1, 1966, and September 1, 1967, determine and proclaim the amount of quota numbers which remain unused at the end of the fiscal year ending on June 30, 1965, June 30, 1966, and June 30, 1967, respectively, and are available for distribution pursuant to subsection (d) of this section.

(d) Quota numbers not issued or otherwise used during the previous fiscal year, as determined in accordance with subsection (c) hereof, shall be transferred to an immigration pool. Allocation of numbers from the pool and from national quotas shall not together exceed in any fiscal year the numerical limitations in subsection (a) of this section. The immigration pool shall be made available to immigrants otherwise admissible under the provisions of this Act who are unable to obtain prompt issuance of a preference visa due to oversubscription of their quotas, or subquotas as determined by the Secretary of State. Visas and conditional entries shall be allocated from the immigration pool within the percentage limitations and in the order of priority specified in section 203 without regard to the quota to which the alien is chargeable.

(e) The immigration pool and the quotas of quota areas shall terminate June 30, 1968. Thereafter immigrants admissible under the provisions of this Act who are subject to the numerical limitations of subsection (a) of this section shall be admitted in accordance with the percentage limitations and in the order of priority specified in section 203. ...

Sec. 2. Section 202 of the Immigration and Nationality Act ... is amended to read as follows:

(a) No person shall receive any preference or priority or be discriminated against in the issuance of an immigrant visa because of his race, sex, nationality, place of birth, or place of residence, ... Provided, That the total number of immigrant visas and the number of conditional entries made available to natives of any single foreign state under paragraphs (1) through (8) of section 203(a) shall not exceed 20,000 in any fiscal year: Provided further, That the foregoing proviso shall not operate to reduce the number of immigrants who may be admitted under the quota of any quota area before June 30, 1968.

(b) Each independent country, self-governing dominion, mandated territory, and territory under the international trusteeship system of the United Nations, other than the United States and its outlying possessions shall be treated as a separate foreign state for the purposes of the numerical limitation set forth in the proviso to sub section (a) of this section when approved by the Secretary of State. All other inhabited lands shall be attributed to a foreign state specified by the Secretary of State. For the purposes of this Act the foreign state to which an immigrant is chargeable shall be determined by birth within such foreign state except that (1) an alien child, when accompanied by his alien parent or parents, may be charged to the same foreign state as the accompanying parent or of either accompanying parent if such parent has received or would be qualified for an immigrant visa, if necessary to prevent the separation of the child from the accompanying parent or parents, and if the foreign state to which such parent has been or would be chargeable has not exceeded the numerical limitation set forth in the proviso to subsection (a) of this section for that fiscal year; (2) if an alien is chargeable to a different foreign state from that of his accompanying spouse, the foreign state to which such alien is chargeable may, if necessary to prevent the separation of husband and wife, be determined by the foreign state of the accompanying spouse, if such spouse has received or would be qualified for an immigrant visa and if the foreign state to which such spouse has been or would be chargeable has not exceeded the numerical limitation set forth in the proviso to subsection (a) of this section for that fiscal year; (3) an alien born in the United States shall be considered as having been born in the country of which he is a citizen or subject, or if he is not a citizen or subject of any country then in the last foreign country in which he had his residence as determined by the consular officer; (4) an alien born within any foreign state in which neither of his parents was born and in which neither of his parents had a residence at the time of such alien's birth may be charged to the foreign state of either parent.

(c) Any immigrant born in a colony or other component or dependent area of a foreign state unless a special immigrant as provided in section 101(a) (27) or an immediate relative of a United States citizen as specified in section 201(b), shall be chargeable, for the purpose of limitation set forth in section 202(a), to the foreign state, except that the number of persons born in any such colony or other component or dependent area overseas from the foreign state chargeable to the foreign state in any one fiscal year shall not exceed 1 per centum of the maximum number of immigrant visas available to such foreign state.

(d) In the case of any change in the territorial limits of foreign states, the Secretary of State shall, upon recognition of such change, issue appropriate instructions to all diplomatic and consular offices.

SEC. 3. Section 203 of the Immigration and Nationality Act ... is amended to read as follows:

Sec. 203

(a) Aliens who are subject to the numerical limitations specified in section 201(a) shall be allotted visas or their conditional entry authorized, as the case may be, as follows:

(1) Visas shall be first made available, in a number not to exceed 20 per centum of the number specified in section 201(a) (ii), to qualified immigrants who are the unmarried sons or daughters of citizens of the United States.

(2) Visas shall next be made available, in a number not to exceed 20 per centum of the number specified in section 201(a) (ii), plus any visas not required for the classes specified in paragraph (1), to qualified immigrants who are the spouses, unmarried sons or unmarried daughters of an alien lawfully admitted for permanent residence.

(3) Visas shall next be made available, in a number not to exceed 10 per centum of the number specified in section 201(a) (ii), to qualified immigrants who are members of the professions, or who because of their exceptional ability in the sciences or the arts will substantially benefit prospectively the national economy, cultural interests, or welfare of the United States.

(4) Visas shall next be made available, in a number not to exceed 10 per centum of the number specified in section 201(a) (ii), plus any visas not required for the classes specified in paragraphs (1) through (3), to qualified immigrants who are the married sons or the married daughters of citizens of the United States.

(5) Visas shall next be made available, in a number not to exceed 24 per centum of the number specified in section 201(a) (ii), plus any visas not required for the classes specified in paragraphs (1) through (4), to qualified immigrants who are the brothers or sisters of citizens of the United States.

(6) Visas shall next be made available, in a number not to exceed 10 per centum of the number specified in section 201(a) (ii), to qualified immigrants who are capable of performing specified skilled or unskilled labor, not of a temporary or seasonal nature, for which a shortage of employable and willing persons exists in the United States.

(7) Conditional entries shall next be made available by the Attorney General, pursuant to such regulations as he may prescribe and in a number not to exceed 6 per centum of the number specified in section 201(a) (ii), to aliens who satisfy an Immigration and Naturalization Service officer at an examination in any non-Communist or non-Communist-dominated country, (A) that (i) because of persecution or fear of persecution on account of race, religion, or political opinion they have fled (I) from any Communist or Communist-dominated country or area, or (II) from any country within the general area of the Middle East, and (ii) are unable or unwilling to return to such country or area on account of race, religion, or political opinion, and (iii) are not nationals of the countries or areas in which their application for conditional entry is made; or (B) that they are persons uprooted by catastrophic natural calamity as defined by the President who are unable to return to their usual place of abode. For the purpose of the foregoing the term 'general area of the Middle East' means the area between and including (1) Libya on the west, (2) Turkey on the north, (3) Pakistan on the east, and (4) Saudi Arabia and Ethiopia on the south: Provided, That immigrant visas in a number not exceeding one-half the number specified in this paragraph may be made available, in lieu of conditional entries of a like number, to such aliens who have been continuously physically present in the United States for a period of at least two years prior to application for adjustment of status.

(8) Visas authorized in any fiscal year, less those required for issuance to the classes specified in paragraphs (1) through (6) and less the number of conditional entries and visas made available pursuant to paragraph (7), shall be made available to other qualified immigrants strictly in the chronological order in which they qualify. Waiting lists of applicants shall be maintained in accordance with regulations prescribed by the Secretary of State. No immigrant visa shall be issued to a nonpreference immigrant under this paragraph, or to an immigrant with a preference under paragraph (3) or (6) of this subsection, until the consular officer is in receipt of a determination made by the Secretary of Labor pursuant to the provisions of section 212(a) (14).

(9) A spouse or child as defined in section 101(b) (1) (A), (B), (C), (D), or (E), shall, if not otherwise entitled to an immigrant status and the immediate issuance of a visa or to conditional entry under paragraphs (1) through (8), be entitled to the same status, and the same order of consideration provided in subsection (b), if accompanying, or following to join, his spouse or parent.

(b) In considering applications for immigrant visas under subsection (a) consideration shall be given to applicants in the order in which the classes of which they are members are listed in subsection (a).

(c) Immigrant visas issued pursuant to paragraphs (1) through (6) of subsection (a) shall be issued to eligible immigrants in the order in which a petition in behalf of each such immigrant is filed with the Attorney General as provided in section 204.

(d) Every immigrant shall be presumed to be a non-preference immigrant until he establishes to the satisfaction of the consular officer and the immigration officer that he is entitled to a preference status under paragraphs (1) through (7) of subsection (a), or to a special immigrant status under section 101 (a) (27), or that he is an immediate relative of a United States citizen as specified in section 201(b). In the case of any alien claiming in his application for an immigrant visa to be an immediate relative of a United States citizen as specified in section 201(b) or to be entitled to preference immigrant status under paragraphs (1) through (6) of subsection (a), the consular officer shall not grant such status until he has been authorized to do so as provided by section 204.

(e) For the purposes of carrying out his responsibilities in the orderly administration of this section, the Secretary of State is authorized to make reasonable estimates of the anticipated numbers of visas to be issued during any quarter of any fiscal year within each of the categories of subsection (a), and to rely upon such estimates in authorizing the issuance of such visas. The Secretary of State, in his discretion, may terminate the registration on a waiting list of any alien who fails to evidence his continued intention to apply for a visa in such manner as may be by regulation prescribed.

(f) The Attorney General shall submit to the Congress a report containing complete and detailed statement of facts in the case of each alien who conditionally entered the United States pursuant to subsection (a) (7) of this section. Such reports shall be submitted on or before January 15 and June 15 of each year.

(g) Any alien who conditionally entered the United States as a refugee, pursuant to subsection (a) (7) of this section, whose conditional entry has not been terminated by the Attorney General pursuant to such regulations as he may prescribe, who has been in the United States for at least two years, and who has not acquired permanent residence, shall forthwith return or be returned to the custody of the Immigration and Naturalization Service and shall thereupon be inspected and examined for admission into the United States, and his case dealt with in accordance with the provisions of sections 235, 236, and 237 of this Act.

(h) Any alien who, pursuant to subsection (g) of this section, is found, upon inspection by the immigration officer or after hearing before a special inquiry officer, to be admissible as an immigrant this Act at the time of his inspection and examination, except for the fact that he was not and is not in possession of the documents required by section 212(a) (20), shall be regarded as lawfully admitted to the United States for permanent residence as of the date of his arrival.

SEC. 4. Section 204 of the Immigration and Nationality Act (66 Stat. 176; 8 U.S.C. 1154) is amended to read as follows:

SEC. 204. (a) Any citizen of the United States claiming that an alien is entitled to a preference status by reason of the relationships described in paragraphs (1), (4), or (5) of section 203(a), or to an immediate relative status under section 201(b), or any alien lawfully admitted for permanent residence claiming that an alien is entitled to a preference status by reason of the relationship described in section 203(a) (2), or any alien desiring to be classified as a preference immigrant under section 203(a) (3) (or any person on behalf of such an alien), or any person desiring and intending to employ within the United States an alien entitled to classification as a preference immigrant under section 203(a) (6), may file a petition with the Attorney General for such classification. The petition shall be in such form as the Attorney General may by regulations prescribe and shall contain such information and be supported by such documentary evidence as the Attorney General may require. The petition shall be made under oath administered by any individual having authority to administer oaths, if executed in the United States, but, if executed outside the United States, administered by a consular officer or an immigration officer.

(b) After an investigation of the facts in each case, and after consultation with the Secretary of Labor with respect to petitions to accord a status under section 203(a) (3) or (6), the Attorney General shall, if he determines that the facts stated in the petition are true and that the alien in behalf of whom the petition is made is an immediate relative specified in section 201 (b) or is eligible for a preference status under section 203(a), approve the petition and forward one copy thereof to the Department of State. The Secretary of State shall then authorize the consular officer concerned to grant the preference status.

(c) Notwithstanding the provisions of subsection (b) no more than two petitions may be approved for one petitioner in behalf of a child as defined in section 101(b) (1) (E) or (F) unless necessary to prevent the separation of brothers and sisters and no petition shall be approved if the alien has previously been accorded a nonquota or preference status as the spouse of a citizen of the United States or the spouse of an alien lawfully admitted for permanent residence, by reason of a marriage determined by the Attorney General to have been entered into for the purpose of evading the immigration laws.

(d) The Attorney; General shall forward to the Congress a report on each approved petition for immigrant status under sections 203(a) (3) or 203(a) (6) stating the basis for his approval and such facts as were by him deemed to be pertinent in establishing the beneficiary's qualifications for the preferential status. Such reports shall be submitted to the Congress on the first and fifteenth day of each calendar month in which the Congress is in session.

(e) Nothing in this section shall be construed to entitle an immigrant, in behalf of whom a petition under this section is approved, to enter the United States as a preference immigrant under section 203(a) or as an immediate relative under section 201(b) if upon his arrival at a port of entry in the United States he is found not to be entitled to such classification.

Sec. 5. Section 205 of the Immigration and Nationality Act … is amended to read as follows:

SEC. 205.

The Attorney General may, at any time, for what he deems to be good and sufficient cause, revoke the approval of any petition approved by him under section 204. Such revocation shall be effective as of the date of approval of any such petition. In no case, however, shall such revocation have effect unless there is mailed to the petitioner's last known address a notice of the revocation and unless notice of the revocation is communicated through the Secretary of State to the beneficiary of the petition before such beneficiary commences his journey to the United States. If notice of revocation is not so given, and the beneficiary applies for admission to the United States, his admissibility shall be determined in the manner provided for in sections 235 and 236.

Sec. 6. Section 206 of the Immigration and Nationality Act … is amended to read as follows:

SEC. 206.

If an immigrant having an immigrant visa is excluded from admission to the United States and deported, or does not apply for admission before the expiration of the validity of his visa, or if an alien having an immigrant visa issued to him as a preference immigrant is found not to be a preference immigrant, an immigrant visa or a preference immigrant visa, as the case may be, may be issued in lieu thereof to another qualified alien.

GLOSSARY

International trusteeship: "Trust territories" were established by the United Nations in 1945 as a means of assisting former League of Nations mandates, territory formerly held by the Axis nations in World War II, and other lands voluntarily joining the program to move toward self-determination. Each was placed under the stewardship of a U.N. member nation. The last trusteeship, Palau in the Pacific Ocean, voted to become independent from its United States trusteeship in 1993 and became a sovereign nation the following year.

Non-preference immigrant: An immigrant that does not fall within one of the categories identified for priority preferential placement under U.S. immigration law.

Self-governing dominion: A self-governing land that is usually associated with a group of other such lands or a separate nation. For example, Canada was a dominion within the British Commonwealth.

Document Analysis

The 1965 law established a new maximum number of immigrants who could be admitted each year—290,000—along with the procedures on how they were to be admitted and responsibility for overseeing the process. Reversing previous precedents, the law clearly stated that "No person shall receive any preference or priority or be discriminated against in the issuance of an immigrant visa because of his race, sex, nationality, place of birth, or place of residence." Revising somewhat the priority listing of the earlier McCarran-Walter Act of 1952, the new legislation gave precedence to the unification of families, defining exactly what relationships would be honored and in what order. Likewise, the manner in which children of aliens were to be recorded was changed somewhat so that each was to be considered as originating in their country of birth except that a child accompanying one or both parents could be charged to either of their places of origin if that was necessary to prevent the separation of family members. The law went on to specify the priority for distributing visas to relatives: no more than twenty percent to unmarried children of citizens; twenty percent to spouses and unmarried children of permanent residents; ten percent to married children o U.S. citizens; and 24 percent to siblings of U.S. citizens.

Secondary preference of not more than the percent would go to those people arriving with education and skills that would be of benefit to the United States. In addition, up to another ten percent could be granted to people "capable of performing specified skilled or unskilled labor, not of a temporary or seasonal nature, for

which a shortage of employable and willing persons exists in the United States." To qualify for the latter the Secretary of Labor had to issue a certification that the skill in question was in fact in short supply in the United States.

Notably, in a substantive departure from laws earlier in the century the old national origins quotas were discarded. Instead, 170,000 visas were to be granted to people applying from the Eastern Hemisphere and 120,000 from the Western Hemisphere. The former specific quotas by country of origin were replaced by a cap of 20,000 visas per country for the Eastern Hemisphere and no specific cap for nations in the Western Hemisphere, although this was the first time that a numerical restriction was placed on people entering from the Western Hemisphere. But these restrictions were more flexible than it might first appear because the immediate relatives of U.S. citizens over the age of 21 were not to be counted toward any of the new quotas; thus, more people would be able to enter the country than the 290,000 total per year.

Refugees were accorded a low status, but that did not mean that they were necessarily being given less consideration since there remained other ways, such as temporary asylum legislation, under which they could gain entry. However, any refugee who had been in the country for two years without either being approved for permanent residence or had the conditional status of the admittance eliminated by the Attorney General was to be placed back into the general pool of applicants and processed by the Immigration and Naturalization Service according to the other provisions of the law.

Finally, the law continued the previous provisions that

(1) alien born in the U.S.would be attributes to the country of one of its parents and (2) all applications would be considered "non-preference" immigrants unless the individual could prove qualification under one of the preference categories.

Essential Themes

The Immigration and Nationality Act of 1965 established a cap of 290,000 visas per year, thus retaining the previous idea of limiting the overall number of arrivals, but eliminated the restrictive nationality-based quotas enacted in 1921 and 1924. It replaced the latter with general quotas for nations and revised the 1952 preference list to privilege family relationships and education/skills beneficial to the country. In other ways it also marked a substantial change of course from previous immigration legislation in that it made it much easier for people from Asia and Africa to enter the country. This action was in keeping with the concern for civil rights prevalent at the time, and also for establishing positive international relations with these areas due to the diplomatic requirements of the Cold War. Its popularity at the time can be seen in the fact that 85 percent of Republicans and 74 percent of Democrats in Congress voted in favor of the bill.

Although supporters of the law claimed that it would not result in any significant change in the demographic composition of the nation, the elimination of restrictions on entry from Asia and Africa, as well as the liberal policy toward the Western Hemisphere, in fact brought a noticeable change. Prior to adoption of the law about 68 percent of immigrants during the decade of the 1950s originated in Northern and Western Europe and Canada. During the decades of the 1970s and 1980s 47.9 percent were from Latin America and another 35.2 percent from Asia—a total of 83.1 percent. Similarly, the new regulations opened the way for a general increase in the number of immigrants. Whereas between 1960 and 1970 about eleven percent of the U.S. population growth was traceable to immigration, this increased to 33 percent in the 1970s and 39 percent in the following decade.

Bibliography and Additional Reading

Garbiel J. Chin, "The Civil Rights Revolution Comes to Immigration Law: A New Look at the Immigration and Nationality Act of 1965," *North Carolina Law Review*, Vol. 75 (1996), 273-345.

Roger Daniels, *Coming to America: A History of Immigration and Ethnicity in American Life* (New York: Harper Collins Publishers, 1990).

Nathan Glazer, ed., *Clamor at the Gates: The New American Immigration* (San Francisco: Institute for Contemporary Studies, 1985).

Edward P. Hutchinson, *Legislative History of American Immigration Policy, 1798-1965* (Philadelphia: University of Pennsylvania Press, 1981).

David M. Reimers, "An Unintended Reform: The 1965 Immigration Act and Third World Immigration to the United States," *Journal of American Ethnic History*, Vol. 3 (1983), 9-28.

EXECUTIVE AND JUDICIAL ACTIONS

Under the Constitution, Congress is responsible of legislating, for creating law. If both the House of Representatives and the Senate adopt a bill, it is sent to the President for signature. The President may sign, with the signed bill then becoming established law, or refuse to sign in which case the bill is vetoed and does not become law. However, Congress has an opportunity to pass the bill over the President's veto provided that it can achieve a two-thirds majority vote in each house. If this happens, the bill becomes law without the President's signature. But it is also possible for the executive branch of government to influence or initiate policies that have an effect on immigrants through use of either the power of the President's "bully pulpit" or through executive orders. Additionally, the Supreme Court has the authority to overturn legislation by declaring it unconstitutional, and in that way exerting its own influence on immigration policy. This section provides examples of both executive actions and federal court decisions that have had a decided effect on U.S. immigration policy.

Presidents can exert moral suasion to influence policy as seen in President Woodrow Wilson's annual message to Congress in 1915. In it he commented extensively on immigration, especially on his belief that some of those who had been welcomed as naturalized citizens had nevertheless maintained their loyalty to their previous nation rather than the United States. He was very blunt in identifying this as a threat to American security. In so doing, he exerted the influence of his office in favor of efforts to restrict immigration which eventually led to the restrictive immigration legislation of 1921 and 1924. Presidents can also influence immigration policy through use of their veto power over federal legislation. Such was the case with President Harry Truman's veto of the Immigration Act of 1952. In his accompanying message he provided his reasons for the veto, taking issue with Congress's attempt to continue the previous

policy of a blanket exclusion of people based on the nation they were coming from rather than factors specific to the individual. Finally, presidents may also issue executive orders relating to the departments within their purview. One such case was President Franklin D. Roosevelt's Executive Order 9066. Controversial from the moment it was issued, it provided for the incarceration of people of Japanese ancestry during World War II. What was so controversial was that it not only applied to aliens, but also to U.S. citizens of Japanese ancestry who had not even been accused of any crime much less convicted.

One of the first successful uses of the federal courts to protect immigrant rights can be seen in *Ho Ah Kow v. Nunan*. Although the issue at stake was a law believed to unfairly discriminate against Chinese in California, other questions also arose such as whether or not the local municipal authorities had the legal right to impose the penalties in question. This was also one of the first tests of the application of the new Fourteenth Amendment and the "equal protection" clause to the states and their political subdivisions.

A similar issue arose in Texas regarding the authority of local school districts when it came to the education of children whose parents had entered the country illegally. With a growing number the children of these illegals entering local schools, and thus increasing the educational expenses, opposition arose. One school district moved to charge these students tuition to ease the financial burden on the district, arguing that since they were not legally residents of the district they would be subject to tuition in the same manner as any other non-resident. Although this was consistent with the Higher Education Act of 1965 which required that federal financial aid be provided only to legal residents of the United States, a Mexican immigrant filed suit in *Plyler v. Doe*. The decision would change federal policy toward the children of illegal immigrants, even those born outside the United States who themselves were in the country illegally.

Finally, as the question of illegal immigration rose to the fore as a popular political issue, controversy erupted over enforcement of the immigration statues. Many people believed that responsibility rested with President Barack Obama's decision not to enforce existing U.S. immigration laws. This led some individual states to attempt enforcement themselves. One of those was Arizona which had been particularly impacted by the costs associated with the rise in illegal immigration. As a remedy, the state adopted its own laws designed to enforce the federal legislation being disregarded by the executive branch. In an odd turn of events, the federal government filed suit against Arizona arguing that the state lacked the authority to enforce federal law, thus its legislation was unconstitutional. It further argued that the action by Arizona's legislature violated the equal protection clause of the Fourteenth Amendment. The case was adjudicated in *Arizona v. United States*.

■ *Ho Ah Kow v. Nunan*

Date: 1879
Author: Stephen J. Field
Genre: Court Decision

Summary Overview

Beginning in the late 1860s, both *de facto* and *de jure* discrimination aimed at Asian residents in California began to increase. The economic recession of the 1870s saw acts of this nature escalate as "foreigners" were blamed for the shortage of jobs and other societal problems. With the largest Chinese community in the state, San Francisco led this nativist movement by mandating that all Asian children attend an "Oriental School" that it established. In another instance, police began selectively enforcing a Cubic Air Ordinance that required a certain amount of space per occupant in a boarding house, knowing full well that lower rent establishments catering to newer immigrants such as the Chinese would not meet this standard. In 1870 the city's Board of Supervisors adopted another law that made it illegal to carry baskets hung on a pole, a uniquely Chinese cultural characteristic, while using a sidewalk.

Overt discrimination intensified in 1873 with the adoption of three more biased ordinances. One of these forbade the removal of bones from the county, a law aimed at the Chinese practice of sending the remains of the deceased back to China for burial. A second regulation required a fee of $2 per quarter for laundries using a horse and wagon, but a $15 fee for those using no horse or wagon; the Chinese were the only launders providing their services on foot. The final act required jailers to shave the heads of all male inmates to a maximum depth of one inch. Again this fell most heavily on the Chinese.

Defining Moment

With the ascension of the Manchu to hegemony in China during the 17th century, male members of the subjugated Han people, who today comprise 93 percent of the Chinese population, were forced to wear their hair in a queue to signify their deference. Refusal was penalized with death. Over time, the queue, often referred to in the United States as a "pigtail," took on the sanction of cultural tradition. In 19th century California, braided queues that reached the waist, or even lower, were commonplace and clearly associated with the Chinese.

The passage of the "Queue Ordinance," often known as the "Pigtail Ordinance," has sometimes been explained as a means of keeping the Chinese *out* of jail since it was believed that poor Chinese were prone to committing minor offences to avail themselves of the bed and free meals that the prisons provided. By mandating that hair be cut upon incarceration, the argument goes, the Chinese would be less likely to find it appealing and the jail populations would be reduced. Another explanation that has been offered is that the law was intended to promote hygiene by combatting lice and fleas.

Sheriff Matthew Nunan took his position and his duties seriously, immediately enforcing the new law on all inmates. One of these was a Chinese laborer named Ho Ah Kow who had been arrested for violation of the Cubic Air Ordinance. When his queue was removed he filed a legal action claiming that the act was a violation of his rights and had caused him irreparable harm. The court's final decision was authored by Justice Stephen J. Field.

Author Biography

A native of Haddam, Connecticut, Stephen Johnson Field graduated from Williams College in 1837 before reading law and being admitted to the New York bar four years later. With the Gold Rush he left for California arriving in San Francisco in December 1849. Field opened a law office but only a year after his arrival was already an elected member of the California State Assembly. In 1857 he was defeated as a candidate for the United States Senate, but did win the canvass for the California Supreme Court. Field's entry onto the court came at a time of great turmoil arising from conflicting land claims between Anglo settlers and those who asserted previous ownership under Mexican law. In these cases he gained a reputation for often siding with the Mexican claimants.

Although these actions won for Field many enemies, President Abraham Lincoln appointed him to the U.S. Circuit Court in California in 1863, and remarkably an associate justice of the U.S. Supreme Court just two weeks later.

Many of Field's opinions on the Supreme Court exhibited a support for individual freedoms, including joining the majority in *Ex Parte Milligan* which found that Lincoln's suspension of habeas corpus during the Civil War had been unconstitutional. He is often credited with first forming the basis for what became the "liberty of contract" theory by arguing that the Fourteenth Amendment protected a person's right to enter into whatever contract the person might wish. His other contribution was called "substantive due process" which in affect expanded the power of the federal court to review state laws. Yet, despite his early reputation for upholding personal liberties, he concurred in declaring the Chinese Exclusion Act to be constitutional, refused to interpret the Fourteenth Amendment to protect people of African ancestry from discrimination by the states and supported the majority in the *Plessy v. Ferguson* case in 1896 which found that segregated facilities for blacks and whites was constitutional, establishing the "separate but equal" principle that survived until *Brown v. the Board of Education* in 1954.

Field resigned from the bench in December 1897 and passed away in Washington, D.C., on April 9, 1899.

HISTORICAL DOCUMENT

The validity of this ordinance is denied by the plaintiff on two grounds: 1. That it exceeds the authority of the board of supervisors, the body in which the legislative power of the city and county is vested; and 2. That it is special legislation imposing a degrading and cruel punishment upon a class of persons who are entitled, alike with all other persons within the jurisdiction of the United States, to the equal protection of the laws. We are of opinion that both these positions are well taken....

The cutting off the hair of every male person within an inch of his scalp, on his arrival at the jail, was not intended and cannot be maintained as a measure of discipline or as a sanitary regulation. The act by itself has no tendency to promote discipline, and can only be a measure of health in exceptional cases. Had the ordinance contemplated a mere sanitary regulation it would have been limited to such cases and made applicable to females as well as to males, and to persons awaiting trial as well as to persons under conviction. The close cutting of the hair which is practiced upon inmates of the state penitentiary, like dressing them in striped clothing, is partly to distinguish them from others, and thus prevent their escape and facilitate their recapture. They are measures of precaution, as well as parts of a general system of treatment prescribed by the directors of the penitentiary under the authority of the state, for parties convicted of and imprisoned for felonies. Nothing of the kind is prescribed or would be tolerated with respect to persons confined in a county jail for simple misdemeanors, most of which are not of a very grave character. For the discipline or detention of the plaintiff in this case, who had the option of paying a fine of ten dollars, or of being imprisoned for five days, no such clipping of the hair was required. It was done to add to the severity of his punishment....

The claim, however, put forth that the measure was prescribed as one of health is notoriously a mere pretense. A treatment to which disgrace is attached, and which is not adopted as a means of security against the escape of the prisoner, but merely to aggravate the severity of his confinement, can only be regarded as a punishment additional to that fixed by the sentence. If adopted in consequence of the sentence it is punishment in addition to that imposed by the court; if adopted without regard to the sentence it is wanton cruelty.

In the present case, the plaintiff was not convicted of any breach of a municipal regulation, nor of violating any provision of the consolidation act. The punishment which the supervisors undertook to add to the fine imposed by the court was without semblance of authority. The legislature had not conferred upon them the right to change or add to the punishments which it deemed sufficient for offenses; nor had it bestowed upon them the right to impose in any case a punishment of the character inflicted in this case. They could no more direct that the queue of the plaintiff should be cut off than that the punishments mentioned should be inflicted. Nor could they order the hair of any one, Mongolian or other person, to be clipped within an inch of his scalp. That measure was beyond their power....

The second objection to the ordinance in question is equally conclusive. It is special legislation on the part of the supervisors against a class of persons who, under the constitution and laws of the United States, are entitled to the equal protection of the laws. The ordinance was intended only for the Chinese in San Francisco. This was avowed by the supervisors on its passage, and was so understood by everyone. The ordinance is known in the community as the "Queue Ordinance," being so designated from its purpose to reach the queues of the Chinese, and it is not enforced against any other persons. The reason advanced for its adoption, and now urged for its continuance, is, that only the dread of the loss of his queue will induce a Chinaman to pay his fine. That is to say, in order to enforce the payment of a fine imposed upon him, it is necessary that torture should be superadded to imprisonment. Then, it is said, the Chinaman will not accept the alternative, which the law allows, of working out his fine by his imprisonment, and the state or county will be saved the expense of keeping him during the imprisonment. Probably the bastinado, or the knout, or the thumbscrew, or the rack, would accomplish the same end; and no doubt the Chinaman would prefer either of these modes of torture to that which entails upon him disgrace among his countrymen and carries with it the constant dread of misfortune and suffering after death. It is not creditable to the humanity and civilization of our people, much less to their Christianity, that an ordinance of this character was possible. The class character of this legislation is none the less manifest because of the general terms in which it is expressed. The statements of supervisors in debate on the passage of the ordinance cannot, it is true, be resorted to for the purpose of explaining the meaning of the terms used; but they can be resorted to for the purpose of ascertaining the general object of the legislation proposed, and the mischiefs sought to be remedied. Besides, we cannot shut our eyes to matters of public notoriety and general cognizance. When we take our seats on the bench we are not struck with blindness, and forbidden to know as judges what we see as men; and where an ordinance, though general in its terms, only operates upon a special race, sect or class, it being universally understood that it is to be enforced only against that race, sect or class, we may justly conclude that it was the intention of the body adopting it that it should only have such operation, and treat it accordingly. We may take notice of the limitation given to the general terms of an ordinance by its practical construction as a fact in its history, as we do in some cases that a law has practically become obsolete. If this were not so, the most important provisions of the constitution, intended for the security of personal rights, would, by the general terms of an enactment, often be evaded and practically annulled. The complaint in this case shows that the ordinance acts with special severity upon Chinese prisoners, inflicting upon them suffering altogether disproportionate to what would be endured by other prisoners if enforced against them. Upon the Chinese prisoners its enforcement operates as "a cruel and unusual punishment."

Many illustrations might be given where ordinances, general in their terms, would operate only upon a special class, or upon a class, with exceptional severity, and thus incur the odium and be subject to the legal objection of intended hostile legislation against them. We have, for instance, in our community a large number of Jews. They are a highly intellectual race, and are generally obedient to the laws of the country. But, as is well known, they have peculiar opinions with respect to the use of certain articles of food, which they cannot be forced to disregard without extreme pain and suffering. They look, for example, upon the eating of pork with loathing. It is an offense against their religion, and is associated in their minds with uncleanness and impurity. Now, if they should in some quarter of the city overcrowd their dwellings and thus become amenable, like the Chinese, to the act concerning lodging-houses and sleeping apartments, an ordinance of the supervisors requiring that all prisoners confined in the county jail should be fed on pork would be seen by everyone to be leveled at them; and, notwithstanding its general terms, would be regarded as a special law in its purpose and operation. During various periods of English history, legislation, general in its character, has often been enacted with the avowed purpose of imposing special burdens and restrictions upon Catholics; but that legislation has since been regarded as not less odious and obnoxious to animadversion than if the persons at whom it was aimed had been particularly designated. But in our country hostile and discriminating legislation by a state against persons of any class, sect, creed or nation, in whatever form it may be expressed, is forbidden by the fourteenth amendment of the constitution. That amendment in its first section declares who are citizens of the United States, and then enacts that no state shall make or enforce any law which shall abridge their privileges and immunities. It further declares that no state shall deprive any person (dropping the distinctive term citizen) of life, liberty or property, without due process of law, nor deny to any person the equal protection of the laws. This inhibition upon the state applies to all the instrumentalities and agencies employed in the administration of its government, to its executive, legislative and judicial departments, and to the subordinate legislative bodies of counties and cities. And the equality of protection thus assured to everyone whilst within the United States, from whatever country he may have come, or of whatever race or color he may be, implies not only that the courts of the country shall be open to him on the same terms as to all others for the security of his person or property, the prevention or redress of wrongs and the enforcement of contracts; but that no charges or burdens shall be laid upon him which are not equally borne by others, and that in the administration of criminal justice he shall suffer for his offenses no greater or different punishment....

We are aware of the general feeling—amounting to positive hostility—prevailing in California against the Chinese, which would prevent their further immigration hither and expel from the state those already here. Their dissimilarity in physical characteristics, in language, manners and religion would seem, from past experience, to prevent the possibility of their assimilation with our people. And thoughtful persons, looking at the millions which crowd the opposite shores of the Pacific, and the possibility at no distant day of their pouring over in vast hordes among us, giving rise to fierce antagonisms of race, hope that some way may be devised to prevent their further immigration. We feel the force and importance of these considerations; but the remedy for the apprehended evil is to be sought from the general government, where, except in certain cases, all power over the subject lies. To that government belong exclusively the treaty-making power and the power to regulate commerce with foreign nations, which includes intercourse as well as traffic, and, with the exceptions presently mentioned, the power to prescribe the conditions of immigration or importation of persons. ... For restrictions necessary or desirable in these matters, the appeal must be made to the general government; and it is not believed that the appeal will ultimately be disregarded. Be that as it may, nothing can be accomplished in that direction by hostile and spiteful legislation on the part of the state, or of its municipal bodies, like the ordinance in question—legislation which is unworthy of a brave and manly people. Against such legislation it will always be the duty of the judiciary to declare and enforce the paramount law of the nation.

GLOSSARY

Animadversion: A critical remark or public censure.

Bastinado: A punishment or torture that involves the beating of the soles of the feet with a cane or other such instrument.

Cognizance: Awareness or notice, as in to take notice of something.

Consolidation: In legal terminology, when a number of actions are brought based on the same policy they may be consolidated into a single ruling.

Knout: A whip, usually containing multiple thongs, used to inflict punishment.

Odium: Hatred or disgust directed toward a person or thing; contempt or discredit attaching to something

Explanation and Analysis of the Document

The basis for this case was a complaint by the plaintiff, Ho Ah Kow, that Sheriff Matthew Nunan, the defendant, had inflicted upon him a cruel and degrading punishment when he enforced an ordinance adopted by the San Francisco Board of Supervisors requiring that the hair of those incarcerated must be cut. Justice Field begins his opinion by stating the grounds upon which the plaintiff asserts that the ordinance was unconstitutional. There were two: First that the ordinance issued by the Board of Supervisors exceeded its legal authority, and second that it provided for a "cruel" punishment that is clearly aimed at one group of people and thus violates the constitutional guarantee of "equal protection" in the Fourteenth Amendment.

The defense contended that the ordinance was enacted for legitimate reasons. The Sanitation Ordinance adopted in 1870 was designed to prevent overcrowding in San Francisco's tenement houses. The penalty for violation of the required space provisions of the law was a fine or one week in prison. One of the unintended consequences of this was that the large Chinese population, frequently found in violation of the law because their low economic status required them to live in the cheap tenements, often chose jail because they lacked the funds to pay the fine or because, as some writers have claimed, the prospect of a week in a cleaner room with three meals a day was more appealing. This led to overcrowding in the prisons. Given the congestion, the defense argued that the purposes of the ordinance were to enforce discipline in the now overloaded prison system and to ensure proper sanitation conditions in the congested jail by preventing the spread of lice and fleas.

Justice Field addressed both claims at the beginning of his opinion, finding that "The cutting off the hair of every male person within an inch of his scalp, on his arrival at the jail, was not intended and cannot be maintained as a measure of discipline or as a sanitary regulation. The act by itself has no tendency to promote discipline, and can only be a measure of health in exceptional cases." For the purpose to actually be directed toward reasons of sanitation, Field observed, "it would have been limited to such cases and made applicable to females as well as to males, and to persons awaiting trial as well as to persons under conviction." Rather, he observed that, like providing striped clothing for inmates, the head saving of male adults was actually designed to distinguish them from non-inmates. In the case of the particular application to the defendant, there was no valid reason for the cutting of the hair since the state allowed for this procedure for those incarcerated for felonies, but the defendant was only charged with a misdemeanor and would be released in a few days. Since this was not required, Field reasoned that "A treatment to which disgrace is attached, and which is not adopted as a means of security against the escape of the prisoner, but merely to aggravate the severity of his confinement, can only be regarded as a punishment additional to that fixed by the sentence. If adopted in consequence of the sentence it is punishment in addition to that imposed by the court; if adopted without regard to the sentence it is wanton cruelty." That is, regardless of whether the hair cutting was imposed as an addition to the sentence, or with no connection to the sentence, it was applied to the defendant without any legal authority.

This brought Field to the question of whether the Board

of Supervisors actually had the authority to impose sentences at all. The justice observed that the state legislature had conferred no such authority on the city or the city's penal system "to change or add to the punishments." Likewise, it had no authority whatever to impose a penalty of hair cutting. But Field went well beyond these legal rulings in his written decision. He found that, based on comments made at the time of its passage, the action of the Board of Supervisors in adopting the original ordinance was unquestionably designed to be applied to the Chinese as a specific group. Further evidence of this, he stated, was that in practice the ordinance was only applied to the Chinese, as anyone could readily ascertain. Taking particular note of Chinese cultural norms, Field found that the punishment "entails upon [male Chinese] disgrace among his countrymen and carries with it the constant dread of misfortune and suffering after death. It is not creditable to the humanity and civilization of our people, much less to their Christianity, that an ordinance of this character was possible." Such consideration of the cultural values of an immigrant group was indeed rare in American jurisprudence at that time. By doing so, the justice was able to conclude that the ordinance operated with "special severity" on Chinese inmates and therefore should be considered "a cruel and unusual punishment."

Field next cited the Fourteenth Amendment provision which states that no state may "deny to any person within its jurisdiction the equal protection of the laws." After giving several examples of minority religious or other groups within American society, Field concluded that the law applied to all state executive, judicial, and legislative subdivisions and agencies and required the "equality of protection thus assured to everyone whilst within the United States, from whatever country he may have come, or of whatever race or color he may be." After commenting at length on the popular feelings against the Chinese in California, he concluded that proper authority for rectifying the miscarriage of justice lay with the federal government since it had the constitutional authority over immigration. In any case, as a final commentary on the original ordinance Field declared that such an act "is unworthy of a brave and manly people."

As a result of his victory, the offending provision was invalidated and Ho Ah Kow received a settlement of $10,000, which was quite a large amount at a time when the average laborer made about $421 per year.

Essential Themes

Justice Field heard the *Ho Ah Kow* case while serving on the California circuit as Supreme Court justices were then required to do. The first issue Field faced was whether the Board of Supervisors in fact had the authority to adopt the so-called Queue Ordinance. This was in some respects a typical case of that era where the provisions of state constitutions were being tested and the application of the Fourteenth Amendment was in its relative infancy. The Board of Supervisors had the authority that was vested in it when it was created by special legislation combining the city and county governments. Field found that the Board had no authority to impose penalties other than fines, forfeiture, and imprisonment. This did not extend to prescribing a penalty of hair cutting. Further, since the Board of Health had statutory responsibility for sanitary conditions in the county prison, neither the Board of Supervisors nor the prison officials had any such authority.

In 1879 when the case was heard, the Fourteenth Amendment had only been adopted eleven years earlier and its application was in some respects still debated between the federal and state governments and in the courts. Field clearly asserted the principle of federal preeminence over state laws, which was already established, but went on to address the issue of whether the Bill of Rights applied to the states and whether the "equal protection" clause could be invoked in a local city case where the ordinance, at least on its face, applied to everyone. His finding that the "equal protection" clause applied to states, and all of their various levels of administration, remains in effect today. Likewise, his ruling that, despite seemingly neutral language, where a law in practice had an adverse effect on a single group it in fact violated the equal protection clause of the Fourteenth Amendment. Equally important, the equal protection clause applied to everyone within the jurisdiction of the United States—citizens and non-citizens as well.

Bibliography and Further Reading

Richard P. Cole and Gabriel J. Chin, "Emerging from the Margins of Historical Consciousness: Chinese Immigrants and the History of American Law," *Law and History Review*, Vol. 17, no. 2 (Summer 1999), 325-64.

Alf Hiltebeitel, ed., *Hair: Its Power and Meaning in Asian Cultures* (Albany: State University of New York Press, 1998).

Paul Kens, *Justice Stephen Field: Shaping Liberty from the Gold Rush to the Gilded Age* (Lawrence, KS: University Press of Kansas, 1997).

Charles J. McClain, *In Search of Equality: The Chinese Struggle against Discrimination in Nineteenth-Century America* (Berkeley: University of California Press, 1994).

■ Woodrow Wilson's Third Annual Message to Congress

Date: December 7, 1915
Author: Woodrow Wilson
Genre: Speech

Summary Overview

By 1880 America's cities were already feeling the strain of overpopulation from the beginning of what would be the mass immigration of millions of Europeans over the next four decades. In response, nativist organizations lobbying for restrictions on entry began to grow in number and membership. The American Protective Association numbered some 500,000 members arguing not only against the number of people entering the country but also who they were, particularly singling out Catholics, Jews, and those from Southern and Eastern Europe as undesirables. The Immigration Restriction League harnessed the financial, intellectual, and political influence of New England's Protestant elite to carry the fight against unrestrained immigration into the halls of Congress, while on the west coast the focus of nativism was the Chinese.

Labor unions joined the chorus calling for restriction, arguing that cheap foreign labor was taking American jobs and reducing wages. The Chinese Exclusion Act was the first major nativist victory, followed periodically thereafter by limitations on various categories of people based on criteria such as physical ailments and political beliefs. When nativists made a strong push for a literacy test and other limiting provisions in 1906, opponents were able to stall the move by calling for the creation of a committee to study the issue. The result was the United States Immigration Commission, also known as the Dillingham Commission. Its report, issued in 41 volumes, supported restriction specifically of people from Southern and Eastern Europe, arguing that they were a menace to American labor, were largely incapable of benefitting from American education, and could not be readily assimilated.

Defining Moment

While the Dillingham Commission reports were being released Europe plunged into the slaughter of World War I. With the United States initially neutral, the nation's

population was somewhat divided in its feelings. Most tended to favor the British and French because of the ancestral links of the majority of the population, but German Americans, Irish Americans, and those tracing their lineage to the Austro-Hungarian Empire often supported the Central Powers because of continuing family contacts in those countries or, as in the case of Irish Americans, historical anti-British feelings.

As Germany began to perceive official American neutrality beginning to shift somewhat, if only unofficially, toward its enemies the German government made diplomatic efforts to keep the United States neutral, but also began to take more overt action through espionage and sabotage. Federal agents claimed to have thwarted several plots planned by German agents, as well as uncovering a plan to purchase American passports to be used as covers for spies and saboteurs. Virtually all of the plots that had any basis in fact involved German agents acting on behalf of their government rather than German Americans. Since the United States was not yet actively in the war, in 1915 German Americans were free to voice their support of their ancestral land. Only a handful of the millions of German Americans were ever even accused of engaging in disloyal espionage or sabotage, much less convicted of anything. Nonetheless, the a prevalent fear among many Americans was that the large German American community, both aliens and U.S. citizens, would take an active part in the war on behalf of Germany. This fear can be seen in a portion of President Woodrow Wilson's annual message to Congress in January 1915.

Author Biography

Thomas Woodrow Wilson was born in Virginia in 1856 to a family that supported the Confederacy during the Civil War. After earning a doctorate in political science at The Johns Hopkins University in Baltimore he embarked on an academic career that eventually led to the presidency of Princeton University where he refused to admit students of African ancestry. Elected governor of New Jersey in 1910 as a Democrat, he moved on to the presidency when the Republican Party split its vote between William Howard Taft and Theodore Roosevelt, the first Southerner elected to the presidency since 1848. Although considered a leader in the Progressive movement by many, he proved to be a blatant racist who instituted strict segregation in the executive branch and several other government offices, supported Jim Crow laws in the South, and lauded the racist film *Birth of a Nation* based on *The Clansman*, a book by Thomas Dixon who had been one of Wilson's students. When a group of black leaders complained to him he is said to have responded that "segregation is not a humiliation but a benefit, and ought to be so regarded by you gentlemen."

Nor was it only African ancestry that Wilson considered inferior. An advocate of eugenics who was also anti-Catholic, in his *A History of the American People* he characterized the immigration beginning in the 1870s demeaningly as "multitudes of men of the lowest class from the south of Italy and men of the meaner sort out of Hungary and Poland, men out of the ranks where there was neither skill nor energy nor any initiative of quick intelligence; and they came in numbers which increased from year to year, as if the countries of the south of Europe were disburdening themselves of the more sordid and hapless elements of their population, the men whose standards of life and of work were such as American workmen had never dreamed of hitherto."

During World War I he promoted the Espionage Act of 1917 and the Sedition Act of 1918 which were used to suppress anti-war, labor, and many immigrant publications and organizations, as well as deny the use of the U.S. mail to publications deemed subversive such as the newsletter of the Industrial Workers of the World and various immigrant labor unions. To gain the support of Irish Americans he promised he would intercede on behalf of a free Ireland once the war was over, but then reneged on the promise and when Irish leaders complained he accused Irish Americans and German Americans, without any evidence whatsoever, of being disloyal to the United States during the war and for failing to support his effort to establish a League of Nations. Regarding the latter, he complained publicly that "There is an organized propaganda against the League of Nations and against the treaty proceeding from exactly the same sources that the organized propaganda proceeded from which threatened this country here and there with disloyalty, and I want to say, I cannot say too often, any man who carries a hyphen about with him carries a dagger that he is ready to plunge into the vitals of this Republic whenever he gets ready." It was within the context of this vision of race and immigration that he gave his 1915 State of the Union Address.

HISTORICAL DOCUMENT

Since I last had the privilege of addressing you on the state of the Union the war of nations on the other side of the sea, which had then only begun to disclose its portentous proportions, has extended its threatening and sinister scope until it has swept within its flame some portion of every quarter of the globe, not excepting our own hemisphere, has altered the whole face of international affairs, and now presents a prospect of reorganization and reconstruction such as statesmen and peoples have never been called upon to attempt before.

We have stood apart, studiously neutral. It was our manifest duty to do so. Not only did we have no part or interest in the policies which seem to have brought the conflict on; it was necessary, if a universal catastrophe was to be avoided, that a limit should be set to the sweep of destructive war and that some part of the great family of nations should keep the processes of peace alive, if only to prevent collective economic ruin and the breakdown throughout the world of the industries by which its populations are fed and sustained. It was manifestly the duty of the self-governed nations of this hemisphere to redress, if possible, the balance of economic loss and confusion in the other, if they could do nothing more. In the day of readjustment and recuperation we earnestly hope and believe that they can be of infinite service.

In this neutrality, to which they were bidden not only by their separate life and their habitual detachment from the politics of Europe but also by a clear perception of international duty, the states of America have become conscious of a new and more vital community of interest and moral partnership in affairs, more clearly conscious of the many common sympathies and interests and duties which bid them stand together. ...

I have spoken to you to-day, Gentlemen, upon a single theme, the thorough preparation of the nation to care for its own security and to make sure of entire freedom to play the impartial role in this hemisphere and in the world which we all believe to have been providentially assigned to it. I have had in my mind no thought of any immediate or particular danger arising out of our relations with other nations. We are at peace with all the nations of the world, and there is reason to hope that no question in controversy between this and other Governments will lead to any serious breach of amicable relations, grave as some differences of attitude and policy have been land may yet turn out to be. I am sorry to say that the gravest threats against our national peace and safety have been uttered within our own borders. There are citizens of the United States, I blush to admit, born under other flags but welcomed under our generous naturalization laws to the full freedom and opportunity of America, who have poured the poison of disloyalty into the very arteries of our national life; who have sought to bring the authority and good name of our Government into contempt, to destroy our industries wherever they thought it effective for their vindictive purposes to strike at them, and to debase our politics to the uses of foreign intrigue. Their number is not great as compared with the whole number of those sturdy hosts by which our nation has been enriched in recent generations out of virile foreign stock; but it is great enough to have brought deep disgrace upon us and to have made it necessary that we should promptly make use of processes of law by which we may be purged of their corrupt distempers. America never witnessed anything like this before. It never dreamed it possible that men sworn into its own citizenship, men drawn out of great free stocks such as supplied some of the best and strongest elements of that little, but how heroic, nation that in a high day of old staked its very

life to free itself from every entanglement that had darkened the fortunes of the older nations and set up a new standard here, that men of such origins and such free choices of allegiance would ever turn in malign reaction against the Government and people who had welcomed and nurtured them and seek to make this proud country once more a hotbed of European passion. A little while ago such a thing would have seemed incredible. Because it was incredible we made no preparation for it. We would have been almost ashamed to prepare for it, as if we were suspicious of ourselves, our own comrades and neighbors! But the ugly and incredible thing has actually come about and we are without adequate federal laws to deal with it. I urge you to enact such laws at the earliest possible moment and feel that in doing so I am urging you to do nothing less than save the honor and self-respect of the nation. Such creatures of passion, disloyalty, and anarchy must be crushed out. They are not many, but they are infinitely malignant, and the hand of our power should close over them at once. They have formed plots to destroy property, they have entered into conspiracies against the neutrality of the Government, they have sought to pry into every confidential transaction of the Government in order to serve interests alien to our own. It is possible to deal with these things very effectually. I need not suggest the terms in which they may be dealt with.

I wish that it could be said that only a few men, misled by mistaken sentiments of allegiance to the governments under which they were born, had been guilty of disturbing the self-possession and misrepresenting the temper and principles of the country during these days of terrible war, when it would seem that every man who was truly an American would instinctively make it his duty and his pride to keep the scales of judgment even and prove himself a partisan of no nation but his own. But it cannot. There are some men among us, and many resident abroad who, though born and bred in the United States and calling themselves Americans, have so forgotten themselves and their honor as citizens as to put their passionate sympathy with one or the other side in the great European conflict above their regard for the peace and dignity of the United States. They also preach and practice disloyalty. No laws, I suppose, can reach corruptions of the mind and heart; but I should not speak of others without also speaking of these and expressing the even deeper humiliation and scorn which every self-possessed and thought- fully patriotic American must feel when lie thinks of them and of the discredit they are daily bringing upon us.

GLOSSARY

Debase: To reduce in value or quality; to cheapen.

Distemper: A person who is in ill-humor or otherwise unbalanced.

Malignant: Something dangerous, malevolent, malicious, or invasive.

Manifest: That which is obvious, clear, or readily understood.

Portentous: Something ominous, threatening, or otherwise to be viewed as a warning.

Document Analysis

With World War I underway, President Wilson reminded his listeners of the dangers threatening not only Europe but the rest of the world including the Western Hemisphere, and also that the official position of the United States was one of neutrality. This was, he reminded listeners, necessary to prevent the war from widening and also because it was the traditional U.S.policy toward Europe.

In a portion of the speech not included here, Wilson went on to discuss the natural shared interests of the United States and the other nations of the Western Hemisphere which he refers to as friendly "Pan-Americanism." He then spends considerable time explaining his plans for preparing America for defense if it becomes necessary, the requirements that will be necessary for both the army and navy, the cost of the buildup, and how he expects to pay for it. As part of this he also mentioned the necessity of maintaining a positive policy toward Puerto Rico and the Philippines, which the United States had taken from Spain as a result of the Spanish-American War. With these topics explored, the president turned to another issue which we see in the excerpt above—America's immigrant community.

While the country is at peace with all of the other nations of the world, Wilson expressed concern about what he called "the gravest threat against our national peace and safety," immigrant citizens welcomed into America who "have poured the poison of disloyalty into the very arteries of our national life; who have sought to bring the authority and good name of our Government into con- tempt, to destroy our industries wherever they thought it effective for their vindictive purposes to strike at them, and to debase our politics to the uses of foreign intrigue." Though acknowledging that "their number is not great," he asserted that it was nevertheless enough that the nation must "be purged of their corrupt distempers." He especially bemoaned that those welcomed to America and afforded all of its benefits could "malign" the "Government and people who had welcomed and nurtured them and seek to make this proud country once more a hotbed of European passion."

Wilson claimed that these disloyal people had "formed plots to destroy property, they have entered into conspiracies against the neutrality of the Government, they have sought to pry into every confidential transaction of the Government in order to serve interests alien to our own." No evidence was offered to support the assertions. And he also claimed that these actions were not limited to a few, but "some men among us, and many resident abroad who, though born and bred in the United States and calling themselves Americans, have so forgotten themselves and their honor as citizens as to put their passionate sympathy with one or the other side in the great European conflict above their regard for the peace and dignity of the United States. They also preach and practice disloyalty."

With these words, and these accusations, Wilson declared publicly that the security of the United States was being undermined by some citizens, even native-born citizens, who owed their allegiance to European powers rather than their own nation. In this, he contributed to the upsurge in nativist sentiment and the eventual restrictionist legislation of 1921 and 1924.

Essential Themes

The rising tide of nativism, especially in the wake of the release of the Dillingham Commission reports, brought forth intensified calls for a literacy test, for a reduction in immigration from selected countries, and for a reduction or even a complete stoppage of all European immigration. Rather than quell the public's fears and arrest the anti-immigrant feelings, Wilson's specific identification of not only immigrants, but native-born citizens, of European origin as being disloyal only fanned the flames prejudice and intolerance. It would not be the last time, for in the wake of World War I Wilson later placed much of the blame for opposition to his League of Nations proposal to ethnic minorities, specifically Irish Americans and German Americans.

It would also not be the last time that a United States president openly supported restriction by casting aspersions on the loyalty of naturalized citizens and their supposed racial inferiority. When Warren G. Harding became president in 1921 he summoned a special session of Congress to consider new immigration legislation for the specific purpose of not only limiting the number of arrivals but also denying entry to specific peoples identified by the Dillingham Commission as unassimilable. This was supported by another future president, Calvin Coolidge, who commented that "Biological law tells us that certain divergent people will not mix or blend."

Bibliography and Additional Reading

Arthur S. Link, *Woodrow Wilson and the Progressive Era, 1910-1917* (New York: Harper, 1954).

Hans Vought, "Woodrow Wilson, Ethnicity, and the Myth of American Unity," in Patrick Gerster and Nicholas Cords, eds., *Myth America: A Historical Anthology*, Volume II (New York: Brandywine Press, 1997).

Kathleen L. Wolgemuth, "Woodrow Wilson and Federal Segregation," *The Journal of Negro History*, Vol. 44, no. 2 (1959), 158-73.

■ Executive Order 9066

Date: February 19, 1942
Author: Franklin D. Roosevelt
Genre: Executive Order

Summary Overview

Relations between the United States and Japan had never been particularly cordial. As Asians, Japanese in America were subject to much of the discrimination aimed at the Chinese, especially on the Pacific coast. Since the Japanese government considered itself the protector of Japanese both at home and abroad, it took great offense at the treatment of its émigrés in the U.S. Although the two nations inked a treaty in 1894 by which Japanese were legally allowed to enter the U.S. and were guaranteed the same rights as American citizens, anti-Asian sentiment continued to ferment. When the San Francisco school board ordered all Japanese to attend segregated Asian schools in 1906, Japan vigorously protested this as a violation of the treaty. The resulting compromise, usually called the "Gentlemen's Agreement," although it was anything but gentlemanly, guaranteed protection for Japanese in the United States in return for the Japanese government restricting the issuance of documents allowing its subjects to go to the U.S.

Tensions were compounded with the growing commercial rivalry of the two nations in Asia, despite the fact that both at least publicly endorsed the "Open Door" principle. When the Russo-Japanese War broke out, President Theodore Roosevelt successfully mediated an end to the conflict, but many Japanese resented his "meddling," convinced that if the war had continued they would have won more concessions. In 1905 the two nations attempted to quell each other's fears with the Taft-Katsura Memorandum by which the U.S. recognized Japanese special interests in Korea and the Japanese renounced any intention to interfere with American interests in the Philippines. Despite this, apprehensions escalated beginning in 1915 when Japan began making demands on China. The Lansing-Ishii Agreement of 1917 attempted to placate both sides with the U.S. acknowledging Japanese special interest in Manchuria in return for a Japanese pledge not to interfere with U.S. commerce in China.

Defining Moment

Strained relations between the U.S. and Japan rose dramatically when the Japanese army took permanent control of Manchuria in 1931. When the League of Nations condemned Japan as an aggressor, it walked out of the League in 1933. Four years later it invaded China. President Franklin D. Roosevelt responded by sending aid to China to help it resist the invasion. Japan reacted by sinking the U.S. gunboat *Panay* as a warning to America to stay out of the conflict. When the U.S., Britain, and the Netherlands joined in a boycott in an attempt to force Japanese withdrawal from China by denying it desperately needed oil, Japan determined to take what it needed even if it meant war with the three Western powers. The attack on Pearl Harbor was an attempt to neutralize the U.S. Pacific Fleet so that Japan could safely invade the oil-rich areas of Southeast Asia.

Naturally, the Japanese attack on America, especially without a prior declaration of war, greatly enraged Americans toward the Asian nation and, by extension, those of Japanese ancestry in the United States. In 1941 there were approximately 120,000 people of Japanese ancestry residing along the Pacific coast, approximately two-thirds of whom were American citizens. Aside from these, the largest concentration was in Hawaii where over 150,000 people of Japanese ancestry accounted for more than one-third of the total population. Given the "sneak" attack on Hawaii and the anti-Japanese stories appearing in its wake, it is not surprising that many government officials, especially those connected with the armed forces whose responsibility it was to keep Hawaii and the western states safe, became concerned that some of these people might engaged in espionage or sabotage. The result was Executive Order 9066.

Author Biography

Although signed by President Franklin Roosevelt, actual authorship of the Executive Order lay with Henry Stimson and John McCloy. Stimson was born into a wealthy family in New York City in 1867 and graduate Phi Beta Kappa from Yale University. He earned his law degree from Harvard University in 1890. A Republican, he served as Secretary of War under William Howard Taft, Governor-General of the Philippines under Calvin Coolidge, and Secretary of State for Herbert Hoover. In the latter position he pursued a policy of opposing Japanese expansion in the Pacific that came to be known as the Stimson Doctrine. In 1940, FDR recalled Stimson to the position of Secretary of War in an effort at bipartisanship. Stimson was known for supporting U.S. intervention in the war against Germany. John McCloy was born in Philadelphia in 1895 and graduated from Amherst College. After leaving Harvard to serve in World War I, he returned to earn his law degree in 1921. Another Republican who joined the Roosevelt administration, he served as Assistant Secretary of War.

Following the attack on Pearl Harbor some military officials, fearing possible espionage and sabotage activities in regions with large Japanese populations, urged that they be removed from sensitive areas. The suggestion was opposed by the Justice Department and, at least initially, Stimson. Increasing pressure from the military, Pacific coast politicians, and McCloy eventually convinced Stimson to support the proposal. In fact, McCloy's biographer, Kai Bird, wrote that "More than any individual, McCloy was responsible for the decision, since the President had delegated the matter to him through Stimson." Once Executive Order 9066 was issued, Stimson and McCloy urged the evacuation of all Japanese from the Hawaiian Islands, but this was quickly deemed unfeasible since they constituted such a large portion of the islands' population and labor force.

After the war Stimson retired in 1945 to write his memoirs. He died in West Hill, New York, in October 1950. McCloy went on to become president of the World Bank and U.S. High Commissioner for Germany. He served as chair of the Chase Manhattan Bank and the Council on Foreign Relations and was a member of the Warren Commission investigating the assassination of President John F. Kennedy. He died in Stamford, Connecticut, in March 1989.

HISTORICAL DOCUMENT

Whereas the successful prosecution of the war requires every possible protection against espionage and against sabotage to national-defense material, national-defense premises, and national-defense utilities as defined in Section 4, Act of April 20, 1918, 40 Stat. 533, as amended by the Act of November 30, 1940, 54 Stat. 1220, and the Act of August 21, 1941, 55 Stat. 655 (U.S.C., Title 50, Sec. 104);

Now, therefore, by virtue of the authority vested in me as President of the United States, and Commander in Chief of the Army and Navy, I hereby authorize and direct the Secretary of War, and the Military Commanders whom he may from time to time designate, whenever he or any designated Commander deems such action necessary or desirable, to prescribe military areas in such places and of such extent as he or the appropriate Military Commander may determine, from which any or all persons may be excluded, and with respect to which, the right of any person to enter, remain in, or leave shall be subject to whatever restrictions the Secretary of War or the appropriate Military Commander may impose in his discretion. The Secretary of War is hereby authorized to provide for residents of any such area who are excluded therefrom, such transportation, food, shelter, and other accommodations as may be necessary, in the judgment of the Secretary of War or the said Military Commander, and until other arrangements are made, to accomplish the purpose of this order. The designation of military areas in any region or locality shall supersede designations of prohibited and restricted areas by the Attorney General under the Proclamations of December 7 and 8, 1941, and shall supersede the responsibility and authority of the Attorney General under the said Proclamations in respect of such prohibited and restricted areas.

I hereby further authorize and direct the Secretary of War and the said Military Commanders to take such other steps as he or the appropriate Military Commander may deem advisable to enforce compliance with the restrictions applicable to each Military area hereinabove authorized to be designated, including the use of Federal troops and other Federal Agencies, with authority to accept assistance of state and local agencies.

I hereby further authorize and direct all Executive Departments, independent establishments and other Federal Agencies, to assist the Secretary of War or the said Military Commanders in carrying out this Executive Order, including the furnishing of medical aid, hospitalization, food, clothing, transportation, use of land, shelter, and other supplies, equipment, utilities, facilities, and services.

This order shall not be construed as modifying or limiting in any way the authority heretofore granted under Executive Order No. 8972, dated December 12, 1941, nor shall it be construed as limiting or modifying the duty and responsibility of the Federal Bureau of Investigation, with respect to the investigation of alleged acts of sabotage or the duty and responsibility of the Attorney General and the Department of Justice under the Proclamations of December 7 and 8, 1941, prescribing regulations for the conduct and control of alien enemies, except as such duty and responsibility is superseded by the designation of military areas hereunder.

GLOSSARY

Executive Order: A directive issued by the president to the executive branch of government to implement federal laws or policies or to interpret existing laws or policies. Executive Orders have the force of law when originating in the Constitutional powers delegated to the President or in authority delegated by Congress.

Supersede: To take the place of; to replace.

Explanation and Analysis of the Document

The Executive Order begins with a statement of why it is deemed necessary and a citation of the specific legislation that authorizes its issuance, primarily those dealing with the authority of the President as commander-in-chief of the armed forces. It delegates responsibility for enforcement to the Secretary of War and the "Military Commanders," specifically excluding the Attorney General, but allows them the discretion to enforce the Order only when they deem "such action necessary or desirable." This allowed local military commanders of the various theaters and areas to determine for themselves if sufficient reason existed to implement the policy.

Assuming that the military leader believed there was sufficient cause, then the Executive Order gave the officer authority to determine a geographic area within which "any or all persons may be excluded" or subject to any restrictions the officer believed necessary. Essentially, any geographic area of any extent under any military commander could, by simple order of that person, be designated as a restricted area within which people could be removed or their movements into and out of the area restricted by whatever requirements that commander might authorize. Should it become necessary, the Order requires "all Executive Departments, independent establishments and other Federal Agencies" to assist in whatever way necessary "including the furnishing of medical aid, hospitalization, food, clothing, transportation, use of land, shelter, and other supplies, equipment, utilities, facilities, and services." This provision was later modified by Executive Order 9102 which conveyed responsibility for the resulting internment camps and their occupants to the War Relocation Authority.

Once an area was declared restricted, the responsible authorities were to "provide for residents" who had been "excluded therefrom, such transportation, food, shelter, and other accommodations as may be necessary, in the judgment of the Secretary of War or the said Military Commander, and until other arrangements are made, to accomplish the purpose of this order." To implement this policy the responsible officers were authorized to use "Federal troops and other Federal Agencies, with authority to accept assistance of state and local agencies."

Nowhere in the document does it specifically mention those of Japanese ancestry, however Presidential Proclamation No. 2525 of December 7, 1941, identified Japanese as enemy aliens. This was followed on the following day by Presidential Proclamations No. 2526 and 2527 which likewise identified Germans and Italians as enemy aliens. In all three cases enemy aliens were "liable to restraint, or to give security, or to remove and depart from the United States" in a manner prescribed by the

WESTERN DEFENSE COMMAND AND FOURTH ARMY
WARTIME CIVIL CONTROL ADMINISTRATION
Presidio of San Francisco, California
April 1, 1942

INSTRUCTIONS
TO ALL PERSONS OF
JAPANESE
ANCESTRY
Living in the Following Area:

All that portion of the City and County of San Francisco, State of California, lying generally west of the north-south line established by Junipero Serra Boulevard, Worchester Avenue, and Nineteenth Avenue, and lying generally north of the east-west line established by California Street, to the intersection of Market Street, and thence on Market Street to San Francisco Bay.

All Japanese persons, both alien and non-alien, will be evacuated from the above designated area by 12:00 o'clock noon Tuesday, April 7, 1942.

No Japanese person will be permitted to enter or leave the above described area after 8:00 a. m., Thursday, April 2, 1942, without obtaining special permission from the Provost Marshal at the Civil Control Station located at:

1701 Van Ness Avenue
San Francisco, California

The Civil Control Station is equipped to assist the Japanese population affected by this evacuation in the following ways:

1. Give advice and instructions on the evacuation.

2. Provide services with respect to the management, leasing, sale, storage or other disposition of most kinds of property including: real estate, business and professional equipment, buildings, household goods, boats, automobiles, livestock, etc.

3. Provide temporary residence elsewhere for all Japanese in family groups.

4. Transport persons and a limited amount of clothing and equipment to their new residence, as specified below.

The Following Instructions Must Be Observed:

1. A responsible member of each family, preferably the head of the family, or the person in whose name most of the property is held, and each individual living alone, will report to the Civil Control Station to receive further instructions. This must be done between 8:00 a. m. and 5:00 p. m., Thursday, April 2, 1942, or between 8:00 a. m. and 5:00 p. m., Friday, April 3, 1942.

Sign posted notifying people of Japanese descent to report for relocation government. It is also interesting to note that the Attorney General is specifically excluded from the process, which may have been intentional since the Justice Department had voiced some early concerns over the constitutionality of any such restriction when the idea was initially suggested.

Essential Themes

This was not the first time that extraordinary presidential or legislative action had been taken in time of crisis. President Abraham Lincoln had suspended the writ of habeas corpus at the beginning of the Civil War even though the Supreme Court later found his action unconstitutional. During World War I the Sedition Act provided penalties for "disloyal, profane, scurrilous, or abusive language" used in reference to the President, Congress, government officials or the form of government of the United States regardless of protests that this legislation trampled on the rights to free speech and freedom on the press. Yet, very few people objected to Executive Order 9066 given the circumstances under which it was issued.

Since Executive Order 9066 gave military commanders discretion over application, Lt. Gen. John L. DeWitt, leading the Western Command, immediately began implementation, later testifying to Congress that "They are a dangerous element. There is no way to determine their loyalty.... It makes no difference whether he is an American citizen, he is still a Japanese. American citizenship does not necessarily determine loyalty." Approximately 112,000 Japanese were sent to internment camps which operated until 1944, 62 percent of them American citizens who had not even been accused of any crime, much less convicted. The camps were located in Arizona, Arkansas, California, Colorado, Idaho, Utah, and Wyoming. Yet, in Hawaii, where more than a third of the population was of Japanese ancestry, no such action was taken. Instead, between 1,200 and 1,800 people were interned who were resident aliens where there was some perceived probable cause. That was only about 1.2 percent of those on the islands.

In 1944 in the case of *Korematsu v. the United States*, the Supreme Court found Executive Order 9066 to be within the constitutional authority of the president. However, four years later President Harry Truman signed into law the Japanese-American Evacuation Claims Act providing $28 million to Japanese business owners who lost their property as a result of the internments. In 1976 President Gerald Ford officially revoked Executive Order 9066 and in 1988 President Ronald Reagan signed the Civil Liberties Act into law providing an official apology for the internment of Japanese during the war and a payment of $20,000 in compensation to each internee who was an American citizen or permanent resident. Eventually, 82,219 survivors or their heirs were identified, receiving $1,644,380,000 in total payments.

Bibliography and Further Reading

John Armor and Peter Wright, *Manzanar* (New York: Times Books, 1988).

Maisie Conrat, Richard Conrat and Dorothea Lange, *Executive Order 9066: The Internment of 110,000 Japanese Americans* (San Francisco: California Historical Society, 1972).

Roger Daniels, *Prisoners Without Trial: Japanese Americans in World War II* (New York: Hill and Wang, 2004).

Lawson Fusao Inada, *Only What We Could Carry: The Japanese American Internment Experience* (San Francisco: California Historical Society, 2000).

Peter Irons, *Justice at War: The Story of the Japanese American Internment Cases* (New York: Oxford University Press, 1983).

Greg Robinson, *By Order of the President: FDR and the Internment of Japanese Americans* (Cambridge, MA: Harvard University Press, 2001).

Toyo Suyemoto and Susan B. Richardson, *I Call to Remembrance: Toyo Suyemoto's Years of Internment* (New Brunswick, NJ: Rutgers University Press, 2007).

■ Presidential Veto of the McCarran-Walter Bill

Date: June 25, 1952
Author: Harry S Truman
Genre: Presidential Veto Message

Summary Overview

Immigration had been a major national issue from the 1880s through 1924 when quotas were established limiting both the number of people admissible per year and the nationalities that could enter the country. World War II found the United States allied against Fascist Germany and militarist Japan with some of the very nations whose citizens America was largely rejecting as undesirables—Russia, Poland, Greece, and later Italy. The end of World War II found hundreds of thousands of refugees in Western Europe, many of whom did not want to return to their Eastern European homelands which had come under Communist rule. Foremost among these were some 240,000 veterans of the Polish army that had fought with the Allies against Germany but, with the Soviet Union in control of Poland, now preferred to remain in the West.

The refugee question quickly brought the immigration issue once again into the national spotlight. Led by various ethnic organizations in the United States, lobbying efforts sought to influence the government to modify its strict quota system to permit the entrance of refugees from the areas in Eastern Europe then under Communist control. As a direct result of these efforts, Congress passed the Displaced Persons Acts in 1948 and 1950 and a special law allowing Polish veterans into the country. Thus, between 1945 and 1954 some 178,000 Poles entered the country.

Despite the momentary opening of America's doors, the restrictive quota system remained in place and there were those who sought to keep it that way.

Defining Moment

In the wake of World War II, Cold War tensions rose. Beginning it 1950 the Korean War was the first major ongoing military conflict between the Communist bloc and the West. By 1952, Eastern Europe was firmly in the grasp of the Soviet Union and in China the Communist forces of Mao Zedong had defeated the U.S.-backed Nationalists of Chiang Kai-shek, forcing them to retreat to the island of Taiwan off the coast of China. Many Americans were very much afraid of the spread of Communism and radicalism, which provided a context for efforts to review the immigration laws with an eye toward keeping out potential threats from the nations on the other side of the Cold War divide.

To address the immigration issue Senator Patrick McCarran of Nevada and Representative Francis Walter of Pennsylvania proposed the Immigration and Naturalization Act of 1952, often referred to simply as the McCarran-Walter Act. The bill retained the national origins quotas from earlier legislation but proposed to add a system of preferences. First priority was to be given to immigrants with special skills of use to the U.S. or relatives of U.S. citizens who were to be admitted without restriction. Additionally, because of fears of the spread of communism, the legislation gave the federal government the authority to bar suspected radicals and subversives from entry into the country and to deport immigrants and naturalized citizens identified as subversives. The bill passed the House and the Senate. From there it went to the desk of President Harry S Truman.

Author Biography

Harry S Truman was born in Lamar, Missouri, in 1884, but grew up in Independence where he attended the local high school. He worked briefly on the railroad and then as a bank clerk and farmer, and served in the state's national Guard for six years. When the United States entered World War I he saw combat as a captain in the field artillery in France. Following the war he managed a clothing store, but it soon failed. Elected to a county judgeship in 1922, he lost a bid for re-election, but was successful in seeking a judgeship in 1926 and again four years later. Although enjoying a reputation for honesty he conversely came under the wing of the Democratic political boss Thomas Pendergast who supported him in his early career and during his successful run for the U.S. Senate in 1934. He rose to national prominence as chair of the Senate Special Committee to Investigate the National Defense Program where he ferreted out corruption in government contracting during World War II.

Elected as vice president to Franklin Roosevelt in 1944, he had served less than three months when the president's death thrust him into leadership of the nation during the closing months of World War II. Certainly his most difficult decision was whether or not to use the atomic bomb, which he knew nothing about until after FDR's death. In the postwar years he fol-

lowed a foreign policy of containment, which became known as the Truman Doctrine, and supported the Marshall Plan for rebuilding Europe. At home the former Missouri senator surprised many by championing African American rights. In 1948 he used executive orders to ban racial discrimination in federal hiring, order the desegregation of the armed forces, and establish the Committee on Civil Rights. Additionally, against the advice of many he opted to recognize the new Jewish state of Israel. He was drawn into the immigration debate when the McCarran-Walter Bill appeared on his desk for signature.

HISTORICAL DOCUMENT

To the House of Representatives:

I return herewith, without my approval, H.R. 5678, the proposed Immigration and Nationality Act.

In outlining my objections to this bill, I want to make it clear that it contains certain provisions that meet with my approval. This is a long and complex piece of legislation. It has 164 separate sections, some with more than 40 subdivisions. It presents a difficult problem of weighing the good against the bad, and arriving at a judgment on the whole.

H.R. 5678 is an omnibus bill which would revise and codify all of our laws relating to immigration, naturalization, and nationality.

A general revision and modernization of these laws unquestionably is needed and long overdue, particularly with respect to immigration. But this bill would not provide us with an immigration policy adequate for the present world situation. Indeed, the bill, taking all its provisions together, would be a step backward and not a step forward. In view of the crying need for reform in the field of immigration, I deeply regret that I am unable to approve H.R. 5678.

In recent years, our immigration policy has become a matter of major national concern. Long dormant questions about the effect of our immigration laws now assume first rate importance. What we do in the field of immigration and naturalization is vital to the continued growth and internal development of the United States— to the economic and social strength of our country—

which is the core of the defense of the free world. Our immigration policy is equally, if not more important to the conduct of our foreign relations and to our responsibilities of moral leadership in the struggle for world peace.

In one respect, this bill recognizes the great international significance of our immigration and naturalization policy, and takes a step to improve existing laws. All racial bars to naturalization would be removed, and at least some minimum immigration quota would be afforded to each of the free nations of Asia.

I have long urged that racial or national barriers to naturalization be abolished. This was one of the recommendations in my civil rights message to the Congress on February 2, 1948. On February 19, 1951, the House of Representatives unanimously passed a bill to carry it out.

But now this most desirable provision comes before me embedded in a mass of legislation which would perpetuate injustices of long standing against many other nations of the world, hamper the efforts we are making to rally the men of East and West alike to the cause of freedom, and intensify the repressive and inhumane aspects of our immigration procedures. The price is too high, and in good conscience I cannot agree to pay it.

I want all our residents of Japanese ancestry, and all our friends throughout the far East, to understand this point clearly. I cannot take the step I would like to take, and strike down the bars that prejudice has erected against them, without, at the same time, establishing new discriminations against the peoples of Asia and approving harsh and repressive measures directed at all who seek a new life within our boundaries. I am sure that with a little more time and a little more discussion in this country the public conscience and the good sense of the American people will assert themselves, and we shall be in a position to enact an immigration and naturalization policy that will be fair to all.

In addition to removing racial bars to naturalization, the bill would permit American women citizens to bring their alien husbands to this country as non-quota immigrants, and enable alien husbands of resident women aliens to come in under the quota in a preferred status. These provisions would be a step toward preserving the integrity of the family under our immigration laws, and are clearly desirable.

The bill would also relieve transportation companies of some of the unjustified burdens and penalties now imposed upon them. In particular, it would put an end to the archaic requirement that carriers pay the expenses of aliens detained at the port of entry, even though such aliens have arrived with proper travel documents.

But these few improvements are heavily outweighed by other provisions of the bill which retain existing defects in our laws, and add many undesirable new features.

The bill would continue, practically without change, the national origins quota system, which was enacted, into law in 1924, and put into effect in 1929. This quota system—always based upon assumptions at variance with our American ideals—is long since out of date and more than ever unrealistic in the face of present world conditions.

This system hinders us in dealing with current immigration problems, and is a constant handicap in the conduct of our foreign relations. As I stated in my message to Congress on March 24, 1952, on the need for an emergency program of immigration from Europe, "Our present quota system is not only inadequate to most present emergency needs, it is also an obstacle to the development of an enlightened and satisfactory immigration policy for the long-run future."

The inadequacy of the present quota system has been demonstrated since the end of the war, when we were compelled to resort to emergency legislation to admit displaced persons. If the quota system remains unchanged, we shall be compelled to resort to similar emergency legislation again, in order to admit any substantial portion of the refugees from communism or the victims of overcrowding in Europe.

With the idea of quotas in general there is no quarrel. Some numerical limitation must be set, so that immigration will be within our capacity to absorb. But the overall limitation of numbers imposed by the national origins quota system is too small for our needs today, and the country by country limitations create a pattern that is insulting to large numbers of our finest citizens, irritating to our allies abroad, and foreign to our purposes and ideals.

The overall quota limitation, under the law of 1924, restricted annual immigration to approximately 150,000. This was about one-seventh of one percent of our total population in 1920. Taking into account the growth in population since 1920, the law now allows us but one-tenth of one percent of our total population. And since the largest national quotas are only partly used, the number actually coming in has been in the neighborhood of one-fifteenth of one percent. This is far less than we must have in the years ahead to keep up with the growing needs of the Nation for manpower to maintain the strength and vigor of our economy.

The greatest vice of the present quota system, however, is that it discriminates, deliberately and intentionally, against many of the peoples of the world. The purpose behind it was to cut down and virtually eliminate immigration to this country from Southern and Eastern Europe. A theory was invented to rationalize this objective. The theory was that in order to be readily assimilable, European immigrants should be admitted in proportion to the numbers of persons of their respective national stocks already here as shown by the census of 1920. Since Americans of English, Irish and German descent were most numerous, immigrants of those three nationalities got the lion's share—more than two-thirds—of the total quota. The remaining third was divided up among all the other nations given quotas.

The desired effect was obtained. Immigration from the newer sources of Southern and Eastern Europe was reduced to a trickle. The quotas allotted to England and Ireland remained largely unused, as was intended. Total quota immigration fell to a half or a third—and sometimes even less—of the annual limit of 154,000. People from such countries as Greece, or Spain, or Latvia were virtually deprived of any opportunity to come here at all, simply because Greeks or Spaniards or Latvians had not come here before 1920 in any substantial numbers.

The idea behind this discriminatory policy was, to put it baldly, that Americans with English or Irish names were better people and better citizens than Americans with Italian or Greek or Polish names. It was thought that people of West European origin made better citizens than Rumanians or Yugoslavs or Ukrainians or Hungarians or Baits or Austrians. Such a concept is utterly unworthy of our traditions and our ideals. It violates the great political doctrine of the Declaration of Independence that "all men are created equal." It denies the humanitarian creed inscribed beneath the Statue of Liberty proclaiming to all nations, "Give me your tired, your poor, your huddled masses yearning to breathe free."

It repudiates our basic religious concepts, our belief in the brotherhood of man, and in the words of St. Paul that "there is neither Jew nor Greek, there is neither bond nor free .... for ye are all one in Christ Jesus."

The basis of this quota system was false and unworthy in 1924. It is even worse now. At the present time, this quota system keeps out the very people we want to bring in. It is incredible to me that, in this year of 1952, we should again be enacting into law such a slur on the patriotism, the capacity, and the decency of a large part of our citizenry.

Today, we have entered into an alliance, the North Atlantic Treaty, with Italy, Greece, and Turkey against one of the most terrible threats mankind has ever faced. We are asking them to join with us in protecting the peace of the world. We are helping them to build their defenses, and train their men, in the common cause. But, through this bill we say to their people: You are less worthy to come to this country than Englishmen or Irishmen; you Italians, who need to find homes abroad in the hundreds of thousands—you shall have a quota of 5,645; you Greeks, struggling to assist the helpless victims of a communist civil war—you shall have a quota of 308; and you Turks, you are brave defenders of the Eastern flank, but you shall have a quota of only 225!

Today, we are "protecting" ourselves, as we were in 1924, against being flooded by immigrants from East-

ern Europe. This is fantastic. The countries of Eastern Europe have fallen under the communist yoke—they are silenced, fenced off by barbed wire and minefields—no one passes their borders but at the risk of his life. We do not need to be protected against immigrants from these countries—on the contrary we want to stretch out a helping hand, to save those who have managed to flee into Western Europe, to succor those who are brave enough to escape from barbarism, to welcome and restore them against the day when their countries will, as we hope, be free again. But this we cannot do, as we would like to do, because the quota for Poland is only 6,500, as against the 138,000 exiled Poles, all over Europe, who are asking to come to these shores; because the quota for the now subjugated Baltic countries is little more than 700—against the 23,000 Baltic refugees imploring us to admit them to a new life here; because the quota for Rumania is only 289, and some 30,000 Rumanians, who have managed to escape the labor camps and the mass deportations of their Soviet masters, have asked our help. These are only a few examples of the absurdity, the cruelty of carrying over into this year of 1952 the isolationist limitations of our 1924 law.

In no other realm of our national life are we so hampered and stultified by the dead hand of the past, as we are in this field of immigration. We do not limit our cities to their 1920 boundaries—we do not hold our corporations to their 1920 capitalizations—we welcome progress and change to meet changing conditions in every sphere of life, except in the field of immigration.

The time to shake off this dead weight of past mistakes is now. The time to develop a decent policy of immigration—a fitting instrument for our foreign policy and a true reflection of the ideals we stand for, at home and abroad—is now. In my earlier message on immigration, I tried to explain to the Congress that the situation we face in immigration is an emergency—that it must be met promptly. I have pointed out that in the last few years, we have blazed a new trail in immigration, through our Displaced Persons Program. Through the combined efforts of the Government and private agencies, working together not to keep people out, but to bring qualified people in, we summoned our resources of good will and human feeling to meet the task. In this program, we have found better techniques to meet the immigration problems of the 1950's.

None of this fruitful experience of the last three years is reflected in this bill before me. None of the crying human needs of this time of trouble is recognized in this bill. But it is not too late. The Congress can remedy these defects, and it can adopt legislation to meet the most critical problems before adjournment.

The only consequential change in the 1924 quota system which the bill would make is to extend a small quota to each of the countries of Asia. But most of the beneficial effects of this gesture are offset by other provisions of the bill. The countries of Asia are told in one breath that they shall have quotas for their nationals, and in the next, that the nationals of the other countries, if their ancestry is as much as 50 percent Asian, shall be charged to these quotas.

It is only with respect to persons of oriental ancestry that this invidious discrimination applies. All other persons are charged to the country of their birth. But persons with Asian ancestry are charged to the countries of Asia, wherever they may have been born, or however long their ancestors have made their homes outside the land of their origin. These provisions are without justification.

I now wish to turn to the other provisions of the bill, those dealing with the qualifications of aliens and immigrants for admission, with the administration of the laws, and with problems of naturalization and nationality. In these provisions too, I find objections that preclude my signing this bill.

The bill would make it even more difficult to enter our country. Our resident aliens would be more easily separated from homes and families under grounds of deportation, both new and old, which would specifically be made retroactive. Admission to our citizenship would be made more difficult; expulsion from our citizenship would be made easier. Certain rights of native born, first generation Americans would be limited. All our citizens returning from abroad would be subjected to serious risk of unreasonable invasions of privacy. Seldom has a bill exhibited the distrust evidenced here for citizens and aliens alike—at a time when we need unity at home, and the confidence of our friends abroad.

We have adequate and fair provisions in our present law to protect us against the entry of criminals. The changes made by the bill in those provisions would result in empowering minor immigration and consular officials to act as prosecutor, judge and jury in determining whether acts constituting a crime have been committed. Worse, we would be compelled to exclude certain people because they have been convicted by "courts" in communist countries that know no justice. Under this provision, no matter how construed, it would not be possible for us to admit many of the men and women who have stood up against totalitarian repression and have been punished for doing so. I do not approve of substituting totalitarian vengeance for democratic justice. I will not extend full faith and credit to the judgments of the communist secret police.

The realities of a world, only partly free, would again be ignored in the provision flatly barring entry to those who made misrepresentations in securing visas. To save their lives and the lives of loved ones still imprisoned, refugees from tyranny sometimes misstate various details of their lives. We do not want to encourage fraud. But we must recognize that conditions in some parts of the world drive our friends to desperate steps. An exception restricted to cases involving misstatement of country of birth is not sufficient. And to make refugees from oppression forever deportable on such technical grounds is shabby treatment indeed.

Some of the new grounds of deportation which the bill would provide are unnecessarily severe. Defects and mistakes in admission would serve to deport at any time because of the bill's elimination, retroactively as well as prospectively, of the present humane provision barring deportations on such grounds five years after entry. Narcotic drug addicts would be deportable at any time, whether or not the addiction was culpable, and whether or not cured. The threat of deportation would drive the addict into hiding beyond the reach of cure, and the danger to the country from drug addiction would be increased.

I am asked to approve the reenactment of highly objectionable provisions now contained in the Internal Security Act of 1950—a measure passed over my veto shortly after the invasion of South Korea. Some of these provisions would empower the Attorney General to deport any alien who has engaged or has had a purpose to engage in activities "prejudicial to the public interest" or "subversive to the national security." No standards or definitions are provided to guide discretion in the exercise of powers so sweeping. To punish undefined "activities" departs from traditional American insistence on established standards of guilt. To punish an undefined "purpose" is thought control.

These provisions are worse than the infamous Alien Act of 1798, passed in a time of national fear and distrust of foreigners, which gave the President power to deport any alien deemed "dangerous to the peace and safety of the United States." Alien residents were thoroughly frightened and citizens much disturbed by that threat to liberty.

Such powers are inconsistent with our democratic ideals. Conferring powers like that upon the Attorney General is unfair to him as well as to our alien residents. Once fully informed of such vast discretionary powers vested in the Attorney General, Americans now would and should be just as alarmed as Americans were in 1798 over less drastic powers vested in the President.

Heretofore, for the most part, deportation and exclusion have rested upon findings of fact made upon evidence. Under this bill, they would rest in many instances upon the "opinion" or "satisfaction" of immigration or consular employees. The change from objective findings to subjective feelings is not compatible with our system of justice. The result would be to restrict or eliminate judicial review of unlawful administrative action.

The bill would sharply restrict the present opportunity of citizens and alien residents to save family members from deportation. Under the procedures of present law, the Attorney General can exercise his discretion to suspend deportation in meritorious cases. In each such case, at the present time, the exercise of administrative discretion is subject to the scrutiny and approval of the Congress. Nevertheless, the bill would prevent this discretion from being used in many cases where it is now available, and would narrow the circle of those who can obtain relief from the letter of the law. This is most unfortunate, because the bill, in its other provisions, would impose harsher restrictions and greatly increase the number of cases deserving equitable relief.

Native-born American citizens who are dual nationals would be subjected to loss of citizenship on grounds not applicable to other native-born American citizens. This distinction is a slap at millions of Americans whose fathers were of alien birth.

Children would be subjected to additional risk of loss of citizenship. Naturalized citizens would be subjected to the risk of denaturalization by any procedure that can be found to be permitted under any State law or practice pertaining to minor civil law suits. Judicial review of administrative denials of citizenship would be severely limited and impeded in many cases, and completely eliminated in others. I believe these provisions raise serious constitutional questions. Constitutionality aside, I see no justification in national policy for their adoption.

Section 401 of this bill would establish a Joint Congressional Committee on Immigration and Nationality Policy. This committee would have the customary powers to hold hearings and to subpoena witnesses, books, papers and documents. But the Committee would also be given powers over the Executive branch which are unusual and of a highly questionable nature. Specifically, section 401 would provide that "The Secretary of State and the Attorney General shall without delay submit to the Committee all regulations, instructions, and all other information as requested by the Committee relative to the administration of this Act."

This section appears to be another attempt to require the Executive branch to make available to the Congress administrative documents, communications between the President and his subordinates, confidential files, and other records of that character. It also seems to imply that the Committee would undertake to supervise or approve regulations. Such proposals are not consistent with the Constitutional doctrine of the separation of powers.

In these and many other respects, the bill raises basic questions as to our fundamental immigration and naturalization policy, and the laws and practices for putting that policy into effect.

Many of the aspects of the bill which have been most widely criticized in the public debate are reaffirmations or elaborations of existing statutes or administrative procedures. Time and again, examination discloses that the revisions of existing law that would be made by the bill are intended to solidify some restrictive practice of our immigration authorities, or to overrule or modify some ameliorative decision of the Supreme Court or other Federal courts. By and large, the changes that would be made by the bill do not depart from the basically restrictive spirit of our existing laws—but intensify and reinforce it.

These conclusions point to an underlying condition which deserves the most careful study. Should we not undertake a reassessment of our immigration policies and practices in the light of the conditions that face us in the second half of the twentieth century? The great popular interest which this bill has created, and the criticism which it has stirred up, demand an affirmative answer. I hope the Congress will agree to a careful reexamination of this entire matter.

To assist in this complex task, I suggest the creation of a representative commission of outstanding Americans to examine the basic assumptions of our immigration policy, the quota system and all that goes with it, the effect of our present immigration and nationality laws, their administration, and the ways in which they can be brought in line with our national ideals and our foreign policy.

Such a commission should, I believe, be established by the Congress. Its membership should be bi-partisan and divided equally among persons from private life and persons from public life. I suggest that four members be appointed by the President, four by the President of the Senate, and four by the Speaker of the House of Representatives. The commission should be given sufficient funds to employ a staff and it should have adequate powers to hold hearings, take testimony, and obtain information. It should make a report to the President and to the Congress within a year from the time of its creation.

Pending the completion of studies by such a commission, and the consideration of its recommendations by the Congress, there are certain steps which I believe it is most important for the Congress to take this year.

First, I urge the Congress to enact legislation removing racial barriers against Asians from our laws. Failure to take this step profits us nothing and can only have serious consequences for our relations with the peoples of the far East. A major contribution to this end would be the prompt enactment by the Senate of H.R. 403. That bill, already passed by the House of Representatives, would remove the racial bars to the naturalization of Asians.

Second, I strongly urge the Congress to enact the temporary, emergency immigration legislation which I recommended three months ago. In my message of March 24, 1952, I advised the Congress that one of the gravest problems arising from the present world crisis is created by the overpopulation in parts of Western Europe. That condition is aggravated by the flight and expulsion of people from behind the iron curtain. In view of these serious problems, I asked the Congress to authorize the admission of 300,000 additional immigrants to the United States over a three year period. These immigrants would include Greek nationals, Dutch nationals, Italians from Italy and Trieste, Germans and persons of German ethnic origin, and religious and political refugees from communism in Eastern Europe. This temporary program is urgently needed. It is very important that the Congress act upon it this year. I urge the Congress to give prompt and favorable consideration to the bills introduced by Senator Hendrickson and Representative Celler (S. 3109 and H.R. 7376), which will implement the recommendations contained in my message of March 24.

I very much hope that the Congress will take early action on these recommendations. Legislation to carry them out will correct some of the unjust provisions of our laws, will strengthen us at home and abroad, and will serve to relieve a great deal of the suffering and tension existing in the world today.

GLOSSARY

Bi-partisan: In political or government usage, the term refers to cooperation or compromise on some issue between two political parties or factions who usually take opposing positions.

Displaced persons: A person forced to become a refugee, usually because of war, oppression, or some natural disaster. The term was mostly applied to about 850,000 such refugees who lived for a time in displaced persons camps in Europe before being relocated following World War II.

Iron curtain: Coined by Winston Churchill, the term is a metaphor for the political border separating the Soviet occupied nations in Europe from those aligned with the Western powers.

Omnibus bill: A bill that is submitted to a legislative body as a single unit although it is made up of two or more proposals, usually on varied subjects. The purpose is to have a single vote on the entirety of the bill.

Totalitarianism: A form of government in which a centralized authority exercises absolute control over its citizens and their activities.

Document Analysis

Truman begins his veto message by noting how important the issue is, that he agrees with some of the provisions, but unfortunately he finds other stipulations in the bill that he cannot accept. This is a typical problem with large omnibus bills that combine multiple provisos on a number of varied topics. In this instance, after weighing the positive and negative elements contained in the bill, the president determined that he was unable to sign it into law. He stressed that this is particularly unfortunate because removing some older immigration and naturalization requirements or limitations would be important in supporting the moral leadership of the United States in the world.

The president's major opposition to the bill was that it "would perpetuate injustices of long standing against many other nations of the world, hamper the efforts we are making to rally the men of East and West alike to the cause of freedom, and intensify the repressive and inhumane aspects of our immigration procedures." Yet, the way the bill is written he is unable to eliminate some injustices without creating others. He prefers, and believes the American people would favor, that all discrimination be eliminated.

Truman notes some aspects of the bill that he likes, but then explains in detail those to which he objects. The first concern he cites is that the bill would retain the national origins quotas from the 1920s which he believed were not in accord with American ideals and "unrealistic

in the face of present world conditions." This system, he argued, is a roadblock to addressing current immigration issues while also being "a constant handicap in the conduct of our foreign relations." As examples of the latter he pointed to the difficulty of taking in refugees from Communism seeking to live in freedom because of both the national origins provisions already in effect and the low quota of total immigrants that could be admitted each year. But, he contends, the "greatest vice" in the system is the discriminatory nature of the quotas applied to people from Southern and Eastern Europe. This discrimination, and the spurious reasoning behind it, Truman found to be "utterly unworthy of our traditions and our ideals. It violates the great political doctrine of the Declaration of Independence that 'all men are created equal.' It denies the humanitarian creed inscribed beneath the Statue of Liberty proclaiming to all nations, 'Give me your tired, your poor, your huddled masses yearning to breathe free.' It repudiates our basic religious concepts, our belief in the brotherhood of man."

The president found that while making "common cause" with nations like Italy, Greece, and Turkey in the North Atlantic Treaty Organization the national origins quotas severely limit anyone wishing to enter the U.S. as an immigrant from those very countries leaving the impression that somehow they were "less worthy" than others. Further, he argues that rather than restrict those behind the iron curtain who are not allowed to emigrate anyway, the U.S. ought to "stretch out a helping hand, to save those who have managed to flee into Western Europe, to succor those who are brave enough to escape from barbarism, to welcome and restore them against the day when their countries will, as we hope, be free again." For all of these reasons he finds the continuance of these nationality quotas unacceptable.

Beyond these concerns the veto letter also challenges requirements that would be applied retroactively to make it easier to deport immigrants, to break up families, as well as other conditions that would make entry and attainment of citizenship more difficult. One particular exclusion would prohibit the entry of people convicted of a crime "even if they were judged in 'courts' in communist countries that know no justice." Similarly, if people gave false information in an attempt to flee a totalitarian regime, that could be used against them to deny entry into the U.S. He concluded: "Seldom has a bill exhibited the distrust evidenced here for citizens and aliens alike—at a time when we need unity at home, and the confidence of our friends abroad." In arbitrary and sweeping punishment, Truman claims the new law is "worse than the infamous Alien Act of 1798, passed in a time of national fear and distrust of foreigners, which gave the President power to deport any alien deemed 'dangerous to the peace and safety of the United States.'" Under the new bill, evidence would not be required for deportation, only "opinion" or the "satisfaction" of government officials. Truman also objected to some of the administrative provisions of the bill, but he reserved his most pointed remarks for the portions he believed "inconsistent with our democratic ideals." In this spirit, the president closed by recommending that Asians be allowed to enter the country and become citizens and that Congress enact temporary emergency legislation he suggested several months earlier to address the blatant discrimination in existing laws.

Essential Themes

The McCarran-Walter Act had two primary purposes: (1) to organize and to modernize immigration law and (2) to fight subversion by making it easier for the government to deny entry to or deport anyone whose presence it believed would be detrimental to U.S. security. In fact, in 2016 some of the law's provisions were still being used in the fight against international terrorism, while others that had been eliminated were restored in the Patriot Act in 2001.

Although Truman vetoed the bill as "un-American" and discriminatory, Congress overrode the veto by a vote of 278 to 113 in the House and 57 to 26 in the Senate. Because of this the nationality quotas enacted in 1921 and confirmed in 1924 were carried forward, requirements for citizenship tightened, and the preference for those from the British Isles and Germany allotted more than 67 percent of the total quota slots available. These provisions would not be eliminated until 1965. Just as the Red Scare at the end of World War I contributed to the erecting of the original barriers, the Cold War that emerged from the second world conflagration influenced the retention and redefinition of those quotas. Although it did eliminate restrictions on Asians, it also made it more difficult for many hoping to flee communism.

Yet, while retaining the quotas, the act also created a hierarchy of priorities based on the need for professionals and skilled workers, reunification of nuclear families, accommodation of spouses and unmarried children of resident aliens, and other relatives of citizens and permanent residents. On the other hand, the "undesirable aliens" provisions led to the denial of visas to a number of internationally renowned literary figures accused of holding communist sympathies including Nobel laureates Doris Lessing, Gabriel García Márquez, and Pablo Neruda.

Bibliography and Additional Reading

Marion T. Bennett, "The Immigration and Nationality (McCarran-Walter) Act of 1952, as Amended to 1965," *Annals of the American Academy of Political and Social Science*, Vol. 367 (September 1966), 127-36.

Carl J. Bon Tempo, *Americans at the Gate: The United States and Refugees During the Cold War* (Princeton, NJ: Princeton University Press, 2008).

Alicia J. Campi, *The McCarran-Walter Act: A Contradictory Legacy on Race, Quotas, and Ideology* (Washington, DC: Immigration Policy Center, 2004).

Roger Daniels, *Guarding the Golden Door: American Immigration Policy and Immigrants Since 1882* (New York: Hill & Wang, 2004).

Daniel J. Tichenor, *Dividing Lines: The Politics of Immigration Control in America* (Princeton, NJ: Princeton University Press, 2002).

■ *Plyler v. Doe*

Date: June 15, 1982
Author: William J. Brennan, Jr.
Genre: Court Opinion

Summary Overview

By 1980 estimates on the number of immigrants illegally in the United States hovered between a low of about two million and a high of around four million. Naturally this became a political issue with the debate largely centering on economics, especially whether this large labor force was a drain on the American economy or had a positive effect. Arguments for the former usually centered around the idea that, in the words of a Cornell University study, "Illegal immigrants compete for employment and income opportunities with citizen workers, usually low-wage-earning minorities, women, and youth." Arguments in favor of illegals having a positive effect mostly reasoned that they "took jobs Americans did not want" and contributed to the economy through increasing demand for products and the payment of sales and other taxes for which they received little if any benefits.

Another concern was that the increase in people illegally in the country created a large a growing class open to exploitation because they were largely without enforceable rights. As the Cornell study phrased it: "Some of the jobs are substandard. Employers often take advantage of people who are grateful for anything they receive. Those illegal immigrants who work under exploitive conditions take jobs that most of our citizens would not tolerate, so they are not taking food off a citizen's table per se. Yet this is certainly no excuse for allowing their mistreatment to continue, nor is it reason to condone the existence of explicitly illegal job classes. If it is legally and morally wrong for citizens to work under unfair conditions, it is also wrong for illegal aliens to do so."

These arguments dominated the debate well into the 1980s, eventually having an effect on the 1986 Immigration Reform and Control Act designed by the administration of President Ronald Reagan as an attempt to address the issue by providing an "amnesty" for illegals with no other criminal record while at the same time attempting stricter enforcement of immigration laws in the future.

Defining Moment

The rise in the number of immigrants in the country illegally had an uneven effect on individual states since some had very few within their borders while others saw that population surge. Among the latter was Texas. Between 1970 and 1980 the number of foreign-born residents in Texas increased by 176.1 percent from 310,000 to 856,000. According to Immigration and Naturalization Service estimates, between 420,000 and 450,000 of these latter number were in the country illegally. This placed a strain on public services, housing, competition for employment (especially among the lower economic classes), and various other socio-economic institutions including public education.

By the early 1970s it was estimated that the largest cost to the state of Texas from illegal immigration was in the expense incurred in educating children in the country without authorization. Faced with rising costs, in May 1975 the state legislature adopted a new education law denying enrollment to children not "legally admitted" to the country and at the same time authorizing the withholding of state funding from any such students. When, subsequently, Superintendent James Plyler of the Tyler Independent School District ruled a student unable to prove their citizenship or legal resident status would have to pay a $1,000 tuition, a group of students from Mexico filed a class action suit in federal court to overturn the requirement because it violated their right to a free public education. Known as *Plyler v. Doe*, the U.S. Supreme Court handed down its decision in the case on June 15, 1982.

Author Biography

The author of the court's majority opinion was Justice William J. Brennan, Jr. Born in Newark, New Jersey, to Irish parents in 1906, he graduated from Harvard Law School. After working as a trail attorney focusing on labor cases he served as an officer in the U.S. Army during World War II. Following the war the New Jersey governor appointed him to the state's Superior Court in 1949 and its Supreme Court two years later. Despite being a liberal Democrat, he was appointed to the U.S. Supreme Court by Republican President Dwight D. Eisenhower in 1956.

Brennan quickly established a record of support for civil rights, the one-person one-vote principle, and *Roe v. Wade*, while opposing the death penalty. Brennan once explained his approach to the bench: "We current Justices read the Constitution in the only way that we can: as twentieth century Americans. We look to the history of the time of framing and to the intervening history of interpretation. But the ultimate question must be: What do the words of the text mean in our time. For the genius of the Constitution rests not in any static meaning it might have had in a world that is dead and gone, but in the adaptability of its great principles to cope with current problems and current needs." He was what many today might call an "activist judge" who looked to modern applications rather than original intent and in that respect has been criticized by some for "legislating from the bench." He was also criticized for his rulings in two cases where he found that desecration of the American flag was protected as a First Amendment free speech. Following his retirement in 1990 he taught at Georgetown University Law Center until 1994 and was awarded the Presidential Medal of Freedom by President Bill Clinton in 1993. He died in Arlington, Virginia, on July 24, 1997.

HISTORICAL DOCUMENT

The question presented by these cases is whether, consistent with the Equal Protection Clause of the Fourteenth Amendment, Texas may deny to undocumented school-age children the free public education that it provides to children who are citizens of the United States or legally admitted aliens.

Since the late 19th century, the United States has restricted immigration into this country. Unsanctioned entry into the United States is a crime, and those who have entered unlawfully are subject to deportation. But despite the existence of these legal restrictions, a substantial number of persons have succeeded in unlawfully entering the United States, and now live within various States, including the State of Texas.

In May 1975, the Texas Legislature revised its education laws to withhold from local school districts any state funds for the education of children who were not "legally admitted" into the United States. The 1975 revision also authorized local school districts to deny enrollment in their public schools to children not "legally admitted" to the country. These cases involve constitutional challenges to those provisions.

This is a class action, filed in the United States District Court for the Eastern District of Texas in September 1977, on behalf of certain school-age children of Mexican origin residing in Smith County, Tex., who could not establish that they had been legally admitted into the United States. The action complained of the exclusion of plaintiff children from the public schools of the Tyler Independent School District. The Superintendent and members of the Board of Trustees of the School District were named as defendants; the State of Texas intervened as a party-defendant. After certifying a class consisting of all undocumented school-age children of Mexican origin residing within the School District, the District Court preliminarily enjoined defendants from denying a free education to members of the plaintiff class. In December 1977, the court conducted an extensive hearing on plaintiffs' motion for permanent injunctive relief.

In considering this motion, the District Court made extensive findings of fact. The court found that neither § 21.031 nor the School District policy implementing it had "either the purpose or effect of keeping illegal aliens out of the State of Texas." Respecting defendants' further claim that § 21.031 was simply a financial measure designed to avoid a drain on the State's fisc, the court recognized that the increases in population resulting from the immigration of Mexican nationals into the United States had created problems for the public schools of the State, and that these problems were exacerbated by the special educational needs of immigrant Mexican children. The court noted, however, that the increase in school enrollment was primarily attributable to the admission of children who were legal residents. It also found that while the "exclusion of all undocumented children from the public schools in Texas would eventually result in economies at some level," funding from both the State and Federal Governments was based primarily on the number of children enrolled. In net effect then, barring undocumented children from the schools would save money, but it would "not necessarily" improve "the quality of education." The court further observed that the impact of § 21.031 was borne primarily by a very small subclass of illegal aliens, "entire families who have migrated illegally and — for all practical purposes — permanently to the United States." Finally, the court noted that under current laws and practices "the illegal alien of today may well be the legal alien of tomorrow," and that without an education, these undocumented children, "[a]lready disadvantaged as a result of poverty, lack of English-speaking ability, and undeniable racial prejudices, ... will become permanently locked into the lowest socio-economic class."

The District Court held that illegal aliens were entitled to the protection of the Equal Protection Clause of the Fourteenth Amendment, and that § 21.031 violated that Clause. Suggesting that "the state's exclusion of undocumented children from its public schools ... may well be the type of invidiously motivated state action for which the suspect classification doctrine was designed," the court held that it was unnecessary to decide whether the statute would survive a "strict scrutiny" analysis because, in any event, the discrimination embodied in the statute was not supported by a rational basis. The District Court also concluded that the Texas statute violated the Supremacy Clause.

The Court of Appeals for the Fifth Circuit upheld the District Court's injunction. The Court of Appeals held that the District Court had erred in finding the Texas statute pre-empted by federal law. With respect to equal protection, however, the Court of Appeals affirmed in all essential respects the analysis of the District Court, concluding that § 21.031 was "constitutionally infirm regardless of whether it was tested using the mere rational basis standard or some more stringent test." We noted probable jurisdiction.

In re Alien Children Education Litigation

During 1978 and 1979, suits challenging the constitutionality of § 21.031 and various local practices undertaken on the authority of that provision were filed in the United States District Courts for the Southern, Western,

and Northern Districts of Texas. Each suit named the State of Texas and the Texas Education Agency as defendants, along with local officials. In November 1979, the Judicial Panel on Multi-district Litigation, on motion of the State, consolidated the claims against the state officials into a single action to be heard in the District Court for the Southern District of Texas. A hearing was conducted in February and March 1980. In July 1980, the court entered an opinion and order holding that § 21.031 violated the Equal Protection Clause of the Fourteenth Amendment. *In re Alien Children Education Litigation*, the court held that "the absolute deprivation of education should trigger strict judicial scrutiny, particularly when the absolute deprivation is the result of complete inability to pay for the desired benefit." The court determined that the State's concern for fiscal integrity was not a compelling state interest; that exclusion of these children had not been shown to be necessary to improve education within the State; and that the educational needs of the children statutorily excluded were not different from the needs of children not excluded. The court therefore concluded that § 21.031 was not carefully tailored to advance the asserted state interest in an acceptable manner. While appeal of the District Court's decision was pending, the Court of Appeals rendered its decision. Apparently on the strength of that opinion, the Court of Appeals, on February 23, 1981, summarily affirmed the decision of the Southern District. ...

The Fourteenth Amendment provides that "[n]o State shall. . . deprive any person of life, liberty, or property, without due process of law; nor deny to any person within its jurisdiction the equal protection of the laws." Appellants argue at the outset that undocumented aliens, because of their immigration status, are not "persons within the jurisdiction" of the State of Texas, and that they therefore have no right to the equal protection of Texas law. We reject this argument. Whatever his status under the immigration laws, an alien is surely a "person" in any ordinary sense of that term. Aliens, even aliens whose presence in this country is unlawful, have long been recognized as "persons" guaranteed due process of law by the Fifth and Fourteenth Amendments. Indeed, we have clearly held that the Fifth Amendment protects aliens whose presence in this country is unlawful from invidious discrimination by the Federal Government.

Appellants seek to distinguish our prior cases, emphasizing that the Equal Protection Clause directs a State to afford its protection to persons within its jurisdiction while the Due Process Clauses of the Fifth and Fourteenth Amendments contain no such assertedly limiting phrase. In appellants' view, persons who have entered the United States illegally are not "within the jurisdiction" of a State even if they are present within a State's boundaries and subject to its laws. Neither our cases nor the logic of the Fourteenth Amendment supports that constricting construction of the phrase "within its jurisdiction." We have never suggested that the class of persons who might avail themselves of the equal protection guarantee is less than coextensive with that entitled to due process. To the contrary, we have recognized that both provisions were fashioned to protect an identical class of persons, and to reach every exercise of state authority.

"The Fourteenth Amendment to the Constitution is not confined to the protection of citizens. It says: 'Nor shall any state deprive any person of life, liberty, or property without due process of law; nor deny to any person within its jurisdiction the equal protection of the laws.' These provisions are universal in their application, to all persons within the territorial jurisdiction, without regard to any differences of race, of color, or of nationality; and the protection of the laws is a pledge of the protection of equal laws."

In concluding that "all persons within the territory of the United States," including aliens unlawfully present, may invoke the Fifth and Sixth Amendments to challenge actions of the Federal Government, we reasoned from the understanding that the Fourteenth Amendment was designed to afford its protection to all within the boundaries of a State. Our cases applying the Equal Protection Clause reflect the same territorial theme. "Manifestly, the obligation of the State to give the protection of equal laws can be performed only where its laws operate, that is, within its own jurisdiction. It is there that the equality of legal right must be maintained. That obligation is imposed by the Constitution upon the States severally as governmental entities, — each responsible for its own laws establishing the rights and duties of persons within its borders."

There is simply no support for appellants' suggestion that "due process" is somehow of greater stature than "equal protection" and therefore available to a larger class of persons. To the contrary, each aspect of the Fourteenth Amendment reflects an elementary limitation on state power. To permit a State to employ the phrase "within its jurisdiction" in order to identify subclasses of persons whom it would define as beyond its jurisdiction, thereby relieving itself of the obligation to assure that its laws are designed and applied equally to those persons, would undermine the principal purpose for which the Equal Protection Clause was incorporated in the Fourteenth Amendment. The Equal Protection Clause was intended to work nothing less than the abolition of all caste-based and invidious class-based legislation. That objective is fundamentally at odds with the power the State asserts here to classify persons subject to its laws as nonetheless excepted from its protection.

Although the congressional debate concerning § 1 of the Fourteenth Amendment was limited, that debate clearly confirms the understanding that the phrase "within its jurisdiction" was intended in a broad sense to offer the guarantee of equal protection to all within a State's boundaries, and to all upon whom the State would impose the obligations of its laws. Indeed, it appears from those debates that Congress, by using the phrase "person within its jurisdiction," sought expressly to ensure that the equal protection of the laws was provided to the alien population. Representative Bingham reported to the House the draft resolution of the Joint Committee of Fifteen on Reconstruction that was to become the Fourteenth Amendment. Two days later, Bingham posed the following question in support of the resolution:

> "Is it not essential to the unity of the people that the citizens of each State shall be entitled to all the privileges and immunities of citizens in the several States? Is it not essential to the unity of the Government and the unity of the people that all persons, whether citizens or strangers, within this land, shall have equal protection in every State in this Union in the rights of life and liberty and property?"

Senator Howard, also a member of the Joint Committee of Fifteen, and the floor manager of the Amendment in the Senate, was no less explicit about the broad objectives of the Amendment, and the intention to make its provisions applicable to all who "may happen to be" within the jurisdiction of a State:

> "The last two clauses of the first section of the amendment disable a State from depriving not merely a citizen of the United States, but any person, whoever he may be, of life, liberty, or property without due process of law, or from denying to him the equal protection of the laws of the State. This abolishes all class legislation in the States and does away with the injustice of subjecting one caste of persons to a code not applicable to another. ... It will, if adopted by the States, forever disable every one of them from passing laws trenching upon those fundamental rights and privileges which pertain to citizens of the United States, and to all persons who may happen to be within their jurisdiction."

Use of the phrase "within its jurisdiction" thus does not detract from, but rather confirms, the understanding that the protection of the Fourteenth Amendment extends to anyone, citizen or stranger, who is subject to the laws of a State, and reaches into every corner of a State's territory. That a person's initial entry into a State, or into the United States, was unlawful, and that he may for that reason be expelled, cannot negate the simple fact of his presence within the State's territorial perimeter. Given such presence, he is subject to the full range of obligations imposed by the State's civil and criminal laws. And until he leaves the jurisdiction—either voluntarily, or involuntarily in accordance with the Constitution and laws of the United States—he is entitled to the equal protection of the laws that a State may choose to establish.

Our conclusion that the illegal aliens who are plaintiffs in these cases may claim the benefit of the Fourteenth Amendment's guarantee of equal protection only begins the inquiry. The more difficult question is whether the Equal Protection Clause has been violated by the refusal of the State of Texas to reimburse local school boards for the education of children who cannot demonstrate that their presence within the United States is lawful, or by the imposition by those school boards of the burden of tuition on those children. It is to this question that we now turn.

The Equal Protection Clause directs that "all persons similarly circumstanced shall be treated alike." But so too, "[t]he Constitution does not require things which are different in fact or opinion to be treated in law as though they were the same." The initial discretion to determine what is "different" and what is "the same" resides in the legislatures of the States. A legislature must have substantial latitude to establish classifications that roughly approximate the nature of the problem perceived, that accommodate competing concerns both public and private, and that account for limitations on the practical ability of the State to remedy every ill. In applying the Equal Protection Clause to most forms of state action, we thus seek only the assurance that the classification at issue bears some fair relationship to a legitimate public purpose.

But we would not be faithful to our obligations under the Fourteenth Amendment if we applied so deferential a standard to every classification. The Equal Protection Clause was intended as a restriction on state legislative action inconsistent with elemental constitutional premises. Thus we have treated as presumptively invidious those classifications that disadvantage a "suspect class," or that impinge upon the exercise of a "fundamental right." With respect to such classifications, it is appropriate to enforce the mandate of equal protection by requiring the State to demonstrate that its classification has been precisely tailored to serve a compelling governmental interest. In addition, we have recognized that certain forms of legislative classification, while not facially invidious, nonetheless give rise to recurring constitutional difficulties; in these limited circumstances we have sought the assurance that the classification reflects a reasoned judgment consistent with the ideal of equal protection by inquiring whether it may fairly be viewed as furthering a substantial interest of the State. We turn to a consideration of the standard appropriate for the evaluation of § 21.031.

Sheer incapability or lax enforcement of the laws barring entry into this country, coupled with the failure to establish an effective bar to the employment of undocumented aliens, has resulted in the creation of a substantial "shadow population" of illegal migrants — numbering in the millions — within our borders. This situation raises the specter of a permanent caste of undocumented resident aliens, encouraged by some to remain here as a source of cheap labor, but nevertheless denied the benefits that our society makes available to citizens and lawful residents. The existence of such an underclass presents most difficult problems for a Nation that prides itself on adherence to principles of equality under law.

The children who are plaintiffs in these cases are special members of this underclass. Persuasive arguments support the view that a State may withhold its beneficence from those whose very presence within the United States is the product of their own unlawful conduct. These arguments do not apply with the same force to classifications imposing disabilities on the minor children of such illegal entrants. At the least, those who elect to enter our territory by stealth and in violation of our law should be prepared to bear the consequences, including, but not limited to, deportation. But the children of those illegal entrants are not comparably situated. Their "parents have the ability to conform their conduct to societal norms," and presumably the ability to remove themselves from the State's jurisdiction; but the children who are plaintiffs in these cases "can affect neither their parents' conduct nor their own status." Even if the State found it expedient to control the conduct of adults by acting against their children, legislation directing the onus of a parent's misconduct against his children does not comport with fundamental conceptions of justice.

"[V]isiting ... condemnation on the head of an infant is illogical and unjust. Moreover, imposing disabilities on the ... child is contrary to the basic concept of our system that legal burdens should bear some relationship to individual responsibility or wrongdoing. Obviously, no child is responsible for his birth and penalizing the ... child is an ineffectual — as well as unjust — way of deterring the parent."

Of course, undocumented status is not irrelevant to any proper legislative goal. Nor is undocumented status an absolutely immutable characteristic since it is the product of conscious, indeed unlawful, action. But § 21.031 is directed against children, and imposes its discriminatory burden on the basis of a legal characteristic over which children can have little control. It is thus difficult to conceive of a rational justification for penalizing these children for their presence within the United States. Yet that appears to be precisely the effect of § 21.031.

Public education is not a "right" granted to individuals by the Constitution. But neither is it merely some governmental "benefit" indistinguishable from other forms of social welfare legislation. Both the importance of education in maintaining our basic institutions, and the lasting impact of its deprivation on the life of the child, mark the distinction. The "American people have always regarded education and [the] acquisition of knowledge as matters of supreme importance." We have recognized "the public schools as a most vital civic institution for the preservation of a democratic system of government," and as the primary vehicle for transmitting "the values on which our society rests." "[A]s ... pointed out early in our history, ... some degree of education is necessary to prepare citizens to participate effectively and intelligently in our open political system if we are to preserve freedom and independence." And these historic "perceptions of the public schools as inculcating fundamental values necessary to the maintenance of a democratic political system have been confirmed by the observations of social scientists." In addition, education provides the basic tools by which individuals might lead economically productive lives to the benefit of us all. In sum, education has a fundamental role in maintaining the fabric of our society. We cannot ignore the significant social costs borne by our Nation when select groups are denied the means to absorb the values and skills upon which our social order rests.

In addition to the pivotal role of education in sustaining our political and cultural heritage, denial of education to some isolated group of children poses an affront to one of the goals of the Equal Protection Clause: the abolition of governmental barriers presenting unreasonable obstacles to advancement on the basis of individual merit. Paradoxically, by depriving the children of any disfavored group of an education, we foreclose the means by which that group might raise the level of esteem in which it is held by the majority. But more directly, "education prepares individuals to be self-reliant and self-sufficient participants in society." Illiteracy is an enduring disability. The inability to read and write will handicap the individual deprived of a basic education each and every day of his life. The inestimable toll of that deprivation on the social, economic, intellectual, and psychological well-being of the individual, and the obstacle it poses to individual achievement, make it most difficult to reconcile the cost or the principle of a status-based denial of basic education with the framework of equality embodied in the Equal Protection Clause. What we said 28 years ago in *Brown v. Board of Education*, still holds true:

"Today, education is perhaps the most important function of state and local governments. Compulsory school attendance laws and the great expenditures for education both demonstrate our recognition of the importance of education to our democratic society. It is required in the performance of our most basic public responsibilities, even service in the armed forces. It is the very foundation of good citizenship. Today it is a principal instrument in awakening the child to cultural values, in preparing him for later professional training, and in helping him to adjust normally to his environment. In these days, it is doubtful that any child may reasonably be expected to succeed in life if he is denied the opportunity of an education. Such an opportunity, where the state has undertaken to provide it, is a right which must be made available to all on equal terms."

These well-settled principles allow us to determine the proper level of deference to be afforded § 21.031. Undocumented aliens cannot be treated as a suspect class because their presence in this country in violation of federal law is not a "constitutional irrelevancy." Nor is education a fundamental right; a State need not justify by compelling necessity every variation in the manner in which education is provided to its population. But more is involved in these cases than the abstract question whether § 21.031 discriminates against a suspect class, or whether education is a fundamental right. Section 21.031 imposes a lifetime hardship on a discrete class of children not accountable for their disabling status. The stigma of illiteracy will mark them for the rest of their lives. By denying these children a basic education, we deny them the ability to live within the structure of our civic institutions, and foreclose any realistic possibility that they will contribute in even the smallest way to the progress of our Nation. In determining the rationality

of § 21.031, we may appropriately take into account its costs to the Nation and to the innocent children who are its victims. In light of these countervailing costs, the discrimination contained in § 21.031 can hardly be considered rational unless it furthers some substantial goal of the State.

It is the State's principal argument, and apparently the view of the dissenting Justices, that the undocumented status of these children *vel non* establishes a sufficient rational basis for denying them benefits that a State might choose to afford other residents. The State notes that while other aliens are admitted "on an equality of legal privileges with all citizens under non-discriminatory laws," the asserted right of these children to an education can claim no implicit congressional imprimatur. Indeed, in the State's view, Congress' apparent disapproval of the presence of these children within the United States, and the evasion of the federal regulatory program that is the mark of undocumented status, provides authority for its decision to impose upon them special disabilities. Faced with an equal protection challenge respecting the treatment of aliens, we agree that the courts must be attentive to congressional policy; the exercise of congressional power might well affect the State's prerogatives to afford differential treatment to a particular class of aliens. But we are unable to find in the congressional immigration scheme any statement of policy that might weigh significantly in arriving at an equal protection balance concerning the State's authority to deprive these children of an education.

The Constitution grants Congress the power to "establish an uniform Rule of Naturalization." Drawing upon this power, upon its plenary authority with respect to foreign relations and international commerce, and upon the inherent power of a sovereign to close its borders, Congress has developed a complex scheme governing admission to our Nation and status within our borders. The obvious need for delicate policy judgments has counseled the Judicial Branch to avoid intrusion into this field. But this traditional caution does not persuade us that unusual deference must be shown the classification embodied in § 21.031. The States enjoy no power with respect to the classification of aliens. This power is "committed to the political branches of the Federal Government." Although it is "a routine and normally legitimate part" of the business of the Federal Government to classify on the basis of alien status, and to "take into account the character of the relationship between the alien and this country," only rarely are such matters relevant to legislation by a State.

As we recognized in *De Canas v. Bica*, the States do have some authority to act with respect to illegal aliens, at least where such action mirrors federal objectives and furthers a legitimate state goal. In *De Canas*, the State's program reflected Congress' intention to bar from employment all aliens except those possessing a grant of permission to work in this country. In contrast, there is no indication that the disability imposed by § 21.031 corresponds to any identifiable congressional policy. The State does not claim that the conservation of state educational resources was ever a congressional concern in restricting immigration. More importantly, the classification reflected in § 21.031 does not operate harmoniously within the federal program.

To be sure, like all persons who have entered the United States unlawfully, these children are subject to deportation. But there is no assurance that a child subject to deportation will ever be deported. An illegal entrant might be granted federal permission to continue to reside in this country, or even to become a citizen. In light of the discretionary federal power to grant relief from deportation, a State cannot realistically determine that any particular undocumented child will in fact be deported until after deportation proceedings have been completed. It would of course be most difficult for the State to justify a denial of education to a child enjoying an inchoate federal permission to remain.

We are reluctant to impute to Congress the intention to withhold from these children, for so long as they are present in this country through no fault of their own, access to a basic education. In other contexts, undocumented status, coupled with some articulable federal policy, might enhance state authority with respect to the treatment of undocumented aliens. But in the area of special constitutional sensitivity presented by these cases, and in the absence of any contrary indication fairly discernible in the present legislative record, we perceive no national policy that supports the State in denying these children an elementary education. The State may borrow the federal classification. But to jus-

tify its use as a criterion for its own discriminatory policy, the State must demonstrate that the classification is reasonably adapted to "the purposes for which the state desires to use it."

Appellants argue that the classification at issue furthers an interest in the "preservation of the state's limited resources for the education of its lawful residents." Of course, a concern for the preservation of resources standing alone can hardly justify the classification used in allocating those resources. The State must do more than justify its classification with a concise expression of an intention to discriminate. Apart from the asserted state prerogative to act against undocumented children solely on the basis of their undocumented status—an asserted prerogative that carries only minimal force in the circumstances of these cases—we discern three colorable state interests that might support § 21.031.

First, appellants appear to suggest that the State may seek to protect itself from an influx of illegal immigrants. While a State might have an interest in mitigating the potentially harsh economic effects of sudden shifts in population, § 21.031 hardly offers an effective method of dealing with an urgent demographic or economic problem. There is no evidence in the record suggesting that illegal entrants impose any significant burden on the State's economy. To the contrary, the available evidence suggests that illegal aliens underutilize public services, while contributing their labor to the local economy and tax money to the state fisc. The dominant incentive for illegal entry into the State of Texas is the availability of employment; few if any illegal immigrants come to this country, or presumably to the State of Texas, in order to avail themselves of a free education. Thus, even making the doubtful assumption that the net impact of illegal aliens on the economy of the State is negative, we think it clear that "[c]harging tuition to undocumented children constitutes a ludicrously ineffectual attempt to stem the tide of illegal immigration," at least when compared with the alternative of prohibiting the employment of illegal aliens.

Second, while it is apparent that a State may "not ... reduce expenditures for education by barring [some arbitrarily chosen class of] children from its schools, appellants suggest that undocumented children are appropriately singled out for exclusion because of the special burdens they impose on the State's ability to provide high-quality public education. But the record in no way supports the claim that exclusion of undocumented children is likely to improve the overall quality of education in the State. As the District Court in No. 80-1934 noted, the State failed to offer any "credible supporting evidence that a proportionately small diminution of the funds spent on each child [which might result from devoting some state funds to the education of the excluded group] will have a grave impact on the quality of education." And, after reviewing the State's school financing mechanism, the District Court in No. 80-1538 concluded that barring undocumented children from local schools would not necessarily improve the quality of education provided in those schools. Of course, even if improvement in the quality of education were a likely result of barring some number of children from the schools of the State, the State must support its selection of this group as the appropriate target for exclusion. In terms of educational cost and need, however, undocumented children are "basically indistinguishable" from legally resident alien children.

Finally, appellants suggest that undocumented children are appropriately singled out because their unlawful presence within the United States renders them less likely than other children to remain within the boundaries of the State, and to put their education to productive social or political use within the State. Even assuming that such an interest is legitimate, it is an interest that is most difficult to quantify. The State has no assurance that any child, citizen or not, will employ the education provided by the State within the confines of the State's borders. In any event, the record is clear that many of the undocumented children disabled by this classification will remain in this country indefinitely, and that some will become lawful residents or citizens of the United States. It is difficult to understand precisely what the State hopes to achieve by promoting the creation and perpetuation of a subclass of illiterates within our boundaries, surely adding to the problems and costs of unemployment, welfare, and crime. It is thus clear that whatever savings might be achieved by denying these children an education, they are wholly insubstantial in light of the costs involved to these children, the State, and the Nation.

If the State is to deny a discrete group of innocent children the free public education that it offers to other children residing within its borders, that denial must be justified by a showing that it furthers some substantial state interest. No such showing was made here. Accordingly, the judgment of the Court of Appeals in each of these cases is Affirmed.

GLOSSARY

Appellant: A person who appeals a judicial decision to a higher court.

Equal Protection Clause: This is a reference to Section 1 of the Fourteenth Amendment which prohibits any state from enacting any law to "deny to any person within its jurisdiction the equal protection of the laws."

Fisc: From the Latin word "fiscus" which referred to the state treasury; today this is usually used in legal documents and refers to a treasury.

In re: A legal term meaning "in the matter of" when referring to a law or legal case.

Injunction: A court order preventing a person or entity from undertaking some action. For example, an "injunction" might be used to prevent a strike or to prevent a law from being enforced while it undergoes court review.

Vel non: A legal term referring to the existence or nonexistence of an issue requiring judicial resolution.

Document Analysis

Justice Brennan framed the case in *Plyler v. Doe* as a question of whether denying the school-age children of parents who were not legal residents of the United States a free public education violated the Equal Protection Clause of the Fourteenth Amendment. As context for the issue, he recognized that United States law regulated entry into the country; hence, anyone in the country who was not legally there was committing a crime and thus subject to deportation. Despite this, a large number of people were nevertheless in the country illegally, especially in Texas where the legislature addressed the economic problem this created by requiring that state funds for education could only be used to support legal residents. Anyone else would be required to pay tuition.

Looking at an earlier decision, Brennan noted that the U.S. District Court for the Eastern District of Texas had found that the law in question was not intended to keep illegal aliens out of the state and that the rationale of fiscal savings had not been proven. In that decision the District Court determined that most of the increase in cost to the school district in question came from the enrollment of the children of legal residents and the number of children of illegal immigrants was small enough as to not make a significant difference, especially since federal and state funding was based on student population. Therefore, children of parents who were not legally in the country were counted in the formula for state aid and did not constitute a significantly large expense to the district. Further, the court found no reason to believe the Texas law would result in any improvement to overall "the quality of education." With these findings of "fact," the District Court concluded that "illegal aliens were entitled to the protection of the Equal Protection Clause of the Fourteenth Amendment," that the discrimination resulting from the Texas law had no "rational basis," and that the Texas law also violated the Supremacy Clause of the Constitution by making laws regarding immigration which was the purview of the federal government. This ruling was later upheld by the Court of Appeals for the Fifth Circuit which, though denying that the Texas statute conflicted with federal law, agreed that the plaintiffs were entitled to equal protection.

One of the main arguments in favor of the Texas law was that the children of illegal aliens were not within the "jurisdiction" of the United States since they did not have legal status to be in the country. The court found this argument baseless since, as it said, "Whatever his status under the immigration laws, an alien is surely a 'person' in any ordinary sense of that term. Aliens, even aliens whose presence in this country is unlawful, have long been recognized as 'persons' guaranteed due process of law by the Fifth and Fourteenth Amendments." It further affirmed that the Fourteenth Amendment "is not confined to the protection of citizens. The court then went on to provide historical precedents to support its conclusions, including quotations from the debates that took place surrounding the adoption of the Fourteenth Amendment.

The Fourteenth Amendment was specifically made applicable to the various states to preclude them from adopting any measures that conflicted with the guarantees provided in the Constitution. The court's ruling continues on to assert that the "lax enforcement of the laws" resulted in "the creation of a substantial 'shadow population' of illegal migrants" the result is a "permanent caste of undocumented resident aliens." This condition creates a class which the state of Texas was attempting to exempt from the Equal Protection Clause because of the statue at least in part the result of failure to enforce federal immigration law. Failing to provide this group equal protection was therefore discriminatory. While the court opined that "Persuasive arguments support the view that a State may withhold its beneficence from those whose very presence within the United States is the product of their own unlawful conduct," this was not the case with the children of illegal aliens since their residence in the country was not of their own volition but that of their parents. In other words, it was not the children who chose to enter illegally, it was their parents, thus the children were here "through no fault of their own" and should not be penalized.

Although the court found that education was not a "right" granted under the Constitution, it was so fundamental to the institutions and social fabric of the nation that to deprive a group of educational opportunity was equivalent to saddling that group with a permanent disadvantage. For support the court quoted from the momentous *Brown v. Board of Education* decision of 1954: "Today, education is perhaps the most important function of state and local governments. ... It is the very foundation of good citizenship. Today it is a principal instrument in awakening the child to cultural values, in preparing him for later professional training, and in helping him to adjust normally to his environment. In these days, it is doubtful that any child may reasonably be expected to succeed in life if he is denied the opportunity of an education. Such an opportunity, where the state has undertaken to provide it, is a right which must be made available to all on equal terms."

Essential Themes

In 1965 the Higher Education Act required that federal financial aid be provided only to legal residents of the United States. The *Pyler v. Doe* decision was by the slimmest 5-4 margin and was limited in effect to K-12 public education, thus it did not directly overturn the 1965 statute dealing with post-secondary education. This division continued in the Illegal Immigration Reform and Immigrant Responsibility Act (1996) which required that "an alien who is not lawfully present in the United States shall not be eligible on the basis of residence within a State (or a political subdivision) for any postsecondary education benefit unless a citizen or national of the United States is eligible for such a benefit (in no less an amount, duration, and scope) without regard to whether the citizen or national is such a resident." This was reinforced in the same year by the Personal Responsibility and Work Opportunity Reconciliation Act by which "An alien who is not a qualified alien is not eligible for any Federal public benefit" including "postsecondary education." Despite these prohibitions, some states have adopted laws to circumvent the restrictions by basing assistance not on residence but on having successfully completed high school.

Despite the *Plyler* decision, since 1982 some states have attempted to circumvent the ruling. In 1994 California voters adopted Proposition 187, which prohibited the enrollment of illegal aliens in an public elementary or secondary school, but this was later overturned by a federal court. In 2006 a school district in Illinois attempted to deny attendance to a student illegally in

the country, but backed down when threatened with the withholding of state funding. In 2001 Alabama adopted a law requiring that school officials verify the legal immigration status of any alien students, but enforcement of the legislation was blocked by the federal courts. Similar attempts will no doubt continue as long as the federal government continues to refrain from enforcement of the immigration laws and the expense of educating the children of those in the country illegally continues to pose a financial burden on state and local communities.

Bibliography and Additional Reading

John W. Borkowski, *Legal Issues for School Districts Related to the Education of Undocumented Children* (Washington, DC: The National School Boards Association and the National Education Association, 2009).

Roxanne L. Doty, *The Law into Their Own Hands: Immigration and the Politics of Exceptionalism* (Tucson: University of Arizona Press, 2009).

Maria Pabon Lopez, "Reflections on educating Latino and Latina undocumented children: Beyond *Plyler v. Doe*," *Seton Hall Law Review*, Vol. 35, no. 4 (2005), ------.

Michael A. Olivas, "The Story of *Plyler v. Doe*, The Education of Undocumented Children, and The Polity," in *Immigration Stories*, eds. David Martin and Peter Schuck (Eagan, MN: Foundation Press, 2005).

Carlos R. Soltero, "Plyler v. Doe (1982) and Educating Children of Illegal Alien," in *Latinos and American Law: Landmark Supreme Court Cases* (Austin, TX: University of Texas Press, 2006), 118–32.

■ *Arizona v. the United States*

Date: June 25, 2012
Authors: Anthony Kennedy and Antonin Scalia
Genre: Court Decision

Summary Overview

By the 1980s the increasing number of illegal aliens in the United States led to mounting calls for immigration reform. In response, in 1986 Congress passed, and President Ronald Reagan signed, the Immigration Reform and Control Act which contained two major provisions. The first was designed to provide amnesty to aliens who had been in the country since January 1982 or had completed ninety days of agricultural employment between May 1985 and May 1986. The result was the legalization of about three million people. The goal of the second portion of the act was to prevent future illegal entry by making it unlawful to hire or protect illegal aliens. However, the Democratically-controlled Congress refused to provide adequate funding for the enforcement provisions. The result was that aliens continued to enter the country illegally, or overstay legal visas, in escalating numbers.

Ten years after this attempt Congress adopted the Illegal Immigrant Reform and Immigrant Responsibility Act which provided for increased hiring of Border Patrol and Immigration and Naturalization Service agents. The new law strengthened penalties for illicit entry, called for a fence to be erected in San Diego, established an electronic verification system for allowing employers to verify immigration status, and included a provision allowing state law enforcement officers to apply the immigration law. Once again, however, lack of full funding hampered enforcement of the law. Although Article II of the Constitution requires that the president "take Care that the Laws be faithfully executed" when Barack Obama assumed that office he adopted a policy of ignoring enforcement of the existing immigration laws resulting, by 2011, in there being an estimated 11.6 million illegal aliens in the country.

Defining Moment

With the increase in illegal aliens came an escalation in crime and the costs associated with the investigation, apprehension, and incarceration of the guilty parties. Both of these—the crimes and the costs—bore heavily on the individual states where they occurred. Between 2008 and 2014, although only 5.6 percent of the population of Arizona, California, Florida, New York, and Texas was comprised of illegal immigrants, 38 percent of murder convictions were by members of that group. According to data from the Government Accountability Office (GAO) over 90 percent of incarcerated aliens were in the country illegally. Much of this burden fell on Arizona.

GAO data from a March 2011 report indicated that between 2003 and 2009 the number of incarcerated criminal aliens in Arizona rose from 14,941 in 2003 to 17,488, an increase of 17 percent. In 2008 about 11 percent of all inmates in Arizona prisons were illegal immigrants, 30 percent of whom were convicted of drug offenses and 11 percent of assault. The GAO estimated that nationally it cost $1.6 billion to support incarcerated criminal aliens in 2009. In Arizona in the same year it cost state taxpayers $14,093 for each incarcerated person. The Center for Immigration Studies estimated that in 2009 illegal immigrants in Maricopa County, Arizona, the location of Phoenix, constituted 8.9 percent of the population but were responsible for 21.8 percent of the felonies. In that county alone, incarceration cost some $44 million for that single year. As the danger and financial costs spiraled upward, the Arizona legislature adopted SB 1070 providing for the state to assume enforcement of existing immigration laws, with the House approving 35-21 (all Republicans voting yes and all Democrats voting no) and the Senate favoring it by 17-11 (one Republican crossing over to vote no and two Democrats voting yes). Once SB 1070 was introduced, a public poll found that 71 percentage of Arizonans supported the legislation. When the federal government took legal action against the Arizona statute, nine other states filed legal briefs supporting Arizona's law.

Author Biography

The documents here were authored by two Supreme Court justices, Anthony Kennedy and Antonin Scalia. Kennedy was born in Sacramento, California, graduated from Harvard Law School, and was appointed to the court by President Ronald Reagan. Generally considered to be a swing vote on a politically divided court, he actually demonstrated consistency in supporting individual rights, racial equality, and freedom of speech. He co-authored a majority opinion in a case that reaffirmed the right of women to seek an abortion, supported LGBT rights including the right to same-sex marriage, and the right of prisoners held in Guantanamo Bay to habeas corpus.

Scalia was born in Trenton, New Jersey. Like Kennedy, he also obtained his law degree at Harvard Law School and was appointed to the court by President Reagan. A leading advocate of interpreting the Constitution in the context of its original intent, he became known as the intellectual leader of strict constructionism, a meticulous questioner, and a ready wit. On the bench he has been described as a moderate conservative, supporting the application of the death penalty and the individual's right to bear arms, while dissenting from laws that drew distinctions between classes of people and opposing the court's affirmation of the constitutionality of the Affordable Care Act, also known as Obamacare.

The first document in this section is the majority opinion written by Justice Kennedy. It is followed by the opinion of Justice Scalia which dissents from the majority on a portion of the legal points contained in the majority opinion.

HISTORICAL DOCUMENT

To address pressing issues related to the large number of aliens within its borders who do not have a lawful right to be in this country, the State of Arizona in 2010 enacted a statute called the Support Our Law Enforcement and Safe Neighborhoods Act. The law is often referred to as S. B. 1070, the version introduced in the state senate. Its stated purpose is to "discourage and deter the unlawful entry and presence of aliens and economic activity by persons unlawfully present in the United States." The law's provisions establish an official state policy of "attrition through enforcement." Ibid. The question before the Court is whether federal law preempts and renders invalid four separate provisions of the state law.

I

The United States filed this suit against Arizona, seeking to enjoin S. B. 1070 as preempted. Four provisions of the law are at issue here. Two create new state offenses. Section 3 makes failure to comply with federal alien-registration requirements a state misdemeanor. Section 5, in relevant part, makes it a misdemeanor for an unauthorized alien to seek or engage in work in the State; this provision is referred to as §5(C). Two other provisions give specific arrest authority and investigative duties with respect to certain aliens to state and local law enforcement officers. Section 6 authorizes officers to arrest without a warrant a person "the officer has probable cause to believe . . . has committed any public offense that makes the person removable from the United States."–Section 2(B) provides that officers who conduct a stop, detention, or arrest must in some circumstances make efforts to verify the person's immigration status with the Federal Government.

The United States District Court for the District of Arizona issued a preliminary injunction preventing the four provisions at issue from taking effect. The Court of Appeals for the Ninth Circuit affirmed. It agreed that the United States had established a likelihood of success on its preemption claims. The Court of Appeals was unanimous in its conclusion that §§3 and 5(C) were likely preempted. Judge Bea dissented from the decision to uphold the preliminary injunction against §§2(B) and 6. This Court granted certiorari to resolve important questions concerning the interaction of state and federal power with respect to the law of immigration and alien status.

II

The Government of the United States has broad, undoubted power over the subject of immigration and the status of aliens. This authority rests, in part, on the

National Government's constitutional power to "establish an uniform Rule of Naturalization," U.S.Const., Art. I, §8, cl. 4, and its inherent power as sovereign to control and conduct relations with foreign nations.

The federal power to determine immigration policy is well settled. Immigration policy can affect trade, investment, tourism, and diplomatic relations for the entire Nation, as well as the perceptions and expectations of aliens in this country who seek the full protection of its laws. Perceived mistreatment of aliens in the United States may lead to harmful reciprocal treatment of American citizens abroad.

It is fundamental that foreign countries concerned about the status, safety, and security of their nationals in the United States must be able to confer and communicate on this subject with one national sovereign, not the 50 separate States. This Court has reaffirmed that "[o]ne of the most important and delicate of all international relationships . . . has to do with the protection of the just rights of a country's own nationals when those nationals are in another country."

Federal governance of immigration and alien status is extensive and complex. Congress has specified categories of aliens who may not be admitted to the United States. Unlawful entry and unlawful reentry into the country are federal offenses. Once here, aliens are required to register with the Federal Government and to carry proof of status on their person. Failure to do so is a federal misdemeanor. Federal law also authorizes States to deny noncitizens a range of public benefits; and it imposes sanctions on employers who hire unauthorized workers.

Congress has specified which aliens may be removed from the United States and the procedures for doing so. Aliens may be removed if they were inadmissible at the time of entry, have been convicted of certain crimes, or meet other criteria set by federal law. Removal is a civil, not criminal, matter. A principal feature of the removal system is the broad discretion exercised by immigration officials. Federal officials, as an initial matter, must decide whether it makes sense to pursue removal at all. If removal proceedings commence, aliens may seek asylum and other discretionary relief allowing them to remain in the country or at least to leave without formal removal.

Discretion in the enforcement of immigration law embraces immediate human concerns. Unauthorized workers trying to support their families, for example, likely pose less danger than alien smugglers or aliens who commit a serious crime. The equities of an individual case may turn on many factors, including whether the alien has children born in the United States, long ties to the community, or a record of distinguished military service. Some discretionary decisions involve policy choices that bear on this Nation's international relations. Returning an alien to his own country may be deemed inappropriate even where he has committed a removable offense or fails to meet the criteria for admission. The foreign state may be mired in civil war, complicit in political persecution, or enduring conditions that create a real risk that the alien or his family will be harmed upon return. The dynamic nature of relations with other countries requires the Executive Branch to ensure that enforcement policies are consistent with this Nation's foreign policy with respect to these and other realities.

Agencies in the Department of Homeland Security play a major role in enforcing the country's immigration laws. United States Customs and Border Protection (CBP) is responsible for determining the admissibility of aliens and securing the country's borders. In 2010, CBP's Border Patrol apprehended almost half a million people. Immigration and Customs Enforcement (ICE), a second agency, "conducts criminal investigations involving the enforcement of immigration-related statutes." ICE also operates the Law Enforcement Support Center. LESC, as the Center is known, provides immigration status information to federal, state, and local officials around the clock. ICE officers are responsible "for the identification, apprehension, and removal of illegal aliens from the United States." Hundreds of thousands of aliens are removed by the Federal Government every year.

The pervasiveness of federal regulation does not diminish the importance of immigration policy to the States. Arizona bears many of the consequences of unlawful immigration. Hundreds of thousands of deportable aliens are apprehended in Arizona each year. Unauthorized aliens who remain in the State comprise, by one estimate, almost six percent of the population. And in the State's most populous county, these aliens are reported to be responsible for a disproportionate share of serious crime.

Statistics alone do not capture the full extent of Arizona's concerns. Accounts in the record suggest there is an "epidemic of crime, safety risks, serious property damage, and environmental problems" associated with the influx of illegal migration across private land near the Mexican border. Brief for Petitioners 6. Phoenix is a major city of the United States, yet signs along an interstate highway 30 miles to the south warn the public to stay away. One reads, "DANGER—PUBLIC WARNING—TRAVEL NOT RECOMMENDED / Active Drug and Human Smuggling Area / Visitors May Encounter Armed Criminals and Smuggling Vehicles Traveling at High Rates of Speed." The problems posed to the State by illegal immigration must not be underestimated.

These concerns are the background for the formal legal analysis that follows. The issue is whether, under pre-emption principles, federal law permits Arizona to implement the state-law provisions in dispute.

III

Federalism, central to the constitutional design, adopts the principle that both the National and State Governments have elements of sovereignty the other is bound to respect. From the existence of two sovereigns follows the possibility that laws can be in conflict or at cross-purposes. The Supremacy Clause provides a clear rule that federal law "shall be the supreme Law of the Land; and the Judges in every State shall be bound thereby, any Thing in the Constitution or Laws of any State to the Contrary notwithstanding." Under this principle, Congress has the power to preempt state law. There is no doubt that Congress may withdraw specified powers from the States by enacting a statute containing an express preemption provision.

State law must also give way to federal law in at least two other circumstances. First, the States are precluded from regulating conduct in a field that Congress, acting within its proper authority, has determined must be regulated by its exclusive governance. The intent to displace state law altogether can be inferred from a framework of regulation "so pervasive . . . that Congress left no room for the States to supplement it" or where there is a "federal interest . . . so dominant that the federal system will be assumed to preclude enforcement of state laws on the same subject."

Second, state laws are preempted when they conflict with federal law. This includes cases where "compliance with both federal and state regulations is a physical impossibility," and those instances where the challenged state law "stands as an obstacle to the accomplishment and execution of the full purposes and objectives of Congress." In preemption analysis, courts should assume that "the historic police powers of the States" are not superseded "unless that was the clear and manifest purpose of Congress."

The four challenged provisions of the state law each must be examined under these preemption principles.

IV

Section 3 of S. B. 1070 creates a new state misdemeanor. It forbids the "willful failure to complete or carry an alien registration document . . . in violation of 8 United States Code section 1304(e) or 1306(a)." In effect, §3 adds a state-law penalty for conduct proscribed by federal law. The United States contends that this state enforcement mechanism intrudes on the field of alien registration, a field in which Congress has left no room for States to regulate.

The Court discussed federal alien-registration requirements in *Hines v. Davidowitz*, 312 U.S.52. In 1940, as international conflict spread, Congress added to federal immigration law a "complete system for alien registration." The new federal law struck a careful balance. It punished an alien's willful failure to register but did not require aliens to carry identification cards. There were also limits on the sharing of registration records and fingerprints. The Court found that Congress intended the federal plan for registration to be a "single integrated and all-embracing system." Because this "complete scheme . . . for the registration of aliens" touched on foreign relations, it did not allow the States to "curtail or complement" federal law or to "enforce additional or auxiliary regulations." As a consequence, the Court ruled that Pennsylvania could not enforce its own alien-registration program.

The present regime of federal regulation is not identical to the statutory framework considered in Hines, but it remains comprehensive. Federal law now includes a requirement that aliens carry proof of registration. Other aspects, however, have stayed the same. Aliens who remain in the country for more than 30 days must apply for registration and be fingerprinted. Detailed information is required, and any change of address has to be reported to the Federal Government. The statute continues to provide penalties for the willful failure to register.

The framework enacted by Congress leads to the conclusion here, as it did in Hines, that the Federal Government has occupied the field of alien registration. The federal statutory directives provide a full set of standards governing alien registration, including the punishment for noncompliance. It was designed as a "'harmonious whole.'" Where Congress occupies an entire field, as it has in the field of alien registration, even complementary state regulation is impermissible. Field pre-emption reflects a congressional decision to foreclose any state regulation in the area, even if it is parallel to federal standards.

Federal law makes a single sovereign responsible for maintaining a comprehensive and unified system to keep track of aliens within the Nation's borders. If §3 of the Arizona statute were valid, every State could give itself independent authority to prosecute federal registration violations, "diminish[ing] the [Federal Government]'s control over enforcement" and "detract[ing] from the 'integrated scheme of regulation' created by Congress." Even if a State may make violation of federal law a crime in some instances, it cannot do so in a field (like the field of alien registration) that has been occupied by federal law.

Arizona contends that §3 can survive preemption because the provision has the same aim as federal law and adopts its substantive standards. This argument not only ignores the basic premise of field preemption—that States may not enter, in any respect, an area the Federal Government has reserved for itself—but also is unpersuasive on its own terms. Permitting the State to impose its own penalties for the federal offenses here would conflict with the careful framework Congress adopted. Were §3 to come into force, the State would have the power to bring criminal charges against individuals for violating a federal law even in circumstances where federal officials in charge of the comprehensive scheme determine that prosecution would frustrate federal policies.

There is a further intrusion upon the federal scheme. Even where federal authorities believe prosecution is appropriate, there is an inconsistency between §3 and federal law with respect to penalties. Under federal law, the failure to carry registration papers is a misdemeanor that may be punished by a fine, imprisonment, or a term of probation. This state framework of sanctions creates a conflict with the plan Congress put in place. See Wisconsin Dept., *supra*, at 286 ("[C]onflict is imminent whenever two separate remedies are brought to bear on the same activity" (internal quotation marks omitted)).

These specific conflicts between state and federal law simply underscore the reason for field preemption. As it did in Hines, the Court now concludes that, with respect to the subject of alien registration, Congress intended to preclude States from "complement[ing] the federal law, or enforc[ing] additional or auxiliary regulations."

Unlike §3, which replicates federal statutory requirements, §5(C) enacts a state criminal prohibition where no federal counterpart exists. The provision makes it a state misdemeanor for "an unauthorized alien to knowingly apply for work, solicit work in a public place or perform work as an employee or independent contractor" in Arizona. Violations can be punished by a $2,500 fine and incarceration for up to six months. The United States contends that the provision upsets the balance struck by the Immigration Reform and Control Act of 1986 (IRCA) and must be preempted as an obstacle to the federal plan of regulation and control.

When there was no comprehensive federal program regulating the employment of unauthorized aliens, this Court found that a State had authority to pass its own laws on the subject. In 1971, for example, California passed a law imposing civil penalties on the employment of aliens who were "not entitled to lawful residence in the United States if such employment would have an adverse effect on lawful resident workers." *De Canas v. Bica* recognized that "States possess broad authority under their police powers to regulate the employment relationship to protect workers within the State." At that point, however, the Federal Government had expressed no more than "a peripheral concern with [the] employment of illegal entrants."

Current federal law is substantially different from the regime that prevailed when *De Canas* was decided. Congress enacted IRCA as a comprehensive framework for "combating the employment of illegal aliens." The law makes it illegal for employers to knowingly hire, recruit, refer, or continue to employ unauthorized workers. It also requires every employer to verify the employment authorization status of prospective employees. These requirements are enforced through criminal penalties and an escalating series of civil penalties tied to the number of times an employer has violated the provisions.

This comprehensive framework does not impose federal criminal sanctions on the employee side (i.e., penalties on aliens who seek or engage in unauthorized work). Under federal law some civil penalties are imposed instead. With certain exceptions, aliens who accept unlawful employment are not eligible to have their status adjusted to that of a lawful permanent resident. Aliens also may be removed from the country for having engaged in unauthorized work. In addition to specifying these civil consequences, federal law makes it a crime for unauthorized workers to obtain employment through fraudulent means. Congress has made clear, however, that any information employees submit to indicate their work status "may not be used" for purposes other than prosecution under specified federal criminal statutes for fraud, perjury, and related conduct.

The legislative background of IRCA underscores the fact that Congress made a deliberate choice not to impose criminal penalties on aliens who seek, or engage in, unauthorized employment. A commission established by Congress to study immigration policy and to make recommendations concluded these penalties would be "unnecessary and unworkable." Proposals to make unauthorized work a criminal offense were debated and discussed during the long process of drafting IRCA. But Congress rejected them. In the end, IRCA's framework reflects a considered judgment that making criminals out of aliens engaged in unauthorized work—aliens who already face the possibility of employer exploitation because of their removable status—would be inconsistent with federal policy and objectives.

IRCA's express preemption provision, which in most instances bars States from imposing penalties on employers of unauthorized aliens, is silent about whether additional penalties may be imposed against the employees themselves. But the existence of an "express pre-emption provisio[n] does not bar the ordinary working of conflict pre-emption principles" or impose a "special burden" that would make it more difficult to establish the preemption of laws falling outside the clause.

The ordinary principles of preemption include the well-settled proposition that a state law is preempted where it "stands as an obstacle to the accomplishment and execution of the full purposes and objectives of Congress." [The] Arizona law would interfere with the careful balance struck by Congress with respect to unauthorized employment of aliens. Although §5(C) attempts to achieve one of the same goals as federal law—the deterrence of unlawful employment—it involves a conflict in the method of enforcement. The Court has recognized that a "[c]onflict in technique can be fully as disruptive to the system Congress enacted as conflict in overt policy." The correct instruction to draw from the text, structure, and history of IRCA is that Congress decided it would be inappropriate to impose criminal penalties on aliens who seek or engage in unauthorized employment. It follows that a state law to the contrary is an obstacle to the regulatory system Congress chose. Section 5(C) is preempted by federal law.

Section 6 of S. B. 1070 provides that a state officer, "without a warrant, may arrest a person if the officer has probable cause to believe . . . [the person] has committed any public offense that makes [him] removable from the United States." The United States argues that arrests authorized by this statute would be an obstacle to the removal system Congress created.

As a general rule, it is not a crime for a removable alien to remain present in the United States. If the police stop someone based on nothing more than possible removability, the usual predicate for an arrest is absent. When an alien is suspected of being removable, a federal official issues an administrative document called a Notice to Appear. The form does not authorize an arrest. Instead, it gives the alien information about the proceedings, including the time and date of the removal hearing. If an alien fails to appear, an in absentia order may direct removal.

The federal statutory structure instructs when it is appropriate to arrest an alien during the removal process. For example, the Attorney General can exercise discretion to issue a warrant for an alien's arrest and detention "pending a decision on whether the alien is to be removed from the United States." And if an alien is ordered removed after a hearing, the Attorney General will issue a warrant. In both instances, the warrants are executed by federal officers who have received training in the enforcement of immigration law. If no federal warrant has been issued, those officers have more limited authority. They may arrest an alien for being "in the United States in violation of any [immigration] law or regulation," for example, but only where the alien "is likely to escape before a warrant can be obtained."

Section 6 attempts to provide state officers even greater authority to arrest aliens on the basis of possible removability than Congress has given to trained federal immigration officers. Under state law, officers who believe an alien is removable by reason of some "public offense" would have the power to conduct an arrest on that basis regardless of whether a federal warrant has issued or the alien is likely to escape. This state authority could be exercised without any input from the Federal Government about whether an arrest is warranted in a particular case. This would allow the State to achieve its own immigration policy. The result could be unnecessary harassment of some aliens (for instance, a veteran, college student, or someone assisting with a criminal investigation) whom federal officials determine should not be removed.

This is not the system Congress created. Federal law specifies limited circumstances in which state officers may perform the functions of an immigration officer. A principal example is when the Attorney General has granted that authority to specific officers in a formal agreement with a state or local government. Officers covered by these agreements are subject to the Attorney General's direction and supervision. There are significant complexities involved in enforcing federal immigration law, including the determination whether a person is removable. As a result, the agreements reached with the Attorney General must contain written certification that officers have received adequate training to carry out the duties of an immigration officer.

By authorizing state officers to decide whether an alien should be detained for being removable, §6 violates the principle that the removal process is entrusted to the discretion of the Federal Government. A decision on removability requires a determination whether it is appropriate to allow a foreign national to continue living in the United States. Decisions of this nature touch on foreign relations and must be made with one voice.

In defense of §6, Arizona notes a federal statute permitting state officers to "cooperate with the Attorney General in the identification, apprehension, detention, or removal of aliens not lawfully present in the United States." There may be some ambiguity as to what constitutes cooperation under the federal law; but no coherent understanding of the term would incorporate the unilateral decision of state officers to arrest an alien for being removable absent any request, approval, or other instruction from the Federal Government. The Department of Homeland Security gives examples of what would constitute cooperation under federal law. These include situations where States participate in a joint task force with federal officers, provide operational support in executing a warrant, or allow federal immigration officials to gain access to detainees held in state facilities. State officials can also assist the Federal Government by responding to requests for information about when an alien will be released from their custody. But the unilateral state action to detain authorized by §6 goes far beyond these measures, defeating any need for real cooperation.

Congress has put in place a system in which state officers may not make warrantless arrests of aliens based on possible removability except in specific, limited circumstances. By nonetheless authorizing state and local officers to engage in these enforcement activities as a general matter, §6 creates an obstacle to the full purposes and objectives of Congress. Section 6 is preempted by federal law.

Section 2(B) of S. B. 1070 requires state officers to make a "reasonable attempt . . . to determine the immigration status" of any person they stop, detain, or arrest on some other legitimate basis if "reasonable suspicion exists that the person is an alien and is unlawfully present in the United States." The law also provides that "[a]ny person who is arrested shall have the person's immigration status determined before the person is released." Ibid. The accepted way to perform these status checks is to contact ICE, which maintains a database of immigration records.

Three limits are built into the state provision. First, a detainee is presumed not to be an alien unlawfully present in the United States if he or she provides a valid

Arizona driver's license or similar identification. Second, officers "may not consider race, color or national origin . . . except to the extent permitted by the United States [and] Arizona Constitution[s]." Ibid. Third, the provisions must be "implemented in a manner consistent with federal law regulating immigration, protecting the civil rights of all persons and respecting the privileges and immunities of United States citizens."

The United States and its amici contend that, even with these limits, the State's verification requirements pose an obstacle to the framework Congress put in place. The first concern is the mandatory nature of the status checks. The second is the possibility of prolonged detention while the checks are being performed.

Consultation between federal and state officials is an important feature of the immigration system. Congress has made clear that no formal agreement or special training needs to be in place for state officers to "communicate with the [Federal Government] regarding the immigration status of any individual, including reporting knowledge that a particular alien is not lawfully present in the United States." And Congress has obligated ICE to respond to any request made by state officials for verification of a person's citizenship or immigration status. ICE's Law Enforcement Support Center operates "24 hours a day, seven days a week, 365 days a year" and provides, among other things, "immigration status, identity information and real-time assistance to local, state and federal law enforcement agencies."

The United States argues that making status verification mandatory interferes with the federal immigration scheme. It is true that §2(B) does not allow state officers to consider federal enforcement priorities in deciding whether to contact ICE about someone they have detained. In other words, the officers must make an inquiry even in cases where it seems unlikely that the Attorney General would have the alien removed. This might be the case, for example, when an alien is an elderly veteran with significant and longstanding ties to the community.

Congress has done nothing to suggest it is inappropriate to communicate with ICE in these situations, however. Indeed, it has encouraged the sharing of information about possible immigration violations. A federal statute regulating the public benefits provided to qualified aliens in fact instructs that "no State or local government entity may be prohibited, or in any way restricted, from sending to or receiving from [ICE] information regarding the immigration status, lawful or unlawful, of an alien in the United States." The federal scheme thus leaves room for a policy requiring state officials to contact ICE as a routine matter.

Some who support the challenge to §2(B) argue that, in practice, state officers will be required to delay the release of some detainees for no reason other than to verify their immigration status. And it would disrupt the federal framework to put state officers in the position of holding aliens in custody for possible unlawful presence without federal direction and supervision. The program put in place by Congress does not allow state or local officers to adopt this enforcement mechanism.

But §2(B) could be read to avoid these concerns. To take one example, a person might be stopped for jaywalking in Tucson and be unable to produce identification. The first sentence of §2(B) instructs officers to make a "reasonable" attempt to verify his immigration status with ICE if there is reasonable suspicion that his presence in the United States is unlawful. The state courts may conclude that, unless the person continues to be suspected of some crime for which he may be detained by state officers, it would not be reasonable to prolong the stop for the immigration inquiry.

To take another example, a person might be held pending release on a charge of driving under the influence of alcohol. As this goes beyond a mere stop, the arrestee (unlike the jaywalker) would appear to be subject to the categorical requirement in the second sentence of §2(B) that "[a]ny person who is arrested shall have the person's immigration status determined before [he] is released." State courts may read this as an instruction to initiate a status check every time someone is arrested, or in some subset of those cases, rather than as a command to hold the person until the check is complete no matter the circumstances. Even if the law is read as an instruction to complete a check while the person is in custody, moreover, it is not clear at this stage and on this record that the verification process would result in prolonged detention. However the law is interpreted, if §2(B) only requires state officers to conduct a status check during the course of an authorized, lawful detention or after a detainee has been released, the provision likely would survive pre-emption—at least absent some showing that it has other consequences that are adverse to federal law and its objectives. There is no need in this case to address whether reasonable suspicion of illegal entry or another immigration crime would be a legitimate basis for prolonging a detention, or whether this too would be preempted by federal law.

The nature and timing of this case counsel caution in evaluating the validity of §2(B). The Federal Government has brought suit against a sovereign State to challenge the provision even before the law has gone into effect. There is a basic uncertainty about what the law means and how it will be enforced. At this stage, without the benefit of a definitive interpretation from the state courts, it would be inappropriate to assume §2(B) will be construed in a way that creates a conflict with federal law. As a result, the United States cannot prevail in its current challenge. This opinion does not foreclose other preemption and constitutional challenges to the law as interpreted and applied after it goes into effect.

V

Immigration policy shapes the destiny of the Nation. On May 24, 2012, at one of this Nation's most distinguished museums of history, a dozen immigrants stood before the tattered flag that inspired Francis Scott Key to write the National Anthem. There they took the oath to become American citizens. These naturalization ceremonies bring together men and women of different origins who now share a common destiny. They swear a common oath to renounce fidelity to foreign princes, to defend the Constitution, and to bear arms on behalf of the country when required by law. The history of the United States is in part made of the stories, talents, and lasting contributions of those who crossed oceans and deserts to come here.

The National Government has significant power to regulate immigration. With power comes responsibility, and the sound exercise of national power over immigration depends on the Nation's meeting its responsibility to base its laws on a political will informed by searching, thoughtful, rational civic discourse. Arizona may have understandable frustrations with the problems caused by illegal immigration while that process continues, but the State may not pursue policies that undermine federal law.

*　　*　　*

The United States has established that §§3, 5(C), and 6 of S. B. 1070 are preempted. It was improper, however, to enjoin §2(B) before the state courts had an opportunity to construe it and without some showing that enforcement of the provision in fact conflicts with federal immigration law and its objectives.

The judgment of the Court of Appeals for the Ninth Circuit is affirmed in part and reversed in part. The case is remanded for further proceedings consistent with this opinion.

It is so ordered.

Justice Scalia, concurring in part and dissenting in part.

The United States is an indivisible "Union of sovereign States." Today's opinion, approving virtually all of the Ninth Circuit's injunction against enforcement of the four challenged provisions of Arizona's law, deprives States of what most would consider the defining characteristic of sovereignty: the power to exclude from the sovereign's territory people who have no right to be there. Neither the Constitution itself nor even any law passed by Congress supports this result. I dissent.

I

As a sovereign, Arizona has the inherent power to exclude persons from its territory, subject only to those limitations expressed in the Constitution or constitutionally imposed by Congress. That power to exclude has long been recognized as inherent in sovereignty. Emer de Vattel's seminal 1758 treatise on the Law of Nations stated:

"The sovereign may forbid the entrance of his territory either to foreigners in general, or in particular cases, or to certain persons, or for certain particular purposes, according as he may think it advantageous to the state. There is nothing in all this, that does not flow from the rights of domain and sovereignty: every one is obliged to pay respect to the prohibition; and whoever dares violate it, incurs the penalty decreed to render it effectual."

There is no doubt that "before the adoption of the constitution of the United States" each State had the authority to "prevent [itself] from being burdened by an influx of persons." And the Constitution did not strip the States of that authority. To the contrary, two of the Constitution's provisions were designed to enable the States to prevent "the intrusion of obnoxious aliens through other States." The Articles of Confederation had provided that "the free inhabitants of each of these States, paupers, vagabonds and fugitives from justice excepted, shall be entitled to all privileges and immunities of free citizens in the several States." This meant that an unwelcome alien could obtain all the rights of a citizen of one State simply by first becoming an inhabitant of another. To remedy this, the Constitution's Privileges and Immunities Clause provided that "[t]he Citizens of each State shall be entitled to all Privileges and Immunities of Citizens in the several States." But if one State had particularly lax citizenship standards, it might still serve as a gateway for the entry of "obnoxious aliens" into other States. This problem was solved "by authorizing the general government to establish a uniform rule of naturalization throughout the United States." In other words, the naturalization power was given to Congress not to abrogate States' power to exclude those they did not want, but to vindicate it.

Two other provisions of the Constitution are an acknowledgment of the States' sovereign interest in protecting their borders. Article I provides that "[n]o State shall, without the Consent of the Congress, lay any Imposts or Duties on Imports or Exports, except what may be absolutely necessary for executing it's inspection Laws." This assumed what everyone assumed: that the States could exclude from their territory dangerous or unwholesome goods. A later portion of the same section provides that "[n]o State shall, without the Consent of Congress, . . . engage in War, unless actually invaded, or in such imminent Danger as will not admit of delay."

Notwithstanding "[t]he myth of an era of unrestricted immigration" in the first 100 years of the Republic, the States enacted numerous laws restricting the immigra-

tion of certain classes of aliens, including convicted criminals, indigents, persons with contagious diseases, and (in Southern States) freed blacks. State laws not only provided for the removal of unwanted immigrants but also imposed penalties on unlawfully present aliens and those who aided their immigration.

In fact, the controversy surrounding the Alien and Sedition Acts involved a debate over whether, under the Constitution, the States had exclusive authority to enact such immigration laws. Criticism of the Sedition Act has become a prominent feature of our First Amendment jurisprudence, but one of the Alien Acts_also aroused controversy at the time:

"Be it enacted by the Senate and House of Representatives of the United States of America in Congress assembled, That it shall be lawful for the President of the United States at any time during the continuance of this act, to order all such aliens as he shall judge dangerous to the peace and safety of the United States, or shall have reasonable grounds to suspect are concerned in any treasonable or secret machinations against the government thereof, to depart out of the territory of the United States...."

The Kentucky and Virginia Resolutions, written in denunciation of these Acts, insisted that the power to exclude unwanted aliens rested solely in the States. Jefferson's Kentucky Resolutions insisted "that alien friends are under the jurisdiction and protection of the laws of the state wherein they are [and] that no power over them has been delegated to the United States, nor prohibited to the individual states, distinct from their power over citizens." Kentucky Resolutions of 1798, reprinted in J. Powell, Languages of Power: A Sourcebook of Early American Constitutional History 131 (1991). Madison's Virginia Resolutions likewise contended that the Alien Act purported to give the President "a power nowhere delegated to the federal government."

In *Mayor of New York v. Miln*, this Court considered a New York statute that required the commander of any ship arriving in New York from abroad to disclose "the name, place of birth, and last legal settlement, age and occupation ... of all passengers . . . with the intention of proceeding to the said city." After discussing the sovereign authority to regulate the entrance of foreigners described by De Vattel, the Court said:

"The power . . . of New York to pass this law having undeniably existed at the formation of the constitution, the simply inquiry is, whether by that instrument it was taken from the states, and granted to congress; for if it were not, it yet remains with them."

And the Court held that it remains.

II

One would conclude from the foregoing that after the adoption of the Constitution there was some doubt about the power of the Federal Government to control immigration, but no doubt about the power of the States to do so. Since the founding era (though not immediately), doubt about the Federal Government's power has disappeared. Indeed, primary responsibility for immigration policy has shifted from the States to the Federal Government. Congress exercised its power "[t]o establish an uniform Rule of Naturalization." But with the fleeting exception of the Alien Act, Congress did not enact any legislation regulating immigration for the better part of a century. In 1862, Congress passed "An Act to prohibit the 'Coolie Trade' by American Citizens in American Vessels," which prohibited "procuring [Chinese nationals] . . . to be disposed of, or sold, or transferred, for any term of years or for any time whatever, as servants or apprentices, or to be held to service or labor." 12 Stat. 340. Then, in 1875, Congress amended that act to bar admission to Chinese, Japanese, and other Asian immigrants who had "entered into a contract or agreement for a term of service within the United States, for lewd and immoral purposes." An act supplementary to the acts in relation to immigration. And in 1882, Congress enacted the first general immigration statute.

I accept that as a valid exercise of federal power—not because of the Naturalization Clause (it has no necessary connection to citizenship) but because it is an inherent attribute of sovereignty no less for the United States than for the States. As this Court has said, it is an "'accepted maxim of international law, that every sovereign nation has the power, as inherent in sovereignty, and essential to self-preservation, to forbid the entrance of foreigners within its dominions.'" That is why there was no need to set forth control of immigration as one of the enumerated powers of Congress, although an acknowledgment

of that power (as well as of the States' similar power, subject to federal abridgment) was contained in Art. I, §9, which provided that "[t]he Migration or Importation of such Persons as any of the States now existing shall think proper to admit, shall not be prohibited by the Congress prior to the Year one thousand eight hundred and eight...."

In light of the predominance of federal immigration restrictions in modern times, it is easy to lose sight of the States' traditional role in regulating immigration—and to overlook their sovereign prerogative to do so. I accept as a given that State regulation is excluded by the Constitution when (1) it has been prohibited by a valid federal law, or (2) it conflicts with federal regulation—when, for example, it admits those whom federal regulation would exclude, or excludes those whom federal regulation would admit.

Possibility (1) need not be considered here: there is no federal law prohibiting the States' sovereign power to exclude (assuming federal authority to enact such a law). The mere existence of federal action in the immigration area—and the so-called field preemption arising from that action, upon which the Court's opinion so heavily relies, *ante*, at 9–11—cannot be regarded as such a prohibition. We are not talking here about a federal law prohibiting the States from regulating bubble-gum advertising, or even the construction of nuclear plants. We are talking about a federal law going to the core of state sovereignty: the power to exclude. Like elimination of the States' other inherent sovereign power, immunity from suit, elimination of the States' sovereign power to exclude requires that "Congress . . . unequivocally expres[s] its intent to abrogate." Implicit "field preemption" will not do.

Nor can federal power over illegal immigration be deemed exclusive because of what the Court's opinion solicitously calls "foreign countries ['] concern[s] about the status, safety, and security of their nationals in the United States," *ante*, at 3. The Constitution gives all those on our shores the protections of the Bill of Rights—but just as those rights are not expanded for foreign nationals because of their countries' views (some countries, for example, have recently discovered the death penalty to be barbaric), neither are the fundamental sovereign powers of the States abridged to accommodate foreign countries' views. Even in its international relations, the Federal Government must live with the inconvenient fact that it is a Union of independent States, who have their own sovereign powers. This is not the first time it has found that a nuisance and a bother in the conduct of foreign policy. Four years ago, for example, the Government importuned us to interfere with thoroughly constitutional state judicial procedures in the criminal trial of foreign nationals because the international community, and even an opinion of the International Court of Justice, disapproved them. We rejected that request, as we should reject the Executive's invocation of foreign-affairs considerations here. Though it may upset foreign powers—and even when the Federal Government desperately wants to avoid upsetting foreign powers—the States have the right to protect their borders against foreign nationals, just as they have the right to execute foreign nationals for murder.

What this case comes down to, then, is whether the Arizona law conflicts with federal immigration law—whether it excludes those whom federal law would admit, or admits those whom federal law would exclude. It does not purport to do so. It applies only to aliens who neither possess a privilege to be present under federal law nor have been removed pursuant to the Federal Government's inherent authority. I proceed to consider the challenged provisions in detail.

§2(B)

"For any lawful stop, detention or arrest made by a law enforcement official ... in the enforcement of any other law or ordinance of a county, city or town or this state where reasonable suspicion exists that the person is an alien and is unlawfully present in the United States, a reasonable attempt shall be made, when practicable, to determine the immigration status of the person, except if the determination may hinder or obstruct an investigation. Any person who is arrested shall have the person's immigration status determined before the person is released...."

The Government has conceded that "even before Section 2 was enacted, state and local officers had state-law authority to inquire of DHS [the Department of Homeland Security] about a suspect's unlawful status and otherwise cooperate with federal immigration officers." That concession, in my view, obviates the need for further inquiry. The Government's conflict-pre-emption claim calls on us "to determine whether, under the circumstances of this particular case, [the State's] law stands as an obstacle to the accomplishment and execution of the full purposes and objectives of Congress." It is impossible to make such a finding without a factual record concerning the manner in which Arizona is implementing these provisions—something the Government's pre-enforcement challenge has pretermitted. "The fact that [a law] might operate unconstitutionally under some conceivable set of circumstances is insufficient to render it wholly invalid, since we have not recognized an 'overbreadth' doctrine outside the limited context of the First Amendment." And on its face, §2(B) merely tells state officials that they are authorized to do something that they were, by the Government's concession, already authorized to do.

The Court therefore properly rejects the Government's challenge, recognizing that, "[a]t this stage, without the benefit of a definitive interpretation from the state courts, it would be inappropriate to assume §2B will be construed in a way that creates a conflict with federal law." Before reaching that conclusion, however, the Court goes to great length to assuage fears that "state officers will be required to delay the release of some detainees for no reason other than to verify their immigration status." Of course, any investigatory detention, including one under §2(B), may become an "unreasonable . . . seizur[e]." But that has nothing to do with this case, in which the Government claims that §2(B) is pre-empted by federal immigration law, not that anyone's Fourth Amendment rights have been violated. And I know of no reason why a protracted detention that does not violate the Fourth Amendment would contradict or conflict with any federal immigration law.

§6

"A peace officer, without a warrant, may arrest a person if the officer has probable cause to believe . . . [t]he person to be arrested has committed any public offense that makes the person removable from the United States."

This provision of S. B. 1070 expands the statutory list of offenses for which an Arizona police officer may make an arrest without a warrant. If an officer has probable cause to believe that an individual is "removable" by reason of a public offense, then a warrant is not required to make an arrest. The Government's primary contention is that §6 is pre-empted by federal immigration law because it allows state officials to make arrests "without regard to federal priorities." The Court's opinion focuses on limits that Congress has placed on federal officials' authority to arrest removable aliens and the possibility that state officials will make arrests "to achieve [Arizona's] own immigration policy" and "without any input from the Federal Government."

Of course on this pre-enforcement record there is no reason to assume that Arizona officials will ignore federal immigration policy (unless it be the questionable policy of not wanting to identify illegal aliens who have committed offenses that make them removable). As Arizona points out, federal law expressly provides that state officers may "cooperate with the Attorney General in the identification, apprehension, detention, or removal of aliens not lawfully present in the United States." It is consistent with the Arizona statute, and with the "cooperat[ive]" system that Congress has created, for state officials to arrest a removable alien, contact federal immigration authorities, and follow their lead on what to do next. And it is an assault on logic to say that identifying a removable alien and holding him for federal determination of whether he should be removed "violates the principle that the removal process is entrusted to the discretion of the Federal Government." The State's detention does not represent commencement of the removal process unless the Federal Government makes it so.

But that is not the most important point. The most important point is that, as we have discussed, Arizona is entitled to have "its own immigration policy"—including a more rigorous enforcement policy—so long as that does not conflict with federal law. The Court says, as though the point is utterly dispositive, that "it is not a crime for a removable alien to remain present in the United States." It is not a federal crime, to be sure. But there is no reason Arizona cannot make it a state crime for a removable alien (or any illegal alien, for that matter) to remain present in Arizona.

The Court quotes 8 U.S.C. §1226(a), which provides that, "[o]n a warrant issued by the Attorney General, an alien may be arrested and detained pending a decision on whether the alien is to be removed from the United States." But statutory limitations upon the actions of federal officers in enforcing the United States' power to pro-

tect its borders do not on their face apply to the actions of state officers in enforcing the State's power to protect its borders. There is no more reason to read these provisions as implying that state officials are subject to similar limitations than there is to read them as implying that only federal officials may arrest removable aliens. And in any event neither implication would constitute the sort of clear elimination of the States' sovereign power that our cases demand.

The Court raises concerns about "unnecessary harassment of some aliens . . . whom federal officials determine should not be removed." But we have no license to assume, without any support in the record, that Arizona officials would use their arrest authority under §6 to harass anyone. And it makes no difference that federal officials might "determine [that some unlawfully present aliens] should not be removed," ibid. They may well determine not to remove from the United States aliens who have no right to be here; but unless and until these aliens have been given the right to remain, Arizona is entitled to arrest them and at least bring them to federal officials' attention, which is all that §6 necessarily entails. (In my view, the State can go further than this, and punish them for their unlawful entry and presence in Arizona.)

The Government complains that state officials might not heed "federal priorities." Indeed they might not, particularly if those priorities include willful blindness or deliberate inattention to the presence of removable aliens in Arizona. The State's whole complaint—the reason this law was passed and this case has arisen—is that the citizens of Arizona believe federal priorities are too lax. The State has the sovereign power to protect its borders more rigorously if it wishes, absent any valid federal prohibition. The Executive's policy choice of lax federal enforcement does not constitute such a prohibition.

§3

"In addition to any violation of federal law, a person is guilty of willful failure to complete or carry an alien registration document if the person is in violation of 8 [U.S.C.] §1304(e) or §1306(a)."

It is beyond question that a State may make violation of federal law a violation of state law as well. We have held that to be so even when the interest protected is a distinctively federal interest, such as protection of the dignity of the national flag. "[T]he State is not inhibited from making the national purposes its own purposes to the extent of exerting its police power to prevent its own citizens from obstructing the accomplishment of such purposes." Much more is that so when, as here, the State is protecting its own interest, the integrity of its borders. And we have said that explicitly with regard to illegal immigration: "Despite the exclusive federal control of this Nation's borders, we cannot conclude that the States are without any power to deter the influx of persons entering the United States against federal law, and whose numbers might have a discernible impact on traditional state concerns."

The Court's opinion relies upon *Hines v. Davidowitz, supra.* Ante, at 9–10. But that case did not, as the Court believes, establish a "field preemption" that implicitly eliminates the States' sovereign power to exclude those whom federal law excludes. It held that the States are not permitted to establish "additional or auxiliary" registration requirements for aliens. But §3 does not establish additional or auxiliary registration requirements. It merely makes a violation of state law the very same failure to register and failure to carry evidence of registration that are violations of federal law. *Hines* does not prevent the State from relying on the federal registration system as "an available aid in the enforcement of a number of statutes of the state applicable to aliens whose constitutional validity has not been questioned." One such statute is Arizona's law forbidding illegal aliens to collect unemployment benefits. To enforce that and other laws that validly turn on alien status, Arizona has, in Justice Stone's words, an interest in knowing "the number and whereabouts of aliens within the state" and in having "a means of their identification." And it can punish the aliens' failure to comply with the provisions of federal law that make that knowledge and identification possible.

In some areas of uniquely federal concern—e.g., fraud in a federal administrative—this Court has held that a State has no legitimate interest in enforcing a federal scheme. But the federal alien registration system is certainly not of uniquely federal interest. States, private entities, and individuals rely on the federal registration system (including the E-Verify program) on a regular basis. Arizona's legitimate interest in protecting

(among other things) its unemployment-benefits system is an entirely adequate basis for making the violation of federal registration and carry requirements a violation of state law as well.

The Court points out, however, *ante*, at 11, that in some respects the state law exceeds the punishments prescribed by federal law: It rules out probation and pardon, which are available under federal law. The answer is that it makes no difference. Illegal immigrants who violate §3 violate Arizona law. It is one thing to say that the Supremacy Clause prevents Arizona law from excluding those whom federal law admits. It is quite something else to say that a violation of Arizona law cannot be punished more severely than a violation of federal law. Especially where (as here) the State is defending its own sovereign interests, there is no precedent for such a limitation. The sale of illegal drugs, for example, ordinarily violates state law as well as federal law, and no one thinks that the state penalties cannot exceed the federal. As I have discussed, moreover, "field preemption" cannot establish a prohibition of additional state penalties in the area of immigration.

Finally, the Government also suggests that §3 poses an obstacle to the administration of federal immigration law, but "there is no conflict in terms, and no possibility of such conflict, [if] the state statute makes federal law its own."

It holds no fear for me, as it does for the Court, that "[w]ere §3 to come into force, the State would have the power to bring criminal charges against individuals for violating a federal law even in circumstances where federal officials in charge of the comprehensive scheme determine that prosecution would frustrate federal policies." That seems to me entirely appropriate when the State uses the federal law (as it must) as the criterion for the exercise of its own power, and the implementation of its own policies of excluding those who do not belong there. What I do fear—and what Arizona and the States that support it fear—is that "federal policies" of nonenforcement will leave the States helpless before those evil effects of illegal immigration that the Court's opinion dutifully recites in its prologue (*ante*, at 6) but leaves unremedied in its disposition.

§5(C)

"It is unlawful for a person who is unlawfully present in the United States and who is an unauthorized alien to knowingly apply for work, solicit work in a public place or perform work as an employee or independent contractor in this state."

Here, the Court rightly starts with *De Canas v. Bica* which involved a California law providing that "'[n]o employer shall knowingly employ an alien who is not entitled to lawful residence in the United States if such employment would have an adverse effect on lawful resident workers.'" This Court concluded that the California law was not pre-empted, as Congress had neither occupied the field of "regulation of employment of illegal aliens" nor expressed "the clear and manifest purpose" of displacing such state regulation. Thus, at the time *De Canas* was decided, §5(C) would have been indubitably lawful.

The only relevant change is that Congress has since enacted its own restrictions on employers who hire illegal aliens, in legislation that also includes some civil (but no criminal) penalties on illegal aliens who accept unlawful employment. The Court concludes from this (reasonably enough) "that Congress made a deliberate choice not to impose criminal penalties on aliens who seek, or engage in, unauthorized employment," *ante*, at 13. But that is not the same as a deliberate choice to prohibit the States from imposing criminal penalties. Congress's intent with regard to exclusion of state law need not be guessed at, but is found in the law's express pre-emption provision, which excludes "any State or local law imposing civil or criminal sanctions (other than through licensing and similar laws) upon those who employ, or recruitor refer for a fee for employment, unauthorized aliens." Common sense, reflected in the canon *expressio unius est exclusio alterius*, suggests that the specification of pre-emption for laws punishing "those who employ" implies the lack of pre-emption for other laws, including laws punishing "those who seek or accept employment."

The Court has no credible response to this. It quotes our jurisprudence to the effect that an "express pre-emption provisio[n] does not bar the ordinary working of conflict pre-emption principles." True enough—conflict preemption principles. It then goes on say that since "Congress decided it would be inappropriate to impose

criminal penalties on aliens who seek or engage in unauthorized employment," "[i]t follows that a state law to the contrary is an obstacle to the regulatory system Congress chose." All that is a classic description not of conflict pre-emption but of field pre-emption, which (concededly) does not occur beyond the terms of an express pre-emption provision.

The Court concludes that §5(C) "would interfere with the careful balance struck by Congress," but that is easy to say and impossible to demonstrate. The Court relies primarily on the fact that "[p]roposals to make unauthorized work a criminal offense were debated and discussed during the long process of drafting [the Immigration Reform and Control Act of 1986 (IRCA)]," "[b]ut Congress rejected them." There is no more reason to believe that this rejection was expressive of a desire that there be no sanctions on employees, than expressive of a desire that such sanctions be left to the States. To tell the truth, it was most likely expressive of what inaction ordinarily expresses: nothing at all. It is a "naïve assumption that the failure of a bill to make it out of committee, or to be adopted when reported to the floor, is the same as a congressional rejection of what the bill contained."

*　　*　　*

The brief for the Government in this case asserted that "the Executive Branch's ability to exercise discretion and set priorities is particularly important because of the need to allocate scarce enforcement resources wisely." Of course there is no reason why the Federal Executive's need to allocate its scarce enforcement resources should disable Arizona from devoting its resources to illegal immigration in Arizona that in its view the Federal Executive has given short shrift. Despite Congress's prescription that "the immigration laws of the United States should be enforced vigorously and uniformly," Arizona asserts without contradiction and with supporting citations:

"[I]n the last decade federal enforcement efforts have focused primarily on areas in California and Texas, leaving Arizona's border to suffer from comparative neglect. The result has been the funneling of an increasing tide of illegal border crossings into Arizona. Indeed, over the past decade, over a third of the Nation's illegal border crossings occurred in Arizona."

Must Arizona's ability to protect its borders yield to the reality that Congress has provided inadequate funding for federal enforcement—or, even worse, to the Executive's unwise targeting of that funding?

But leave that aside. It has become clear that federal enforcement priorities—in the sense of priorities based on the need to allocate "scarce enforcement resources"—is not the problem here. After this case was argued and while it was under consideration, the Secretary of Homeland Security announced a program exempting from immigration enforcement some 1.4 million illegal immigrants under the age of 30. If an individual unlawfully present in the United States

- "came to the United States under the age of sixteen;

- "has continuously resided in the United States for at least five years . . . ,

- "is currently in school, has graduated from high school, has obtained a general education development certificate, or is an honorably discharged veteran . . . ,

- "has not been convicted of a [serious crime]; and

- "is not above the age of thirty,"

then U.S.immigration officials have been directed to "defe[r] action" against such individual "for a period of two years, subject to renewal." The husbanding of scarce enforcement resources can hardly be the justification for this, since the considerable administrative cost of conducting as many as 1.4 million background checks, and ruling on the biennial requests for dispensation that the nonenforcement program envisions, will necessarily be deducted from immigration enforcement. The President said at a news conference that the new program is "the right thing to do" in light of Congress's failure to pass the Administration's proposed revision of the Immigration Act. Perhaps it is, though Arizona may not think so. But to say, as the Court does, that Arizona contradicts federal law by enforcing applications of the Immigration Act that the President declines to enforce boggles the mind.

The Court opinion's looming specter of inutterable horror—"[i]f §3 of the Arizona statute were valid, every State could give itself independent authority to prosecute federal registration violations"—seems to me not so horrible and even less looming. But there has come to pass, and is with us today, the specter that Arizona and the States that support it predicted: A Federal Government that does not want to enforce the immigration laws as written, and leaves the States' borders unprotected against immigrants whom those laws would exclude. So the issue is a stark one. Are the sovereign States at the mercy of the Federal Executive's refusal to enforce the Nation's immigration laws?

A good way of answering that question is to ask: Would the States conceivably have entered into the Union if the Constitution itself contained the Court's holding? Today's judgment surely fails that test. At the Constitutional Convention of 1787, the delegates contended with "the jealousy of the states with regard to their sovereignty." Through ratification of the fundamental charter that the Convention produced, the States ceded much of their sovereignty to the Federal Government. But much of it remained jealously guarded—as reflected in the innumerable proposals that never left Independence Hall. Now, imagine a provision which included among the enumerated powers of Congress "To establish Limitations upon Immigration that will be exclusive and that will be enforced only to the extent the President deems appropriate." The delegates to the Grand Convention would have rushed to the exits.

As is often the case, discussion of the dry legalities that are the proper object of our attention suppresses the very human realities that gave rise to the suit. Arizona bears the brunt of the country's illegal immigration problem. Its citizens feel themselves under siege by large numbers of illegal immigrants who invade their property, strain their social services, and even place their lives in jeopardy. Federal officials have been unable to remedy the problem, and indeed have recently shown that they are unwilling to do so. Thousands of Arizona's estimated 400,000 illegal immigrants—including not just children but men and women under 30—are now assured immunity from enforcement, and will be able to compete openly with Arizona citizens for employment.

Arizona has moved to protect its sovereignty—not in contradiction of federal law, but in complete compliance with it. The laws under challenge here do not extend or revise federal immigration restrictions, but merely enforce those restrictions more effectively. If securing its territory in this fashion is not within the power of Arizona, we should cease referring to it as a sovereign State. I dissent.

GLOSSARY

Amici Curiae: A Latin phrase meaning "friend of the court," the term refers to anyone not party to a case who files a statement with the court in support of one of the sides in the case.

Asylum: In the context of the legal documents being studied, and international law, "asylum" refers to the granting of refuge to people who have left their country for political reasons.

Certiorari: A Latin word meaning roughly "to be made certain of"; in legal use it refers to the action of a higher court reviewing the findings of a lower court.

Federalism: A system of government in which power is divided between a national ("federal") government and regional governments such as between the national and state governments in the United States or the national and provincial governments in Canada.

Sovereign: Legally, this refers to an independent political entity or the person or group of people who exercise ultimate political authority within the political unit.

Warrant: A document issued by a court, upon probable cause, authorizing police or other government officials to arrest a person, search specific premises, or engage in some other judicial action.

Document Analysis

Justice Kennedy, offering the majority opinion of the Court, began by summarizing the general reasons for the Arizona law in question and the resulting legal action. He identified four issues that the Court reviewed in making its decision. These included (1) making failure to comply with federal immigration law a state offense, (2) making it illegal for someone not in compliance with federal law to work in the state, (3) allowing law enforcement officers to arrest a person without a warrant if the officer "has probable cause to believe ... has committed any public offense that makes the person removable from the United States," and (4) that officers making a "stop, detention, or arrest must in some circumstances make efforts to verify the person's immigration status." Although these were all state actions, the judge noted that the Constitution gives the federal government the authority to enforce immigration policy. He also notes that Congress has traditionally enacted laws that make "unlawful entry" into the U.S. a federal offense. Further, "Once here, aliens are required to register with the Fed-

eral Government and to carry proof of status on their person. Failure to do so is a federal misdemeanor. Federal law also authorizes States to deny noncitizens a range of public benefits; and it imposes sanctions on employers who hire unauthorized workers." For all of these reasons Kennedy began with the basic understanding that the federal government had within its purview the authority to create and enforce U.S. immigration policies.

Despite having just reviewed the legal requirements for aliens seeking to enter and remain in the country, Kennedy next argued that there were variations in circumstances that make deportation "inappropriate," circumstances such as whether the alien was likely to pose a danger, if the alien had "long ties to the community," or if the alien had children who were U.S. citizens. Additionally, deportation may also be intertwined with American foreign relations as extenuating circumstances. While acknowledging that the state of Arizona "bears many of the consequences of unlawful immigration" and that "aliens are reported to be responsible for a disproportionate share of serious crime" and other problems, the justice asserted that the primary issue in question was "whether, under pre-emption principles, federal law permits Arizona to implement the state-law provisions in dispute."

Kennedy explained that any state law conflicting with a federal law was not enforceable because the federal law overrode legislation by any state or court decisions by any state court. "The four challenged provisions of the state law," he concluded, "each must be examined under these preemption principles." Regarding the state statute, Kennedy noted that it created a new misdemeanor and state penalties for violation of federal immigration laws. Under the supremacy clause of the Constitution, the state was precluded from adding additional punishments or from enforcing federal immigration law without specific authorization from federal authorities. Were it otherwise, then "every State could give itself independent authority to prosecute federal registration violations" which would interfere with and reduce federal authority. Although Arizona claimed that it was acting in accord with federal law, Kennedy found that argument immaterial since under the preemption principle states were precluded from taking any action within the purview of federal authority. Secondly, he also found against the state since the state penalties varied from those imposed in federal law.

Presenting the minority opinion, Justice Scalia observed that the United States was a federal union of "sovereign States" and the Court's decision "deprives States of what most would consider the defining characteristic of sovereignty: the power to exclude from the sovereign's territory people who have no right to be there. Neither the Constitution itself nor even any law passed by Congress supports this result." Arizona, or any state, had the right to exclude from within its borders anyone it chose so long as the exclusion did not violate a specific provision in the Constitution or an act of Congress. In support of this position he pointed out that the original states had the authority to exclude people from their territory and that there is nothing in the Constitution that withdraws that authority from them and in fact states had enacted legislation restricting people into their borders throughout the first century of national existence.

Although the federal government had increasingly legislated in the field of immigration since 1862, Scalia argued that this did not in any way remove from the states their sovereign right to legislate regarding immigration and aliens. Similarly, he discounts the majority's argument about the influence of immigration policy on foreign affairs because the "sovereign powers of the States"

cannot be "abridged to accommodate foreign countries' views. ... Even in its international relations, the Federal Government must live with the inconvenient fact that it is a Union of independent States, who have their own sovereign powers." For Scalia, "What this case comes down to, then, is whether the Arizona law conflicts with federal immigration law—whether it excludes those whom federal law would admit, or admits those whom federal law would exclude. It does not purport to do so. It applies only to aliens who neither possess a privilege to be present under federal law nor have been removed pursuant to the Federal Government's inherent authority."

While presenting a detailed refutation of the various arguments of the majority, Scalia notes that the argument against the requirement that law officers check immigration status ignores the fact that Arizona state law allowed this prior to the enactment of the legislation in question and in doing so it had cooperated with the Department of Homeland Security. The new law changed nothing. Similarly, the objection to the provision that "A peace officer, without a warrant, may arrest a person if the officer has probable cause to believe ... [t]he person to be arrested has committed any public offense that makes the person removable from the United States" is not valid because law enforcement officials already have the authority to arrest suspects on the basis of "probable cause." On the contrary, Scalia notes that "federal law expressly provides that state officers may 'cooperate with the Attorney General in the identification, apprehension, detention, or removal of aliens not lawfully present in the United States.'" This, he concludes, "is consistent with the Arizona statute, and with the 'cooperat[ive]' system that Congress has created."

In response to the contention of U.S. attorneys that state actions might not be consistent with federal "priorities," Scalia asserts that this is true, but it is a matter for the state to determine for itself, "particularly if those priorities include willful blindness or deliberate inattention to the presence of removable aliens in Arizona. The State's whole complaint—the reason this law was passed and this case has arisen—is that the citizens of Arizona believe federal priorities are too lax. The State has the sovereign power to protect its borders more rigorously if it wishes, absent any valid federal prohibition. The Executive's policy choice of lax federal enforcement does not constitute such a prohibition." Finally, he argues that although the president may argue that he has the discretion to set priorities when enforcement funding is limited, "there is no reason why the Federal Executive's need to allocate its scarce enforcement resources should disable Arizona from devoting its resources to illegal immigration in Arizona that in its view the Federal Executive has given short shrift. Despite Congress's prescription that 'the immigration laws of the United States should be enforced vigorously and uniformly,' Arizona asserts without contradiction" that federal priorities have resulted in "funneling of an increasing tide of illegal border crossings into Arizona. … Must Arizona's ability to protect its borders yield to the reality that Congress has provided inadequate funding for federal enforcement—or, even worse, to the Executive's unwise targeting of that funding?" He concludes, "to say, as the Court does, that Arizona contradicts federal law by enforcing applications of the Immigration Act that the President declines to enforce boggles the mind."

Essential Themes

Arizona v. the United States is an episode in an ongoing difference of opinion over the demarcation line between federal and state authority that has been continuously argued since the ratification of the Constitution in 1788, only the specific issues change. In this case Arizona sought to enforce immigration law because of what it believed was a clear and present danger presented by a five-fold increase in the number of illegal immigrants in the state between 1990 and 2010. As a result of the increasing burdens imposed on the state, and the refusal of the administration of President Barack Obama to enforce federal immigration laws, the Arizona legislature acted to enforce the laws itself. The Obama administration filed a legal action to prevent this, arguing that only the federal government had authority to make and enforce legislation on immigration. The majority of the U.S. Supreme Court agreed, nullifying the state law since in its judgment the statute conflicted with federal law which had preemptive power.

The court's majority decision effectively removed enforcement of immigration law from the states by finding that it was the sole purview of the federal government. What this decision left unresolved was the question of what recourse a state may have to protect its interests, and those of its citizens, when a presidential administration refuses to fulfill its constitutional obligation to enforce the laws enacted by Congress.

Bibliography and Additional Reading

Joseph Callway, "Constitutional Law—Preemption—Federal Law Preempts Sections of Arizona's Support Our Law Enforcement and Safe Neighborhoods Act," *Cumberland Law Review*, Vol. 43, no. 3 (2013), 591-606.

Tara Helfman, "Obama the Scrivener & the Supine Court," *Commentary*, Vol. 136, no. 5 (December 2013), 28-30.

Roderick M. Hills, Jr., "Arizona v. United States: The Unitary Executive's Enforcement Discretion as a Limit on Federalism," *Cato Supreme Court Review* (2011), 189-218.

Kate M. Manuel and Michael John Garcia, "Arizona v. United States: A Limited Role for States in Immigration Enforcement," Congressional Research Service Report for Congress, R42719, September 10, 2012 (https://www.fas.org/sgp/crs/homesec/R42719.pdf).

Daniel J. Tichenor and Alexandra Filindra, "Raising Arizona v. United States: Historical Patterns of American Immigration Federalism," *Lewis & Clark Law Review*, Vol. 16, no. 4 (Winter 2012), 1215-47.

■ *State of Texas v. United States*

Date: June 23, 2016
Author: Jerry E. Smith
Genre: Court Decision

Summary Overview

Immigration has been a consistent element in American history, although the size and proportion ebbs and flows over time. In 1970 the census reported some 9.6 million immigrants which accounted for 4.7 percent of the population. Over the next forty years both the number and proportion increased steadily, reaching 40 million or 12.9 percent of the population in 1910. This upward trend continued, another million people arriving during 2013 and 1.2 million in the following year. The largest sources in 2014 were India (147,500), China (131,800), Mexico (130,000), Canada (41,200), and the Philippines (40,500).

The escalation in immigration propelled the issue into the national political dialogue with anti-immigration forces calling for reform that would limit the numbers arriving, especially after the economic recession beginning in 2008 dragged on during the succeeding years. Congress attempted to address the issue in 2013 when a bipartisan group of eight Senators negotiated a bill that would provide a path to legalization for those in the country illegally, improved employment verification and work visa systems, and measures to decrease the backlog of people applying for permanent resident status. Although adopted by the Senate, the House failed to act so the measure failed to gain approval.

As calls for action on reform increased, President Barack Obama explained on the Spanish-language television network Univision that "until Congress passes a new law, then I am constrained in terms of what I am able to do." Despite this statement, once it became apparent that the bipartisan bill was not going to be adopted the president, in prepared remarks, vowed to "fix as much of our immigration system as I can on my own, without Congress." On November 20, 2014, in an address to the nation, he announced an executive order establishing the Deferred Action for Parents of Americans and Lawful Permanent Residents (DAPA) program, which was later supplemented with the Deferred Action for Child-

hood Arrivals (DACA) program. These, complemented by two orders from the Secretary of Homeland Security, required officials of the U.S. Immigration and Customs Enforcement to give a low priority to deportations and to defer action in any cases involving parents of U.S. citizens or permanent residents.

Defining Moment

The impact of the new executive order fell most heavily on California, Texas, and New York where more than half of the estimated five million people resided who would have been subject to possible deportation had the president and Department of Homeland Security not acted. According to the Federation for Immigration Reform, there were about 1.8 million illegal aliens living in Texas costing the state's taxpayers an estimated $12.1 billion annually, while taxes paid to the state by those illegals amounted to only $1.27 billion per year. Worse, other studies pointed to a dramatic increase in crimes being committed by illegal immigrants resulting in considerable political pressure for action within the affected states.

Statistics from the U.S. Border Patrol for 2014 affirmed that 52.6 percent of all border crossings that year took place in the Rio Grande Valley. At the same time, this area also accounted for the largest number of drug smuggling cases and the second largest number of felonies associated with immigrants. Because of the inordinate influence of the federal policies on Texas, the state, supported by twenty-six other states, filed suit in the United States District Court for the Southern District of Texas seeking an injunction preventing the implementation of the new Obama administration policy characterizing it as arbitrary and capricious and arguing that it had not been subject to required administrative procedures before being announced and also violated the constitutional limit on executive powers. When the Fifth Circuit Court for the Southern District of Texas issued the injunction, the

Obama administration appealed the decision.

Author Biography

Jerry Edwin Smith was born in Del Rio, Texas, in 1946. He earned a baccalaureate degree from Yale University in 1969 and a law degree from Yale Law School three years later. Following a decade of private practice in Houston where he also served as director of the Harris County Housing authority and chair of the Houston Civil Service Commission, he was appointed city attorney. In June of 1987 President Ronald Reagan nominated him to the U.S. Court of Appeals for the Fifth District with the Senate confirming on December 21, 1987.

On the bench Smith has been described as "an originalist and a textualist," meaning that he believes the role of the judiciary is to apply the original meaning of the Constitution including, of course, the various amendments that have been adopted. In this respect, he bases his rulings on the text of those documents. He wrote the majority "conservative" opinion in Hopwood v. Texas, a decision that ruled against the use of affirmative action criteria in the admissions process for the University of Texas Law School because the school had shown "no compelling justification" why it should "continue to elevate some races over others," but that decision was overturned by the U.S. Supreme Court in 2003. In other cases he was sided with "liberal" justices such as in *East Texas Baptist University v. Burwell* which rejected the religiously-affiliated school's claim that the Affordable Care Act violated the Religious Freedom Restoration Act by requiring contraceptive coverage.

HISTORICAL DOCUMENT

SUPREME COURT OF THE UNITED STATES
No. 15–674
UNITED STATES, ET AL., PETITIONERS v. TEXAS, ET AL.

ON WRIT OF CERTIORARI TO THE UNITED STATES COURT OF APPEALS FOR THE FIFTH CIRCUIT [June 23, 2016]

PER CURIAM.

The judgment is affirmed by an equally divided Court.

▪   ▪   ▪

The Supreme Court's per curia decision affirms the judgment of the Fifth Circuit written by Justice Jerry E. Smith. A large part of the Fifth Circuit's decision of well over 100 pages is taken up with citations of previous cases, federal law, and other supporting evidence, as well as the history of the litigation, procedural matters, and lengthy discussions regarding whether actions by the Secretary of Homeland Security are reviewable. In the interest of space, these portions are deleted in the following document in favor of those that explain the basic arguments and the reasons for the court's decision.

▪   ▪   ▪

The United States appeals a preliminary injunction, pending trial, forbidding implementation of the Deferred Action for Parents of Americans and Lawful Permanent Residents program ("DAPA"). Twenty-six states (the "states") challenged DAPA under the Administrative Procedure Act ("APA") and the Take Care Clause of the Constitution; in an impressive and thorough Memorandum Opinion and Order issued February 16, 2015, the district court enjoined the program on the ground that the states are likely to succeed on their claim that DAPA is subject to the APA's procedural requirements.

The government appealed and moved to stay the injunction pending resolution of the merits. ... Reviewing the district court's order for abuse of discretion, we affirm the preliminary injunction because the states have standing; they have established a substantial likelihood of success on the merits of their procedural and substantive APA claims; and they have satisfied the other elements required for an injunction. ...

The states sued to prevent DAPA's implementation on three grounds. First, they asserted that DAPA violated the procedural requirements of the APA as a substantive rule that did not undergo the requisite notice-and-comment rulemaking. Second, the states claimed that

DHS lacked the authority to implement the program even if it followed the correct rulemaking process, such that DAPA was substantively unlawful under the APA. Third, the states urged that DAPA was an abrogation of the President's constitutional duty to "take Care that the Laws be faithfully executed."

The district court held that Texas has standing. It concluded that the state would suffer a financial injury by having to issue driver's licenses to DAPA beneficiaries at a loss. Alternatively, the court relied on a new theory it called "abdication standing": Texas had standing because the United States has exclusive authority over immigration but has refused to act in that area. The court also considered but ultimately did not accept the notions that Texas could sue as *parens patriae* on behalf of citizens facing economic competition from DAPA beneficiaries and that the state had standing based on the losses it suffers generally from illegal immigration. The court temporarily enjoined DAPA's implementation after determining that Texas had shown a substantial likelihood of success on its claim that the program must undergo notice and comment. Despite full briefing, the court did not rule on the "Plaintiffs' likelihood of success on their *substantive* APA claim or their constitutional claims under the Take Care Clause/separation of powers doctrine." On appeal, the United States maintains that the states do not have standing or a right to judicial review and, alternatively, that DAPA is exempt from the notice-and-comment requirements. The government also contends that the injunction, including its nationwide scope, is improper as a matter of law.

"We review a preliminary injunction for abuse of discretion." A preliminary injunction should issue only if the states, as movants, establish (1) a substantial likelihood of success on the merits, (2) a substantial threat of irreparable injury if the injunction is not issued, (3) that the threatened injury if the injunction is denied outweighs any harm that will result if the injunction is granted, and (4) that the grant of an injunction will not disserve the public interest. ...

The government claims the states lack standing to challenge DAPA. As we will analyze, however, their standing is plain, based on the driver's-license rationale, so we need not address the other possible grounds for standing. As the parties invoking federal jurisdiction, the states have the burden of establishing standing. They must show an injury that is "concrete, particularized, and actual or imminent; fairly traceable to the challenged action; and redressable by a favorable ruling." "When a litigant is vested with a procedural right, that litigant has standing if there is some possibility that the requested relief will prompt the injury-causing party to reconsider the decision that allegedly harmed the litigant." "[T]he presence of one party with standing is sufficient to satisfy Article III's case-or-controversy requirement." We begin by considering whether the states are entitled to "special solicitude".... They are. ...

As we will show, DAPA would have a major effect on the states' fiscs [finances], causing millions of dollars of losses in Texas alone, and at least in Texas, the causal chain is especially direct: DAPA would enable beneficiaries to apply for driver's licenses, and many would do so, resulting in Texas's injury.

Second, DAPA affects the states' "quasi-sovereign" interests by imposing substantial pressure on them to change their laws, which provide for issuing driver's licenses to some aliens and subsidizing those licenses. "[S]tates have a sovereign interest in 'the power to create and enforce a legal code.'" Pursuant to that interest, states may have standing based on (1) federal assertions of authority to regulate matters they believe they control, (2) federal preemption of state law, and (3) federal interference with the enforcement of state law, at least where "the state statute at issue regulate[s] behavior or provide[s] for the administration of a state program" and does not "simply purport to immunize [state] citizens from federal law." Those intrusions are analogous to pressure to change state law. ...

[T]he states are entitled to "special solicitude" in the standing inquiry. ... At least one state—Texas—has satisfied the first standing requirement by demonstrating that it would incur significant costs in issuing driver's licenses to DAPA beneficiaries. Under current state law, licenses issued to beneficiaries would necessarily be at a financial loss. The Department of Public Safety "shall issue" a license to a qualified applicant. A non-citizen "must present ... documentation issued by the appropriate United States agency that authorizes the applicant to be in the United States."

If permitted to go into effect, DAPA would enable at least 500,000 illegal aliens in Texas to satisfy that requirement with proof of lawful presence or employment authorization. Texas subsidizes its licenses and would lose a minimum of $130.89 on each one it issued to a DAPA beneficiary. Even a modest estimate would put the loss at "several million dollars."

Instead of disputing those figures, the United States claims that the costs would be offset by other benefits to the state. It theorizes that, because DAPA beneficiaries would be eligible for licenses, they would register their vehicles, generating income for the state, and buy auto insurance, reducing the expenses associated with uninsured motorists. The government suggests employment authorization would lead to increased tax revenue and decreased reliance on social services.

Even if the government is correct, that does not negate Texas's injury, because we consider only those offsetting benefits that are of the same type and arise from the same transaction as the costs. "Once injury is shown, no attempt is made to ask whether the injury is outweighed by benefits the plaintiff has enjoyed from the relationship with the defendant. Standing is recognized to complain that some particular aspect of the relationship is unlawful and has caused injury." "Our standing analysis is not an accounting exercise...."

Here, none of the benefits the government identifies is sufficiently connected to the costs to qualify as an offset. The only benefits that are conceivably relevant are the increase in vehicle registration and the decrease in uninsured motorists, but even those are based on the independent decisions of DAPA beneficiaries and are not a direct result of the issuance of licenses. ....

In the instant case, the states have alleged an injury, and the government predicts that the later decisions of DAPA beneficiaries would produce offsetting benefits. Weighing those costs and benefits is precisely the type of "accounting exercise" ... in which we cannot engage. Texas has shown injury.

Texas has satisfied the second standing requirement by establishing that its injury is "fairly traceable" to DAPA. It is undisputed that DAPA would enable beneficiaries to apply for driver's licenses, and there is little doubt that many would do so because driving is a practical necessity in most of the state.

The United States urges that Texas's injury is not cognizable, because the state could avoid injury by not issuing licenses to illegal aliens or by not subsidizing its licenses. Although Texas could avoid financial loss by requiring applicants to pay the full costs of licenses, it could not avoid injury altogether. "[S]tates have a sovereign interest in 'the power to create and enforce a legal code,'" and the possibility that a plaintiff could avoid injury by incurring other costs does not negate standing. ...

The United States maintains that Texas's injury is self-inflicted because the state voluntarily chose to base its driver's license policies on federal immigration law. ... First, Texas ... sued after the United States had announced DAPA, which could make at least 500,000 illegal aliens eligible for driver's licenses and cause millions of dollars of losses.... The fact that Texas sued in response to a significant change in the defendants' policies shows that its injury is not self-inflicted.

Second, ... Texas seeks to issue licenses only to those lawfully present in the United States, and the state is required to use federal immigration classifications to do so. ... [T]here is no allegation that Texas passed its driver's license law to manufacture standing. The legislature enacted the law one year before DACA and three years before DAPA was announced, and there is no hint that the state anticipated a change in immigration policy—much less a change as sweeping and dramatic as DAPA. Despite the dissent's bold suggestion that Texas's license plate cost injury "is entirely manufactured by Plaintiffs for this case," the injury is not self-inflicted.

In addition to its notion that Texas could avoid injury, the government theorizes that Texas's injury is not fairly traceable to DAPA because it is merely an incidental and attenuated consequence of the program. But *Massachusetts v. EPA* establishes that the causal connection is adequate. Texas is entitled to the same "special solicitude" as was Massachusetts, and the causal link is even closer here.

For Texas to incur injury, DAPA beneficiaries would have to apply for driver's licenses as a consequence of DHS's action, and it is apparent that many would do so. ... Indeed, treating the availability of changing state law as a bar to standing would deprive states of judicial recourse for many *bona fide* harms. For instance, under that theory, federal preemption of state law could never be an injury, because a state could always change its law to avoid preemption. But courts have often held that states have standing based on preemption. And states could offset almost any financial loss by raising taxes or fees. The existence of that alternative does not mean they lack standing.

This case raises even less doubt about causation, so the result is the same. The matters in which the Supreme Court held that an injury was not fairly traceable to the challenged law reinforce this conclusion. In some of them, the independent act of a third party was a necessary condition of the harm's occurrence, and it was uncertain whether the third party would take the required step. Not so here.

DAPA beneficiaries have strong incentives to obtain driver's licenses, and it is hardly speculative that many would do so if they became eligible. In other cases, in which there was insufficient proof of causation, several factors potentially contributed to the injury, and the challenged policy likely played a minor role.

Far from playing an insignificant role, DAPA would be the primary cause and likely the only one. Without the program, there would be little risk of a dramatic increase in the costs of the driver's license program. This case is far removed from those in which the Supreme Court has held an injury to be too incidental or attenuated. Texas's injury is fairly traceable to DAPA.

Texas has satisfied the third standing requirement, redressability. Enjoining DAPA based on the procedural APA claim could prompt DHS to reconsider the program, which is all a plaintiff must show when asserting a procedural right. And enjoining DAPA based on the substantive APA claim would prevent Texas's injury altogether.

The United States submits that Texas's theory of standing is flawed because it has no principled limit. In the government's view, if Texas can challenge DAPA, it could also sue to block a grant of asylum to a single alien or any federal policy that adversely affects the state, such as an IRS revenue ruling that decreases a corporation's federal taxable income and corresponding state franchise tax liability.

The flaw in the government's reasoning is that *Massachusetts v. EPA* entailed similar risks, but the Court still held that Massachusetts had standing. ... After *Mas-*

sachusetts v. EPA, the answer to those criticisms is that there are other ways to cabin policy disagreements masquerading as legal claims. ...

Because the states are suing under the APA, they "must satisfy not only Article III's standing requirements, but an additional test: The interest [they] assert must be 'arguably within the zone of interests to be protected or regulated by the statute' that [they] say[] was violated." That "test...'is not meant to be especially demanding'" and is applied "in keeping with Congress's 'evident intent' when enacting the APA 'to make agency action presumptively reviewable.'" ...

The interests the states seek to protect fall within the zone of interests of the INA. "The pervasiveness of federal regulation does not diminish the importance of immigration policy to the States," which "bear many of the consequences of unlawful immigration." Reflecting a concern that "aliens have been applying for and receiving public benefits from Federal, State, and local governments at increasing rates," "Congress deemed some *unlawfully present* aliens ineligible for certain state and local public benefits unless the state explicitly provides otherwise." With limited exceptions, unlawfully present aliens are "not eligible for any State or local public benefit."

Contrary to the government's assertion, Texas satisfies the zone of interests test not on account of a generalized grievance but instead as a result of the same injury that gives it Article III standing—Congress has explicitly allowed states to deny public benefits to illegal aliens. Relying on that guarantee, Texas seeks to participate in notice and comment before the Secretary changes the immigration classification of millions of illegal aliens in a way that forces the state to the Hobson's choice of spending millions of dollars to subsidize driver's licenses or changing its statutes. ...

[The government also claims the issue if not reviewable.] Establishing unreviewability is a "heavy burden," and "where substantial doubt about the congressional intent exists, the general presumption favoring judicial review of administrative action is controlling." ...

The United States [argues] for the proposition that the INA expressly prohibits judicial review. But the government's broad reading is contrary to *Reno v. American-Arab Anti-Discrimination Committee*, in which the Court rejected "the unexamined assumption that covers the universe of deportation claims—that it is a sort of 'zipper' clause that says 'no judicial review in deportation cases unless this section provides judicial review.'" The Court emphasized that [this] "applies only to three discrete actions that the Attorney General may take: her 'decision or action' to '*commence* proceedings, *adjudicate* cases, or *execute* removal orders.'"

None of those actions is at issue here—the states' claims do not arise from the Secretary's "decision or action ... to commence proceedings, adjudicate cases, or execute removal orders against any alien"; instead, they stem from his decision to grant lawful presence to millions of illegal aliens on a class-wide basis. Further, the states are not bringing a "cause or claim by or on behalf of any alien"—they assert their own right to the APA's procedural protections. Congress has expressly limited or precluded judicial review of many immigration decisions, including some that are made in the Secretary's "sole and unreviewable discretion," but DAPA is not one of them.

Judicial review of DAPA is consistent with the protections Congress affords to states that decline to provide public benefits to illegal aliens. ... Congress has sought to protect states from "bear[ing] many of the consequences of unlawful immigration." Texas avails itself of some of those protections through Section 521.142(a) of the Texas Transportation Code, which allows the state to avoid the costs of issuing driver's licenses to illegal aliens. ...

At its core, this case is about the Secretary's decision to change the immigration classification of millions of illegal aliens on a class-wide basis. The states properly maintain that DAPA's grant of lawful presence and accompanying eligibility for benefits is a substantive rule that must go through notice and comment, before it imposes substantial costs on them, and that DAPA is substantively contrary to law. The federal courts are fully capable of adjudicating those disputes.

Because the interests that Texas seeks to protect are within the INA's zone of interests, and judicial review is available, we address whether Texas has established a substantial likelihood of success on its claim that DAPA must be submitted for notice and comment. ...

The government advances the notion that DAPA is exempt from notice and comment as a policy statement.

We evaluate two criteria to distinguish policy statements from substantive rules: whether the rule (1) "impose[s] any rights and obligations" and (2) "genuinely leaves the agency and its decision-makers free to exercise discretion." There is some overlap in the analysis of those prongs "because '[i]f a statement denies the decision-maker discretion in the area of its coverage...then the statement is binding, and creates rights or obligations.'" "While mindful but suspicious of the agency's own characterization, we ... focus primarily on whether the rule has binding effect on agency discretion or severely restricts it." "[A]n agency pronouncement will be considered binding as a practical matter if it either appears on its face to be binding, or is applied by the agency in a way that indicates it is binding." ...

Like the DAPA Memo, the DACA Memo instructed agencies to review applications on a case-by-case basis and exercise discretion, but the district court found that those statements were "merely pretext" because only about 5% of the 723,000 applications accepted for evaluation had been denied, and "[d]espite a request by the [district] [c]ourt, the [g]overnment's counsel did not provide the number, if any, of requests that were denied [for discretionary reasons] even though the applicant met the DACA criteria...." The finding of pretext was also based on a declaration by Kenneth Palinkas, the president of the union representing the USCIS employees processing the DACA applications, that "DHS management has taken multiple steps to ensure that DACA applications are simply rubberstamped if the applicants meet the necessary criteria"; DACA's Operating Procedures, which "contain nearly 150 pages of specific instructions for granting or denying deferred action"; and some mandatory language in the DAPA Memo itself. In denying the government's motion for a stay of the injunction, the district court further noted that the President had made public statements suggesting that in reviewing applications pursuant to DAPA, DHS officials who "don't follow the policy" will face "consequences," and "they've got a problem."

The DACA and DAPA Memos purport to grant discretion, but a rule can be binding if it is "applied by the agency in a way that indicates it is binding," and there was evidence from DACA's implementation that DAPA's discretionary language was pretextual. For a number of reasons, any extrapolation from DACA must be done carefully.

First, DACA involved issuing benefits to self-selecting applicants, and persons who expected to be denied relief would seem unlikely to apply. But the issue of self-selection is partially mitigated by the finding that "the [g]overnment has publicly declared that it will make no attempt to enforce the law against even those who are denied deferred action (absent extraordinary circumstances)."

Second, DACA and DAPA are not identical: Eligibility for DACA was restricted to a younger and less numerous population, which suggests that DACA applicants are less likely to have backgrounds that would warrant a discretionary denial. Further, the DAPA Memo contains additional discretionary criteria: Applicants must not be "an enforcement priority as reflected in the [Prioritization Memo]; and [must] present no other factors that, in the exercise of discretion, makes the grant of deferred action inappropriate." DAPA Memo at 4. But despite those differences, there are important similarities: The Secretary "direct[ed] USCIS to *establish a process, similar to DACA,* for exercising prosecutorial discretion," *id.* (emphasis added), and there was evidence that the DACA application process *itself* did not allow for discretion, regardless of the rates of approval and denial.

Instead of relying solely on the lack of evidence that any DACA application had been denied for discretionary reasons, the district court found pretext for additional reasons. It observed that "the 'Operating Procedures' for implementation of DACA contains nearly 150 pages of specific instructions for granting or denying deferred action to applicants" and that "[d]enials are recorded in a 'check the box' standardized form, for which USCIS personnel are provided templates. Certain denials of DAPA must be sent to a supervisor for approval[, and] there is no option for granting DAPA to an individual who does not meet each criterion." The finding was also based on the declaration from Palinkas that, as with DACA, the DAPA application process itself would preclude discretion: "[R]outing DAPA applications through service centers instead of field offices ... created an application process that bypasses traditional in-person investigatory interviews with trained USCIS adjudications officers" and "prevents officers from conducting case-by-case

investigations, undermines officers' abilities to detect fraud and national-security risks, and ensures that applications will be rubberstamped." ...

In summary, the states have established a substantial likelihood of success on the merits of their procedural claim. We proceed to address whether, in addition to that likelihood on the merits, the states make the same showing on their substantive APA claim.

A "reviewing court shall ... hold unlawful and set aside agency action ... found to be—(A) arbitrary, capricious, an abuse of discretion, or otherwise not in accordance with law ... [or] (C) in excess of statutory jurisdiction, authority, or limitations, or short of statutory right." Although the district court enjoined DAPA solely on the basis of the procedural APA claim, "it is an elementary proposition, and the supporting cases too numerous to cite, that this court may affirm the district court's judgment on any grounds supported by the record." Therefore, as an alternate and additional ground for affirming the injunction, we address this substantive issue, which was fully briefed in the district court. ...

In specific and detailed provisions, the INA expressly and carefully provides legal designations allowing defined classes of aliens to be lawfully present and confers eligibility for "discretionary relief allowing [aliens in deportation proceedings] to remain in the country." Congress has also identified narrow classes of aliens eligible for deferred action, including.... Congress has enacted an intricate process for illegal aliens to derive a lawful immigration classification from their children's immigration status: In general, an applicant must (i) have a U.S. citizen child who is at least twenty-one years old, (ii) leave the United States, (iii) wait ten years, and then (iv) obtain one of the limited number of family-preference visas from a United States consulate. Although DAPA does not confer the full panoply of benefits that a visa gives, DAPA would allow illegal aliens to receive the benefits of lawful presence solely on account of their children's immigration status without complying with any of the requirements, enumerated above, that Congress has deliberately imposed. ...

DAPA would make 4.3 million otherwise removable aliens eligible for lawful presence, employment authorization, and associated benefits, and "we must be guided to a degree by common sense as to the manner in which

Congress is likely to delegate a policy decision of such economic and political magnitude to an administrative agency." DAPA undoubtedly implicates "question[s] of deep 'economic and political significance' that [are] central to this statutory scheme; had Congress wished to assign that decision to an agency, it surely would have done so expressly." ...

For the authority to implement DAPA, the government relies in part on ... a provision that does not mention lawful presence or deferred action, and that is listed as a "[m]iscellaneous" definitional provision expressly limited to § 1324a, a section concerning the "Unlawful employment of aliens"—an exceedingly unlikely place to find authorization for DAPA. Likewise, the broad grants of authority in [cites cases]... cannot reasonably be construed as assigning "decisions of vast 'economic and political significance,'" such as DAPA, to an agency.

The interpretation of those provisions that the Secretary advances would allow him to grant lawful presence and work authorization to any illegal alien in the United States—an untenable position in light of the INA's intricate system of immigration classifications and employment eligibility. Even with "special deference" to the Secretary, the INA flatly does not permit the reclassification of millions of illegal aliens as lawfully present and thereby make them newly eligible for a host of federal and state benefits, including work authorization. ...

The states have satisfied the other requirements for a preliminary injunction. They have demonstrated "a substantial threat of irreparable injury if the injunction is not issued." DAPA beneficiaries would be eligible for driver's licenses and other benefits, and a substantial number of the more than four million potential beneficiaries—many of whom live in the plaintiff states—would take advantage of that opportunity. The district court found that retracting those benefits would be "substantially difficult—if not impossible," and the government has given us no reason to doubt that finding.

The states have shown "that the threatened injury if the injunction is denied outweighs any harm that will result if the injunction is granted." The states have alleged a concrete threatened injury in the form of millions of dollars of losses.

The harms the United States has identified are less substantial. It claims that the injunction "obstructs a core Executive prerogative" and offends separation-of-powers and federalism principles. Those alleged harms are vague, and the principles the government cites are more likely to be affected by the resolution of the case on the merits than by the injunction.

Separately, the United States postulates that the injunction prevents DHS from effectively prioritizing illegal aliens for removal. But the injunction "does not enjoin or impair the Secretary's ability to marshal his assets or deploy the resources of the DHS [or] to set priorities," including selecting whom to remove first, and any inefficiency is outweighed by the major financial losses the states face. ...

The district court did not err and most assuredly did not abuse its discretion. The order granting the preliminary injunction is AFFIRMED.

GLOSSARY

Hobson's choice: A situation in which there appears to be a choice, but in reality one is left only with the choice of taking what is offered or nothing at all. Colloquially it means "take it or leave it."

parens patriae: A legal and political concept by which a government or legal authority is regarded as having the responsibility to act as the protector of its citizens. This has been used to argue that a state has the right to sue the federal government on behalf of its citizens to protect their interests.

pretextual: A pretext is a reason given for an action that appears on the surface to be valid but actually has some ulterior motive. For example, if police suspect someone of driving while impaired they might stop the person on the "pretext" of a broken taillight when in fact that only provided a reason for the real action which was to determine if the driver was impaired.

special solicitude: This is a legal claim by which the Supreme Court in *Massachusetts v. EPA* argued that states should be given special consideration in establishing whether or not they have standing to sue the federal government.

zone of interests test: Legally, to have standing to sue the federal government the plaintiff must show that its injury falls under the a concern that is regulated or protected by federal law

Document Analysis

This case deals with an appeal by the Obama administration of a lower court ruling that issued an injunction against enforcement of a Department of Homeland Security policy designed to prevent the deportation of aliens illegally residing in the United States. Among the chief issues in the case was whether the states involved in the original action had a legal standing, and if they did whether the increased costs the state claimed resulted from the action were not in fact self-inflicted by its own policies. Although not specifically called upon to adjudicate the original case, as part of the appeals procedure the court did venture an opinion on whether it was reasonable that the states might prevail at trial because lacking any rational basis for their original case would have provided grounds on which the injunction could be lifted.

The states presented three grounds on which they sought the initial injunction: (1) that the Department of Homeland Security (DHS) policy violated procedural requirements, (2) that the DHS had no authority to issue the new policy, and (3) that the executive actions establishing the Deferred Action for Parents of Americans and Lawful Permanent Residents (DAPA) program was an abrogation of the president's constitutional responsibilities. The court found that Texas had standing to sue because it risked financial injury from the DHS policy and all that was required under law was that one of the plaintiffs establish such standing. In this argument the court also introduced a new legal theory of "abdication standing" which reasoned that Texas had standing in the matter because, although the federal government enjoyed exclusive authority in immigration matters, it had refused to enforce the existing law thereby creating the problem from which relief was being sought.

The court accepted the state argument that implementation of the new DHS policy would result in substantial financial loss to the state. The federal government's attorneys argued that this financial obligation was really of the state's own making because it not only required driver's licenses but chose to subsidize the cost from public funds. Were it not for these state regulations the injury the state claimed would not exist. The United States also argued that even if there was some initial financial impact on the state, this would be outweighed by potential benefits. The court rejected both of these arguments reasoning that the state laws pre-dated the DHS action and were thus not intended to circumvent federal policy and that the government's projection of benefits that may or may not happen and could not be directly tied to the DHS action were not valid.

The court also found that since existing Texas law provided that only legal residents were eligible for driver's licenses, and it relied on federal immigration law for its definitions of legal residency, the DHS action attempted to substitute new criteria for that established by Congress in the Immigration and Naturalization Acts. In this legislation Congress clearly established that "unlawfully present aliens" were not eligible for "certain state and local public benefits unless the state explicitly provides otherwise." As the court pointed out, "Congress has explicitly allowed states to deny public benefits to illegal aliens. Relying on that guarantee, Texas seeks to participate in notice and comment before the Secretary changes the immigration classification of millions of illegal aliens" and therefore the DHS action without the legally required period of notice and comment violates federal law. Also, evidence indicated that the DHS action was merely a "pretext" for non-enforcement since about ninety-five percent of cases it supposedly reviewed were given the deferred status.

After dispensing with the federal government's arguments, and the issue it raised over the propriety of judicial review in this case, the court proceeded to examine whether there was a reasonable expectation that the plaintiffs might prevail in a trial, thereby warranting the injunction. It found that "DAPA would make 4.3 million otherwise removable aliens eligible for lawful presence, employment authorization, and associated benefits." "Common sense," the court noted, argued against the DHS assertion that it had discretionary authority to change the provisions of legislation adopted by Congress which clearly addressed these vary issues. Thus, the court agreed that there was a reasonable expectation that in a trial the plaintiffs would prevail.

Essential Themes

The increasing arrival of people in the United States, both legally and illegally, between 1980 and 2010 propelled immigration to the forefront as a national issue. Beginning with the Immigration Reform and Control Act of 1986, which was supposed to solve the immigration dilemma by providing a path to legalization for those in the country unlawfully in return for stricter immigration enforcement, the Congress adopted several other measures designed to address the issue. The Immigration Act of 1990 set a maximum annual quota for legal immigration and six years later Congress expanded the definition of the crimes for which an immigrant could be deported, added significantly to the number of Border Patrol agents, and established means for "expedited removal" of deportable immigrants. In the REAL ID Act of 2005 Congress required that states verify the citizenship or immigration status of anyone applying for licenses and placed further restrictions on refugees seeking asylum and the habeas corpus rights of immigrants. Quite clearly, the intent of Congress was to closely scrutinize people entering the country and to make sure that they were not accorded equal rights with American citizens.

Some of the matters involved in *State of Texas v. United States* are similar to those in *Arizona v. United States*, es-pecially the fundamental issue of what recourse a state has when it is unduly disadvantaged by the failure of the executive branch of government to enforce the laws sanctioned by Congress. In its argument in this case, Texas contended that there was no federal legislation that conveyed to the executive branch the authority to override federal law in the application of immigration policies to legitimize the residence of immigrants who were not legally in the country. While not deciding the basic issue, since that question was not before the appellate court, the justices did decide that states had standing to sue the federal government and offered its opinion that the merits of the underlying case were such that there was reason to believe the plaintiffs might prevail in the eventual court case on the specific issues.

The case eventually made it to the U.S. Supreme Court in 2016 with the justices divided four to four in their opinions. With no clear majority, the decision of the lower court remained in effect. This kept the issues involved in the original case alive, no doubt for a future Supreme Court to decide.

Bibliography and Additional Reading

Adam B. Cox and Cristina M. Rodríguez, "The President and Immigration Law Redux," *Yale Law Journal*, Vol. 104, no. 155 (2015), 104-225.

Garrett Epps, "U.S. Supreme Court Takes Up *United States v. Texas*," *The Atlantic*, January 21, 2016.

Matt Ford, "A Ruling Against the Obama Administration on Immigration," *The Atlantic*, November 10, 2015.

Hans von Spakovsky, "Texas Judge Delivers Blistering Rebuke of Obama Administration Immigration Lawyers' Misbehavior," *The Daily Signal*, April 8, 2015.

Appendixes

Chronological List

Web Resources

www.nolo.com/

Start at the Immigration Law page of Nolo's website for plain-English explanations of U.S. immigration law, and hundreds of Frequently Asked Questions covering individual fact patterns.. Follow the links to pages covering everything from family-based visas to H-1B and other nonimmigrant visas to the consequences of crimes on one's U.S. immigration status.

www.uscis.gov

U.S. Citizenship and Immigration Services (USCIS, formerly called INS) is the first stop for many types of immigration applications.

www.doleta.gov

Applicants for labor-based visas or green cards, or their employers, will also need to interact with the DOL. Most of the relevant functions are handled by its Employment and Training Administration, at www.doleta.gov. The online system that employers use for obtaining labor certifications is called iCert.

www.justice.gov/eoir

Executive Office for Immigration Review (EOIR). The U.S. immigration court's website is an important source of information on court procedures, forms, and a list of recognized providers of pro bono or low cost legal services.

Bibliography

Adam B. Cox and Cristina M. Rodríguez, "The President and Immigration Law Redux," *Yale Law Journal*, Vol. 104, no. 155 (2015), 104-225.

Alexander Alland, Sr., *Jacob A. Riis: Photographer and Citizen* (Millerton, NY: Aperture Book, 1993).

Alf Hiltebeitel, ed., *Hair: Its Power and Meaning in Asian Cultures* (Albany: State University of New York Press, 1998).

Alicia J. Campi, *The McCarran-Walter Act: A Contradictory Legacy on Race, Quotas, and Ideology* (Washington, DC: Immigration Policy Center, 2004).

Andrew Gyory, *Closing the Gate: Race, Politics, and the Chinese Exclusion Act* (Chapel Hill: University of North Carolina Press, 1998).

Anzia Yezierska, *How I found America: Collected Stories of Anzia Yezierska* (New York: Persea Books, 1991).

———, *Hungry Hearts and Other Stories* (New York: Persea Books, 1985).

———, *The Open Cage: An Anzia Yezierska Collection* (New York: Persea Books, 1979), Alice Kessler-Harris, ed.

Arthur S. Link, *Woodrow Wilson and the Progressive Era, 1910-1917* (New York: Harper, 1954).

Barry R. Chiswick, "Jewish Immigrant Wages in America in 1909: An Analysis of the Dillingham Commission Data," *Explorations in Economic History*, Vol. 29, no. 3 (June 1992), 274-89.

Bill Ong Hing, *Defining America Through Immigration Policy* (Philadelphia: Temple University Press, 2004,), especially Chapter 3.

Bonnie Yochelson and Daniel Czitrom, *Rediscovering Jacob Riis: Exposure Journalism and Photography in Turn-of-the-Century New York* (New York: New Press, 2007).

Carey McWilliams and Matt S. Meier, *North from Mexico: The Spanish-Speaking People of the United States* (New York: Praeger, 1990).

Carl Frederick Wittke, *Refugees of Revolution: The German Forty-Eighters in America* (Philadelphia: University of Pennsylvania Press, 1952).

Carl J. Bon Tempo, *Americans at the Gate: The United States and Refugees During the Cold War* (Princeton, NJ: Princeton University Press, 2008).

Carlos R. Soltero, "Plyler v. Doe (1982) and Educating Children of Illegal Alien," in *Latinos and American Law: Landmark Supreme Court Cases* (Austin, TX: University of Texas Press, 2006), 118–32.

Carol B. Schoen, *Anzia Yezierska* (Boston: Twayne, 1982).

Charles J. McClain, *In Search of Equality: The Chinese Struggle against Discrimination in Nineteenth-Century America* (Berkeley: University of California Press, 1994).

———, *In Search of Equality: The Chinese Struggle against Discrimination in Nineteenth-Century America* (Berkeley: University of California Press, 1994).

Cheesman A. Herrick, *White Servitude in Pennsylvania: Indentured and Redemption Labor in Colony and Commonwealth* (New York: Negro University Press, 1969).

Cheryl Shanks, *Immigration and the Politics of American Sovereignty, 1890-1990* (Ann Arbor: University of Michigan Press, 2001).

Daniel J. Tichenor and Alexandra Filindra, "Raising Arizona v. United States: Historical Patterns of American Immigration Federalism," *Lewis & Clark Law Review*, Vol. 16, no. 4 (Winter 2012), 1215-47.

Daniel J. Tichenor, *Dividing Lines: The Politics of Immigration Control in America* (Princeton, NJ: Princeton University Press, 2002).

Daniel W. Hollis, "'Cotton Ed Smith': Showman or Statesman?" *The South Carolina Historical Magazine*, Vol. 71, no. 4 (October 1970), 235-56.

David Goldberg, *Discontented America: the United States in the 1920s* (Baltimore: The Johns Hopkins University Press, 1999).

David M. Reimers, "An Unintended Reform: The 1965 Immigration Act and Third World Immigration to the United States," *Journal of American Ethnic History*, Vol. 3 (1983), 9-28.

David Rosner, Ronald H. Lauterstein, Jerold M. Michael, "The National Board of Health: 1879–1883," *Public Health Reports*, Vol.126, no 1 (2011), 123-29.

Dennis Wepman, *Immigration: From the Founding of Virginia to the Closing of Ellis Island* (New York: Facts on File, 2002).

Desmond King, *Making Americans: Immigration, Race, and the Origins of the Diverse Democracy* (Cambridge, MA: Harvard University Press, 2000).

Donald E. Pienkos, *PNA: A Centennial History of the Polish National Alliance of the United States of North America* (Boulder: East European Monographs, distributed by Columbia University Press, 1984)

Edward P. Hutchinson, *Legislative History of American Immigration Policy, 1798-1965* (Philadelphia: University of Pennsylvania Press, 1981).

Edward R. Kantowicz, *Polish American Politics in Chicago: 1888-1940* (Chicago: University of Chicago Press, 1975).

Eric Foner, *Free Soil, Free Labor, Free Men: The Ideology of the Republican Party Before the Civil War* (New York: Oxford University Press, 1970).

Erika Lee, *At America's Gates: Chinese Immigration During the Era of Exclusion, 1882-1943* (Chapel Hill: University of North Carolina Press, 2007).

Farley Grubb, "The Auction of Redemptioner Servants, Philadelphia, 1771-1804: An Economic Analysis," *The Journal of Economic History*, Vol. 48, no. 3 (September 1988), 583-603.

Fitzhugh Mullan, *Plagues and Politics: The Story of the United States Public Health Service* (New York: Basic Books, 1989).

Francis Russell, *Sacco and Vanzetti: The Case Resolved* (New York: Harper & Row, 1986).

Frank Bardacke, *Trampling Out the Vintage: Cesar Chavez and the Two Souls of the United Farm Workers* (London: Verso, 2011).

Frank G. Franklin, *The Legislative History of Naturalization in the United States* (New York: Arno Press, 1969).

Frank Ried Diffenderffer, *The German Immigration into Pennsylvania Through the Port of Philadelphia from 1700 to 1775 and the Redemptioners* (Baltimore: Genealogical Publishing Co., 1977).

Garbiel J. Chin, "The Civil Rights Revolution Comes to Immigration Law: A New Look at the Immigration and Nationality Act of 1965," *North Carolina Law Review*, Vol. 75 (1996), 273-345.

Garrett Epps, "U.S. Supreme Court Takes Up *United States v. Texas*," *The Atlantic*, January 21, 2016.

Grant Dinehart Langdon, "The Origins of the Homestead Act of 1862," *Journal of the West*, Vol. 51, no. 3 (Summer 2012), 56-61.

Greg Robinson, *By Order of the President: FDR and the Internment of Japanese Americans* (Cambridge, MA: Harvard University Press, 2001).

Gunther Barth, *Bitter Strength: A History of the Chinese in the United States, 1850-1870* (Cambridge, MA: Harvard University Press, 1964).

Hans von Spakovsky, "Texas Judge Delivers Blistering Rebuke of Obama Administration Immigration Lawyers' Misbehavior," *The Daily Signal*, April 8, 2015.

Hans Vought, "Woodrow Wilson, Ethnicity, and the Myth of American Unity," in Patrick Gerster and Nicholas Cords, eds., *Myth America: A Historical Anthology*, Volume II (New York: Brandywine Press, 1997).

Harvey A. Levenstein, "The AFL and Mexican Immigration in the 1920s: An Experiment in Labor Diplomacy," *Hispanic American Historical Review*, Vol. 48, no. 2 (May 1968), 206-19.

Jaap Jacobs, *New Netherland: A Dutch Colony in Seventeenth-Century America* (Ithaca, NY: Cornell University Press, 2009).

Jacob Freund, "The Homestead Act of 1862," *Journal of the West*, Vol. 52, no. 2 (Spring 2013), 16-21.

Jacobus tenBroek, *The Antislavery Origins of the Fourteenth Amendment* (Berkeley: University of California Press, 1951).

James E. Pfander and Theresa R. Wardon, "Reclaiming the Immigration Constitution of the Early Republic: Prospectivity, Uniformity, and Transparency," *Virginia Law Review*, Vol. 96, no. 1 (2010), 359-411.

James E. Starrs, "Once More Unto the Breech: The Firearms Evidence in the Sacco and Vanzetti Case Revisited," *Journal of Forensic Sciences*, 1986, 630-

54, 1050-78.

James H. Kettner, *The Development of American Citizenship, 1608–1870* (Chapel Hill: University of North Carolina Press, 1978).

James S. Pula, *Polish Americans: An Ethnic Community* (New York: Twayne Publishers, 1995).

———, "United States Immigration Policy and the Dillingham Commission," *Polish American Studies*, XXXVII, No. 1 (1980), 5-31.

Janet B. Pascal, *Jacob Riis: Reporter and Reformer* (New York: Oxford University Press, 2005).

John Armor and Peter Wright, *Manzanar* (New York: Times Books, 1988).

John F Keane, *Irish Seattle* (Charleston, SC: Arcadia Publishers, 2007).

John Frederick Whitehead, Johann Carl Büttner, Susan E Klepp, Farley Ward Grubb, and Anne Pfaelzer De Ortiz, *Souls for Sale: Two German Redemptioners Come to Revolutionary America: the Life Stories of John Frederick Whitehead and Johann Carl Büttner* (University Park, PA: Pennsylvania State University Press, 2006).

John Robert Soennichsen, *The Chinese Exclusion Act of 1882* (Santa Barbara, CA: Greenwood, 2011).

John W. Borkowski, *Legal Issues for School Districts Related to the Education of Undocumented Children* (Washington, DC: The National School Boards Association and the National Education Association, 2009).

Joseph B. James, *The Ratification of the Fourteenth Amendment* (Macon, GA: Mercer University Press, 1984).

Joseph Callway, "Constitutional Law—Preemption—Federal Law Preempts Sections of Arizona's Support Our Law Enforcement and Safe Neighborhoods Act," *Cumberland Law Review*, Vol. 43, no. 3 (2013), 591-606.

Judy Yung, Gordon H. Chang, and Him Mark Lai, eds., *Chinese American Voices: From the Gold Rush to the Present* (Berkeley: University of California Press, 2006).

Julia Young, *Mexican Exodus: Emigrants, Exiles, and Refugees of the Cristero War* (New York: Oxford University Press, 2015).

Kate M. Manuel and Michael John Garcia, "Arizona v. United States: A Limited Role for States in Immigration Enforcement," Congressional Research Service Report for Congress, R42719, September 10, 2012 (https://www.fas.org/sgp/crs/homesec/R42719.pdf).

Katherine Benton-Cohen, "Other Immigrants: Mexicans and the Dillingham Commission of 1907-1911," *Journal of American Ethnic History*, Vol. 30, no. 2 (Winter 2011), 33-57.

Kathleen L. Wolgemuth, "Woodrow Wilson and Federal Segregation," *The Journal of Negro History*, Vol. 44, no. 2 (1959), 158-73.

Keith Gandal, *The Virtues of the Vicious: Jacob Riis, Stephen Crane, and the Spectacle of the Slum* (New York: Oxford University Press, 1997).

Kenneth M. Ludmerer, "Genetics, Eugenics and the Immigration Restriction Act of 1924," *Bulletin of the History of Medicine*, Vol. 46, no. 1 (January/February 1972), 59-81.

Lawson Fusao Inada, *Only What We Could Carry: The Japanese American Internment Experience* (San Francisco: California Historical Society, 2000).

Lee Ann Potter and Wynell Schamel, "The Homestead Act of 1862," Social Education, Vol. 61, no. 6 (October 1997), 359-364.

Liping Zhu, *A Chinaman's Chance: The Chinese on the Rocky Mountain Mining Frontier* (Boulder, CO: University Press of Colorado, 1997).

Louise Henriksen, *Anzia Yezierska: A Writer's Life* (New Brunswick: Rutgers University Press, 1988).

Maddalena Marinari, "Divided and Conquered: Immigration Reform Advocates and the Passage of the 1952 Immigration and Nationality Act," *Journal of American Ethnic History*, Vol. 35, no. 3 (Spring 2016), 9-40.

Mae M. Ngai, "The Architecture of Race in American Immigration Law: A Reexamination of the Immigration Act of 1924," *Journal of American History*, Vol. 86, no. 1 (1999), 67-92.

Maisie Conrat, Richard Conrat and Dorothea Lange, *Executive Order 9066: The Internment of 110,000 Japanese Americans* (San Francisco: California Historical Society, 1972).

Margaret C. Jasper, *The Law of Immigration* (Dobbs

Ferry, NY: Oceana Publications, 2000).

Maria Pabon Lopez, "Reflections on educating Latino and Latina undocumented children: Beyond Plyler v. Doe," *Seton Hall Law Review*, Vol. 35, no. 4 (2005).

Marion T. Bennett, "The Immigration and Nationality (McCarran-Walter) Act of 1952, as Amended to 1965," *Annals of the American Academy of Political and Social Science*, Vol. 367 (September 1966), 127-36.

Matt Ford, "A Ruling Against the Obama Administration on Immigration," *The Atlantic*, November 10, 2015.

Matt Meier and Feliciano Rivera, *Mexican Americans/ American Mexicans* (New York: Hill and Wang, 1993)

Michael A. Olivas, "The Story of Plyler v. Doe, The Education of Undocumented Children, and The Polity," in *Immigration Stories*, eds. David Martin and Peter Schuck (Eagan, MN: Foundation Press, 2005).

Michael C. Lemay and Elliott R. Barkan, *U.S. Immigration and Naturalization Laws and Issues: a Documentary History* (Westport, CT: Greenwood, 1999).

Michael Coffey and Terry Golway, *The Irish in America* (New York: Hyperion, 1997).

Michael Glazier, ed., *The Encyclopedia of the Irish in America* (Notre Dame, IN: University of Notre Dame Press, 1999).

Michael LeMay and Elliott Robert Barkan, eds., *U.S. Immigration and Naturalization Laws and Issues: A Documentary History* (Westport, CT: Greenwood Press, 1999).

Moshik Temkin, *The Sacco-Vanzetti Affair: America on Trial* (New Haven: Yale University Press, 2009)

Nathan Glazer, ed., *Clamor at the Gates: The New American Immigration* (San Francisco: Institute for Contemporary Studies, 1985).

Oliver A. Rink, *Holland on the Hudson. An Economic and Social History of Dutch New York* (Ithaca, NY: Cornell University Press, 1986).

Paul Avrich, *Sacco and Vanzetti: The Anarchist Background* (Princeton: Princeton University Press, 1991)

Paul Kens, *Justice Stephen Field: Shaping Liberty from the Gold Rush to the Gilded Age* (Lawrence, KS: University Press of Kansas, 1997).

Peter Condon, "Knownothingism," *The Catholic Encyclopedia* (New York: Robert Appleton Company, 1910).

Peter Irons, *Justice at War: The Story of the Japanese American Internment Cases* (New York: Oxford University Press, 1983).

Peter Matthiessen, *Sal si puedes; Cesar Chavez and the New American Revolution* (New York: Random House, 1969).

Ping Chiu, *Chinese Labor in California, 1850-1880* (Madison: State Historical Society of Wisconsin, 1963).

Ralph Chester Williams, *The United States Public Health Service, 1798-1950* (Washington, DC: Commissioned Officers Association of the United States Public Health Service, 1951).

Ray Allen Billington, *The Protestant Crusade, 1800–1860: A Study of the Origins of American Nativism* (Chicago: Quadrangle Books, 1964).

Reports of the Immigration Commission (Washington: Government Printing Office, 1911). 41 volumes.

Richard Griswold del Castillo and Arnoldo de León, *North to Aztlán: A History of Mexican Americans in the United States* (New York: Twayne Publishers, 1996).

Richard Griswold del Castillo and Richard A. Garcia. *César Chávez: A Triumph of Spirit* (Norman: University of Oklahoma Press, 1995).

Richard O'Connor, *German-Americans: An Informal History* (Boston: Little, Brown, 1968).

Richard P. Cole and Gabriel J. Chin, "Emerging from the Margins of Historical Consciousness: Chinese Immigrants and the History of American Law," *Law and History Review*, Vol. 17, no. 2 (Summer 1999), 325-64.

Richard Plunz, *A History of Housing in New York City* (New York: Columbia University Press, 1990).

Robert A. Divine, *American Immigration Policy, 1924-1952* (New Haven: Yale University Press, 1957).

Robert C. Alexander, "A Defense of the McCarran-Walter Act," *Law and Contemporary Problems*, Vol.

21, no. 2 (Spring, 1956), 382-400.

Robert Ernst, *Immigrant Life in New York City, 1825-1863* (New York: King's Crown Press, 1949).

Robert F. Zeidel, *Immigrants, Progressives, and Exclusion Politics: the Dillingham Commission, 1900-1927* (DeKalb, IL: Northern Illinois University Press, 2004).

Robin West, "Toward an Abolitionist Interpretation of the Fourteenth Amendment," *West Virginia Law Review*, Vol. 94 (Fall 1991), 111–55.

Roderick M. Hills, Jr., "Arizona v. United States: The Unitary Executive's Enforcement Discretion as a Limit on Federalism," *Cato Supreme Court Review* (2011), 189-218.

Roger A. Bruns, *Cesar Chavez and the United Farm Workers Movement* (Santa Barbara, CA: Greenwood, 2011).

Roger Daniels, *Coming to America: A History of Immigration and Ethnicity in American Life* (New York: Harper Collins Publishers, 1990).

———, *Guarding the Golden Door: American Immigration Policy and Immigrants Since 1882* (New York: Hill & Wang, 2004).

———, *Not Like Us: Immigrants and Minorities in America, 1890-1924* (Chicago: Ivan R. Dee, 1997).

———, *Prisoners Without Trial: Japanese Americans in World War II* (New York: Hill and Wang, 2004).

Ronald Takaki, *Strangers From a Different Shore* (Boston: Little, Brown and Company, 1989).

Roxanne L. Doty, *The Law into Their Own Hands: Immigration and the Politics of Exceptionalism* (Tucson: University of Arizona Press, 2009).

Russell Shorto, *The Island at the Center of the World: The Epic Story of Dutch Manhattan and the Forgotten Colony That Shaped America* (New York: Doubleday, 2004).

Sally Ann Drucker, "Yiddish, Yidgin & Yezierska," *Modern Jewish Studies Annual*, Vol. VI (1987), 99-113.

Samuel McSeveney, "Immigrants, the Literacy Test, and Quotas: Selected American History College Textbooks' Coverage of the Congressional Restriction of European Immigration, 1917-1929," *The History Teacher*, Vol. 21 (1987), 41-51.

Seema Sohi, (2013). "Immigration Act of 1917 and

the "Barred Zone," in Xiaojian Zhao and Edward J. W. Park, eds., *Asian Americans: An Encyclopedia of Social, Cultural, Economic, and Political History* (Santa Barbara, CA: ABC-CLIO, 2013).

Stanley Nadel, *Little Germany: Ethnicity, Religion, and Class in New York City, 1845-80* (Urbana: University of Illinois Press, 1990).

Stephen E. Maizlish, "The Meaning of Nativism and the Crisis of the Union: The Know-Nothing Movement in the Antebellum North," in William Gienapp, Stephen E. Maizlish, and John J. Kushma eds., *Essays on American Antebellum Politics, 1840–1860* (College Station, TX: Texas A & M University Press, 1982), 166–98.

Stuart Creighton Miller, *The Unwelcome Immigrant; the American Image of the Chinese, 1785-1882* (Berkeley: University of California Press, 1969).

Susan Ferriss, Ricardo Sandoval, and Diana Hembree, eds., *The Fight in the Fields: Cesar Chavez and the Farmworkers Movement* (New York: Harcourt Brace, 1997).

Susan Tejada, *In Search of Sacco & Vanzetti: Double Lives, Troubled Times, & the Massachusetts Murder Case that Shook the World* (Boston: Northeastern University Press, 2012).

Tara Helfman, "Obama the Scrivener & the Supine Court," *Commentary*, Vol. 136, no. 5 (December 2013), 28-30.

Tibor Frank, "From Nativism to the Quota Laws: Restrictionist Pressure Groups and the US Congress 1879-1924," *Parliaments, Estates and Representation*, November 15, 1995, 143-157.

Timothy J. Meagher, *The Columbia Guide to Irish American History* (New York: Columbia University Press, 2005).

Tom Buk-Swienty, *The Other Half: The Life of Jacob Riis and the World of Immigrant America* (New York: W. W. Norton & Company 2008).

Toyo Suyemoto and Susan B. Richardson, *I Call to Remembrance: Toyo Suyemoto's Years of Internment* (New Brunswick, NJ: Rutgers University Press, 2007).

Trina R. W. Shanks, "The Homestead Act: A Major Asset-building Policy in American History," in Michael Sherraden, ed., *Inclusion in the American*

Dream: Assets, Poverty, and Public Policy (New York: Oxford University Press, 2005), 20-41.

Tyler Anbinder, *City of Dreams: The 400-year Epic History of Immigrant New York* (Boston: Houghton Mifflin Harcourt, 2016).

———, *Nativism and Slavery: The Northern Know Nothings and the Politics of the 1850s* (New York: Oxford University Press, 1992).

Van Cleaf Bachman, *Peltries or Plantations: The Economic Policies of the Dutch West India Company in New Netherland, 1623-1639* (Baltimore: Johns Hopkins Press, 1969).

Victor Greene, *For God and Country: The Rise of Polish and Lithuanian Ethnic Consciousness in America, 1860-1919* (Madison: State Historical Society of Wisconsin, 1975).

William E. Watson and Eugene J. Halus, Jr., *Irish Americans: The History and Culture of a People* (Santa Barbara, CA: ABC-CLIO, 2014).

William J. Perry, *We the People: The Fourteenth Amendment and the Supreme Court* (New York: Oxford University Press, 1999).

William Nelson, *The Fourteenth Amendment: From Political Principle to Judicial Doctrine* (Cambridge, MA: Harvard University Press, 1988).

William R. Tamayo, "Asian Americans and the McCarran-Walter Act," in *Asian Americans and Congress: A Documentary History*, edited by Hyung-chan Kim (Westport, CT: Greenwood Press, 1996), 336-528.

William V. Shannon, *The American Irish: A Political and Social Portrait* (Amherst: University of Massachusetts Press, 1989).

William Young and David E. Kaiser, *Postmortem: New Evidence in the Case of Sacco and Vanzetti* (Amherst, MA: University of Massachusetts Press, 1985).

Yong Chen, *Chinese San Francisco, 1850-1943: A Trans-Pacific Community* (Stanford: Stanford University Press, 2000).

Index

T

Taft-Katsura Memorandum 193
Taiwan 198
Take Care Clause 238, 239
talismanic power 22
Talmudic scholar 57
Teacher's College at Columbia University 58
temporary asylum legislation 177
temporary guest worker visas 77
tenant-houses 36, 38
tenement 35, 36, 37, 38, 39, 40, 41, 42, 43, 44, 45, 57, 58, 68, 185
Tenement-house Building Company 41, 42
Tenement-house Commission 39
Thayer, Judge 71, 74, 75
Thirteenth Amendment 124, 127
threat of deportation 202
thumbscrew 183
Tonningen 16, 17
tract books and plats 121
trades 62, 65, 68
The Transplanted 55
Treaty of Guadalupe-Hidalgo x, 108
Treaty of Tientsin 138
Trescot, William Henry 134
tribal organizations 127
Truman Doctrine 199
Truman, Harry S. 114, 161, 170, 179, 197, 198
tuberculosis 109, 128, 146, 149, 167
Tübingen 26
tuition 179, 207, 211, 214, 216
Tyler Independent School District 207, 208

U

ukaz 58, 59, 60, 62
underdogs 71, 74
underground lodging-houses 38
under-letting 37
"undesirable aliens" provisions 206
undesirables 145, 188, 198
undocumented children 208, 209, 214, 215, 217, 256
unification of families 177
uniform Rule of Naturalization 115, 213, 220, 228
United East India Company 3
United Farm Workers (UFW) 77
United States census ix, 25, 115, 155, 156
United States District Court for the Eastern District of Texas 208

United States Immigration Commission xi, 87, 95, 103, 152, 188
United States Office of Immigration 140
University Club of Boston 71
University of Cracow 48
University of Leiden 3
University of Prague 48
Univision 237
Unsanctioned entry into the United States 208
The Uprooted 55
urban nation 35
urban political machines 35
urban population x, 35
U.S. Circuit Court in California 182
U.S. citizens of Japanese ancestry 179
U.S. Pacific Fleet 193
usurer 60

V

vagrants 38, 124, 146, 167
Vancouver Island 31
van der Donck, Adriaen vii, 1, 3, 13
van Rensselaer, Kiliaen 4
Vanzetti, Bartolomeo v, 2, 69, 70, 249
Vatican 26, 93
Vermont Society of the Sons of the American Revolution 96
Villafalletto, Italy 70
Virginia Resolutions 227
Vogel, Samuel 17
Volkstheater 27, 28
Voting Rights Act 171, 172

W

Wade-Davis Bill 127
walk-ups 44
Walter, Francis 161, 198
want of bread 17
War Brides Act of 1945 xi, 161
War Democrats 119
Ward, Robert DeCourcy 145
Warnenczyk, Wladislas 48
War of 1812 19
war of nations 189
War on Poverty 79
Warren, Charles 145
Washington, George, election 115
Washingtonian 153